ARCHITECTURE AND MATHEMATICS IN ANCIENT EGYPT

In this fascinating new study, architect and Egyptologist Corinna Rossi analyses the relationship between mathematics and architecture in ancient Egypt by exploring the use of numbers and geometrical figures in ancient architectural projects and buildings. While previous architectural studies have searched for abstract 'universal rules' to explain the history of Egyptian architecture, Rossi attempts to reconcile the different approaches of archaeologists, architects and historians of mathematics into a single coherent picture. Using a study of a specific group of monuments, the pyramids, and placing them in the context of their cultural and historical background, Rossi argues that theory and practice of construction must be considered as a continuum, not as two separated fields, in order to allow the original planning process of a building to re-emerge. Highly illustrated with plans, diagrams and figures, this book is essential reading for all scholars of ancient Egypt and the architecture of ancient cultures.

Dr Corinna Rossi is a Junior Research Fellow in Egyptology at Churchill College, Cambridge.

ARCHITECTURE AND
MATHEMATICS IN ANCIENT EGYPT

CORINNA ROSSI

CAMBRIDGE
UNIVERSITY PRESS

CAMBRIDGE UNIVERSITY PRESS
Cambridge, New York, Melbourne, Madrid, Cape Town, Singapore, São Paulo

Cambridge University Press
The Edinburgh Building, Cambridge, CB2 8RU, UK

Published in the United States of America by Cambridge University Press, New York

www.cambridge.org
Information on this title: www.cambridge.org/9780521690539

First published 2003
Reprinted with corrections 2006
First paperback edition 2007

Printed in the United Kingdom at the University Press, Cambridge

A catalogue record for this publication is available from the British Library

ISBN-13 978-0-521-82954-0 hardback
ISBN-13 978-0-521-69053-9 paperback

Contents

Illustrations

Tables

Preface

Mathematics has always played an important role in architecture, in the past just as in the present. Despite this continuity, however, reconstructing exactly how the relationship between architecture and mathematics worked in an ancient culture may prove rather complicated. An investigation into the way architecture and mathematics interacted in the past, in ancient Egypt as well as in other cultures, may be misled by three main sets of tangled problems. The first is generated by our expectations of the results of such a research; the second depends on the reliability of the drawings used to test or 'discover' a theory; and the third stems from the way mathematics is employed during the research.

Regarding the first point, it is evident that in ancient monuments people have found all they wanted to find in terms of mathematical concepts and geometrical figures. A small-scale plan, a ruler, a compass and a bit of imagination are enough to 'discover' several mathematical relationships in the design of any building. This does not imply, however, that the ancient architects based their reasoning on the same points, nor that they were aware of all of the possible interpretations of their plans.

A second point concerns the drawings employed in this type of study. The habit of using mainly plans to analyse the proportions of buildings may produce a dangerous distance between the actual monument and its schematic representation. A plan is a useful and simple way to represent a building, but it includes just a few clues about the elevation, and even less about the masses and materials involved. Defining a building just by means of its plan may be reductive, and discussing its proportions on this basis may be misleading. Another problem related to the use of drawings is their reliability. Precision in architectural surveys has not always been a priority, and graphic reconstructions sometimes have been based on the imagination more than is appropriate.

A third, important point is the way scholars use mathematics. In their search for a 'rule' that would explain the proportions of ancient Egyptian architecture, modern scholars have generally ignored ancient Egyptian mathematics and have based their theories on our modern mathematical system. In some extreme cases, this line of research has led to complicated interpretations based on symbolic and esoteric concepts. These theories do not necessarily provide any useful information about the ancient culture to which they are supposed to refer, but on the other hand they may play an important role in a study of the culture and the historical period that produced them – that is, Europe in the last two centuries. The modern diffusion of a scientific and logical way of thinking seems to have corresponded to a growing need for an imaginary escape into mysterious worlds, where there are still secrets to discover. Egypt, with its impressively oversized architectural remains, its legendary wealth, its obscure and fascinating writing, seems to be the ideal candidate to hide the key of a lost wisdom. Even if the ancient Egyptians would have been flattered by this attitude, the results of this kind of speculation have, unfortunately, little to do with the actual historical and archaeological remains.

This does not mean that there is nothing left to discover; it simply means that we must look in other directions. The structure of this book reflects the existence of two separate channels of research that have taken shape in the last two centuries. Broadly speaking, they can be attributed to the two main groups of scholars who have dealt with ancient Egyptian architecture: architectural historians and Egyptologists. Finding a mathematical rule that would explain the proportions of ancient Egyptian architecture has generally been an idea entertained by architects and architectural historians, who rarely took into account any archaeological or textual evidence. On the other hand, the archaeological and textual evidence usually has been studied in detail by Egyptologists who had no interest in or did not believe in the existence of a more general rule, and so rarely tried to set any piece of architectual evidence into a broader picture.

The search for a rule has the merit of encouraging a perception of the subject from a more general and less particular point of view, but it also is true that the desire to find links, interconnections and similarities has often overstepped the boundaries of rigorous historical interpretation. A combination between these two viewpoints, however, may yield interesting results. Part I of this book is dedicated to the theories suggested in the past to explain the proportions of ancient Egyptian architecture. The discrepancy between the methods used by modern scholars and the ancient mathematical sources proves the inconsistency of many modern interpretations. Part II is dedicated to a detailed analysis of the surviving archaeological evidence on the planning and building process, such as architectural drawings, models and texts. Although this material has already been studied in detail by several scholars, comparisons between documents from different periods, and between the architectural and the mathematical sources, provide new clues about the way mathematics was used by ancient Egyptian architects, scribes and workmen.

Therefore, Part I may be defined as the 'architectural' approach corrected by the Egyptological studies, whereas Part II is based on the inverse combination. Finally, Part III is an attempt to reconcile these two views and prove that the association between them may be extremely productive. A group of monuments, the Old and Middle Kingdom pyramids, have been analysed on the basis of the conclusions drawn at the ends of Parts I and II. The result is a coherent picture which incorporates symbolic needs, theoretical reasoning and practical considerations, while setting aside the complicated implications of some past theories and pointings to new, interesting directions of research.

In conclusion, this study does not aim to discover any secret, nor to find out any formula which might explain the proportions in ancient Egyptian architecture. It is simply an attempt to outline the relationship between architecture and mathematics in ancient Egypt; that is, the way the ancient Egyptians used numbers and geometrical figures when planning and building. My wish is that it will act as a bridge between architects and Egyptologists and will help to set the path for a consistent analysis, in mathematical terms, of future archaeological evidence.

Acknowledgments

This book is the outcome of several years of research that took shape and gained consistency in Cambridge under the guidance of Barry J. Kemp. As my Ph.D. supervisor, he encouraged and supported my research and offered me the possibility of learning from his experience. To him I wish to express my deepest gratitude and respect.

Turning my doctoral dissertation into a book has been made possible by several people and institutions. My manuscript benefited from the comments and suggestions offered by Ian Shaw, Stephen Quirke and Dieter Arnold. The publication has been supervised with an expert hand by Simon Whitmore, patiently edited by Nancy Hynes, and also supported by Helen Barton and Jessica Kuper. My postdoctoral studies have been generously funded by a Junior Research Fellowship at Churchill College, Cambridge, that provided a lively and stimulating environment for interdisciplinary research such as mine.

My doctoral dissertation was funded by the Lady Wallis Budge Fund, offered by Christ's College. My research was supported on a daily basis by the staff of the library of the Faculty of Oriental Studies and occasionally by the Faculty of Classics and the University Library. The section of this book dedicated to the Ptolemaic temples is the result of a separate study, funded by the Gerald Averay Wainwright Near Eastern Archaeological Fund, Oxford.

Over the years, I received useful comments and suggestions from Katherine Spence, Serafina Cuomo, Penelope Wilson, Sarah Clackson, Günter Burkard, Ted Brock and the Theban Mapping Project, Stephen Seydlmayer, Nabil Swelim and Jan Nekovar. Thanks are also due to Sally MacDonald and the Petrie Museum, Carol Andrews, Richard Parkinson and the British Museum, Catharine H. Roehrig and the Metropolitan Museum of Art, Ingeborg Müller and the Staatliche Museen zu Berlin, Enrichetta Leaspo and the Museo Egizio in Turin, and the Dutch Archaeological Institute in Cairo.

In the early years of my research, important figures have been Professor Giulio Pane, with whom I graduated in History of Architecture at the Facoltà di Architettura, Università degli Studi di Napoli Federico II, Professor Rodolfo Fattovich, Rosanna Pirelli and, at the very beginning, Professor Anna Maria Iurza, who taught me Greek and Latin.

I must say a special thanks to Adriano, because there is more to life than just research. Finally, for their unfailing support, I wish to thank my parents, Aldo and Donatella, architects, to whom this book is dedicated.

Abbreviations

AOS	American Oriental Series
ASAE	*Annales du Service des Antiquités de l'Egypte*
ASE	Archaeological Survey of Egypt
AV	Archäologische Veroffentlichungen
BCA	Bulletin de Correspondance Africaine
BdE	Bibliothèque d'Etude
Beiträge Bf	Beiträge zur Ägyptischen Bauforschung und Altertumskunde
BIFAO	*Bulletin de l'Institut Français d'Archéologie Orientale*
BMMA	*Bulletin of the Metropolitan Museum of Art*
BSAE	British School of Archaeology in Egypt
CAJ	*Cambridge Archaeological Journal*
CdE	*Chronique d'Egypte*
CG	*Catalogue Général des Antiquités Egyptiennes du Musée du Caire*
DAIK	Deutsches Archäologisches Institut Kairo
DE	*Discussions in Egyptology*
DFIFAO	Documents de Fouilles de l'Institut Français d'Archéologie Orientale
EA	*Egyptian Archaeology*
EEF	Egypt Exploration Fund
EES	Egypt Exploration Society
ERA	Egyptian Research Account
GM	*Göttinger Miszellen*
HM	*Historia Mathematica*
IFAO	Institut Français d'Archéologie Orientale
JARCE	*Journal of the American Research Center in Egypt*
JEA	*Journal of Egyptian Archaeology*
JEOL	*Jaarbericht ex Oriente Lux*

JSAH	*Journal of the Society of Architectural Historians*
LÄ	Helck Wolfgang and Eberhard Otto (eds.), *Lexikon der Ägyptologie*, Wiesbaden 1975–92.
MIFAO	Mémoires de l'Institut Français d'Archéologie Orientale
MDAIK	*Mitteilungen des Deutschen Archäologischen Instituts Kairo*
NARCE	*Newsletter of the Americal Research Center in Egypt*
OLA	Orientalia Lovaniensia Analecta
PSBA	*Proceedings of the Society of Biblical Archaeology*
RAPH	Recherches d'Archéologie, de Philologie et d'Historie
RdE	*Revue d'Egyptologie*
SAE	Service des Antiquités de l'Egypte
SAK	*Studien zur Altägyptischen Kultur*
TTS	Theban Tombs Series
VA	*Varia Aegyptiaca*
ZÄS	*Zeitschrift für Ägyptische Sprache und Altertumskunde*

Table 1. *Schematic chronology of Ancient Egypt*

Historical Period	Dynasty	Approximate dates	Kings and Queens mentioned in the text
Early Dynastic Period	Dynasty 0	3100–3000 BC	
	First Dynasty	3000–2750 BC	
	Second Dynasty	2750–2686 BC	Hetepsekhemwy, Ninetjer
Old Kingdom	Third Dynasty	2686–2600 BC	Djoser, Sekhemkhet, Khaba
	Fourth Dynasty	2600–2450 BC	Snefru, Khufu (Cheops), Djedefra, Khafra (Chefren), Menkaura (Mykerinos), Shepseskaf, Nebka (?)
	Fifth Dynasty	2450–2300 BC	Userkaf, Sahura, Neferirkara, Shepseskara, Raneferef, Neuserra, Menkauhor, Djedkara-Isesi, Unas
	Sixth Dynasty	2300–2181 BC	Teti, Pepi I, Merenra, Pepi II
First Intermediate Period	Seventh Dynasty	no historical evidence	
	Eighth Dynasty	2180–2160 (?) BC	Iby
	Ninth/Tenth Dynasty (Herakleopolis)	2160–2025 (?) BC	
	Eleventh Dynasty (Thebes)	2160–2025 BC	Nebhetepra Mentuhotep
Middle Kingdom	Eleventh Dynasty (all Egypt)	2025–1976 BC	
	Twelfth Dynasty	1976–1794 BC	Amenemhat I, Senusret I, Amenemhat II, Senusret II, Senusret III, Amenemhat III, Amenemhat IV
	Thirteenth Dynasty	1794–1700 BC	Ameny-Qemau, Khendjer, Merneferra-Ay
Second Intermediate Period	Fourteenth Dynasty	chronology uncertain, some dynasties were contemporary	
	Fifteenth Dynasty (Hyksos rulers in Lower Egypt)		
	Sixteenth Dynasty		
	Seventeenth Dynasty (Thebes)	1650–1550 (?) BC	Kamose

(*cont.*)

Table 1. (*cont.*)

Historical Period	Dynasty	Approximate dates	Kings and Queens mentioned in the text
New Kingdom	Eigtheenth Dynasty	1550–1292 BC	Ahmose, Tuthmosis I, Hatshepsut, Tuthmosis III, Amenhotep III, Amarna Period, Tutankhamun
	Amarna Period	1351–1334 BC	Akhenaton (Amenhotep IV)
	Nineteenth Dynasty	1292–1185 BC	Seti I, Ramses II, Merenptah, Seti II, Siptah, Tawosret
	Twentieth Dynasty	1186–1069 BC	Sethnakht, Ramses III, Ramses IV, Ramses V, Ramses VI, Ramses IX
Third Intermediate Period	Twenty-first Dynasty	1069–945 BC	
	Twenty-second Dynasty	945–735 BC	
	Twenty-third Dynasty	818–715 BC	
	Twenty-fourth Dynasty ('Saite')	727–715 BC	
	Twenty-fifth Dynasty (from Napata)	747–664 (?) BC	
Late Period	Twenty-sixth Dynasty	664–525 BC	
First Persian Period	Twenty-seventh Dynasty	525–404 BC	
Late Dynastic Period	Twenty-eighth Dynasty	404–399 BC	
	Twenty-ninth Dynasty	399–380 BC	
	Thirtieth Dynasty	380–343 BC	Nectanebo I, Nectanebo II
Second Persian Period	Persian kings	343–332 BC	
Macedonian Period	Macedonian Dynasty	332–304 BC	Alexander the Great
Ptolemaic Period	Ptolemaic Dynasty	304–30 BC	Ptolemy, Ptolemy II, Ptolemy III, Ptolemy VI, Ptolemy VIII, Ptolemy X, Ptolemy XI, Ptolemy XII, Cleopatra VII
Roman Period	Roman Emperors	30 BC – 395 AD	Augustus
Byzantine Period		395–640 AD	
Islamic Period		640–1517 AD	
Ottoman Period		1517–1805 AD	
Khedival Period		1805–1919 AD	
Monarchy		1919–1953 AD	
Republic		1953-today	

Part I

Proportions in ancient Egyptian architecture

Harmony and proportions in architecture

Throughout the whole history of architecture, the concept of harmony has been the subject of numerous studies and long-lasting discussions.[1] Harmony may be defined as a correspondence between parts, the result of the composition (or the division) of a whole into consonant parts. Its ancient link with music, where 'agreeable' combinations of sounds can be read as mathematical relationships, seems to seal the connection between harmony and mathematics. In art and architecture, however, this correspondence is not easily described. Although it is undeniable that a link between architecture and geometry (and therefore mathematics in general) exists, in different periods the nature of this connection has been identified and judged in different ways.

To Pythagoras and the Pythagoreans is attributed the discovery that tones can be measured in space – that is, that musical consonances correspond to ratios of small whole numbers. If two strings vibrate in the same conditions, the resulting sounds depend on the ratios between their length. The ratio 1:2, for instance, generates a difference of one octave (diapason), the ratio 2:3 produces an interval of one fifth (diapente), and the ratio 3:4 corresponds to a difference of one fourth (diatessaron). The addition of two intervals results in the multiplication of the two numerical ratios, the subtraction corresponds to a division and, therefore, halving an interval equals extracting a square root.

The Pythagorean interest in numbers, as filtered by Plato, generated a tradition that linked philosophy and mathematics in the interpretation of the cosmos. Thus, as Walter Burkert wrote

---

[1] For convenient summaries, see Miloutine Borissavliévitch, *Essai critique sur le principales doctrines relatives à l'esthétique de l'architecture*, Paris: Payot, 1925; Rudolf Wittkower, *Architectural Principles in the Age of Humanism*, London: Academy Editors, 1998, and P. H. Scholfield, *The Theory of Proportion in Architecture*, Cambridge: Cambridge University Press, 1958.

one is *nous* and *ousia*; two is *doxa*; three is the number of the whole – beginning, middle and end; four is justice – equal times equal – but it is also the form of the *tetraktys*, the 'whole nature of numbers' [a 'perfect triangle' made up of the numbers 1, 2, 3 and 4]; five is marriage, as the first combination of odd and even, male and female; seven is opportunity (*kairos*) and also Athena, as the 'virginal' prime number; ten is the perfect number, which comprehends the whole nature of number and determines the structure of the cosmos.[2]

During the European Renaissance interest in the theory of proportion in architecture increased considerably. One of the reasons for this was the rediscovery, in 1414 in the Montecassino Abbey, of the treatise *De Architectura libri decem*, written by the Roman architect Vitruvius in the first century BC, and eventually translated from the Latin into the major European languages during the sixteenth and seventeenth centuries. According to some authors, Vitruvius failed to provide a coherent theory of proportions. P. H. Scholfield, however, has explained that the difficulties in the translation of Latin words which appear to have similar meanings, such as 'symmetria', 'eurythmia', 'proportio' and 'commensus', generated confusion and misunderstanding among scholars and commentators.[3] One of the most important elements in Vitruvius' theory is commensurability: the dimensions of the parts are submultiples of the dimensions of the whole. This seemed to apply especially to the human body, and he suggested that the proportions of a temple ought to be like those of a well-formed human being.[4]

Vitruvius and the Pythagorean-Platonic philosophy of harmonic numbers were the main source of reference for Renaissance architects. In 1534, the painter Titian, the architect Serlio and the humanist Fortunio Spira all approved the project suggested by the Franciscan monk Francesco Giorgi for the proportions of the church of San Francesco della Vigna in Venice, which had been laid out according to Pythagorean and Platonic theories.[5] The Italian architects Palladio and Leon Battista Alberti, although with some differences, followed the same principles and based their architectures on simple ratios of small numbers.

The idea of a universal harmony which ruled microcosm and macrocosm began to decline in the seventeenth century, and was completely overthrown in eighteenth-century England. According to David Hume, beauty was not a quality in things themselves, but existed only in the mind of the person who contemplated them,[6]

---

[2] Walter Burkert, *Lore and Science in Ancient Pythagoreanism*, Cambridge, Mass.: Harvard University Press, 1972, pp. 467–8. In the original text the Greek words are quoted in Greek.

[3] Scholfield, *Theory of Proportion*, pp. 19–20.

[4] Vitruvius, *Ten Books on Architecture*, III.1.1, translated by Ingrid D. Rowland, commentary and illustrations by Thomas Noble Howe, Cambridge: Cambridge University Press, 1999, p. 47; see also figs. 37 and 38.

[5] 'Francesco Giorgi's Memorandum for S. Francesco della Vigna', in Wittkower, *Architectural Principles*, Appendix I, pp. 136–8.

[6] David Hume, 'Of the Standard of Taste' (1777) in Eugene F. Miller (ed.), *Essays: Moral, Political, and Literary*, Indianapolis, Ind.: Liberty Fund, 1987, pp. 226-49.

and Edmund Burke concluded that beauty had nothing to do with calculation and geometry.[7] Even the connection between architecture and music was heavily criticised and dismissed in favour of a more individual point of view influenced by the limitations of human perception.[8] At the same time, the sensation that something belonging to the past had been lost started to appear. William Gilpin sadly wrote that 'the secret is lost. The ancients had it. They well knew the principles of beauty; and had that unerring rule, which in all things adjusted their taste. (. . .) And if we could only discover their *principles of proportions*, we should have the arcanum of the science, and might settle all our disputes about taste with good ease'.[9]

The idea of a universal harmony was revived in the second half of the nineteenth century, together with research, in art and architecture, into a common rule which could link the past to the present.[10] The study of Emeric Henszlmann published in 1860, for example, bears a significant title: *Théorie des proportions appliquées dans l'architecture depuis la XIIe dynastie des rois égyptiens jusq'au XVIe siècle*. The author constructed a series of increasing and decreasing ratios between catheti of right-angled triangles and suggested that these values had been used by the architects of different cultures for millennia.[11] However, in 1863 the French architect and architectural historian Eugène Viollet-le-Duc expressed a different opinion about the nature of harmony. Being a theorist but at the same time a great expert in construction and restoration, he had a more balanced view of the link between abstract mathematics and practical operations. According to him,

going further back and examining the monuments of Ancient Egypt, we also recognize the influence of a harmonic method, but we do not observe the artists of Thebes subjected to a formula; and I confess I should be sorry if the existence of such formulas among artistic peoples could be demonstrated; it would greatly lower them in my estimation; for what becomes of art and the merit of the artist when proportions are reduced to a formulary?[12]

[7] Edmund Burke, *Enquiry into the Origin of our Ideas of the Sublime and Beautiful* (1757), ed. James T. Bolton, Oxford: Blackwell, 1987.

[8] Henry H. Kames, *Elements of Criticism*, Edinburgh: Kincaid & Bell, 1765.

[9] William Gilpin, *Three Essays: On Picturesque Beauty; On Picturesque Travel; And On Sketching Landscape*, London: Blamire, 1792, pp. 32–3.

[10] A useful summary of the theories of this period, together with bibliographical references, can be found in Wittkower, *Architectural Principles*, Appendix II, pp. 139–40.

[11] Emeric Henszlmann, *Théorie des proportions appliquées dans l'architecture depuis la XIIe dynastie des rois égyptiens jusq'au XVIe siècle*, Paris: Bertrand, 1860, p. 1 and fig. 3. The starting point is the right-angle triangle taken from a cube with side-length equal to 1. The sides of the triangle are: the side of the square face (equal to 1), the diagonal of the face, (equal to $\sqrt{2}$) and the diagonal of the cube (equal to $\sqrt{3}$). From these values, Henszlmann created a sequence of increasing and decreasing irrational numbers which were supposedly used by the ancient architects of all periods. As Egyptian monuments, he included pyramids, pylons, some layouts of temples, the tomb of Khnum Hotep at Beni Hasan, the portico of the ambulatory of Thutmosis III and the temple of Khons at Karnak.

[12] Eugène Viollet-le-Duc, *Lectures on Architecture* (*Entretiens sur l'architecture*, Paris 1863), English translation by Benjamin Bucknall, New York: Dover Publications, 1987, pp. 390–1.

The results of the search for a unique rule, especially in the cases when they were summarised in a mathematical formula or a geometrical construction, are quite heterogeneous and often contradictory. Some scholars thought that they had found the solution in a geometrical figure: Viollet-le-Duc himself believed that triangles were the basis of every good architecture,[13] Odilio Wolff favoured the hexagon,[14] Ernst Mössel the circle,[15] and Jay Hambidge the so-called 'root rectangles', that is, rectangles in which the short side was equal to the unity, and the long side respectively to $\sqrt{2}$, $\sqrt{3}$, $\sqrt{4}$ and $\sqrt{5}$.[16] His system, which he referred to as 'Dynamic Symmetry', is also related to the most successful among the geometrical constructions evoked by the scholars of the nineteenth and twentieth centuries: the Golden Section.[17]

This proportion appeared to satisfy all the requests for a proper 'universal rule'. From a mathematical point of view, it could have a relatively simple geometrical construction, but at the same time an extremely complicated theoretical background, which lent itself very well to a symbolic interpretation. Moreover, at the beginning of the twentieth century several scholars suggested that the structure of many natural forms was based on this proportion.[18] In 1854 Adolf Zeising claimed that he had discovered that the Golden Section ruled the proportions of the whole human body (height and breadth, front and back), and that the same occurred in music, poetry, religion and, of course, architecture.[19] In the first half of the twentieth century, Matila Ghyka followed his example and applied the Golden Section to nature and art, explicitly referring to a 'revival of Pythagorean doctrine in science and art'.[20]

Ancient Egyptian architecture, in particular the Giza pyramids, quickly became one of the favourite subjects to which such an approach was applied. Unfortunately, the majority of these theories, on Egypt or other ancient cultures, are based on our modern mathematical system, which is not necessarily similar to the ancient ones.

---

[13] Viollet-le-Duc, *Lectures on Architecture*, IX Entretien.

[14] Odilio Wolff, *Tempelmasse*, Vienna: Schroll and Co., 1912.

[15] Eric Mössel, *Die Proportion in Antike und Mittelalter,* Munich: Beck, 1928.

[16] Jay Hambidge, *The Parthenon and Other Greek Temples: Their Dynamic Symmetry*, New Haven: Yale University Press, 1924. See also *The Elements of Dynamic Symmetry*, New Haven: Yale University Press, 1948 for 'root rectangles'.

[17] This proportion has been known under several names (see note 15 of the next chapter): even if 'extreme and mean ratio' is probably more correct from a mathematical and historical point of view, in this case I prefer to adopt the most famous definition among non-specialistic scholars: the 'Golden Section'.

[18] Theodore Cook, *Spirals in Nature and Art*, London: Murray, 1903; *The Curves of Life*, New York: Holt & Co., 1914; D'Arcy W. Thompson, *On Growth and Form*, Cambridge: Cambridge University Press, 1961 (1917).

[19] Adolf Zeising, *Neue Lehre von den Proportionen des menschlichen Körpers*, Leipzig: Weigel, 1854.

[20] Matila C. Ghyka, *Le Nombre d'Or – Rites et rythmes Pythagoriciens dans le développement de la civilisation occidentale*, Paris: Gallimard, 1931 and *The Geometry of Art and Life*, New York: Dover, 1946, from which this quotation is taken (pp. 168–72). Especially significant are volume I, chapter 1 in volume II, and plates 17–24 in *Le Nombre d'Or*.

Part I is entirely dedicated to this discrepancy, and reflects this in its structure. The first section will focus on the theories suggested to explain the proportions in ancient Egyptian architecture and their mathematical background. In the second section, I will adopt the historically correct mathematical point of view and demonstrate that many of those theories are based upon faulty assumptions.

1

In search of 'the rule' for ancient Egyptian architecture

Triangles and other figures

Three triangles for ancient Egypt

Before the diffusion of the Napoleonic *Description de l'Egypte*, the available information on Egyptian architecture was fragmentary and imprecise, and did not necessarily create a good impression on architectural historians, especially those accustomed to the reproductions of Greek art and architecture. The French architectural historian Quatremère de Quincy, for instance, was not exactly a supporter of ancient Egypt. He believed that ancient Egyptian architecture lacked 'order', meaning a 'system of proportions of forms and ornaments', and that beauty and taste were foreign to it.[1] In his *Dictionnaire Historique d'Architecture*, he wrote that in Egyptian architecture the large size of the construction, the vastness of the composition and the profuseness of signs and objects were due to a lack of science, a lack of creativity, and a lack of taste, respectively.[2] He concluded that the best way to mould someone's taste, to develop a feeling for truth and beauty, was to familiarise them with Greek statuary. But if one wished to prevent this feeling from developing, it would be enough to condemn the person to looking at Egyptian statues.[3] If one looks at the appalling reproductions of Egyptian monuments that accompanied his texts (for example fig. 1), the temptation to agree with him is very strong.

Ancient Egyptian architecture began to be included in the studies on architectural proportions when more reliable reproductions of the monuments became available. In the nineteenth century, drawings from the *Description* and from the publications of early travellers were the sole sources that the architectural historians could use in their studies. Ancient Egyptian texts were being slowly deciphered and by the

---

[1] Antoine C. Quatremère de Quincy, *De l'architecture Egyptienne*, Paris: Barrois, 1803, pp. 214–8 and 222–4.
[2] Antoine C. Quatremère de Quincy, *Dictionnaire Historique d'Architecture*, Paris: Le Clére, 1832, vol. I, p. 572.
[3] Quatremère de Quincy, *Architecture Egyptienne*, p. 224.

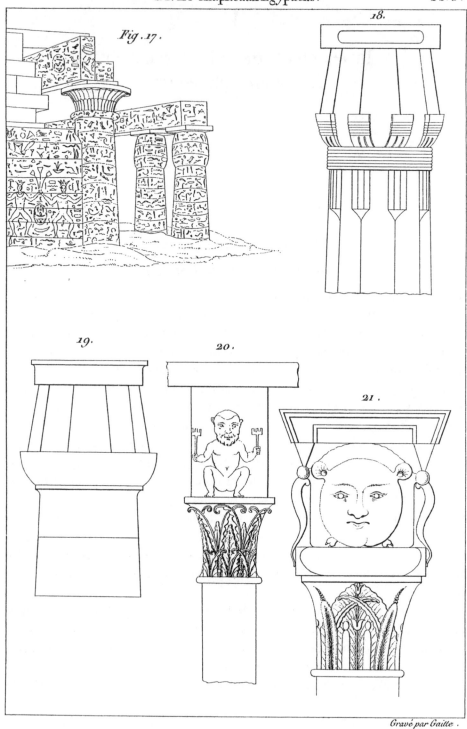

Fig. 1: Early nineteenth-century reproductions of Egyptian monuments (from Quatremère de Quincy, *De l'architecture Egyptienne*, pls. 3 and 10).

Gravé par Gaitte.

Fig. 1: (cont.)

end of the century, among the mass of material accumulated by archaeologists and travellers, ancient architectural drawings started to appear. For a long time, however, the only available material for architectural historians was represented by more or less precise surveys of the archaeological remains.

In general, not many Egyptian monuments were actually taken into account in nineteenth-century studies on architectural proportions. The aim of the nineteenth-century scholars generally was just to connect Egypt to the following history of architecture and to make sure that its monuments harmonised with the rest, rather than study them as a separate subject. In 1854 Zeising dedicated just a paragraph to the Egyptian canon of proportion for the human body. In 1860 Henszlmann started his study with a few observations on the Egyptian Twelfth Dynasty, but his main concern was certainly Greek architecture. In 1924, Hambidge wrote that

Saracenic, Mahomedan, Chinese, Japanese, Persian, Hindu, Assyrian, Coptic, Byzantine, and Gothic art analyses show unmistakably the conscious use of plan schemes and all belong to the same type. Greek and Egyptian art analyses show an unmistakable conscious use of plan schemes of another type. There is no question as to the relative merit of the two types. The latter is immeasurably superior to the former. This is made manifest as soon as the two types are tested by nature.[4]

No practical examples of the application of this theory on actual Egyptian buildings, however, are included in this publication. The first publication to take into account ancient Egyptian textual sources and various archaeological material, and to suggest an interpretation of over fifty Egyptian monuments, was the monograph published in 1965 by Alexander Badawy.

The most successful among the geometrical figures applied to ancient Egyptian architecture (with or without a precise connection with the Golden Section), was the triangle. In particular, three triangles: the 3-4-5, the equilateral and the triangle called 'Egyptian' by Viollet-le-Duc and 8:5 by Choisy and Badawy. The first is a right-angled triangle which belongs to a peculiar group of right-angled triangles in which all the three sides correspond to whole numbers. The second is a triangle with three equal sides, while the third is an isosceles triangle (two sides equal and one different) in which the ratio between the base and the height is about 8:5. Originally, as we shall see in the next paragraph, in Viollet-le-Duc's suggested theory the equilateral and the 'Egyptian' or 8:5 triangle were geometrically connected, the latter depending on the former. But this link was soon forgotten, and the supposed use of the second triangle was later interpreted as an approximation of the Golden Section. The story of the evolution of the theories discussed in the following section is a tale of confusion and misunderstanding among scholars and among geometrical figures, which I will attempt to clarify.

---

[4] Hambidge, *Dynamic Symmetry*, p. xii.

Viollet-le-Duc, Babin and the primeval pyramid

In 1863, Viollet-le-Duc suggested that three triangles were the basis of the design of every good style of architecture: the 3-4-5 triangle, the equilateral triangle and what he called the 'Egyptian' triangle. According to him

[the equilateral triangle] completely satisfies the eye. It presents three equal angles, three equal sides, a division of the circle into three parts, a perpendicular let fall from the vertex dividing the base into two equal parts, and the formation of the hexagon inscribed in a circle and dividing it into six equal parts. No geometrical figure affords more satisfaction to the mind, and none fulfils better those conditions that please the eye, viz., regularity and stability.[5]

The third triangle is strictly connected to the equilateral and, in fact, derives from it. In a pyramid in which the vertical section parallel to the side-length of the base corresponds to an equilateral triangle, the section along the diagonal of the base is the triangle which Viollet-le-Duc called 'Egyptian'[6] (fig. 2). This triangle was also erroneously identified as the vertical section of the pyramid of Khufu, that in turn was believed by Viollet-le-Duc and other scholars to have been derived from the 3-4-5 triangle (fig. 3).

In Viollet-le-Duc's 'Egyptian' triangle the ratio between base and height (which would be an irrational number) can be approximated by means of the ratio 4:2.5 or 8:5. As for the equilateral triangle, Viollet-le-Duc observed that

the relation to 5 in height and 8 in breadth satisfies the eye. Now, while it is difficult to *prove* why a visual sensation is pleasing or displeasing, it is at least possible to define this sensation. As I said above, *dimensions* become *proportions* sensible to the eye, – that is, comparative relations of lengths, breadths, and surfaces, – only as far as there are dissimilarities between these dimensions. The relations of 1 to 2 or of 2 to 4 are not dissimilarities, but equal divisions of similars, reproducing similars. When a method of proportions obliges the designer, so to speak, to give divisions which are as 8 to 5, e.g. 5 being neither the half nor the third, nor the fourth of 8, sustaining a relation to 8 which the eye cannot define, you have already, at the very outset, a means of obtaining the contrasts which are necessary for satisfying the first law of proportions.[7]

Viollet-le-Duc detected the use of the equilateral and the 'Egyptian' triangles in the design of monuments of various periods. Egypt is represented by a portion of a colonnade from the Temple of Khons at Karnak (fig. 4, marked as G), two schemes of distribution of masses in unidentified (ideal?) Egyptian porticos and the

---

[5] Viollet-le-Duc, *Lectures on Architecture*, IX Entretien and figs. 1 to 10 (quotation from *Lectures on Architecture*, pp. 392–3); for a discussion on this theory, see Borissavliévitch, *Essai critique*, pp. 97–120.

[6] Jomard, however, had called 'Egyptian' the 3-4-5 triangle (Edmé F. Jomard, 'Memoire sur le système métrique des anciens Egyptiens', in *Description de l'Egypte, Antiquités, Memoires*, vol. I, Paris: Imprimerie Impèriale, 1809).

[7] Viollet-le-Duc, *Lectures on Architecture*, pp. 405–6.

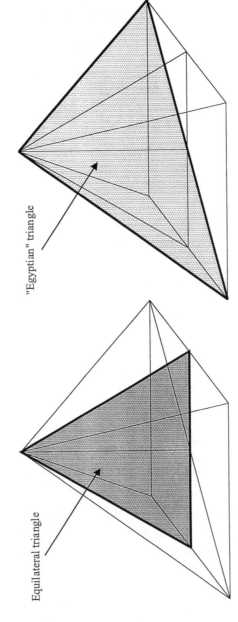

"Egyptian" triangle

Equilateral triangle

Fig. 2: Equilateral and 'Egyptian' triangles according to Viollet-le-Duc.

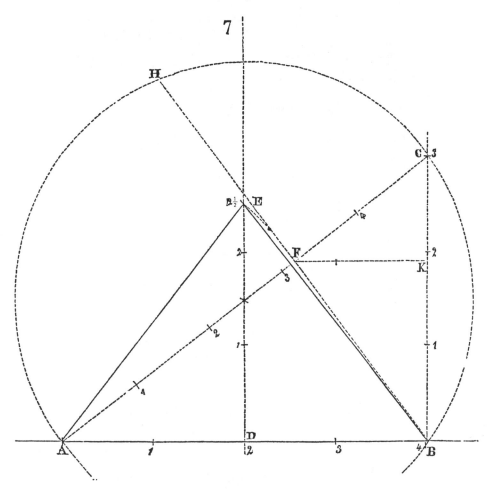

Fig. 3: Construction of the vertical section of the pyramid of Khufu by means of the 3-4-5 triangle according to Viollet-le-Duc (from *Entretiens*, fig. 7).

Pyramid of Khufu. Monuments from other periods include the colonnades of the Greek temples at Corinth, of Concord at Agrigentum, of Egina (fig. 4, A, B and D), and the Parthenon (fig. 5); the Arch of Titus in Rome; a little Roman arch at St. Chamas, in Provence, especially appreciated because apparently entirely designed after an equilateral triangle; the Basilica of Constantine (fig. 6); and the cathedrals of Notre-Dame de Paris and Amiens[8] (fig. 7).

Twenty-seven years later, Babin, an Ingénieur des Ponts-et-Chaussées, published an article in which he followed Viollet-le-Duc's theory about the use of the two

---

[8] For a criticism of Viollet-le-Duc's approach, see for instance August Thiersch, *Die Proportionen in der Architektur*, Handbuch der Architektur 4, Darmstadt: Bergsträsser, 1883.

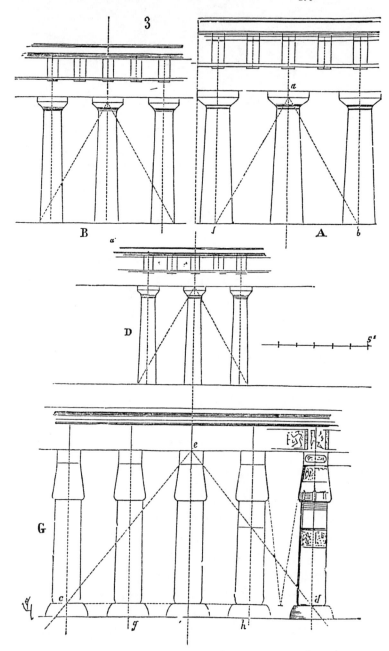

Fig. 4: Proportions obtained by means of equilateral and 'Egyptian' triangles in the temples of Corinth (A), of the Concord at Agrigentum (B), of Egina (D) and of Khons at Karnak (G) according to Viollet-le-Duc (from *Entretiens*, fig. 3).

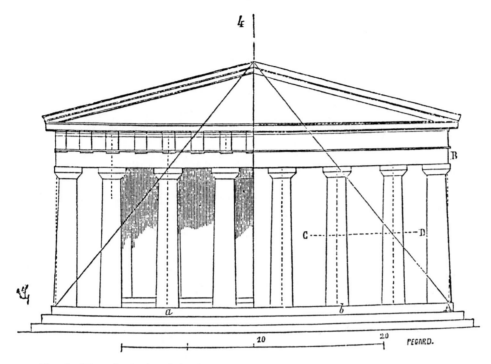

Fig. 5: 'Egyptian' triangle in the design of the façade of the Parthenon according to Viollet-le-Duc (from *Entretiens*, fig. 4).

triangles and applied it to several Greek monuments.[9] Instead of using convenient approximations, he retained the true irrational values of the sides of the 'primeval pyramid' (fig. 8). He observed that in many Greek temples the ratio between the height of the columns and the length of the sanctuary corresponds to one of the following values: $\frac{1}{\sqrt{3}}$, $\frac{\sqrt{2}}{\sqrt{3}}$ and $\sqrt{2}$. These ratios can be found in the two triangles mentioned by Viollet-le-Duc, where the first corresponds to the ratio between half the base and height, the second to the ratio between half the diagonal and the height, and the third to half the diagonal (in the case of a pyramid with side-length equal to 2). The text which explains the relationship between the two triangles and between the 'Egyptian' and the 8:5 (or 4:2.5) triangle is rather obscure and unless the reader had a previous acquaintance with the subject, it is not certain that the connection would appear clear. This is probably what happened to Choisy, whose theory will be explained in the next section.

Babin only investigated Greek temples. He suggested that the Greeks used these triangles both as geometrical figures (as in figure 9) and as sources of numerical ratios between columns and naos (fig. 10). Neither on this occasion, nor in the article

[9] C. Babin, 'Note sur l'emploi des triangles dans la mise en proportion des monuments grecs', *Revue Archéologique* 15 (1890), 82–106.

8

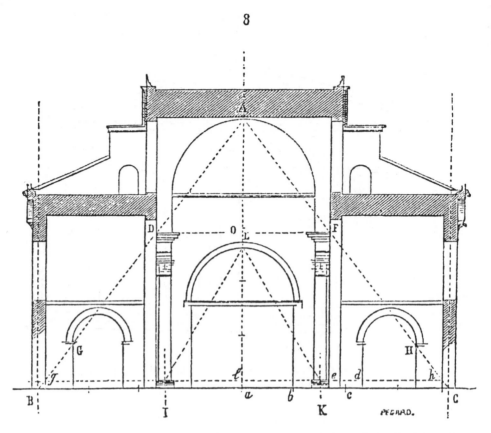

Fig. 6: Equilateral and 'Egyptian' triangles in the design of the Basilica of Constantine according to Viollet-le-Duc (from *Entretiens*, fig. 8).

which he published a year later on the metrology of Achaemenid architecture,[10] did Babin seek to analyse Egyptian monuments. Nevertheless, by acting as a bridge between Viollet-le-Duc and Choisy, his first article seems to have had a significant influence on the development of research on Egyptian architecture.

Choisy and the introduction of the Golden Section

In 1899, the French architectural historian Auguste Choisy published his *Histoire de l'Architecture*, in which a chapter was devoted to ancient Egyptian architecture and a whole paragraph to its proportions.[11] According to him, Egyptian temples appear to have been built using 'rapports d'une remarquable simplicité', such as

---

[10] C. Babin, 'Note sur la métrologie et les proportions dans les monuments achéménides de la Perse', *Revue Archéologique* 17 (1891), 347–79.

[11] Auguste Choisy, *Histoire de l'architecture*, Paris: Gauthier-Villars, 1899, pp. 51–8.

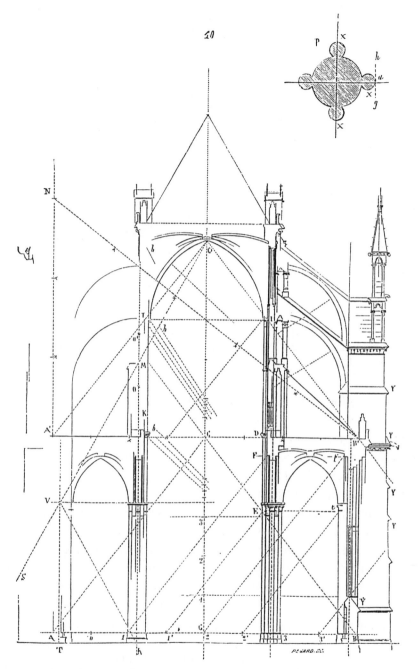

Fig. 7: Proportions of the section of the Cathedral of Amiens according to Viollet-le-Duc (from *Entretiens*, fig. 10).

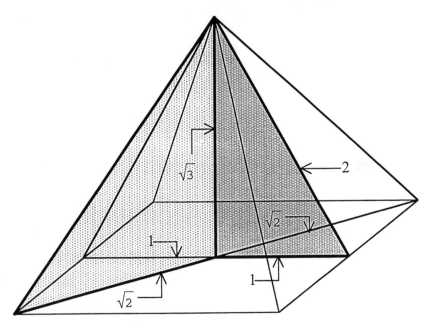

Fig. 8: Dimensions of various elements of a pyramid with side-length of the square base equal to 2 and vertical section (parallel to the side-length) equal to an equilateral triangle.

1:2 or 3:5. He followed the idea that the Egyptians used a number of triangles in the design of their buildings, but included only one drawing, representing the façade of the Eighteenth Dynasty southern peripteral temple at Elephantine, which had been designed, in his opinion, by means of two triangles and a series of 'simple' ratios between the elements (fig. 11). This temple, however, was not a good choice, since both peripteral temples at Elephantine – the northern (which was already in poor condition) and the southern – were completely destroyed in 1822,[12] and it is not clear whether the surviving drawings are correct.[13]

Choisy suggested that the Egyptians used the triangles reproduced in figure 12. The first two triangles are generated by the association of two 3-4-5 triangles (the first by connecting them by means of the cathetus equal to 3, the second by means of the cathetus equal to 4). The importance of the 3-4-5 triangle was due to the fact that, unlike the majority of right-angled triangles, all its sides correspond to

[12] Gardner Wilkinson, *The Architecture of Ancient Egypt*, London: Murray, 1850, p. 80.

[13] In 1933 Borchardt was unable to match the sole surviving inscribed block with the drawings of the *Description*. Nestor l'Hôte, who visited the site with Champollion in 1822, left a perspective of this temple which differs from the *Description* in several details. By the comparison between the two sources, Borchardt concluded that Nestor l'Hôte's drawing was more reliable. Since, however, when Nestor l'Hôte visited the site both peripteral temples had already been destroyed, Borchardt suggested that he might have referred to drawings, now lost, of an earlier traveller (Ludwig Borchardt, *Ägyptische Tempel mit Umgang*, Beiträge Bf 2, Cairo 1938, pp. 95–8, especially note 1, p. 96, and plate 21).

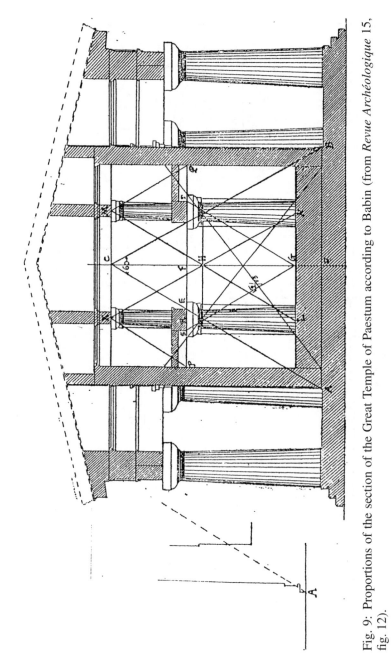

Fig. 9: Proportions of the section of the Great Temple of Paestum according to Babin (from *Revue Archéologique* 15, fig. 12).

MONUMENTS	LARGEUR INTÉRIEURE de la cella. l	HAUTEUR des colonnes H	DIMENSIONS calculées	DIAGRAMME REPRESENTATIF
1) Temple B à Sélinoute a.........	3ᵐ,681	3ᵐ,207 depuis le pavé du péristyle jusqu'au-dessous du chapiteau	$\frac{L}{2}\sqrt{3} = 3{,}187$ au lieu de 3,207 Différ. 0,02	1. Triangle équilatéral.
2) Temple C à Sélinonte a......... hexastyle périptère construit vers 628-604 av. J.-C.	8ᵐ,743	7ᵐ,587 depuis le pavé du péristyle jusqu'au-dessous du chapitenu	$\frac{L}{2}\sqrt{3} = 7{,}569$ au lieu de 7,587 Différ. 0,018	
3) Temple D à Sélinonte a......... hexastyle périptère construit vers 604.	8ᵐ,27	7ᵐ,453 jusqu'au-dessous du tailloir du chapiteau	$\frac{L}{2}\sqrt{3} = 7{,}161$ ou lieu de 7,153 Différ. 0,008	
4) Temple T à Sélinonte a......... pseudo-diptère octostyle construit vers 604.	18ᵐ,04	15ᵐ,615 jusqu'au-dessous du tailloir du chapiteau	$\frac{L}{2}\sqrt{3} = 15{,}622$ au lieu de 15,615 Différ. 0,007	
5) Temple R à Sélinonte a......... hexastyle périptère construit de 444 à 416 av. J.-C.	11ᵐ,78	10ᵐ,187	$\frac{L}{2}\sqrt{3} = 10{,}201$ au lieu de 10,187 Différ. 0,014	
6) Temple de Phigalie b......... hexastyle périptère construit vers 430.	6ᵐ,80	5ᵐ,925	$\frac{L}{2}\sqrt{3} = 5{,}89$ au lieu de 5,925. Différ. 0,035	
7) Temple de Thésée............ hexastyle périptère construit vers 467.	6ᵐ,21	5ᵐ,35 jusqu'au-dessous de l'échine	$\frac{L}{2}\sqrt{3} = 5{,}369$ au lieu de 5,350 Différ. 0,019	

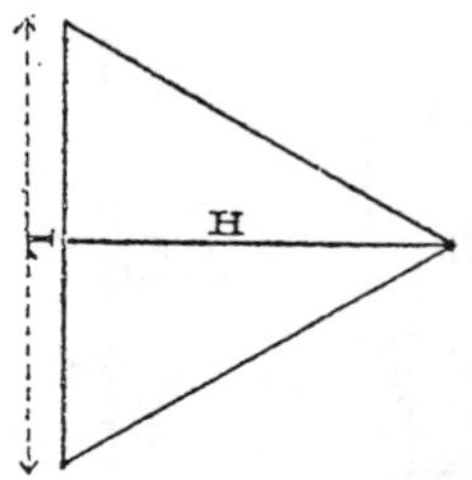

a) Hittorf et Zauth, *Architecture antique de la Sicile.*

b) *Expédition de Morée.*

Fig. 10: Relationship between the dimensions of some Greek temples and the proportions of some triangles according to Babin (from *Revue Archéologique* 15, pp. 91–2).

MONUMENTS	LARGEUR INTÉRIEURE de la cella L	HAUTEUR des colonnes H	DIMENSIONS calculées	DIAGRAMME REPRÉSENTATIF
8) Temple A à Sélinonte a....... hexastyle périptère construit de 444 à 416.	environ 7m,68	6m,235	$L \dfrac{\sqrt{2}}{\sqrt{3}} = 6{,}278$ au lieu de 6,235 Différ. 0,043	II. Triangle égyptien. 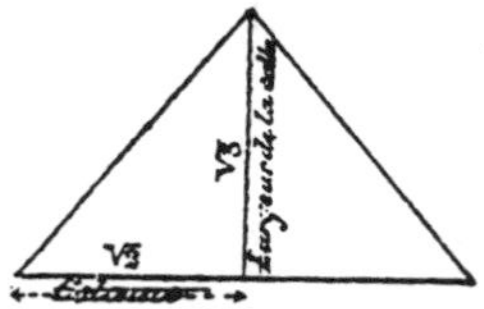
9) Grand temple de Pæstum c... hexastyle périptère construit en 530.	10m,895	8m,89	$L \dfrac{\sqrt{2}}{\sqrt{3}} = 8{,}901$ au lieu de 8,89 Différ. 0,011	
10) Temple de Jupiter à Égine d . hexastyle périptère construit vers 480.	6m,44	5m,27	$L \dfrac{\sqrt{2}}{\sqrt{3}} = 5{,}264$ au lieu de 2,570 Différ. 0,009	III. Triangle égyptien.
11) Temple S à Sélinonte a....... construit de 628 à 604.	7m,201	8m,776 jusqu'au - dessous du tailloir	$L \dfrac{\sqrt{2}}{\sqrt{2}} = 8{,}814$ au lieu de 8,776 Différ. 0,038	
12) Temple d'Héra à Olympie e....	8m,34	5m,21	$\dfrac{L}{2} \dfrac{5}{4} = 5{,}21$	IV. Base 4. Hauteur 2,5. 
13) Temple de Diane à Éphèse f...	21m,236	16m,998	$\dfrac{5}{4} H = 21{,}247$ au lieu de 21,236 Différ. 0,011	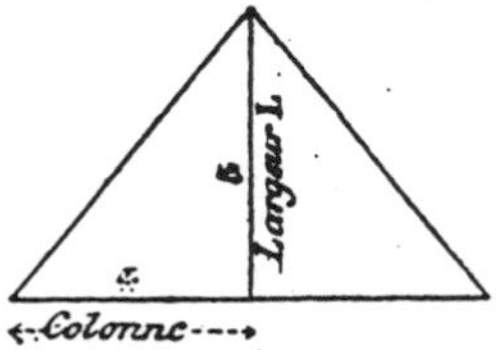
14) Temple de la Concorde....... à Agrigente g IVe siècle av. J.-C.	7m,40	fût de la colonne 5m,93	$\dfrac{5}{4} H = 7{,}41$ au lieu de 7,40 Différ. 0,010	V. Base 4. Hauteur 2,5.

a) Hittorf et Zanth, *Architecture antique de la Sicile*.
c) Labrouste, *Restitution des temples de Pæstum*.
d) C. Garnier, *Restitution du temple d'Égine*.
e) *Ausgrabungen zu Olympia.*
f) Wood, *Discoveries at Ephesus*.
g) Gærtner, *Vue des principaux monuments grecs de la Sicile.*

Fig. 10: (*cont.*)

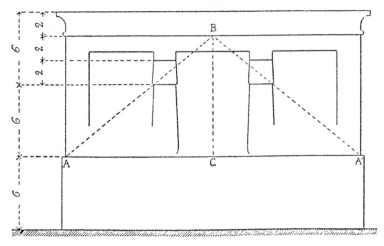

Fig. 11: Design of the façade of the southern peripteral chapel at Elephantine according to Choisy (from *Histoire de l'architecture*, fig. 1).

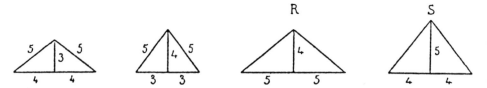

Fig. 12: Triangles used by the Egyptians according to Choisy (from *Histoire de l'architecture*, fig. 3).

whole numbers. Therefore, joining three sides respectively 3, 4 and 5 units long provided a simple method to construct a right angle. Choisy considered also the third and fourth triangles (labelled R and S) as derivative of the 3-4-5, but with no clear geometrical reason. They do contain the numbers 4 and 5, but are constructed by associating two right-angled triangles in which the catheti are equal to 4 and 5 and the hypotenuse is equal to the irrational number 6.403 . . ., that has nothing to do with the 3-4-5 triangle and all its implications.

   According to Choisy, the Egyptians used also three other triangles: the equilateral triangle, the triangle corresponding to the vertical section along the diagonal of a pyramid such as Khufu's, 'where the outline is an equilateral triangle'; and the triangle 'in which the height is given by the division of the base into mean and extreme ratio'. The second triangle (corresponding to S) is Viollet-le-Duc's 'Egyptian' triangle (the hint about the pyramid of Khufu is wrong, since the proportions of this pyramid are completely different, but the relationship between the two sections of the same pyramidal solid is correct). The third triangle is generated by the 'mean and extreme ratio' – that is, another name for the Golden Section.

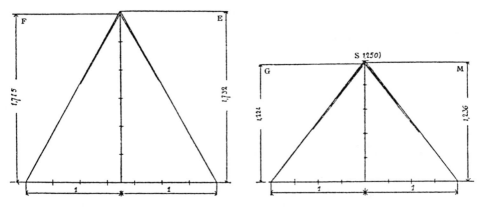

Fig. 13: Constructions of equilateral and 'Egyptian' triangles according to Choisy (from *Histoire de l'architecture*, fig. 4).

Choisy observed that the use of triangles might appear contradictory to the use of modules and simple ratio, but that in fact these two methods were related to each another (fig. 13). To construct an equilateral triangle, for example, they drew a triangle in which the base was equal to 7 and the height to 6 units (even better if the ratio was 8:7). In order to approximate the mean and extreme ratio, Choisy vaguely suggested the adoption of the ratios 5:3 and 8:5 (the former is mentioned in the text and the latter is actually used in the drawing).

In conclusion, as early as the end of the nineteenth century, from all these theories three triangles emerge as potentially significant for the study of proportions in ancient Egyptian architecture: the 3-4-5, the equilateral and the 'Egyptian' triangle. To be precise, it is not the 'Egyptian' triangle, but its approximation, the 8:5 triangle, that will be widely used by the late scholars, as we shall see in the next chapter.

The Golden Section

The origin and definitions of the Golden Section

Before we move to a detailed analysis of the theories based on the Golden Section, it is necessary to introduce a few basic mathematical concepts which will act as a guide to the following sections.[14] The Golden Section has been known under different names,[15] and can be visualised in various ways. Figure 14 shows two

---

[14] For extensive explanations on symbolic aspects, see Ghyka, *Nombre d'Or*, vol. I, chapters 1–2; Ghyka, *Geometry of Art and Life*, chapters 1–2; André VandenBroeck, *Philosophical Geometry*, Rochester, NY: Inner Traditions International, 1972, especially pp. 62–4; Robert Lawlor, *Sacred Geometry, Philosophy and Practice*, London: Thames and Hudson, 1982, especially pp. 44–64.

[15] The name 'Golden Section' was coined by Ohm in 1834 or 35. This proportion has been known under a variety of names: *divina proportione* for Luca Pacioli (1509), *proportio divina* for Kepler (1608 and 1611), the *golden medial*, the *medial section* and the *golden mean* (David H. Fowler, 'A generalisation of the Golden Section', *Fibonacci Quarterly* 20/2 (1982), 146–58, especially 146–7).

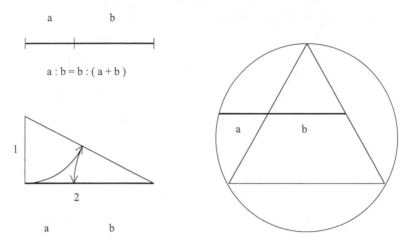

Fig. 14: Subdivision of a segment according to the Golden Section and two geometrical constructions of the same proportion (the latter drawn after Fowler, *Plato's Academy*, p. 105, note 3.5b).

possible geometrical constructions of this proportion, probably the simplest and the most striking.

In general, a proportion may be defined as a relation among four magnitudes, or as an equality of two ratios:

$$a{:}b = c{:}d \tag{1}$$

A proportion is called 'continuous' if there is a common term between the ratios:

$$a{:}b = b{:}c \tag{2}$$

If $c = a + b$, it is possible to establish a proportion which involves two terms only, instead of the four of the first example and the three of the second:

$$a{:}b = b{:}(a{+}b) \tag{3}$$

that is, the ratio between two terms is equal to the ratio between the larger term and the sum of the two.

In $a{:}b = b{:}c$, then $b^2 = ac$, whereas in $a{:}b = b{:}(a + b)$ then $b^2 = ab + a^2$. These conditions are visualised in figure 15, where the lower scheme represents the geometrical properties of the Golden Section: if we assume that $b = 1$, the semidiagonal of the square can be easily calculated as $\frac{\sqrt{5}}{2}$. Therefore, the smaller term is equal to $\frac{\sqrt{5}}{2} - \frac{1}{2}$, while the sum is equal to $\frac{\sqrt{5}}{2} + \frac{1}{2} = 1.618033989 \ldots$: this irrational number, usually defined by the Greek letter ϕ, is the numerical value of the Golden Section.

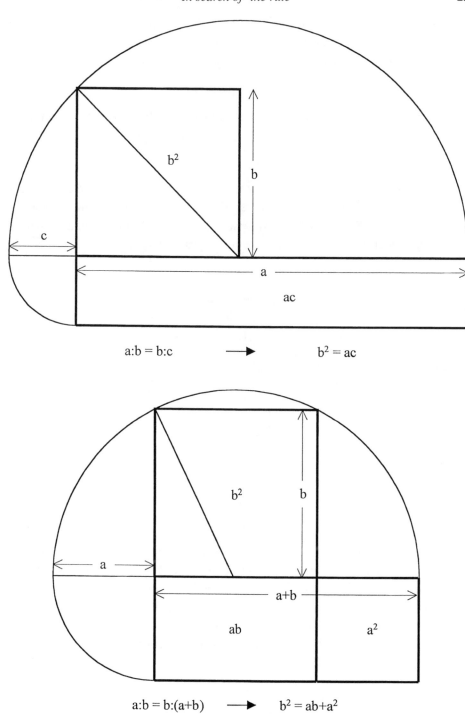

Fig. 15: Visualisation of the relationship among elements of a continuous proportion, above, and of the Golden Section, below (drawn after Vandenbroeck, *Philosophical Geometry*, figs. 25g and h).

Another important point is the connection with the numerical series named after the Italian scholar Leonardo from Pisa, also called Fibonacci (1175–1240). It is a series of numbers in which each term is the sum of the two previous:

1, 2, 3, 5, 8, 13, 21, 34, 55, 89, 144, 233, 377, 610, 987, . . .

If a different start is chosen, we may obtain other series,[16] such as, for example:

1, 3, 4, 7, 11, 18, 29, 47, . . .
1, 4, 5, 9, 14, 23, 37, 60, . . .

and so on. These series share an important characteristic; the sequence of consecutive ratios between each term and its antecedent tends in the limit to the number ϕ, equal to 1.618033989 . . . , which expresses the Golden Section. The approximation is very rough for low numbers, but converges very quickly, especially in the Fibonacci Series:

$$\frac{2}{1} = 2$$

$$\frac{3}{2} = 1.5$$

$$\frac{5}{3} = 1.667\ldots$$

$$\frac{8}{5} = 1.6$$

$$\frac{13}{8} = 1.625\ldots$$

$$\frac{21}{13} = 1.615\ldots$$

$$\frac{34}{21} = 1.619\ldots$$

and so on

The Fibonacci Series is also related to the so-called gnomonic expansion, which takes place when a figure, added to an original figure, generates a resultant figure which is similar to the original; that is, the size changes, but the proportions remain the same (which is more or less what happens in the Fibonacci Series). The gnomonic growth can be visualised by means of spirals: figure 16 shows a spiral based on the $\sqrt{5}$ generated by the ratio between the series 1, 3, 4, 7, 11, 18, 29, 47 . . . and 1, 2, 3, 5, 8, 13, 21, 34, ...

---

[16] These are also called Lucas numbers (for a detailed explanation, see Steven Vajda, *Fibonacci and Lucas Numbers, and the Golden Section*, Chichester: Ellis Horwood, 1989, chapters 4, 13 and 14).

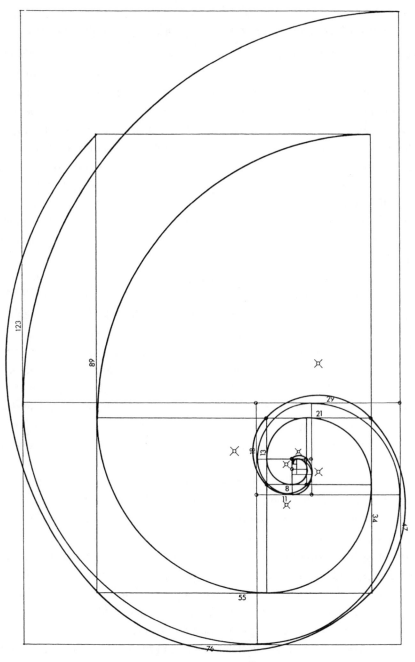

Fig. 16: Gnomonic growth visualised as a $\sqrt{5}$ spiral (from Lawlor, *Sacred Geometry*, fig. 6.1).

The Golden Section and ancient Egyptian art and architecture

Concerning ancient Egypt, in many cases, the Golden Section-based geometrical constructions appear to be based on very unlikely starting points. Sometimes, however, they seem to rely upon more convincing details. Before turning to Badawy's theory, the most convincing and substantial of all, here is a brief review of some interpretations suggested by other scholars. It is worth starting with an example to which we shall return later, the representation from the Ptolemaic tomb of Petosiris (about 300 BC) which is shown in figure 17.[17] Robert Lawlor noticed that the right-angled triangle, which represents the sloping side of mountainous desert and which occupies the right lower portion of the scene, seems to be designed after the Golden Section: that is, if the base of the triangle is 1, the other cathetus is equivalent to φ (fig. 18, left). Another, more complex interpretation by the same author is shown in figure 18, right.[18]

Among other scholars, it is worth mentioning Matila Ghyka, who included in his publications a few rather vague examples of Egyptian monuments, including a scheme of an unidentified Egyptian temple (after Mössel), four schemes simply called 'tracés harmoniques égyptiens' (fig. 19) and a rough sketch of the pyramid of Khufu (fig. 20).[19] Over a century later, Else C. Kielland analysed a number of statues and reliefs and claimed to have found that they were all designed according to the Golden Section. Quoting Ghyka, she optimistically concludes that 'the φ-proportion was highly esteemed by the Pythagoreans, whose dependence on the Egyptians is well known. But no Egyptologist has ever found it mentioned in any hieroglyphic text, which does not exclude the possibility of its being found in the future'.[20]

One of the most famous theories on the proportions of ancient Egyptain architecture and art is that suggested by Schwaller de Lubicz. He believed that the Egyptian canon for the representations of the human body depended on a system based on musical harmony, π and φ, in which horizontal guide-lines marked the position of specific anatomical points of the body. He suggested that there was a strict correspondence between vital centres of the human body and significant points in the layout of the temple of Luxor (fig. 21).[21] It is interesting to note that this theory represents yet another version of the recurrent idea of the existence of parallels between sacred buildings and human body, an idea that links Vitruvius, Francesco di Giorgio Martini, Viollet-le-Duc, and the nineteenth-century division

---

[17] Gustave Lefebvre, *Le tombeau de Petosiris*, Cairo: SAE, 1923, plates 28, 31 and 32.
[18] Lawlor, *Sacred Geometry*, pp. 54–5.   [19] Ghyka, *Nombre d'Or*, plates 30a, 27 and 44.
[20] Else C. Kielland, *Geometry in Egyptian Art*, London: Tiranti, 1955 (quotation from p. 13). She later extended her conclusions to Greek art (*Geometry in Greek Art*, Oslo: Dreyer, 1983).
[21] René A. Schwaller de Lubicz, *Le Temple de l'Homme*, Paris: Caractères, 1957, pp. 490–505.

Fig. 17: Scene from the east wall of the chapel of the Ptolemaic tomb of Petosiris (drawn after Lefebvre, *Petosiris*, pl. 32).

of a building-organism into structure-skeleton and a façade-skin.[22] Robert Lawlor continued and extended Schwaller de Lubicz's theories, putting forward as examples some two-dimensional representations of the throne of Osiris ('clearly depicted as the square of 4, as it transforms into the square of 5 through the principle of $\sqrt{5}$ on which all the ϕ proportion rests'[23]), the gnomonic expansion of the

---

[22] See, for example, Philip Steadman, *The Evolution of Designs*, Cambridge Urban and Architectural Studies 5, Cambridge: Cambridge University Press, 1979, chapters 2, 3 and 4 and figs. 4 and 8.

[23] Lawlor, *Sacred Geometry*, p. 72; see also Schwaller de Lubicz, *Temple de l'Homme*, pp. 157–8.

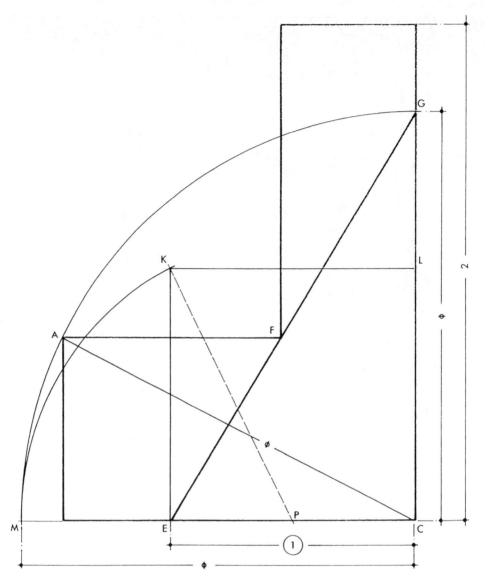

Fig. 18: Two interpretations of the geometrical figures in a scene from the tomb
of Petosiris by Lawlor and Lamy (from Lawlor, *Sacred Geometry*, pp. 54–5).

temple of Luxor (fig. 22) and four different geometrical schemes based on ϕ for
the Osireion, the peculiar temple built by Seti I at Abydos (fig. 23).[24]

The apotheosis of the Golden Section-based theories is represented by the results
of the research of Fournier de Corats. Starting from the pyramid of Khufu (fig. 24),
he calculated eight values, which he called 'Rapports de Divine Harmonie', and

---

[24] Lawlor, *Sacred Geometry*, pp. 61–2 and 73.

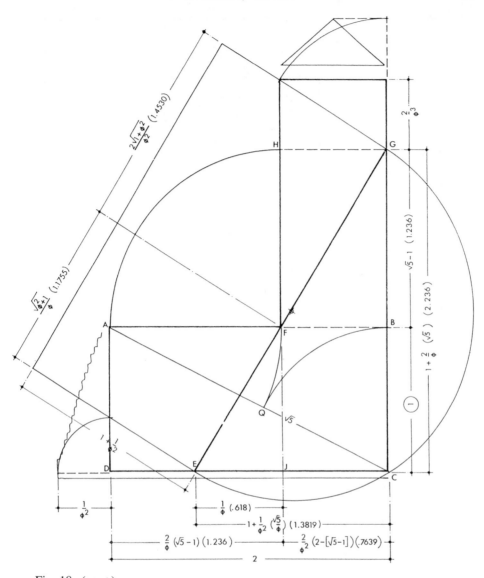

Fig. 18: (*cont.*)

applied these ratios, labelled by letters, to examples of art and architecture of any size and period, ranging from (obviously) the pyramid of Khufu to a New Kingdom brooch, from some columns from the temple of Karnak to the Ptolemaic zodiac from the temple of Dendera (figs. 25 and 26).[25]

[25] A. Fournier des Corats, *La proportion égyptienne et les rapports de divine harmonie*, Paris: Trédaniel, 1957.

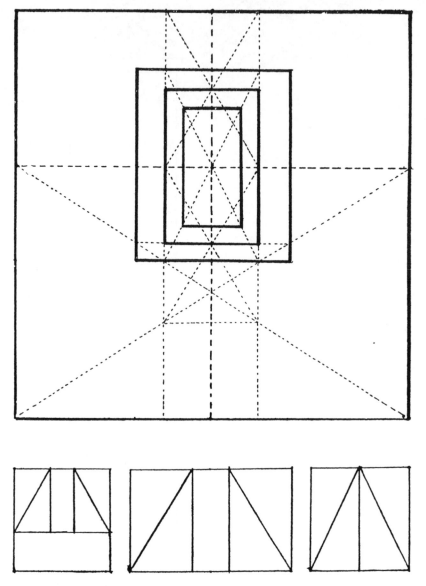

Fig. 19: 'Tracés harmoniques égyptiens' according to Ghyka (from *Le Nombre d'Or*, pl. 27).

The theory of Alexander Badawy

In 1965 Alexander Badawy, the Egyptian architect and Egyptologist, suggested the most convincing theory based on the Golden Section. Following Mössel, he assumed that this proportion had been one of the main devices used by the Egyptians in the layout of their buildings. However, he abandoned Mössel's circles and based his

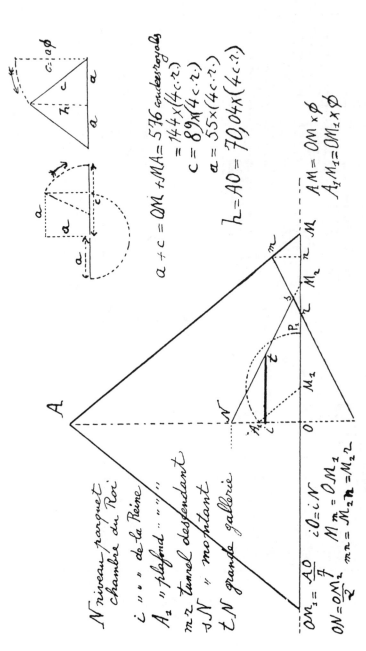

Fig. 20: Sketch of the proportions of the pyramid of Khufu, according to Ghyka (from *Le Nombre d'Or*, pl. 54).

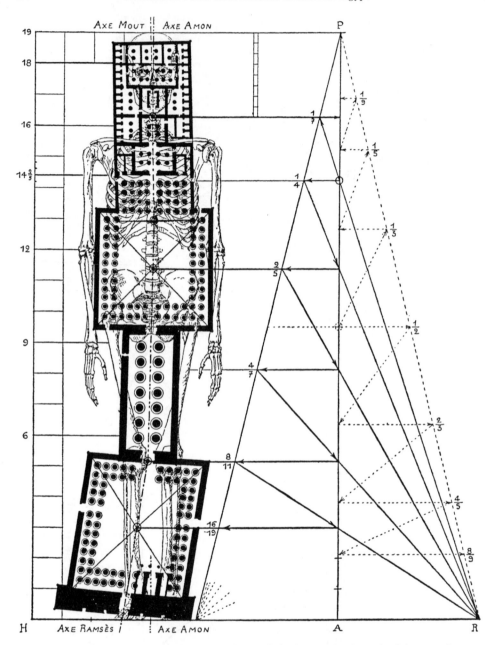

Fig. 21: Parallel between the proportions of the human body and of the temple of Luxor at the time of the Nineteenth Dynasty according to Schwaller de Lubicz (from *Temple de l'Homme*, fig. 138).

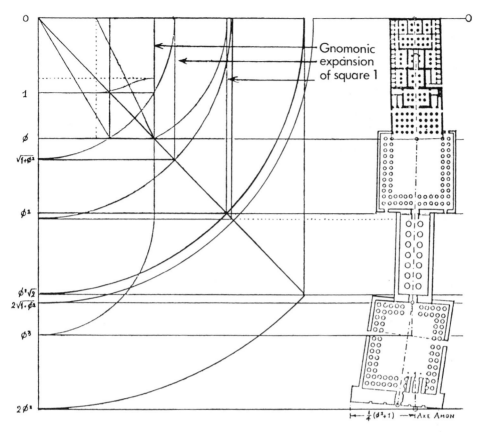

Fig. 22: Gnomonic expansion of the temple of Luxor (from Lawlor, *Sacred Geometry*, p. 73).

theory on other geometrical figures. According to Badawy, the Egyptians used a number of right-angled triangles, plus the square and the rectangle, to design plans and elevations of their monuments.[26] These triangles included the right-angled triangle in which the sides are 3, 4 and 5 unit; long; the isosceles triangle in which the basis is equal to 8 and the height to 5 units; and the isosceles triangles in which the height is 1, 2 or 4 times the base, that he called 1:2, 1:4 and 1:8 triangles. In addition, the square was used to construct a telescopic sequence of spaces, called the 'prismatic pillar', or was used in connection with the 8:5 triangle (fig. 27).

Badawy suggested that the Egyptians achieved the Golden Section by means of the Fibonacci Series 1, 2, 3, 5, 8, 13, 21, 34, 55. . . . According to his theory, they adopted the ratio 8:5 (in which 8 and 5 are numbers of the Fibonacci Series), which gives 1.6 as a result, as a good approximation for ϕ (that is, 1.618033989 . . .).

[26] Alexander Badawy, *Ancient Egyptian Architectural Design. A Study of the Harmonic System*, Near Eastern Studies 4, Berkeley: University of California Press, 1965, pp. 19–40.

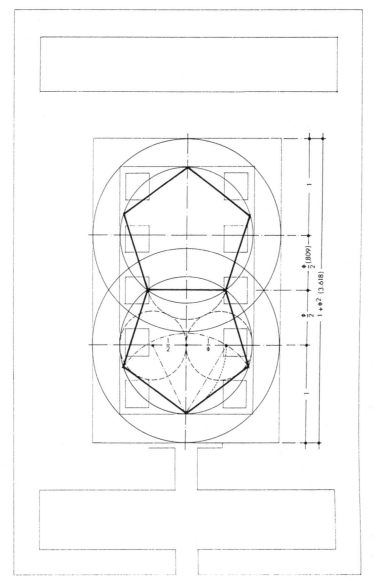

Fig. 23: An interpretation based on φ of the plan of the Osireion (Nineteenth Dynasty) by Lawlor and Lamy (from Lawlor, *Sacred Geometry*, p. 61).

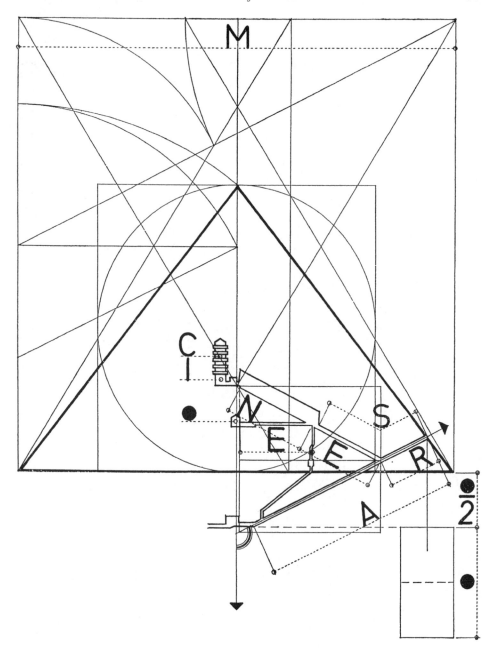

Fig. 24: Vertical section of the pyramid of Khufu showing the use of the eight 'Ratios of Divine Harmony' according to Fournier des Corats (from *Proportion égyptienne*, fig. 24).

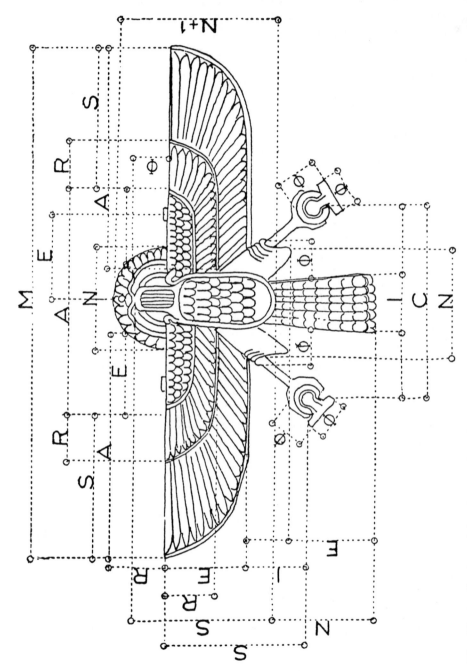

Fig. 25: Application of the eight Ratios of Divine Harmony to a New Kingdom brooch (above) and to the body of the goddess Nut from the Ptolemaic Dendera Zodiac (below) according to Fournier des Corats (from *Proportion égyptienne*, figs. 37 and 48).

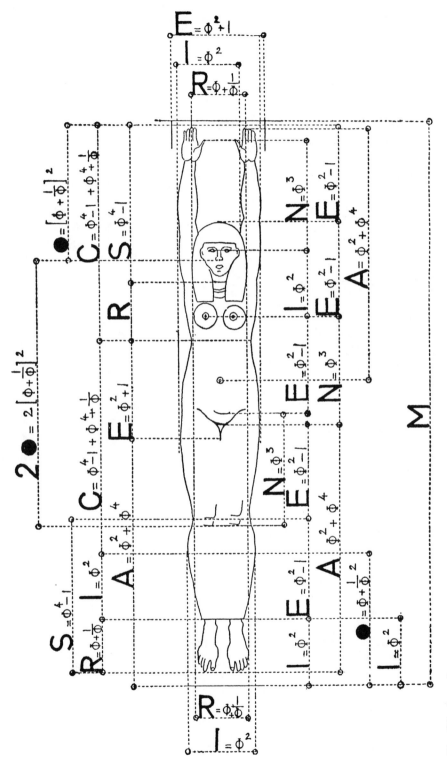

Fig. 25: *(cont.)*

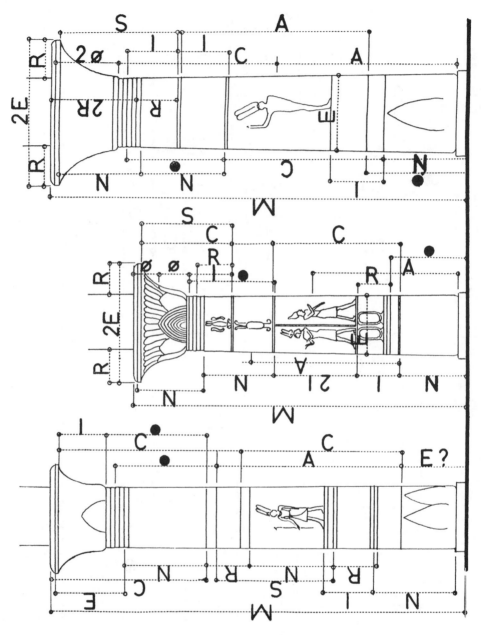

Fig. 26: Application of the eight Ratios of Divine Harmony to some columns of the temple of Amon at Karnak according to Fournier des Corats (from *Proportion égyptienne*, fig. 41).

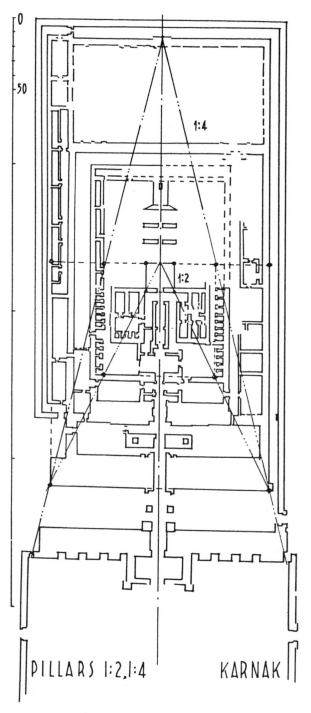

Fig. 27: Pillars 1:2, 1:4, 1:8 and prismatic pillar according to Badawy (from *Architectural Design*, figs. 6, 7 and 8).

PILLAR 1:8

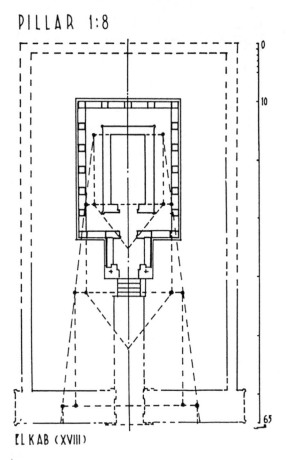

EL KAB (XVIII)

Fig. 27: (*cont.*)

In the layout of their buildings the architects used either the Fibonacci Series or, more often, a network of isosceles triangles in which the basis was equal to 8 units and the height to 5, thus approximating the Golden Section by means of a practical and not very complicated device.[27]

The process of planning would have been as follows. The architects would have traced the central axis of symmetry, then used the 1:2, 1:4 and 1:8 triangles to fix some special points of the plan (fig. 28). The next step would have been the 'constructional diagram', usually a combination of squares and triangles which were supposed to define the general outline of the building. Finally

[27] Badawy also suggested that the Egyptians used the 8:5 triangle to construct the heptagon, which he connected to the emblem of the goddess Seshat, who is often represented performing foundation ceremonies with the king. Her head is surmounted by seven radiating lancets, from which a vertical piece of cord descends, which Badawy assimilated to the heptagon. It may be noted, however, that although there are seven lancets, they are disposed, together with the cord, in eight symmetrical directions – not seven. The figure described by them would therefore be an octagon, rather than a heptagon.

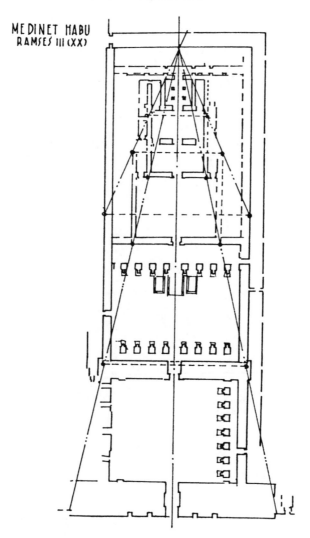

MEDINET HABU
RAMSES III (XX)

Fig. 27: (*cont.*)

a network of scissor-like shapes based on the sides of 8:5 triangles set along the longitudinal axis provided, at their intersections with the transverse or longitudinal sides of rooms, related points of reference indicating the location of some features. Thus the angles, doorways, columns, or piers are found to be interrelated in plan, while similar details, such as architraves, tori, capitals, and the axes of columns, doorways, or even panels are delimited in elevation.[28]

With this system, Badawy successfully analysed more than fifty-five plans and a few elevations of Egyptian monuments from the Predynastic to the Ptolemaic

---

[28] Badawy, *Ancient Egyptian Architectural Design*, pp. 34–5.

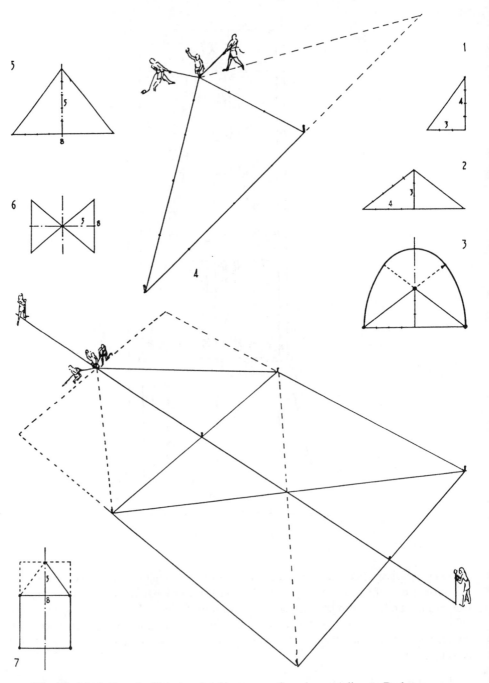

Fig. 28: Method to design triangles by means of cords according to Badawy (*Architectural Design*, fig. 2).

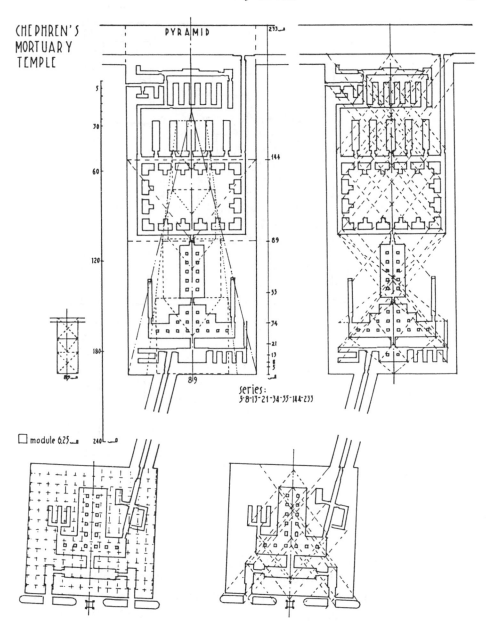

CHEPHREN'S
MORTUARY
TEMPLE

PYRAMID

series:
5·8·13·21·34·55·144·233

module 6.25

Fig. 29: Analysis of the plan of the mortuary temple of Khafra (Fourth Dynasty), according to Badawy (from *Architectural Design*, pl. 2).

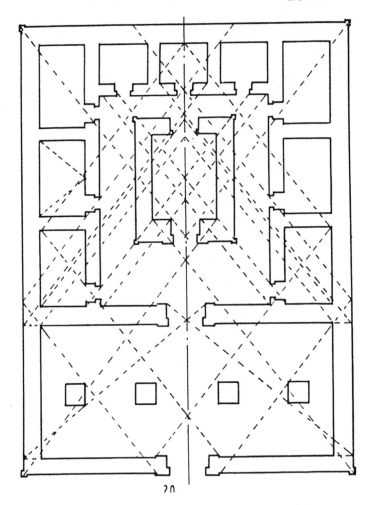

Fig. 30: Analysis of the reconstructed plan of the temple of Senusret I at Tôd
(Twelfth Dynasty), according to Badawy (from *Architectural Design*, pl. 9).

Period, including civil, funerary and religious architecture (figs. 29, 30, 32 and
34–7). His theory seems able to explain many factors. It suggests that a single set of
rules was used throughout the entire history of Egyptian architecture (and beyond),
that all of these rules were related to one another, that the Golden Section was
among them, and that the Egyptians could have achieved these results using their
own mathematical system and practical tools. All of these points, however, are open
to criticism.

First of all, Badawy's theory is hampered by the usual problems relating to the use
of drawings, such as their small scale and their inaccuracy. In many plans of large
buildings it is impossible to check the precision of the geometrical constructions,
because the thickness of the lines employed in the drawing can make a significant

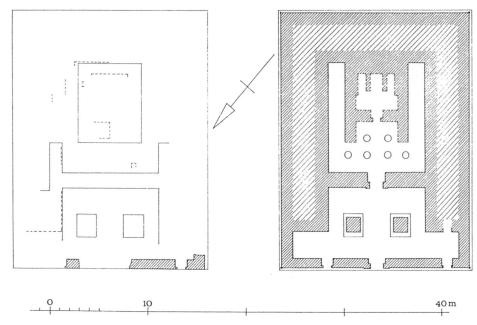

Fig. 31: Actual archaeological remains of the temple of Senusret I at Tôd (Twelfth Dynasty) and reconstruction of the original plan by Arnold (from Arnold, *MDAIK* 31, fig. 4).

difference. In the cases of intersection of two lines (for example, two sides of an 8:5 triangle, or a triangle and a particular element of the building), a small-scale drawing may hide very well a discrepancy of a couple of metres (see, for example, fig. 34). Moreover, Badawy readily employed more or less heavily reconstructed plans, such as Bisson de la Roque's plan of the Middle Kingdom temple at Tôd[29] (later re-interpreted by Arnold,[30] compare figs. 30 and 31), Lavers' plan of the Sanctuary of the Great Aten Temple at Amarna[31] reconstructed by comparing the representations found in the Amarna tombs with the very denuded archaeological remains[32] (compare figs. 32 and 33), and the already mentioned peripteral temple at Elephantine – probably not the most reliable bases for a study on proportions.

From a geometrical point of view, the methods suggested by Badawy for the use of each figure are often independent from one another. The constructions of 8:5, 1:2, 1:4, 3-4-5 triangles, prismatic pillar and square module have nothing in common with one another from a geometrical point of view. Furthermore, many lines which cross the plans published by Badawy correspond to the plans because

[29] Fernand Bisson de la Roque, *Tôd (1934 à 1936)*, FIFAO 17, Cairo: IFAO, 1937, pp. 6–7 and fig. 6.
[30] Dieter Arnold, 'Bemerkungen zu den frühen Tempeln von El-Tôd', *MDAIK* 31 (1975), 175–86, especially 184–6.
[31] J. D. S. Pendlebury, *The City of Akhenaten III*, London: EES, 1951, pp. 5–10 and pls. 7–9, 25 and 26.
[32] Barry J. Kemp, 'The Sanctuary of the Great Aten Temple', *Amarna Reports IV*, London: EES, 1987, chapter 8.

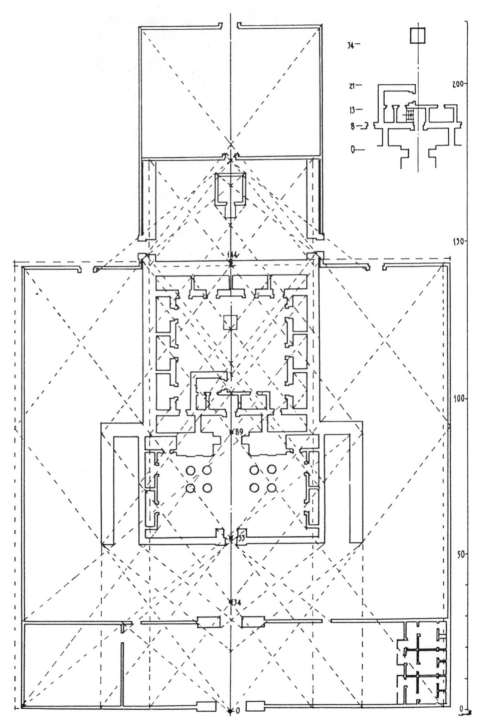

Fig. 32: Analysis of the plan of the Sanctuary of the Great Aten Temple at Amarna
(Eighteenth Dynasty), by means of a network of 8:5 triangles according to Badawy
(from *Architectural Design*, pl. 21).

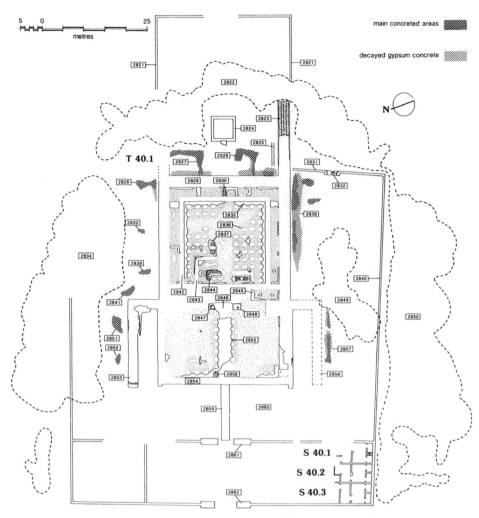

5   0   25

metres

main concreted areas

decayed gypsum concrete

N

2821   2821

2822

2823

2824

2825

T 40.1   2826

2827   2831

2828   2829   2830

2832

2835   2838

2833   2836

2837

2834

2839   2840

2842 2844 2845

2841   2843   2846   2849

2847   2848   2850

2851

2852   2855

2857

2853   2856   2858

2854

2859   2860

2861   S 40.1

S 40.2

2862   S 40.3

Fig. 33: Plan of the actual archaeological remains of the Sanctuary of the Great
Aten Temple at Amarna (Eighteenth Dynasty) according to the 1986 survey
(courtesy of the Egypt Exploration Society).

they were drawn after them, but they would not be of great use if they had to be
the starting point of the design. There is not a fixed correspondence between the
network of lines and the various elements of the buildings, as Badawy himself
admitted, and the resulting plan is often quite different from the combination of
lines describing triangles and squares. In fact in many cases, after using all of the
different geometrical constructions, the ancient architects still would have been
left with many basic details of the whole building to be established. Finally, it
may be observed that the easiest way to outline a rectangular hall would be by means

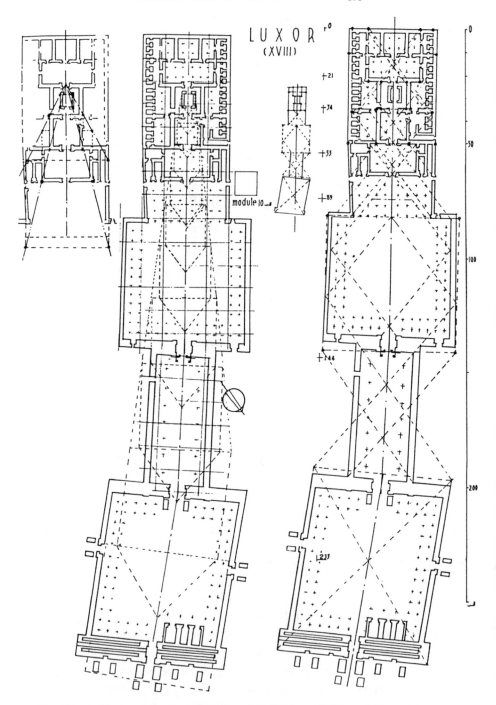

Fig. 34: Analysis of the plan of the temple of Luxor (Eighteenth Dynasty), according to Badawy (from *Architectural Design*, pl. 29).

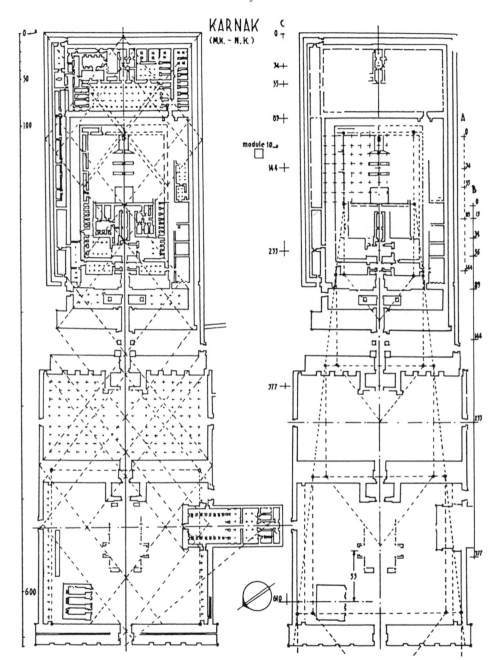

Fig. 35: Analysis of the plan of the temple of Karnak, New Kingdom, according to Badawy (from *Architectural Design*, pl. 26).

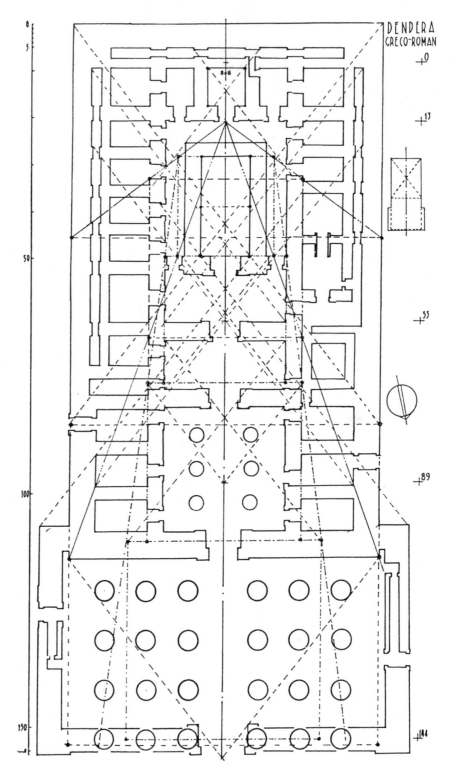

Fig. 36: Analysis of the plan of the Ptolemaic temple at Dendera according to Badawy (from *Architectural Design*, pl. 43).

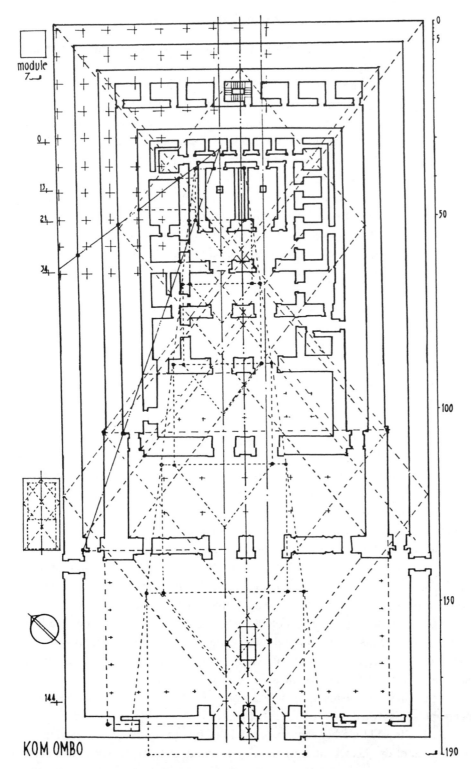

Fig. 37: Analysis of the plan of the Ptolemaic temple at Kom Ombo according to Badawy (from *Architectural Design*, pl. 42).

of a rectangle, rather than by four independent networks of different triangles overlapping one another.

The fact that the ancient Egyptian architects did not use scale drawings while planning their buildings rules out the possibility that the triangles which Badawy 'read' on the plans were a trace of the planning process on papyrus. At the same time, the use of triangles in the practice of construction would be far more complicated than it seems at first glance. All of the geometrical figures mentioned by Badawy seem simple when they are called 1:2, 1:4, 1:8 or 8:5. However, especially in the case of the 8:5 triangle, whenever the basis or the height do not correspond to a number of cubits easy to handle, a significant amount of calculation would have been required in order to construct the rest of the triangle. If we consider that, moreover, the 8:5 triangle seldom corresponds to a single space, the complications increase even more. Finally, it would not help to consider Badawy's triangles simply as ratios between longitudinal and transversal dimensions, thus ignoring the triangular shape of his diagrams. In this way, without the sloping sides of a triangle connecting them, it would become really difficult to justify why a certain length along the axis should be related to a certain breadth.

Another point of Badawy's theory that fails to convince from a geometrical point of view is the relationship between the constructions of the 3-4-5 and the 8:5 triangles. In the case of the 3-4-5 triangle, it has been suggested that a cord, whatever its length, could have been divided into 12 regular intervals ($3 + 4 + 5 = 12$) and then tied around three pegs in order to obtain a 3-4-5 triangle on the ground. Badawy extended this idea to the 8:5 triangle (fig. 28), but, in this case, this process would be difficult to use. The dimensions of the three sides of an 8:5 triangle, in fact, do not amount to easy numbers, since the sloping sides correspond to irrational numbers. This misunderstanding may have derived from Choisy's confused presentation of these triangles discussed above, where he created a connection that had no sound geometrical reasons to exist. Even if Badawy did not comment upon this point, his theory might be still rescued by suggesting that the Egyptians adopted an approximated value for the sum of the three sides, thus approximating ϕ twice, once with the adoption of the 8:5 triangle, and once with the adoption of an approximated version of the 8:5 triangle. It remains to be established, however, how these figures were drawn on the ground. The hypotheses about the use of cords in architecture will be examined in Part II, and will prove extremely difficult to support for large-scale plans.

Despite these criticisms, Badawy's schemes seem to work. No one else has ever been able to apply a theory to over fifty plans of Egyptian buildings, and his method has been followed by other scholars. Jean Lauffray, for instance, analysed the plan of the chapel of Hakoris at Karnak (Twenty-ninth Dynasty, early fourth century BC) using a geometrical construction based on ϕ and a network of 8:5 triangles, and

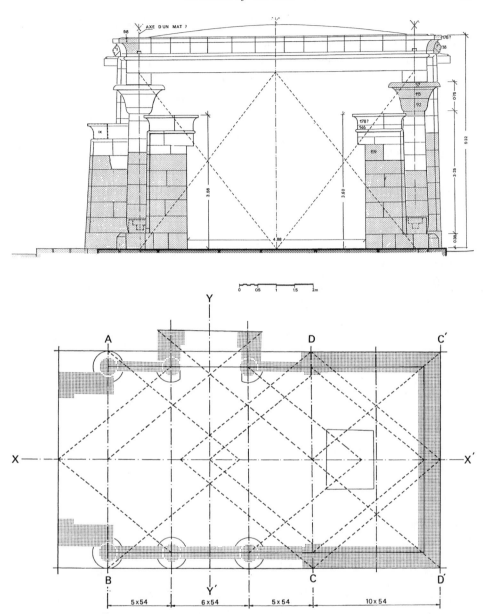

Fig. 38: Analysis of the plan and reconstruction of the western façade of the chapel of Hakoris at Karnak (Twenty-ninth Dynasty) based on a network of 8:5 triangles, according to Lauffray (from *Chapelle d'Achôris*, figs. 9 and 34).

then even reconstructed the monument according to these ideas (fig. 38)[33]; Friedrich Hinkel detected the use of the ratio 8:5 in several later Meroitic monuments.[34] It is important to note, however, that the buildings studied by Lauffray and Hinkel belong to a period when the cultural interconnections across the Mediterranean were much stronger than they had been in the past, and therefore the cultural background of these monuments may have been different (I will go back to this point later).

In conclusion, the most interesting point of Badawy's theory is the use of the 8:5 triangle, which corresponds to the most successful among the geometrical constructions listed above, whereas all the others may be dismissed without losing any significant detail. The 8:5 triangle raises many questions. Its geometrical construction and practical use are difficult (although not impossible) to explain, but the main objection lies at a deeper level of the discussion, at a basic point which Badawy did not take into account. He thought that the 8:5 triangle could have been a simple and practical device to approximate the convergence of the Fibonacci Series to ϕ, thus implying that the Egyptian knew ϕ and performed this calculation. However, he did not go far enough as to prove it.

---

[33] Jean Lauffray, *Karnak d'Egypte, domaine du divin*, Paris: Centre National de la Recherche Scientifique, 1979, pp. 221–6 and *La chapelle d'Achôris à Karnak*, vol. I, Paris: Recherche sur les Civilisations, 1995, pp. 24–6 and 61–3.

[34] Friederich W. Hinkel, 'The Process of Planning in Meroitic Architecture', in Davies W. V. (ed.), *Egypt and Africa*, London: British Museum and Egypt Exploration Society, 1993, pp. 220–5; see also Hinkel, 'The Royal Pyramids of Meroe. Architecture, Construction and Reconstruction of a Sacred Landscape', *Sudan and Nubia* 4 (2000), 11–26.

2

Mathematics and architecture in ancient Egypt

Ancient Egyptian mathematics

The mathematical sources and their language

One of the most common faults of the modern approach to the problem of proportions in ancient architecture is the adoption of a mathematical system which
is chronologically inappropriate. As we have seen, many of the modern theories
involving the Golden Section in the interpretation of ancient Egyptian art and architecture are based on the calculation of φ according to our mathematical system.
The ancient Egyptians, however, used a different mathematical language, adopted
different methods and expressed the results in a different way. If a calculation works
or a pattern appears in our own mathematical system, this does not imply that exactly the same would happen in theirs. Moreover, in some cases the question to ask
is not only if a method would have worked in a certain mathematical system, but
also if *that* method would have been produced and adopted by *that* mathematical
mentality.

Our main sources for defining the ancient Egyptian mathematical system are a
number of mathematical texts written on papyri, ostraca and leather dating from
the second half of the Middle Kingdom to the Second Intermediate Period (*c.* 1800
to 1600 BC), the most important of which are the Rhind Mathematical Papyrus[1]
(usually abbreviated as RMP), the Moscow Mathematical Papyrus,[2] the Kahun
Papyri[3] and the Egyptian Mathematical Leather Roll.[4] The computational procedure

---

[1] Eric T. Peet, *The Rhind Mathematical Papyrus*, Liverpool: University Press; London: Hodder and Stoughton,
  1923; Arnold B. Chace, Ludlow Bull, Henry P. Manning, *The Rhind Mathematical Papyrus*, Oberlin: Mathematical Association of America, 1929; Gay Robins and Charles Shute, *The Rhind Mathematical Papyrus*, London:
  British Museum, 1987.
[2] W. W. Struve, 'Mathematischer Papyrus des Staatlichen Museums der Schönen Künste in Moskau', *Studien und
  Quellen zur Geschichte der Mathematik, Astronomie und Physik*, part A, vol. I (1930).
[3] Francis L. Griffith, *The Petrie Papyri: Hieratic Papyri from Kahun and Gurob*, London: University College,
  1897.
[4] S. R. K. Glanville, 'The Mathematical Leather Roll in the British Museum', *JEA* 13 (1927), 232–8.

adopted by the Middle Kingdom scribes survived well into the Graeco-Roman period and beyond, as is attested by a set of Demotic papyri dating from the third century BC to the second century AD,[5] and a number of Coptic and Byzantine texts.[6]

These documents do not correspond to our idea of a mathematical textbook or treatise. Apart from a few cases, they do not contain formulae or general rules that may be applied to solve problems. They contain, instead, table texts, such as the doubling of unit fractions, and problem texts, the majority of which (but not all of them) have a practical character, such as the division of loaves among men, the calculation of the area of a field or the volume of a granary, and so on. Annette Imhausen has recently studied the mechanisms underlying the scribes' calculations and has been able to identify and compare the algorithms used in various Middle Kingdom texts containing different types of mathematical problems.[7]

As for numerical system, the Egyptians used integers (that is, whole numbers) and fractions, but only the so-called unit fractions, with 1 as a numerator and any number as a denominator, such as $\frac{1}{2}$, $\frac{1}{15}$, $\frac{1}{42}$ or $\frac{1}{140}$, with the exception of the fraction $\frac{2}{3}$. Ratios such as $\frac{3}{5}$, for instance, were expressed by means of a sum of unit fractions. At least from the Middle Kingdom onwards,[8] this representation was never $\frac{1}{5} + \frac{1}{5} + \frac{1}{5}$ but could be, for example, $\frac{1}{2} + \frac{1}{10}$. In many cases it happens that more than one representation exists, that is, more than one combination of unit fractions can be used to express the same quantity. The ratio $\frac{3}{5}$, for instance, apart from the 2-term combination $\frac{1}{2} + \frac{1}{10}$, can be also expressed by means of seven 3-term combinations or one hundred and five 4-term combinations,[9] and so on. The Egyptians were aware of this possibility and, even if the mechanism that regulated their decisions is not entirely clear, they appear to have preferred short combinations of fractions with even and small denominators.[10]

In ancient Egypt multiplications were performed by doubling the initial number, and divisions by halving it. In other words, the progression 1, 2, 4, 8, 16, 32, 64, ... in which each term is twice the previous one, was used to perform multiplications

[5] Richard A. Parker, *Demotic Mathematical Papyri*, Providence, R.I.: Brown University Press; London: Humphries, 1972; Wilbur K. Knorr, 'Techniques of Fractions in Ancient Egypt and Greece', *HM* 9 (1982), 133–71.

[6] For the use of unit fractions in Coptic and Byzantine texts, see for example Monika R. M. Hasitzka, *Neue Texte und Dokumentation zum Koptisch-Unterricht*, Mitteilungen aus der Papyrussammlung der Nationalbibliothek (later Österreichischen Nationalbibliothek) in Wien XVIII, Vienna: Hollinek, 1990, pp. 265–84 and 302–12; and Herbert Thompson, 'A Byzantine Table of Fractions', *Ancient Egypt* 2 (1914), 52–4.

[7] Annette Imhausen, *Ägyptische Algorithmen. Ein Untersuch zu den mittelägyptischen mathematischen Aufgabentexten*, Ägyptologische Abhandlungen, Wiesbaden: Harrassowitz, 2003.

[8] For the Old Kingdom see David P. Silverman, 'Fractions in the Abusir Papyri', *JEA* 61 (1975), 248–9.

[9] For denominators lower than 1,000.

[10] Richard J. Gillings, *Mathematics at the Time of the Pharaohs*, Cambridge, Mass.: MIT Press, 1972, pp. 45–70, criticised by M. Bruckheimer and Y. Salomon, 'Some Comments on R. J. Gillings' Analysis of the 2/n Table in the Rhind Papyrus', *HM* 4 (1977), 445–52. See also Kurt Vogel, *Vorgriechische Mathematik* I, Hannover: Schroedel; Paderborn: Schöningh, 1959, p. 42 and Knorr, *HM* 9, pp. 136–7.

and its reciprocal 1, $\frac{1}{2}$, $\frac{1}{4}$, $\frac{1}{8}$, $\frac{1}{16}$ ... to perform divisions. In some cases, the short succession $\frac{2}{3}$, $\frac{1}{3}$, $\frac{1}{6}$, in which each term is half the previous one, too, was also used.[11] A property of the progression 1, 2, 4, 8, 16, 32, 64, ... is that any integer can be expressed by means of the sum of some of its terms, and this is how ancient Egyptian multiplication worked. For instance, in order to calculate 17×13, the scribe would have doubled 17 until the next multiplier (1, 2, 4, etc.) would have exceeded the multiplicand (13). Then he would find that $1 + 4 + 8 = 13$, would tick these numbers, add the corresponding results ($17 + 68 + 136 = 221$) and write the result below:

$$
\begin{array}{llllll}
/ & 1 & \times & 17 & = & 17 \\
 & 2 & \times & 17 & = & 34 \\
/ & 4 & \times & 17 & = & 68 \\
/ & 8 & \times & 17 & = & 136 \\
\hline
\text{Total} & 13 & \times & 17 & = & 221
\end{array}
$$

The knowledge of other numerical series has been suggested on the basis of other mathematical problems,[12] but it is important to mention the fact that no mathematical source contains any trace of the Fibonacci Series 1, 2, 3, 5, 8, 13, ... (or of any similar series based on the same method of accretion, such as 1, 3, 4, 7, 11, 18, ... or 1, 4, 5, 9, 14, 23, ... and so on). Architectural remains, unfortunately, do not help, since Badawy's few drawings showing the use of the Fibonacci Series in architecture are not particularly convincing. In general, as in the cases of other geometrical figures, the Fibonacci numbers often mark points which do not correspond to any particular element of the building and do not seem to have been used according to a consistent rule.

Another important corollary of the adoption of the 'correct' mathematical point of view is the use of the original units of measurements in the interpretation of the ancient monuments. The ancient Egyptian unit of measurement was the cubit, divided into palms, which in turn were divided into 4 fingers. The 'small cubit' corresponded to the forearm and was divided into 6 palms (or 24 fingers), but in architecture the unit of measurement generally adopted was the 'royal cubit', corresponding to 7 palms (or 28 fingers).[13] Unless otherwise stated, in this text

---

[11] Gillings, *Mathematics*, pp. 16–20 and 166–7; Robins and Shute, *Rhind Mathematical Papyrus*, pp. 22–4. See also Knorr, *HM* 9, pp. 136–40.

[12] RMP 40, 64 and 79, and Kahun Papyrus IV.3. Gillings suggested that the Egyptians, after the progression 1, 2, 4, 8, 16, 32, 64 ... , might have used other similar series, such as 3, 9, 27, 81, 243, 729 ... , in which each term is multiplied by 3, or 4, 16, 64, 256, 1024, 4096 ... , in which each term is multiplied by 4, and so on (Gillings, *Mathematics*, pp. 166–80).

[13] In addition to Reiner Hannig, *Grosses Handworterbuch Agyptisch-Deutsch*, Mainz: von Zabern, 1995, from which the information given by table 2 is taken, see also Karl Richard Lepsius, *Die Alt-Aegyptische Elle (aus den Abhandlungen der Königlichen Akademie der Wissenschaften 1865)*, Berlin 1865 and Adelheid Schlott-Schwab, *Die Ausmasse Ägyptens nach altägyptischen Texte*, Ägypten und Altes Testament 3, Wiesbaden: Harrassowitz, 1981. See also *Preliminary Report on Czechoslovak Excavation in the Mastaba of Ptahshepses at Abusir*, Prague: Charles University, 1976.

'cubit' will always refer to the royal cubit. A schematic summary of the ancient Egyptian units of measurement is shown in table 2.

In fact, the best results to date in terms of 'reading' the plans of ancient Egyptian buildings have been achieved by Dieter Arnold, who adopted the ancient cubit to explain the design of ancient Egyptian monuments on several occasions.[14] From his studies it appears that the ancient Egyptians generally laid out their plans on the basis of simple numbers of cubits, palms and fingers (fig. 39). As we shall see in Part II, this agrees entirely with the nature of the ancient Egyptian architectural drawings that have survived until today.

On φ, π and other anachronisms

The extant mathematical documents provide enough material to reconstruct various aspects of ancient Egyptian mathematics. Nevertheless, the way we interpret these sources is not neutral. For instance, modern scholars often speak of the ancient Egyptians as being able to use an approximation of φ or π. Such an evolutionary vision of mathematics, however, may be misleading. It is true that some of our modern mathematical methods come from an ancient practice, but it is also true that reading history backwards may produce strange distortions. Let us analyse three examples: the Pythagorean triplets; the calculation of the area of the circle; and the Golden Section.

The so-called 'Pythagorean triplets' are triplets of integers which correspond to the three sides of right-angled triangles. The most famous case is the already mentioned right-angled triangle in which the sides are 3, 4 and 5 units long, but there are many more. These triplets also represent a straightforward case of the so-called theorem of Pythagoras, since it is easy to calculate, for instance, that $3^2 + 4^2 = 5^2$ $(9 + 16 = 25)$.

Pythagoras and the Pythagoreans are surrounded by an aura of myth that makes it difficult to distinguish between their actual achievements and those discoveries attributed to them by later legend.[15] At any rate, it is an established fact that they had a special interest in numbers, and they appear to have developed a mathematical system in which numbers are represented by figures made with pebbles, called *psephoi*. It has been suggested that it was on the basis of this method that Pythagoras

---

[14] See for example Dieter Arnold, *Der Tempel des Königs Mentuhotep von Deir el-Bahari*, vol. I: Architektur und Deutung, AV 8, Mainz: Von Zabern, 1974; *The Temple of Mentuhotep at Deir el-Bahari from the Notes of Herbert Winlock*, Metropolitan Museum of Art Egyptian Expedition 21, New York: Metropolitan Museum of Art, 1979, pp. 29–31; *Der Pyramidenbezirk des Königs Amenemhet III. in Dahschur*, AV 53, Mainz: Von Zabern, 1987, p. 63; and Dieter Arnold and Dorothea Arnold, *Der Tempel Qasr el-Sagha*, AV 27, Mainz: Von Zabern, 1979.

[15] Burket, *Lore and Science*, chapter 2.

Table 2. *List of ancient Egyptian units of measurements*

Units of measurement	Egyptian name	Measure	Egyptian mutual value	Value expressed in modern units	Comments and further bibliographical details
cubit (royal)	*mḥ*	length	7 palms	*c.* 52.5 cm	Principal unit of measurement in architecture (see also Arnold, *Mentuhotep*, pp. 29–31)
cubit (small)	*mḥ*	length	6 palms	*c.* 45 cm	Length of the forearm
remen	*rmn*	length	5 cubits	*c.* 37.5 cm	Secondary subdivision found on New Kingdom votive cubit rods
djeser	*ḏsr*	length	4 palms	*c.* 30 cm	
large hands-breadth	*pḏ-ꜥꜣ*	length	$3\frac{1}{2}$ palms	*c.* 25 cm	
small hands-breadth	*pḏ-šsr*	length	3 palms	*c.* 22.5 cm	
palm	*šsp*	length	$\frac{1}{7}$ royal cubit, $\frac{1}{6}$ small cubit	*c.* 7.5 cm	Breadth of the palm
finger	*ḏbꜥ*	length	$\frac{1}{28}$ royal cubit, $\frac{1}{4}$ palm	*c.* 1.875 cm	Breadth of a finger
khet (rod)	*ḥt*	length	100 cubits	*c.* 52.5 m	Also called 'rod of cord', might refer to actual cords 100 cubits long
river-measure	*itrw*	length	20,000 cubits	*c.* 10.5 km	See also Schott-Schwab, *Ausmasse Ägyptens*, pp. 101–45
foot(?)	*ṯbt*	length		*c.* 9 cm (?)	Dubious, attested only twice in the Fifth Dyn. mastaba of Ptahshepses at Abusir (*Preliminary Report on Czechoslovak Excavation*, p. 83)
kha-ta	*ḫꜣ-tꜣ*	area	100,000 square cubits	*c.* 27,565 m2	
setat	*sṯꜣt*	area	1 square *khet* (10,000 square cubits)	*c.* 2,756.5 m2	
kha	*ḫꜣ*	area	1,000 square cubits	*c.* 275.65 m2	
ta	*tꜣ*	area	100 square cubits	*c.* 27.565 m2	
remen	*rmn*	area	$\frac{1}{2}$ *ta*, 50 square cubits	*c.* 13.7 m2	
heseb	*ḥsb*	area	$\frac{1}{2}$ *remen*, 25 square cubits	*c.* 6.8 m2	
sa	*sꜣ*	area	$\frac{1}{2}$ *heseb*, 12.5 square cubits	*c.* 3.4 m2	
deny	*dny*	volume	1 cubic cubit		
neby	*nby*	volume(?)			
khar (sack)	*ḫꜣr*	capacity	10 hekat	*c.* 48 litres	$\frac{2}{3}$ of a cubic cubit
	ipt-n-pr	capacity	50 hinu	*c.* 24 litres	
quadruple-*hekat*	*ḥḳꜣt-fdw, ipt*	capacity	40 hinu	*c.* 19.2 litres	
double-*hekat*	*ḥḳꜣty*	capacity		*c.* 9.6 litres	
hekat	*ḥḳꜣt*	capacity		*c.* 4.8 litres	Also divided into $\frac{1}{2}$, $\frac{1}{4}$, $\frac{1}{8}$, $\frac{1}{16}$, $\frac{1}{32}$ and $\frac{1}{64}$ (so-called Horus-Eye Fractions)
dja	*ḏꜣ*	capacity	$\frac{2}{3}$ hinu	*c.* 0.33 litres	
hinu	*hnw*	capacity	$\frac{1}{10}$ hekat, 32 ro	0.48 litre	
ro	*r*	volume	$\frac{1}{320}$ hekat	0.015 litre	
deben	*dbn*	weight		*c.* 13.6 grammes in OK and MK; *c.* 91 grammes in NK	
kite	*ḳdt*	weight	$\frac{1}{10}$ deben		
shenaty	*šnꜥty*	value	$\frac{1}{12}$ deben		Measured the value of silver

Unless otherwise stated, data taken from Hannig, *Handwörterbuch Ägyptisch-Deutsch* and *LÄ*, 'Maße un Gewichte (Pharaonische Zeit)'.

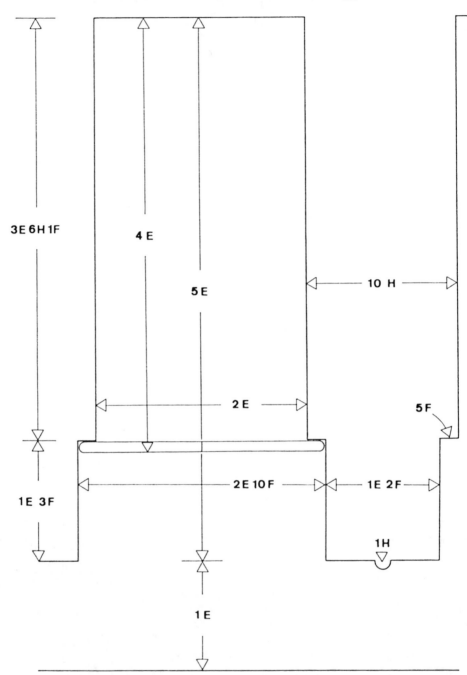

Fig. 39: Examples of Dieter Arnold's studies: the dimensions of some architectural elements in the temple of Mentuhotep at Deir el-Bahari (left, from *Der Tempel des Königs Mentuhotep*, figs. 6, 7 and 20) and the dimensions of one of the chapels in the Middle Kingdom temple of Qasr el-Sagha in cubits (E), palms (H) and fingers (F) (right, from Arnold and Arnold, *Qasr el-Sagha*, pl. 27b).

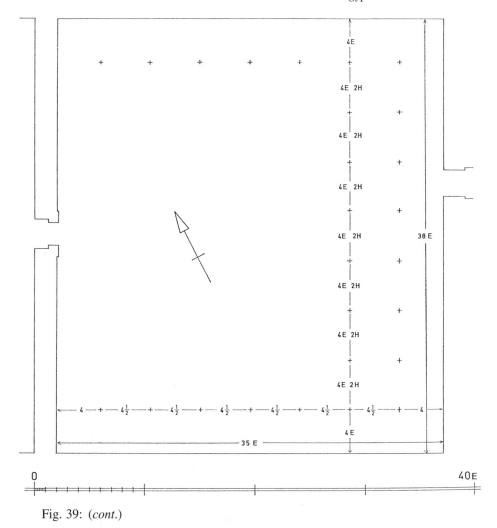

Fig. 39: (*cont.*)

might have derived the formula, attributed to him by a later tradition, to calculate a triplet starting from any odd number.[16]

In Euclid's *Elements* (written around 300 BC) we find the formulation of the so-called theorem of Pythagoras to which we are accustomed: 'in right-angled triangles the square on the side subtending the right angle is equal to the squares on the sides containing the right angle',[17] that is, a theorem valid for *any* right-angled triangle. The triplets certainly correspond to special cases of the general theorem,

---

[16] Thomas L. Heath, *The Thirteen Books of Euclid's Elements*, Cambridge: Cambridge University Press, 1926, vol. I, pp. 349–60; Wilbur R. Knorr, *The Evolution of the Euclidean Elements*, Dordrecht/Boston: Reidel, 1975, pp. 154–61.

[17] Euclid, *Elements*, Book I, Proposition 47, English translation by Thomas L. Heath, Great Books of the Western World 10, Chicago: Encyclopaedia Britannica, Inc., 1990, p. 28.

but their knowledge and use may have developed independently and proceeded side by side with the more general cases. The Babylonians apparently used the equivalent of the theorem of Pythagoras as early as 1800 BC,[18] and a number of triplets are listed on the Old Babylonian tablet called Plimpton 322.[19]

In Egypt the first unambiguous evidence of the use of the theorem of Pythagoras is a Demotic papyrus dating to the third century BC, where, apart from one exception, the numbers involved correspond to three triplets.[20] An earlier use of some triplets independently from the more general Greek formulation of the theorem is not clearly attested by any mathematical source, but may be inferred by other clues. As we shall see in Part III, some triplets might have been used as early as the Old Kingdom as a practical device in the construction of some pyramids, with or without any symbolic meaning attached to them.

The insistence of the late Greek sources to link the 3-4-5 triangle to ancient Egypt may well reflect part of the truth. The most quoted passage to prove the link between the 3-4-5 triangle and the ancient Egyptians is from Plutarch's *Isis and Osiris*:

the better and more divine nature consists of three elements – what is spiritually intelligible, the material and the element derived from these, which the Greeks call the cosmos. Plato is wont to call what is spiritually intelligible the form and the pattern of the father; and the material he calls the mother, the nurse, and the seat and place of creation, while the fruit of both he calls the offspring and creation. One might suppose that the Egyptians liken the nature of the universe especially to this supremely beautiful of the triangles which Plato also in the Republic seems to have used in devising his wedding figure. That triangle has a vertical of three units of length, a base of four, and an hypotenuse of five, which is equal, when squared, to the squares of the other two sides. The vertical should thus be likened to the male, the base to the female, and the hypotenuse to their offspring; and one should similarly view Osiris as the origin, Isis as the receptive element, and Horus as the perfect achievement. The number three is the first and perfect odd number; four is the square of the even number two; five is analogous partly to the father and partly to the mother, being made up of a triad and a dyad.[21]

Plutarch lived in the late first–early second century AD, and the cultural background to which he referred was a mixture of Egyptian and Greek sources with a strong Platonic influence. There is no reason to distrust what Plutarch wrote, but

[18] Helmuth Gericke, *Mathematik in Antike und Orient*, Wiesbaden: Fourier, 1992, p. 33.
[19] Otto E. Neugebauer and A. Sachs, *Mathematical Cuneiform Texts*, New Haven: American Oriental Society and the American Schools of Oriental Research, 1945, pp. 38–41; Jöran Friberg, 'Methods and Tradition of Babylonian Mathematics', *HM* 8 (1981), 277–318; Derek J. de Solla Price, 'The Babylonian "Pythagorean Triangle" Tablet', *Centaurus* 10 (1964), 1–13; Eleanor Robson, 'Neither Sherlock Holmes nor Babylon: A Reassessment of Plimpton 322', *HM* 28 (2001), 167–206.
[20] Parker, *Demotic Mathematical Papyri*, pp. 3–4 and 35–40. See also Richard J. Gillings, 'The Mathematics of Ancient Egypt', in *Dictionary of Scientific Biography*, vol. xv, Supplement 1, New York: Scribner, 1978, p. 690.
[21] Plutarch, *De Iside et Osiride*, English translation by J. Gwyn Griffiths, Cardiff: University of Wales Press, 1970, chapter 56, 373E–F, 374A, pp. 205–8 and 509.

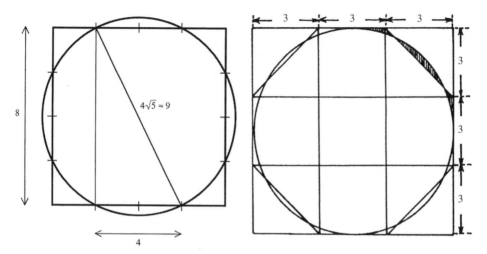

Fig. 40: The calculation of the area of the circle, based on RMP problem 48, according to Robins and Shute (left, drawn after *Rhind Mathematical Papyrus*, fig. 10) and Gillings (right, from *Mathematics*, fig. 13.6).

what the Egyptians (and Greeks) thought about the 3-4-5 triangle at that time is not necessarily what they had thought twenty centuries earlier. In conclusion, the Old Kingdom architects may have used some Pythagorean triplets, but this does not imply that the Old Kingdom architects were the creators of the Pythagorean symbolism of numbers or were aware of all the mathematical implications of Euclid's formulation of the theorem of Pythagoras.

Another interesting example of development of a mathematical concept is the calculation of the area of the circle. According to the Rhind Mathematical Papyrus (RMP), the method to find the area of a circle is to subtract one-ninth of the diameter and square the rest. This rather synthetic statement has been explained in different ways. Hermann Engels,[22] followed by Gay Robins and Charles Shute,[23] suggested that the Egyptians drew a square which intersected the circle at a quarter and three quarters of its side (fig. 40, left). This solution, however simple it may appear, is not easy to explain in practice, and in fact Robins and Shute's proof is entirely based on the knowledge of π and on a confident familiarity with the theorem of Pythagoras (for which, as we have seen, we have no evidence earlier than the third century BC – that is, at least thirteen centuries after the RMP).

Instead, according to Kurt Vogel,[24] followed by Richard Gillings,[25] what the scribe did was to calculate the area of an octagon that intersected the circumference. This polygon was not a regular octagon; that is, it did not have eight equal sides, but

[22] Hermann Engels, 'Quadrature of the Circle in Ancient Egypt', *HM* 4 (1977), 137–40.
[23] Robins and Shute, *Rhind Mathematical Papyrus*, pp. 44–6.
[24] Vogel, *Vorgriechische Mathematik*, vol. I, p. 66.   [25] Gillings, *Mathematics*, pp. 142–4.

was generated by 'cutting off' at 45° the edges of a square whose sides had been divided into three equal parts (fig. 40, right). This also explains the careful choice by the scribe of a diameter of 9 units of measurements in four out of five RMP problems, easily divisible into three parts. The area of the circle is well approximated by the area of such an octagon, that corresponds to an 8×8 square.

Now if we look at one of the methods adopted by the Greek mathematicians to square the circle, we find the same idea, that is, that the area of a polygon could approximate the area of the circle.[26] For instance, Bryson's argument (fourth century BC), as reported by Themistius, may have been that 'a circle is greater than all inscribed polygons and less than circumscribed ones; the polygon drawn between those inscribed in and circumscribed about the circle is greater than all inscribed ones and less than all circumscribed ones; therefore, this polygon and the circle are equal to one another'.[27] As it happened, we do not know if and how Bryson planned to measure this polygon.

The approximation of the circle by means of a polygon provides also the foundation for Archimedes' famous Propositions 1 and 3, written in the mid-third century BC. The first says that 'the area of any circle is equal to a right-angled triangle in which one of the sides about the right angle is equal to the radius, and the other to the circumference of the circle', and is demonstrated by inscribing and circumscribing the circumference by means of polygons.[28] The second proposition is simply a consequence of the third and it is not accompanied by any demonstration, while the third says that 'the perimeter of every circle is three-times the diameter and further it exceeds by [a line] less than a seventh part of the diameter but greater than ten seventy-first [parts of the diameter]'.[29] Translated into our modern mathematical language, this means that in any circle the ratio between the circumference and the diameter (which *we* now call π) is less than $3 + \frac{1}{7}$ but greater than $3 + \frac{10}{71}$.

However, as David Fowler observed,

Archimedes clearly does *not* here consider the ratio of circumference to diameter as a numerical quantity. Also the phrase 'ten seventy-first parts' seems to refer to the line obtained by concatenating ten copies of the seventy-first parts of the diameter, rather than the common fraction $\frac{10}{71}$; it is a *line*, not a number.[30]

Greek mathematics up to the second century BC was, as Fowled pointed out, non-arithmetised; that is, it used words to describe lines, figures and various manipulations. In modern mathematics, lines are identified by means of their length,

---

[26] See, for instance, Wilbur K. Knorr, 'Archimede's Dimensions of the Circle: A View of the Genesis of the Extant Text', *Archive for History of Exact Sciences* 35/4 (1986), 281–324.

[27] Ian Mueller, 'Aristotle and the Quadrature of the Circle', in Norman Kretzmann (ed.), *Infinity and Continuity in Ancient and Medieval Thought*, Ithaca and London: Cornell University Press, 1982, p. 161.

[28] Archimedes, *Measurement of a Circle*, English translation by Thomas L. Heath, Great Books of the Western World 10, Chicago: Encyclopaedia Britannica, Inc., 1990, pp. 447–51.

[29] David H. Fowler, *The Mathematics of Plato's Academy*, Oxford: Oxford University Press, 1987, p. 241.

[30] Fowler, *Plato's Academy*, p. 241; see also pp. 8–13.

figures by means of their area, and ratios between quantities by means of quotients of the two numbers that represent them. The theorem attributed to Pythagoras, where the sum of the squares of the catheti of a triangle are equal to the square of the hypotenuse, becomes $a^2 + b^2 = c^2$, and the ratio between circumference and diameter becomes π. It may be worth remembering that π was proved to be irrational only in 1768, and to be transcendental in 1882, and that therefore Archimedes himself did not think in terms of π as we do today.

Going back to the area of the circle in ancient Egypt, virtually none of the authors mentioned above escaped the temptation to conclude that, whatever the precise method employed by the Egyptians, they had found a 'good' approximation for π. However, does it really make sense to talk about the approximation of a concept or a number that did not exist in the Egyptian mind? The method used by the Egyptians (take $\frac{1}{9}$ from the diameter and square the rest) had nothing to do with the ratio between circumference and diameter, now expressed by π.

Finally, let us go back to the problem of ϕ and the Golden Section. First of all, it is essential to mention that there is no direct evidence in any ancient Egyptian written mathematical source of any arithmetic calculation or geometrical construction which could be classified as the Golden Section. The 'only direct, explicit and unambiguous surviving references'[31] to this proportion in early Greek mathematics, philosophy and literature are contained in Euclid's *Elements* (third century BC). The definition is to be found at the beginning of Book VI: 'a straight line is said to have been cut in extreme and mean ratio when, as the whole line is to the greater segment, so is the greater to the less'.[32] That is, a segment is divided into two parts according to this proportion if the ratio between the shorter and the longer part is the same as existing between the longer part and the whole (see fig. 14).

As we have seen, in the ancient Egyptian mathematical sources there is no trace of the Fibonacci Series either. It is true that the way the Egyptians dealt with other geometrical progressions is not incompatible with the basic concept of the Fibonacci Series, where each term is given by the sum of the two previous terms. The link with the calculation of ϕ, however, is not straightforward. While in our system each ratio between consecutive Fibonacci numbers is expressed by means of a single number, in the ancient Egyptian system each ratio can be expressed by means of several combinations of unit fractions.

Elsewhere[33] Christopher Tout and I have argued that, in theory, an ancient scribe might have calculated probably not more than the first ten ratios of consecutive terms (the denominators grow very quickly and generate very small fractions). Again in theory, he might have found a way to express the results in such a way that

[31] Fowler, *Fibonacci Quarterly* 20/2, p. 148.
[32] Euclid, *Elements*, Book VI, Definition 2, quoted from the English translation, p. 99.
[33] Corinna Rossi and Christopher A. Tout, 'Were the Fibonacci Series and the Golden Section known in ancient Egypt?', *Historia Mathematica* 29 (2002), 101–13.

the convergence was visible. Even if he did that, however, we must ask whether he would have taken any interest in it. We say that the sequence converges to a limit because we have the concept of the irrational number φ, but there is no evidence that the ancient Egyptians had a similar idea. It might even be suggested that they would not have liked the concept of the convergence to a number they could not reach, since the mathematical sources seem to indicate that the Egyptians were particularly fond of the completion to the unity.[34]

In conclusion, the convergence to φ, and φ itself as a number, do not fit with the extant Middle Kingdom mathematical sources. It cannot be excluded that the Golden Section was, at some point, brought to Egypt by the Greeks. From Alexandria, Euclid's *Elements* or a similar treatise seems to have travelled as far as Elephantine, where a group of ostraca dating to the late third century BC have been found. Their contents have been identified as the rather complex construction of a regular icosahedron inscribed within a sphere, possibly taken from Euclid's *Elements* 13.16.[35]

At any rate, as we have seen, the definitions of this proportion which can be found in Greek texts have nothing to do with the calculation of φ and the Fibonacci Series (which, in fact, derives its name from a Medieval scholar). In Euclid's *Elements*, the definition of extreme and mean ratio quoted earlier is followed by examples of manipulations of geometrical figures based on this proportion, such as 'if a straight line be cut in extreme and mean ratio, the square on the greater segment added to half of the whole is five times the square of the half'.[36] If, as seems likely, the Golden Section was known in Egypt in the Graeco-Roman period, it must be borne in mind that the types of definitions, the language and the approach to this proportion must have been similar to what we find in Euclid, rather than to what modern scholars have suggested.

Intention, coincidence or tendency?

Triangles and architecture

A careful study of the ancient Egyptian and Greek sources then delivers a fatal blow to the vast majority of the Golden Section-based theories. However, some aspects highlighted by the discussion on this and other proportions need further clarification. Why, for example, do some theories appear to work even if they are

---

[34] For the problems on the completion to 1 see Peet, *Rhind Mathematical Papyrus*, pp. 53–60; Gillings, *Mathematics*, chapter 8; Robins and Shute, *Rhind Mathematical Papyrus*, pp. 19–21. For the series of Horus-Eye fractions converging to 1 see Peet, *Rhind Mathematical Papyrus*, pp. 25–6; Gillings, *Mathematics*, pp. 210–1; Robins and Shute, *Rhind Mathematical Papyrus*, pp. 14–5.

[35] Jürgen Mau and Wolfgang Müller, 'Mathematische Ostraka aus der Berliner Sammlung', *Archiv für Papyrusforschung* 17 (1962), 1–10.

[36] Euclid, *Elements*, Book XIII, Proposition 1, quoted from the English translation, p. 369.

clearly based on anachronistic concepts? The discussion in this chapter will rotate around the thin line dividing intention, coincidence and tendency in the choice of a geometrical figure or pattern. As we shall see, in some cases it is not easy for us to make a distinction.

Let us start with the triangle, which has been the most successful of the geometrical figures employed in the attempts to explain the proportions of ancient architecture. Ancient Egyptian architecture, in particular (at least according to Badawy's theory) appears to have been entirely dependent on this geometrical figure. Apart from the contemporary interpretations of the modern surveys, what evidence really exists on the use of this geometrical figure in ancient Egyptian architecture?

The ancient Egyptian word for 'triangle' was *sepedet* (*śpdt*), 'the pointed' figure[37] (from *śpd* that also means 'sharp' and 'effective'). A four-sided figure such as rectangle or a square, instead, was called *ifed* (*ifd*),[38] clearly coming from *ifedw* (*ifdw*), the number four, referring to the number of its sides or corners. It is interesting to note that, differently from the square, the triangle was named after its pointed appearance, rather than after the number of its components.[39]

Although sloping lines have often inspired more or less convincing geometrical analyses,[40] the sole, 'real', unmistakable triangles in ancient Egyptian architecture are embodied in the pyramids. The first attempt to build a true pyramid was carried out around 2400 BC by Snefru, whose first project was a pyramid with its vertical section (parallel to the side of the base) probably corresponding to an equilateral triangle. As we shall see in detail in Part III, structural problems forced the architects to reduce the slope twice, and the result is the so-called Bent Pyramid. Apart from later developments in the choice of the slope of pyramids, which depended on many factors, the equilateral triangle seems to have occupied an important place in the mind of the ancient architects, since they chose it as the shape for their first project of a new type of monument.

---

[37] See for instance RMP problem 51.

[38] See for instance RMP problem 44 for *ifd* referring to a square, and RMP problem 49 for *ifd* referring to a rectangle.

[39] Peet, *Rhind Mathematical Papyrus*, especially p. 91.

[40] Perrot and Chipiez interpreted the sloping lines which so often recur in the Egyptian monuments as strictly related to pyramidal forms. They published two drawings in which two rectangular buildings with sloping walls are seen as truncated pyramids (Georges Perrot and Charles Chipiez, *A History of Art in Ancient Egypt*, vol. I, London: Chapman and Hall, 1833, figs. 58 and 59). An interpretation of the triangular shape of the apron often worn by ancient Egyptians in two-dimensional representations was attempted by Schwaller de Lubicz (*Temple de l'Homme*, vol. I, chapter 6, figs. 145B and D). Robins, however, noted that the measurements of the aprons used by Schwaller de Lubicz for his calculations were wrong (Gay Robins and Charles Shute, 'Mathematical Bases of Ancient Egyptian Architecture and Graphic Art', *HM* 12 (1985), 107–22, especially 118–9) and proved, in general, that the aprons were not necessarily perceived as triangles. The two oblique lines were generally treated separately by the artists, and their slope (like the slope of other oblique elements of the composition, such as crowns or staffs) corresponded to lines drawn between specific points of the square grid which acted as a guide for the artists (Gay Robins, 'The Slope of the Front of the Royal Apron', *DE* 3 (1985), 49–56; also *Proportion and Style in Ancient Egyptian Art*, London: Thames and Hudson, 1994, pp. 219–227, especially p. 222).

A tantalising coincidence is that the first model of the Bent Pyramid corresponds to what I have called Viollet-le-Duc's 'primeval pyramid'. Its section along the diagonal, therefore, can be approximated by an 8:5 triangle. Viollet-le-Duc, however, could not have been aware of this link, because the first suggestion of the existence of this early stage of the Bent Pyramid dates to 1964, and the remains of three unfinished pyramids with the same slope were studied later. Moreover, it is not clear to me whether his primeval pyramid is just a theoretical geometrical figure or whether its proportions were inspired by the classic sources on ancient Egyptian pyramids.[41]

Going back to ancient Egypt, the slope of a pyramid was calculated along the face, but the corner must have been the object of careful observations, if not calculations, since it was the only visible straight line which could be followed to check that the monument was not rotating during construction. This means that the Egyptians must have been acquainted with what we call the section of the pyramid along the diagonal of its base, which, in the case of the first project of the Bent Pyramid, would correspond to an 'Egyptian' triangle, well approximated by an 8:5 triangle. The idea that they acknowledged the special properties of this particular triangle, however, would be difficult to support. In pyramid building, the evidence of an independent use of the 8:5 triangle as vertical section parallel to the base is non-existent. This triangle, therefore, seems only able to bask in the reflected glory of the equilateral triangle, which in turn, however, does not amount to much. As we shall see in Part III, after Snefru's first attempt (which must have been remembered by several generations of architects, to judge from the ensuing careful search for a 'safe' slope), the slope corresponding to an equilateral triangle appears to have been used in possibly four Middle Kingdom minor pyramids only. Other triangles, including the 3-4-5, proved definitely more successful.

Badawy claimed to have found another trace of the importance of the equilateral and the 8:5 triangle in a number of amulets in the shape of a mason's level.

---

[41] Viollet-le-Duc did not include any bibliography on the subject. Among the classical writers, he might have referred to Diodorus Siculus, who wrote that 'the largest [pyramid] is in the form of a square and has a base length on each side of seven plethra and a height of over six plethra' (Diodorus, *Historical Library*, I.63.4, English translation by C. H. Oldfather, London: Heinemann; Cambridge, Mass.: Harvard University Press, 1946, vol. I, pp. 214–17). This is, more or less, the approximation suggested by Choisy for an equilateral triangle. Neither in Diodorus, nor in any other classical writer, however, does the section along the diagonal appear to have attracted a particular interest: Herodotus wrote that the pyramid of Khufu had a base equal to height (Herodotus, *Histories*, II.126, English translation by A. D. Godley, London: Heinemann; Cambridge, Mass.: Harvard University Press, 1946 (1922), vol. I, p. 427); Strabo wrote that the height of pyramids exceeded their bases (Strabo, *Geography*, XVII.1.33; English translation by Horace L. Jones, London: Heinemann; Cambridge, Mass.: Harvard University Press, 1959, vol. VIII, p. 91); Abd el-Latyf mentioned two possible measurements, one of them corresponding to a triangle in which base and height are equal (quoted by Edmé F. Jomard, 'Remarques at recherches sur les pyramides d'Egypte', in *Description de l'Egypte, Antiquités, Memoires*, vol. II, Paris: Imprimerie Impèriale, 1818, p. 188). The equilateral triangle was mentioned by Vitruvius (*Ten Books on Architecture*, v.6.1 and IX.1.13) and Plutarch (*De Iside at Osiride*, 75, 381D and 75, 381E), but never in connection with pyramidal forms.

Some of them appear to correspond to right-angled triangles, some to equilateral triangles, and some (the majority according to Badawy) to 8:5 triangles.[42] It is true that some amulets represent isosceles triangles flatter than equilateral and right-angled triangles,[43] but their identification as 8:5 triangles is arbitrary.[44] At any rate, they all date to the Late Period, at least nineteen centuries after Snefru's first pyramidal misadventures, with very little in between which could document any outstanding interest in the equilateral triangle or its 'derivative', the 'Egyptian' or 8:5 triangle.

The case of the 3-4-5 triangle is different, as seen later in this book in connection with the use of cords in architecture (Part II) and with the construction of pyramids (Part III). We do not possess any explicit early mathematical source recording its knowledge, but its use as a simple geometrical device is not incompatible with ancient Egyptian mathematics. In practice, it may have been used in the construction of at least eight Old Kingdom pyramids and possibly for small-scale layouts on the ground, as we shall see below.

The only case in which the use of a triangle was postulated on the basis of actual archaeological remains is Karl Georg Siegler's study of the plan and the elevation of the Ptolemaic temple at Kalabsha. During the dismantling of the building, which was moved to another location at the time of the construction of the Aswan Dam, a number of short lines drawn on the foundations came to light. One of them, numbered 29, accompanied by two other marks 29a and 29b, appeared to generate an angle of 60° and was interpreted as the trace of an equilateral triangle used to design the plan. Siegler suggested the use of five different modules in the layout of plan and elevations, and concluded that the position of the triangle was related to one of those square grids (fig. 41).[45]

It may be observed, however, that the 60° lines were marked on the already laid foundations, thus implying that at that point the plan of the building had already been established. Moreover, the plan of the sanctuary of the temple of Kalabsha is extremely simple (three rectangular rooms behind one another entered along a central axis), and it would not be easy to explain in a convincing way the function (practical or aesthetic) of an equilateral triangle laid out across the plan in that position. We may conclude that the presence of these lines is an intriguing coincidence

---

[42] Badawy, *Ancient Egyptian Architectural Design*, p. 42.

[43] See also George A. Reisner, *Amulets*, *CG*, Cairo: SAE, 1907, pp. 59–60 and plate 4; U. Hölscher, *The Excavation of Medinet Habu II: The Temples of the Eighteenth Dynasty*, Chicago: University of Chicago, Oriental Institute, 1939; Carol A. R. Andrews, *Amulets of Ancient Egypt*, London: British Museum, 1994, pp. 85–6.

[44] Among the fourteen examples published by Badawy (two are equilateral triangles), only three seem to have the same slope (about 52°) of an 8:5 triangle, and two seem to be very close to it, whereas the other slopes range from 44° to 55°.

[45] Karl Georg Siegler, *Kalabsha, Architektur und Baugeschichte des Tempels*, AV 1, Berlin: Mann, 1970, pp. 43–9 and pl. 9.

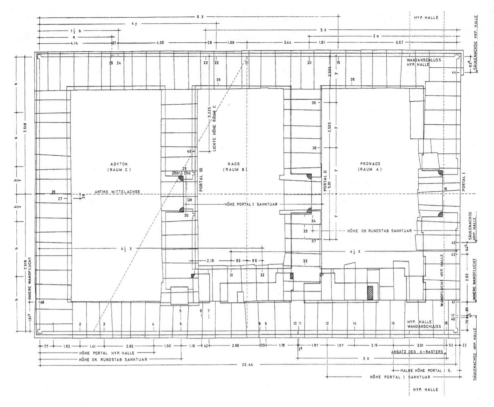

Fig. 41: Interpretation of some marks as traces of an equilateral triangle in the plan of the Roman temple at Kalabsha according to Siegler (from Siegler, *Kalabsha*, pl. 9 and fig. 24).

and has nothing to do with an equilateral triangle. Or we might go further and add another observation: with the adoption of the module x, the sanctuary happens to be 8 units long and 5 units wide, thus incorporating, beside the equilateral triangle, also its derivative, the 8:5 triangle.

But where do we go from here? Apart from the fact that there must be a certain number of cases that can be explained as coincidences, it is also true that without a constant rule, without a reliable mathematical background, and without any certain archaeological evidence, Badawy's 8:5 triangle seems to be able, somehow, to match some plans, and the same happens, in fact, for many theories on proportions, even for those which seem to be mutually exclusive. In general, by looking at Siegler's geometrical analyses (but also at Viollet-le-Duc's, Badawy's, Lauffray's, Hinkel's, Carlotti's[46] and some of Lauer's drawings), the doubt remains

---

[46] Jean-François Carlotti, 'Contribution à l'étude métrologique de quelque monuments du temple d'Amon-Rê à Karnak', *Cahiers de Karnak X*, Paris: Recherche sur les Civilisations, 1995, pp. 65–94.

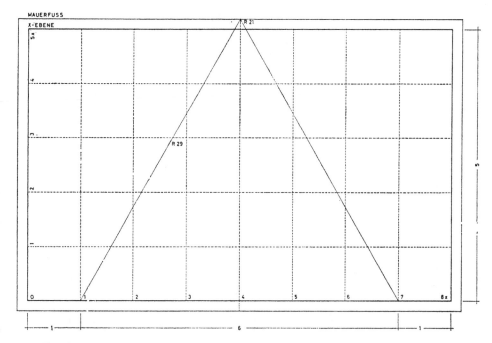

Fig. 41: (*cont.*)

whether what many of these schemes do is, in fact, nothing more than highlighting internal geometrical properties that each layout or elevation, being a geometrical figure itself, possesses. In some cases it is difficult to establish whether they are reconstructions of the process adopted by the ancient architect, or whether they simply underline geometrical connections resulting from the use of certain figures (see, for instance, fig. 42). The possibility of superimposing several geometrical schemes to a plan, as in the case of Mallinson's and Spence's attempts on the Small Aten Temple at Amarna (fig. 43 and fig. 63, the latter included in Part II),[47] implies that each possible scheme represents a possible geometrical analysis *a posteriori* of the plan. Not all of them, however, must necessarily correspond to methods of design adopted by the ancient architects. It is possible, of course, to make a distinction between more or less likely solutions, but in some cases it is impossible to provide a final answer. When dealing with geometrical schemes, in fact, it is not always easy to draw a clear distinction between intention and coincidence, because there is a third possibility: a general human tendency towards certain geometric patterns.

---

[47] Barry J. Kemp and Pamela Rose, 'Proportionality in Mind and Space in Ancient Egypt', *CAJ*, 1:1 (1991), figs. 4, 5 and 6.

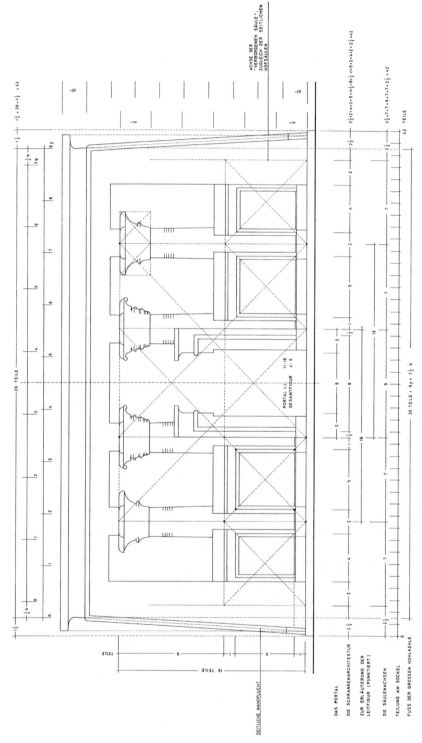

Fig. 42: Interpretation of the design of a façade and a section of the Roman temple at Kalabsha according to Siegler (from Siegler, *Kalabsha*, pls. 21 and 26).

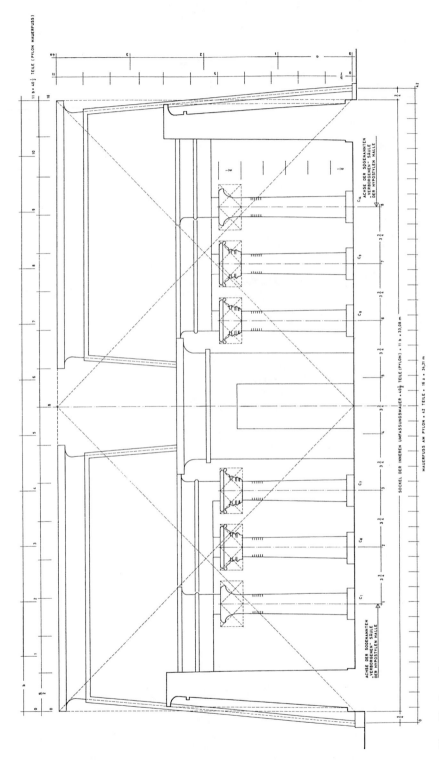

Fig. 42: *(cont.)*

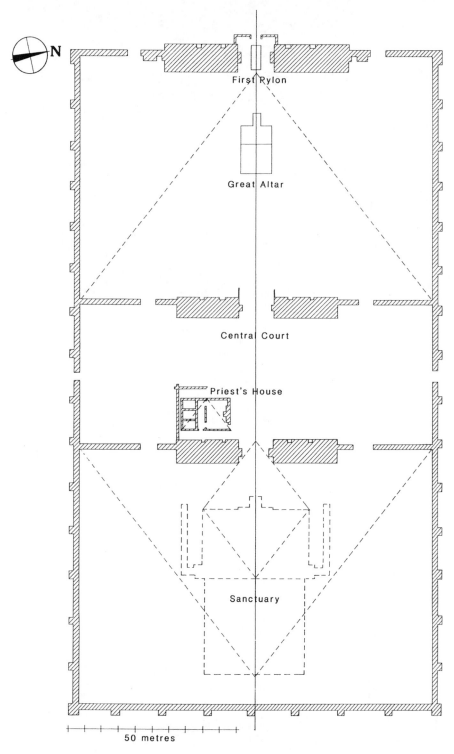

N

First Pylon

Great Altar

Central Court

Priest's House

Sanctuary

50 metres

Fig. 43: Interpretation of the plan of the Small Aten Temple at Amarna (Eighteenth Dynasty), according to Badawy left, and Mallinson, right (from Kemp and Rose, *CAJ* 1, figs. 3 and 5).

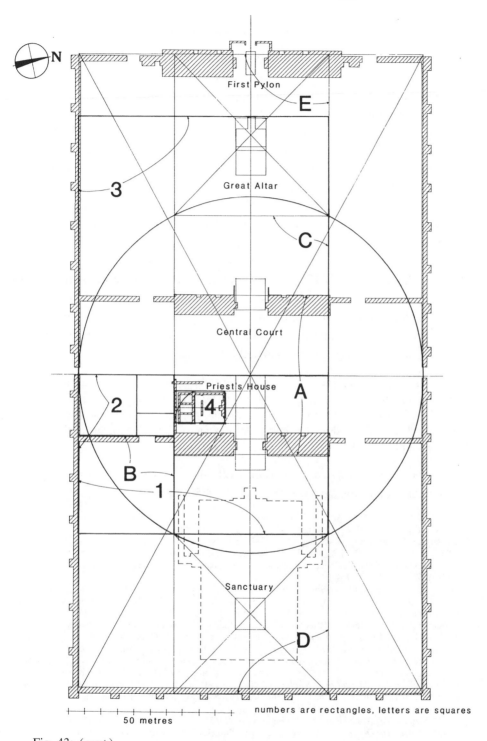

First Pylon

E

Great Altar

3

C

Central Court

Priest's House

A

2

4

B

1

Sanctuary

D

50 metres

numbers are rectangles, letters are squares

N

Fig. 43: (*cont.*)

Psychological experiments and involuntary trends

Since the study of Fechner,[48] a number of psychological experiments have been carried out in order to prove our innate preference for some geometrical figures. Even if the results are not conclusive, it appears that the most successful proportion is, in fact, the Golden Section. Apparently, among Western populations there is a tendency, when asked to provide a series of positive or negative value-judgements on a discrete set of entities, to give a percentage of positive answers corresponding to a value very close to ϕ in comparison with the total number of answers. That is, 'whenever people differentiate one thing into two, they tend to do so in a way that approximates the golden section'.[49] The distinction is made between positive and non-positive judgements, the latter including negative and neutral answers.[50] The experiments carried out by John Benjafield seem to prove this tendency,[51] but the discussion is still open. It is not clear, for example, whether the precise value of the Golden Section (1.618 . . .) is significant itself, or whether it simply falls into a range of values (e.g. 1.5, 1.6 or even 1.75) which are indistinctly preferred.[52] In fact, Rudolf Arnheim attributed the preference for the Golden Section to the characteristics of a certain type of rectangle, rather than to a mathematical ratio. According to him, this preference existed

because a ratio approaching the centric symmetry of the square does not bestow ascendancy on any one direction and therefore looks like a static mass; whereas too great a difference in the two dimensions undermines the equilibrium: the longer dimension is deprived of the counterweight provided by the shorter. A ratio approaching the golden section lets the shape stay in place while giving it a lively inherent tension[53].

As we have seen, over a century earlier Viollet-le-Duc had given more or less the same explanation of the aesthetic value of the 8:5 triangle.

[48] Gustav T. Fechner, *Vorschule der Aesthetik*, Leipzig: Breitkopf and Härtel, 1876.
[49] John Benjafield and J. Adams-Webber, 'The Golden Section Hypothesis', *British Journal of Psychology* 67 (1976), 11–5.
[50] Benjamin Shalit, 'The Golden Section Relation in the Evaluation of Environmental Factors', *British Journal of Psychology* 71 (1980), 39–42.
[51] John Benjafield and Edward Pomeroy, 'A Possible Idea Underlying Interpersonal Descriptions', *British Journal of Social and Clinical Psychology* 17 (1978), 23–35; Edward Pomeroy, John Benjafield, Chris Rowntree and Joanna Kuiack, 'The Golden Section: A Convenient Ideal?', *Social Behaviour and Personality* 9 (1981), 231–4. John Benjafield, 'A Review of Recent Research on the Golden Section', *Empirical Studies of the Arts* 3 (1985), 117–34 and *Cognition*, London: Prentice-Hall International, 1992, pp. 245–7. See also J. M. Hinz and T. M. Nelson, 'Haptic Aesthetic Value of the Golden Section', *Journal of British Psychology* 62 (1971), 217–23: congenitally blind subjects did not show a marked preference for the Golden Section. See also Hans J. Eysenck and Maureen Castle, 'Training in Art as a Factor in the Determination of Preference Judgements for Polygons', *British Journal of Psychology* 61 (1970), 65–81 and Hans J. Eysenck, 'Aesthetic Preferences and Individual Differences', in David O'Hare (ed.), *Psychology of the Arts*, Brighton: Harvester, 1981 for experiments involving polygons and colours.
[52] I. C. McManus, 'The Aesthetics of Simple Figures', *British Journal of Psychology* 71 (1980), 505–24.
[53] Rudolf Arnheim, *The Dynamics of Architectural Forms*, Berkeley/London: University of California Press, 1977, p. 221.

Another important point is the diffusion of this supposed tendency. According to Berlyne, who showed a number of rectangles with different proportions to a group of Canadian and Japanese girls,

neither groups showed a special preference for the golden section rectangle, but the Japanese subjects judged rectangles more favourably, the nearer they approached the square, whereas the Canadian subjects were more partial than them to more elongated rectangles. (. . .) Subjects of both populations, while differing in their evaluations of other rectangles are, in the light of our data, more likely to make a square their first choice than any other rectangle.[54]

He concluded that the Western preference for the Golden Section might be explained, at least in part, by the repeated exposure of the population to its diffused use in Western art since Egyptian and classical antiquity. Since ancient arithmetic and techniques of calculations did not allow complicated calculations, the Golden Section was essentially achieved by means of geometrical constructions.

Benjafield noted that, during his experiments on interpersonal judgement, when people were asked to assign a number of positive and negative labels, the total number of positive labels and the total number of labels of either sort were always, at any stage of the process, three successive terms of the Fibonacci Series.[55] Fibonacci-like series recur in other interesting contexts. In his study of Minoan architecture, Donald Preziosi claimed that the Fibonacci Series 1, 2, 3, 5, 8, 13, . . . was widely used in the design of façades and plans.[56] Roland Fletcher, on the other hand, in his study on space and settlements, detected the use of a similar sequence of numbers in the dimensions of a modern Konkomba settlement in Ghana: the space was arranged according to a series of growing dimensions each equal to the sum of the two previous ones. He found a similar pattern in the archaeological remains of the ancient Egyptian settlement at Deir el-Medina, although in this case the Fibonacci-like sequences appeared to be very short.[57]

Traces of the Golden Section have been found almost everywhere: other examples, not specifically related to architecture, include Virgil's *Aeneid*, Bartok's music and Grimm's fairy tales.[58] Can this instinctive tendency towards the creation of patterns linked to the proportion which we call the Golden Section be assumed

---

[54] D. E. Berlyne, 'The Golden Section and Hedonic Judgement of Rectangles: A Cross-Cultural Study', *Sciences de l'Art – Scientific Aesthetics* 7 (1970), 1–6.

[55] John Benjafield and T. R. G. Green, 'Golden Section Relations in Interpersonal Judgement', *British Journal of Psychology* 69 (1978), pp. 23–35, especially 28–9.

[56] Donald Preziosi, 'Harmonic Design in Minoan Architecture', *Fibonacci Quarterly* 6/6 (1868), 370–84, where he suggested that Minoan workmen employed in the construction of the pyramid of Senusret I might have imported the use of the Fibonacci Series to Crete; see also *Minoan Architectural Design*, Berlin: Mouton, 1983, especially 458–64 and figs. II.44 and IV.30.E.

[57] Roland J. Fletcher, 'Space in Settlements: A Mechanism of Adaptation', Ph.D. thesis, University of Cambridge (1976), pp. 76, 82 and 266.

[58] John Benjafield and Christine Davis, 'The Golden Section and the Structure of Connotation', *Journal of Aesthetics and Art Criticism* 36 (1978), 423–7.

for ancient Egypt, too? Extremely complicated geometrical analyses of artistic and architectural material do not necessarily provide a reliable basis to support this idea: when playing with geometrical figures and numbers without any restraint, it is relatively easy to find what one is expecting to find. Simpler cases, however, may provide interesting material for a discussion.

Cases from ancient Egypt

An involuntary tendency towards patterns related to the Golden Section in ancient Egypt has been studied by Barry Kemp and Pamela Rose,[59] who analysed a number of situations in the light of modern psychological experiments. The so-called 'Calendars of Lucky and Unlucky Days', for example, provide interesting material for a discussion on bipolar judgement: they are calendars for the full year or for a single month only, in which the days are classified either as 'good', or 'bad', or 'good' and 'bad' together, in this case producing a mixed, neutral result.

In the earliest example, a Middle Kingdom calendar for one unspecified month, there seem to be 18 'good', 9 'bad' and 3 neutral days[60]: the ratio between the 'good' days and the total of 'good' and 'not good' ('bad' + neutral) is 0.60, very close to the Golden Section value of 0.618. . . . The papyrus, however, is damaged in respect to the end of three lines which appear to contain a 'good' sign: if in only one case the 'good' was followed by a 'bad' sign,[61] thus giving a mixed (neutral) entry, the total percentage would drop to 0.57.[62] In the three Ramesside calendars including a whole year,[63] each day is divided into three parts, which may be labelled as 'good' or 'bad'. The result is a series of combinations which may be divided into four groups: 'good' days (three 'good' signs), more 'good' than 'bad' days (two 'good' and one 'bad' sign, in different combinations), more bad than good days (two 'bad' and one 'good' sign, in different combinations) and bad days (three 'bad' signs). In the Budge Papyrus (including 357 days), the ratio between the positive signs and the total is $209/357 = 0.585$ . . . , in the Papyrus Sallier IV (including 209 days) is $130/209 = 0.622$ . . . , while in Cairo Papyrus 86637 (including 344 days) is $195/344 = 0.567$ . . . .[64] In these cases, the percentage of 'positive' judgements seems to be very similar to the results of modern psychological experiments: the

---

[59] Kemp and Rose, *CAJ* 1:1, 103–29.

[60] Francis L. Griffith, *Hieratic Papyri from Kahun and Gurob*, London: Quaritch, 1898, p. 62 and pl. 25.

[61] As it was suggested by Warren R. Dawson, 'Some Observations on the Egyptian Calendars of Lucky and Unlucky Days', *JEA* 12 (1926), 260–4.

[62] Kemp and Rose, *CAJ* 1:1, p. 106.

[63] See Dawson, *JEA* 12, 260–4 for data from Budge and Sallier IV Papyri; Abd el-Mohsen Bakir, *The Cairo Calendar n° 86637*, Cairo: Government Press, 1966 for the Cairo Calendar; see Tamás A. Bács, 'Two Calendars of Lucky and Unlucky Days', *SAK* 17 (1990), 41–64 for O. Gardiner 109 and Cairo Calendar, and *LÄ*, vol. IV, pp. 153–6 for general references.

[64] Kemp and Rose, *CAJ* 1:1, 106.

classification of days according to two opposite polarities shows the same 'optimistic' tendency in favour of positive judgements, which, in terms of numerical value, is very close to the data produced by modern experiments.

Artistic and architectural material, however, provides less clear evidence when vigorously examined. Modern psychological experiments on the supposed preference for certain geometrical figures have been carried out on extremely simple examples, such as a group of plain rectangles drawn on paper which are isolated from any context. The attempts at explaining art and architectural design by means of the Golden Section, on the other hand, are usually based on more or less complicated geometrical constructions. In general, art produces relatively small-scale objects in which it should be easier to detect patterns similar to those investigated by modern psychological experiments. It has been suggested, for example, that the length, breadth and depth of a series of boxes or caskets were designed on the basis of the Golden Section.[65] No constant simple formula can be identified, however, and the ratios among the dimensions are uneven, thus excluding a conscious, calculated use of this proportion.

Traces of a voluntary or involuntary use of the Golden Section have been perceived in the canon for the representation of the human body. Square grids were used by the Egyptian artists as a guide for their drawings, and the human body for a long time was drawn as 18 squares high, measured from the ground to the forehead (thus excluding crowns or wigs). At some point, probably during the Twenty-fifth Dynasty, artists turned to another grid system, in which the square was smaller and the height of the human figure measured 21 squares to the upper eyelid (fig. 44). Concerning the first system, it has been noted that the navel was placed along line 11 from the bottom, and that the ratio between 18 (upper point) and 11 produces the value 1.636 . . . , 18 and 11 being, in fact, two terms of a Fibonacci-like series. The same ratio can be found between the height of the junction of the legs and the height of the junction of the armpits. Davis noted that the change to a 21-square grid 'improved' these ratios, the new value being 1.615 . . .[66]

The 18-square grid originated in a number of horizontal lines which Old Kingdom artists used in order to align some points of the bodies. They were used as a guide, rather than as a strict rule, and it may be noted that, in the surviving cases, the navel does not seems to have been regarded as a special point, while the lines marking the junction of the legs and the level of the armpits are usually included.[67] Whether this is enough to suggest that the presence of ratios which happen to be close to the Golden Section was felt to hold a special significance, is difficult to tell. In fact,

---

[65] Kielland, *Egyptian Art*, pp. 108–11 and Kemp and Rose, *CAJ* 1:1, 109–111.
[66] Whitney Davis, *The Canonical Tradition in Ancient Egyptian Art*, Cambridge: Cambridge University Press, 1989, p. 48.
[67] Robins, *Proportion and Style*, figs. 4.1–5.

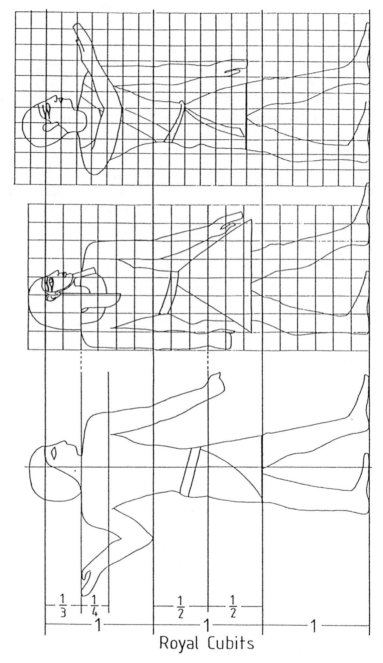

Fig. 44: The development of the square grid system according to Legon (from *DE* 35, fig. 1).

Robins has suggested a reason for the change of the grid which has nothing to do with the Golden Section.[68]

In comparison with art, architecture is related to a completely different kind of perception, and it is worth asking whether the human eye appreciates a golden rectangle in the same way when it is perceived from the outside (that is, either drawn on a two-dimensional surface or shaping a small three-dimensional object) and when it is embodied in a three-dimensional space in which the eye itself is moving.

Matila Ghyka mentioned five cases in which length and breadth of monuments of different periods show a striking correspondence to golden rectangles or seem to have been designed according to geometrical constructions related to the Golden Section.[69] The problem is that, as we shall see in Part II, ancient Egyptian working drawings were not to scale. Therefore, if the preference for a particular geometrical figure is assumed, it is necessary to imply that this was not visualised in advance in a drawing. On the other hand, it is equally difficult to establish whether the proportions of the full-size outline of a building on the ground would stimulate any particular aesthetic consideration. An extreme case is represented by a number of chambers in royal tombs, the outline of which approximates to the Golden Section.[70] In this case, their shape could not be established on the ground and the surviving working drawings of rock-cut tombs seem to suggest that, in general, the final dimensions of the subterranean rooms could be influenced by several factors. Again, it is difficult to say whether their proportions have a specific meaning. Moreover, the third dimension has a significant influence on the creation of an 'agreeable' space. Even if the plan corresponded to a perfectly balanced golden rectangle, an extremely low or high ceiling would certainly make a difference in the perception of that space.

The suspicion remains, therefore, that our detection of some geometrical characteristics in the ancient plans relies too heavily upon our experience of our modern system of representation. It is true that with the aid of a plan we may be able to find clues in royal tombs related to some involuntary tendency towards the use of certain geometrical patterns. But it is also true that we rely too much on plans alone to describe a whole monument. Mark Lehner, for example, suggested that the Amarna Royal Tomb was supposed to be 100 cubits long and that the entrance to the rooms α, β and γ, lies at the point corresponding to the subdivision of the length according to the Golden Section (fig. 45).[71] This is true in plan, but not in

[68] Robins, *Proportion and Style*, pp. 166–9. John Legon, even if starting from different assumptions, arrived at the same conclusions as for the reasons of the change (John Legon, 'Review article – Measurement in Ancient Egypt', *DE* 30 (1994), especially 95–100 and 'The Cubit and the Egyptian Canon of Art', *DE* 35 (1996), 61–76).

[69] Ghyka, *Nombre d'Or*, pp. 73–4, note 1.   [70] Kemp and Rose, *CAJ* 1:1, 119–23 and figs. 7 and 8.

[71] Mark Lehner, 'The Tomb Survey', in Geoffrey T. Martin, *The Royal Tomb at el-'Amarna II*, London: EES, 1989, pp. 5–9.

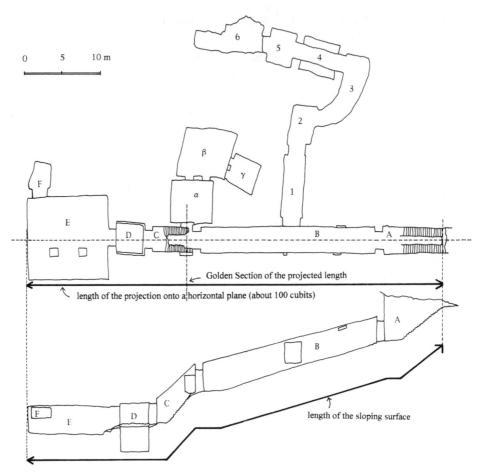

Fig. 45: Plan and section of the Amarna Royal Tomb, showing Lehner's suggestion that the plan was designed after the Golden Section, and the difference between
sloping surfaces and horizontal projection (from Rossi, *JEA* 87, fig. 3).

section. From the comparison between written sources and actual monuments, it
seems that the Egyptians measured the length of sloping corridors along the sloping
surface, rather than as its projection on a theoretical horizontal plane (as we do in
our modern plans). In this case, the length of the tomb would be much more than
100 cubits, and the correspondence to the Golden Section of the entrance to the
secondary funerary apartment would disappear.[72] In order to have a length in plan of
100 cubits, in fact, the ancient architects should have planned the tomb both in plan
and in section. However, no evidence of such a process, either drawn or written, has
survived.

[72] Corinna Rossi, 'Dimensions and Slope of the Royal Tombs', *JEA* 87 (2001), 73–80.

In conclusion, the presence of simple Golden Section-related patterns in ancient Egyptian art and architecture is not as straightforward as it may seem. Where art is concerned, only the scene from the Ptolemaic tomb of Petosiris (fig. 17) is safe to mention as a case where the Golden Section might have been consciously used or at least where this possibility cannot be excluded. The monument belongs to a period when Greek influence is not only possible, but actually tangible in that very tomb; half of the decoration (including the incriminated triangle) was carried out in Egyptian style, and the other half in Greek style. In that particular section of the decoration, only the height and the base of the triangle are important, and it is not necessary to assume that the artists were aware of all the geometrical properties shown in figure 18. I am sure that, if one tries hard, it is possible to imagine at least half a dozen reasons why the Golden Section should have been used to represent the mountain. At the same time, it may be best to bear in mind that there is always the possibility that the proportions of that triangle are just a coincidence.

In general, all the other cases mentioned above do not seem to provide enough evidence to suggest that the Egyptian artists showed a marked preference for simple Golden Section-based geometrical figures. The same applies to architecture. There are cases in which this proportion seems to rule the design in a rather simple way, but it is difficult to establish whether their number is really significant in comparison with all the cases in which this does not actually happen. Concerning the existence of a tendency towards certain geometrical patterns, the nature of the perception of architectural space cannot be easily compared with the results of modern psychological experiments, and the lack of scale drawings among the archaeological evidence makes any attempt to prove this connection difficult. Again, among all the rectangles outlining Egyptian buildings, or described in texts of various periods (see, for example, the Building Texts described in Part II), there are only a few simple golden rectangles. An interesting case is represented by the outline of the central nucleus of the Ptolemaic temples of Edfu and Dendera, which will be discussed in detail in Part II, but in general, for their rectangular outlines the Egyptians seem to have used the entire spectrum of possible proportions, from the square to very elongated shapes. It may be interesting to note that the rectangle very close to a square is not rare, and that the double square, a figure supposedly not very 'pleasing', was also widely adopted. The taste of the Thirtieth Dynasty king Nectanebo I would have probably deeply disappointed Viollet-le-Duc and Arnheim: in both temples founded by this king at Ashmunein the length was twice the breadth.[73]

---

[73] The outlines of these two temples were 60×30 cubits and 220×110 cubits (Günther Roeder, 'Zwei hiero-glyphische Inschriften aus Hermopolis (Ober-Ägypten)', *ASAE* 52 (1954), 403–4 and 410–1).

In conclusion, even discarding the most complicated theories, Golden Section-related geometrical figures and mathematical relationships can be found both in the art and architecture of ancient Egypt. The number of clear cases, however, does not appear to be significant and does not seem to be able to provide a reliable basis for claiming the existence of a marked preference of the ancient Egyptian artists and architects for this proportion. What appears clear, on the contrary, is the modern psychological tendency to find the Golden Section everywhere.

Ancient mathematics and practical operations

As I have shown in Part I, concepts like φ or π did not belong to ancient Egyptian mathematics and therefore could not be used by the ancient Egyptian architects. Their presence in the plans of ancient buildings is mainly due to our modern interpretation of the geometrical figures that compose the plan on paper. However, I am not arguing that mathematics was not involved in ancient Egyptian architecture, but rather that so far we have analysed cases in which the wrong mathematical system was adopted. Before we move on to an analysis of the ancient Egyptian architectural documents on planning and building, we must consider a final point: the supposed existence of a secret knowledge, restricted to a few initiated, concerning rules and symbolic meanings that would have been hidden in some buildings.

In theory, a project might be laid out on the basis of extremely complicated concepts and then the actual construction carried out with a certain degree of approximation. It is also true, however, that ancient Egypt does not reveal evidence for this discrepancy (in fact, I wonder how many other cultures actually do?). At any rate, the total lack of evidence has never prevented people from suggesting more or less complicated theories. Architecture may have a strong symbolic function, and in theory it is possible to suggest that, in their buildings, ancient Egyptian architects hid meaningful mathematical relationships, not immediately perceptible and related to an esoteric knowledge. Such a hypothesis is extremely difficult to test. If it were to be accepted, the idea that only an initiated few had access to a secret knowledge (which was kept well hidden and did not manifest itself anywhere else) undermines any research based on the actual archaeological evidence. It initiates a vicious circle: there is no evidence because there is not supposed to be any.

The problem of the existence of restricted knowledge has been discussed by John Baines, who has analysed sources from the Old Kingdom to the Late Period containing allusions to various degrees of involvement in religious and secular knowledge. The ancient Egyptian title of 'Keeper of the Secrets' is certainly suggestive, but the nature and contents of these 'secrets' is unclear. As Baines pointed out, they 'could be either confidential, or secret in a religious sense; royalty might have some interest in blurring this distinction, because it would place extra sanctions on the confidentiality of the less religious information'.[1] Being the materialisation of religious and royal power, architecture is likely to have been included, at least to some extent, among the restricted subjects. However, in comparison with religion, for example architecture also has an extremely practical aspect which cannot be neglected. The common mathematical problems of builders of all times have always been the same: construction of right angles, alignment of straight lines, calculation of areas to cover, volumes to remove or build, and so on.

On this subject, it is worth reading what the Roman architect Vitruvius wrote in the first century BC, in his treatise *De architectura* (cf. fig. 46):

> if there is a square plot or field with sides of equal length and it needs to be doubled in size, the need will arise for the type of number that cannot be found by means of calculation, but it can be found by drawing a succession of precise lines. Here is a demonstration of the problem: A square plot that is ten feet long and ten feet wide gives an area of 100 square feet. If it is necessary to double this, and make one of 200 square feet, likewise with equal sides, then the question will arise as to how long the side of this square would be, so that from it two hundred feet should correspond to the doubling of the area. It is not possible to find such a number by counting. For if fourteen is established as the measure of each side, then when multiplied the sides will give 196 square feet, if fifteen, 225 square feet. Therefore, it is not discovered by means of numbers. However, if in that original square that was ten feet on a side, a line should be drawn diagonally from corner to corner, so as to divide off two triangles of equal size, each of fifty feet in area, then a square with equal sides should be drawn on the basis of this diagonal line. Thus, whatever the size of the two triangles defined by the diagonal line in the smaller square, each with an area of fifty feet, just so, four such triangles, of the same size and the same number of square feet, will be created in the larger square.[2]

This argument is taken from Plato's *Meno* (written around 390 BC) where Socrates discusses mathematics with a slave-boy,[3] but its origin might be earlier than Greek.[4] It is a convenient method that does not involve any arithmetical calculation (such as the square root of 200, which is not a whole number, being about 14.142136 . . .) but

---

[1] John Baines, 'Restricted Knowledge, Hierarchy and Decorum: Modern Perceptions and Ancient Institutions', *JARCE* 27 (1990), 1–23 (quotation from p. 9).

[2] Vitruvius, *Ten Books on Architecture*, IX.praef.4–5, quoted from the English translation, p. 107.

[3] Plato, *Meno*, English translation by G. M. A. Grube, Indianapolis, Ind.: Hackett, 1976, 82–5.

[4] Richard Gillings suggested that the ancient Egypyians used the same system to double areas and based his conclusions on the double use of the *remen* as a unit of measurement for length and area (cf. table 2). In New Kingdom votive cubit rods, the subdivision of the cubit corresponding to 5 palms is called *remen*, the same name of the unit of measurement that in the Old Kingdom corresponds to half *ta*, that is, 50 square cubits. Gillings suggested that the *remen* corresponded to half the diagonal of a 1-cubit square (that would be a trifle less than 10 palms) and that might have been used to double square areas (Gillings, *Mathematics*, pp. 208–9). Less demanding and more consistent with the other subdivisions of the unit of measurement of areas is Griffith's interpretation of the *remen* as half a *setat* cut into two rectangles (each 100 × 50 cubits), rather than diagonally into two triangles as in Plato's and Vitruvius' example (Francis L. Griffith, 'Notes on Egyptian Weights and Measures', *PSBA* 14 (1891–2), especially 417).

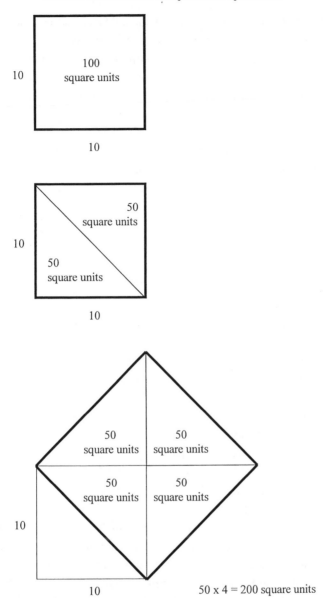

Fig. 46: Geometrical method to double a 100-square unit area.

just an easy geometrical construction. I find the statement that the square root of 200 'cannot be found by counting' quite revealing. It suggests that five centuries after the legendary Pythagoras, and in any case two centuries after Euclid, a practical geometrical approach was still the most likely method to be adopted by an architect.[5]

---

[5] About the concept of mathematics in Vitruvius, see Serafina Cuomo, *Ancient Mathematics*, London/New York: Routledge, 2001, pp. 202–3.

Vitruvius is one of our best sources about ancient Greek and Roman architecture, and it is interesting to note that the mathematics involved in his treatise is very simple. He generally suggested the use of simple numerical ratios in the design of buildings, such as 3:5 and 2:3. The diagonal of a square used as a dimension is mentioned only a couple of times, and even in these cases as the result of a geometrical construction ('make a square whose sides are equal to the width, draw a diagonal line, and whatever the distance of the diagonal, this is the length of the atrium'[6]) rather than the numerical value $\sqrt{2}$, for which he does not seem to display any interest. The equilateral triangle also appears briefly in the chapter dedicated to the Roman theatre, where it is used to establish the design of the plan:

whatever the size of the lower perimeter, locate a centre point and draw a circle around it, and in this circle draw four triangles with equal sides and at equal intervals. These should just touch the circumference of the circle. (By these same triangles, astrologers calculate the harmonies of the stars of the twelve heavenly sings in musical terms.) Of these triangles, take the one whose side will be closest to the performing platform. There, in that area that cuts the curvature of the circle, lay out the *scaenae frons* . . . .[7]

In the Greek theatre the process is the same, but the correct proportions are obtained by means of three squares, instead of four triangles.[8]

In conclusion, because of the adoption of modern mathematical concepts and the expectations that people have of ancient Egypt, complicated solutions seem to gather more credit than simple explanations. From a logical point of view, however, the subject should be approached in the reverse order. I am not saying that there cannot be complicated solutions, but rather that they ought to be considered only after the simple ones have been analysed and discarded, and that (most of all) they ought to be consistent with the cultural and archaeological background. Many of the modern mathematical analyses of ancient Egyptian monuments do not fulfil these conditions. Ancient Egyptian mathematics, its language and its numerical notation points in a different direction from what many modern theories have suggested, and it is this direction that we must follow. Part II is entirely dedicated to the study of ancient Egyptian working drawings and models and to the textual evidence related to the construction of tombs and temples. We shall see that projects and actual buildings (as one would expect) are the product of exactly the same culture which generated the surviving mathematical sources. Moreover, not only are there no traces of the most complicated mathematical methods so far suggested, but a study of the original sources from the 'correct' mathematical point of view highlights connections and methods so far unnoticed.

---

[6] Vitruvius, *Ten Books on Architecture*, vi.3.3, quoted from the English translation, p. 79. See also iv.1.11.
[7] Vitruvius, *Ten Books on Architecture*, vi.6.1, quoted from the English translation, pp. 68–9; see also fig. 83.
[8] Vitruvius, *Ten Books on Architecture*, vi.7.1–2; see also, in the English translation, fig. 84.

Part II

Ancient Egyptian sources: construction and representation of space

Tradition and variations in ancient Egyptian
art and architecture

Ancient Egyptian architects certainly followed a number of rules in the construction of their buildings, but both the nature and the function of these rules must be clarified. Identifying them just as mathematical formulae might be reductive and inappropriate. In general, continuity (real or pretended) is a striking element of ancient Egypt, where revivals of ancient features took place from time to time in both language and the arts. Although forms and tastes did not remain unchanged during the more than thirty centuries of ancient Egyptian history, the link with the past, with what had been done by the ancestors, continued to play a significant role. A good example is the religious text engraved by Shabaka, king of the Twenty-fifth Dynasty, on a stele now at the British Museum, which is said to have been copied from an ancient, worm-eaten document. The style of the text is archaic and resembles the Old Kingdom Pyramid Texts, but it is now generally assumed that it is a much later composition, perhaps even dating to Shabaka's time.[1]

Concerning the arts, it seems that there were archives of traditional sources and models which could be consulted and used. The drawing of a shrine on papyrus, in black ink over a red square grid (fig. 47), might be the only surviving original example of this type of document.[2] The existence of models may also be deduced by several observations. Jean Capart, for example, isolated nine possible models which might have been used by the artists to design the twenty-four birds which are to be found in a scene of hunting in the Old Kingdom chapel of Ti.[3] Textual sources also provide similar evidence. According to the text on a now lost stele

---

[1] Miriam Lichtheim, *Ancient Egyptian Literature*, Berkeley: University of California Press, 1973–80, vol. I, pp. 51–2; vol. III, p. 5; Friedrich Junge, 'Zur Fehldatierung des sog. "Denkmals memphitischer Theologie", oder Der Beitrag der ägyptischen Theologie zur Geistesgeschichte der Spätzeit', *MDAIK* 29 (1973), 195–204.

[2] Legon, *DE* 35, especially 72–3. See also W. M. Flinders Petrie, 'Egyptian Working Drawings', *Ancient Egypt* 1 (1926), 24–7; H. S. Smith and H. M. Stewart, 'The Gurob Shrine Papyrus', *JEA* 70 (1984), 54–64.

[3] Jean Capart, 'Cahiers de modèles', *CdE* 16 (1941), 43–4; in general, see also 'Sur le cahiers de modèles en usage sous l'Ancien Empire', *CdE* 20 (1945), 33–5.

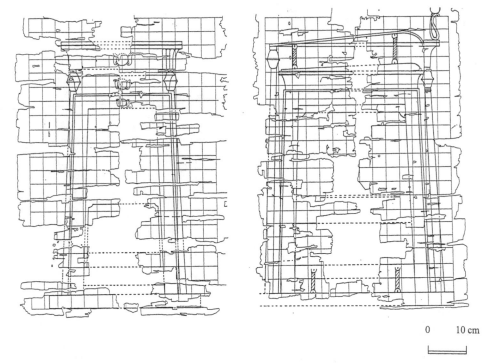

0   10 cm

Fig. 47: Eighteenth Dynasty (?) drawing of a portable shrine on papyrus, (from Clarke and Engelbach, *Ancient Egyptian Masonry*, fig. 48).

from Abydos, Neferhotep I (a king of the Thirteenth Dynasty) consulted ancient papyri held in a library in order to 'know the god in his form' and prepare a new statue[4]. In a text from Edfu, the scheme of the Ptolemaic temple is said to have been established by Imhotep, the architect who over twenty-four centuries earlier built the complex of the step pyramid at Saqqara for Djoser, second king of the Third Dynasty.[5] References to earlier sources are quite common in the so-called Building Texts, which describe the origin and foundation of Ptolemaic temples. As we shall see in subsequent chapters, in this case it is possible to suggest that some of the passages in these texts referred to mathematical rules.

In architecture, symbolic forms and elements were certainly handed down, and their proportions must have been influenced by some basic rules dictated by structural reasons. Besides this, however, the existence of fixed, specific mathematical rules is not easy to demonstrate. As we have seen, it is relatively easy to 'find' more

[4] Hieroglyphic text in Wolfgang Helck, *Historisch-Biographische Texte der 2. Zwischenzeit und neue Texte der 18. Dynastie*, Kleine Ägyptische Texte, Wiesbaden: Harrassowitz, 1983, pp. 21–9; translation in Max Pieper, *Die grosse Inschrift des Königs Neferhotep in Abydos*, Mitteilungen der Vorderasiatisch-aegyptischen Gesellschaft 32, 2, Leipzig: Hinrich, 1929.

[5] Kurt Sethe, *Imhotep, der Asklepios der Aegypter*, Leipzig: Hinrichs, 1902, pp. 15–8.

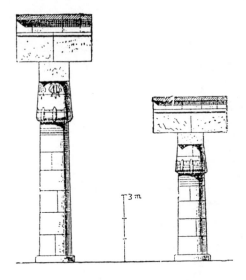

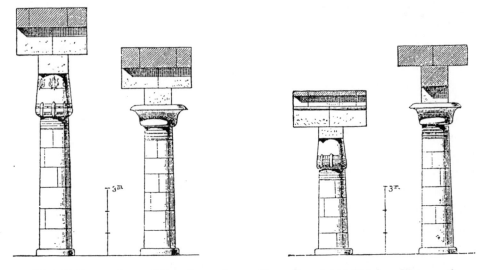

Fig. 48: Proportions of Egyptian columns (from Perrot and Chipiez, *History of Art*, vol. I, figs. 62–4 and 66).

or less complicated mathematical relationships in a plan, if this is what one is looking for. At the same time, in ancient Egyptian architecture it is probably easier to
note the absence of a rule in cases where it would be expected. Perrot and Chipiez,
for example, noted that columns of the same type and of the same diameter might
have different heights, that columns of different types but with the same diameter
had no fixed proportions in comparison with one another, and that the spacing of

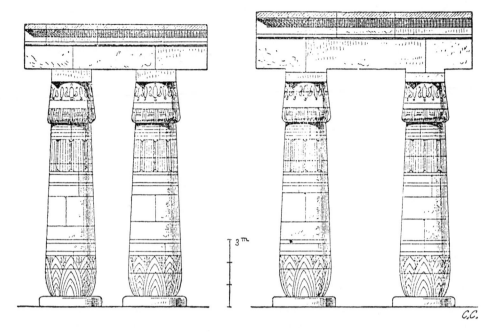

Fig. 48: (*cont.*)

identical columns was not always the same (fig. 48). They concluded that 'in this sense, the art of Egypt was not mathematical'.[6]

In her study on the proportions of human figures, Gay Robins proved that ancient Egyptian artists used square grids to draw human figures, but just as a guide, not as a rigid and fixed device. In fact, they were perfectly able to draw without them, as a number of surviving examples show.[7] The variety in proportions of architectural elements seems to suggest that architects might have had a similar approach to the design of their buildings. They might have had a few basic rules based on a long-established practice of construction that were adopted, changed or combined during the actual building process. The following chapters contain a study of the surviving architectural working drawings and models, and of the texts describing the construction of some monuments, that will help us outline the planning and building process followed by the ancient architects.

---

[6] Perrot and Chipiez, *History of Art*, pp. 99–102; see also Wilkinson, *Architecture of Ancient Egypt*, especially Part II.
[7] Robins, *Proportion and Style*, p. 259.

3

Documents on the planning and building process

Architectural drawings

Representations of buildings and working drawings

Representations of buildings are frequently found in Egyptian art, and in many cases they provide a large amount of information about lost evidence, such as constructional details, overall appearance, function and internal arrangement of space. They sometimes may be the sole clue to the existence of totally destroyed buildings, but often they are not definitive. In many cases the doubts and questions generated by alternative interpretations must remain unanswered.

At first sight, Egyptian representations may seem rather complicated, but they were just based on different graphic rules in comparison with our modern conventions. We use partial representations, as in perspective, where a single point of view is privileged, while the Egyptians preferred to adopt for each object its best point of view, so that nothing could be lost, covered or misunderstood because of an incomplete visual. This is the reason why, for example, they represented the human body in positions which would be difficult to assume, but in which every single part could be perceived from its clearest point of view. The front view of the torso combined with the lateral view of head, arms and legs sometimes produced two-dimensional representations not easy to decipher. In the pose of worship, for example, the two arms were generally represented as if they were raised at different levels, even if in three-dimensional statues they appear to be held at the same height.[1]

The same convention was generally employed to represent groups of objects which overlap one another from a perspective point of view: parallel rows of offerings on tables, or of jars in a room, or of columns of a building, which lay close to

---

[1] Richard H. Wilkinson, *Reading Egyptian Art*, London: Thames and Hudson, 1992, pp. 28–9. Wilkinson even suggested that the hieroglyph for the word 'man', a man sitting on one leg with the other knee raised, represented in fact a man in the typical scribal position with both legs folded beneath him, which was difficult to represent from a lateral point of view (pp. 14–5).

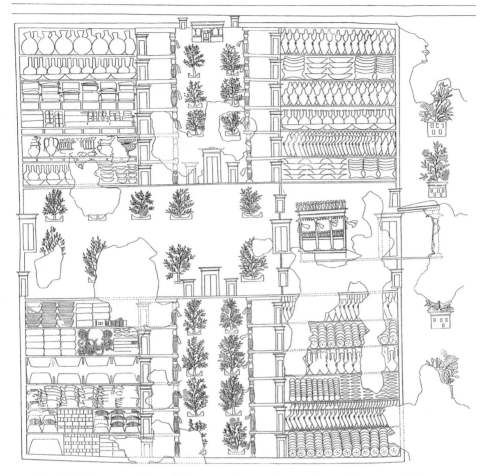

Fig. 49: Representation of the royal granaries and storehouses of Amarna (Eighteenth Dynasty) from the tomb of Meryra (from Davies, *Amarna* I, pl. 31).

one another (i.e. one behind the other from the viewer's perspective), were represented in lines lying one above the other (fig. 49). In this way, not only every single object, but also every single group could be clearly seen and identified. Architectural representations also followed this pattern, combining the plan and elevation of the building. A room was usually represented by means of its more distinctive feature, i.e. its being an 'enclosure', and therefore the best way to convey this impression was the closed outline of the plan. The contents of the room (objects, people, activities, but also architectural elements like doors and columns) were better represented from a frontal point of view, in superimposed registers if necessary (fig. 50).

Another important feature of ancient Egyptian representations, which is common to all subjects, is the expression of importance by means of size: the more important

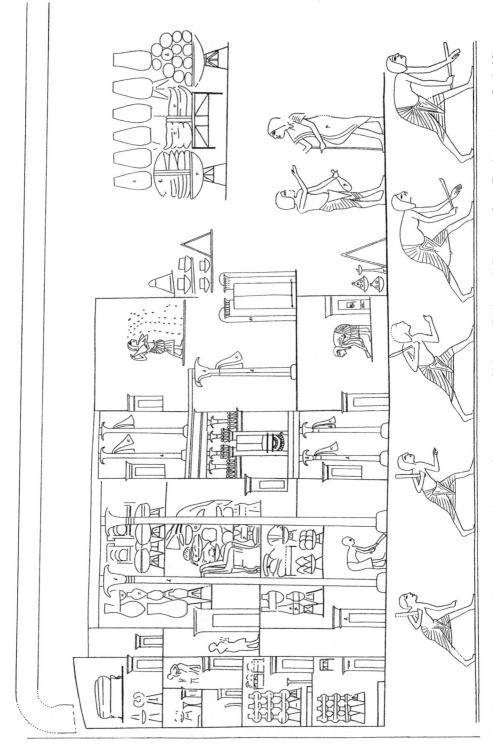

Fig. 50: Representation of an Amarna royal palace from the tomb of Meryra, Eighteenth Dynasty (from Davies, *Amarna* I, pl. 18).

a person or an object is, the bigger it is in the scene. In the case of people, social hierarchy could be expressed by means of dimensional hierarchy,[2] but in the case of buildings or architectural details the interpretation is not that simple. Human beings are, more or less, similar in terms of dimensions, which means that their size in the representations depended simply on their social status (the difference in size visualised very well the power of the 'bigger', i.e. the 'stronger' over the 'smaller', i.e. the 'weaker'). On the other hand, drawings depicting buildings or parts of them show a double degree of complexity. As usual, the feature which is considered prominent in a specific scene is shown on a larger scale, but important parts of buildings could actually have been larger than other, less significant, parts. The main gateway of a temple or a palace might be larger than any other entrance, because of its important symbolic function; moreover, it could be represented even bigger than it was in proportion with the rest of the building, because of the importance it had in a particular scene.

The representations of Akhenaten rewarding his people from the Window of Appearance at Amarna is a good example of the use of this device (fig. 51). The entire scene is arranged to highlight the extreme importance of the king in comparison with the commoners, and the extreme importance of the Window itself in that particular situation. Of course, the king was not five times bigger than his officials, but the Window might have been built to be 'impressive'. Moreover, in this particular occasion it was represented on an even larger scale in relation to the rest of the building.

The representations of the buildings of Amarna, unlike many other cases, can be compared with the actual archaeological remains of the city. Even in this case, however, the task is not particularly easy, since they were decorative descriptions and were not intended to be exact surveys. As Barry Kemp concluded, the representations of the Aten temple, for example, seem to include features from both the Great and the Small Aten Temple; in the case of royal estates, it is difficult to establish to what extent the artist actually knew those buildings and how many fantastic elements he added to them.[3]

In general, all of these representations say very little about the dimensions of these buildings, but they may provide important information about the outline, distribution and function of the constructions involved. The representation of the

[2] See for example Richard H. Wilkinson, *Symbol and Magic in Egyptian Art*, London: Thames and Hudson, 1999 (1994), chapter 2.

[3] On the correspondence between representations and findings see Norman de Garis Davies, *The Rock Tombs of El Amarna* I–VI, ASE 13–18, vol. VI, London, 1903–8, pp. 36–7 and pl. 34; Alexander Badawy, *Le dessin architectural chez les anciens Egyptiens*, Cairo: Imprimerie Nationale, 1948, pp. 110 and 166–81; Barry J. Kemp, 'The Window of Appearance at El-Amarna and the Basic Structure of this City', *JEA* 62 (1976), 81–99; Kemp, *Ancient Egypt. Anatomy of a Civilisation*, London: Routledge, 1989, fig. 90; Kemp, 'The Sanctuary of the Great Aten Temple', *Amarna Reports* IV, London: EES, 1987, chapter 8; Kemp, 'Outlying temples at Amarna', *Amarna Reports* VI, London: EES, 1995, chapter 15.

Fig. 51: Akhenaten rewarding Meryra from the Window of Appearance, Eighteenth Dynasty (from Davies, *Amarna* II, pl. 33).

house of Djehuti-nefer Huia, for instance, shows the full vertical section of a three-storey house with granaries on the top, with a clear section of the floor indicating the way it was built.[4] Another good example is the fragments of a slate tablet, probably belonging to an archive, on which the plan of an Eighteenth Dynasty temple at Heliopolis was represented. Even though the building has completely

---

[4] Ernest Mackay, 'The Origin of Polychrome Borders: A Suggestion', *Ancient Egypt* IV (1916), 169–73.

disappeared, Herbert Ricke was able to suggest two possible reconstructions of its layout by comparing the drawing on the tablet with the plans of other New Kingdom temples[5] (fig. 52). In other cases, however, such as the faded plan of an estate on papyrus from the Ramesseum,[6] not even a tentative reconstruction is possible.

In his *Dessin architectural chez les anciens Egyptiens*, Badawy attempted the reconstruction of the plans of a large number of buildings depicted by Egyptian artists, from predynastic enclosures to New Kingdom temples, from private houses to funerary monuments, also including gardens and military architecture. None of the representations so far mentioned, however, provide precise evidence about the dimensions of the buildings, not even of their proportions,[7] and therefore cannot be considered a primary source for this research. Especially important are, instead, the architectural working drawings which have survived to the present day.[8] Some of them provide dimensional information while others lack precise indications, but together they represent one of our most important sources for understanding the ancient way of laying down a project. They are the trace of the hand of the ancient architect, and represent the intermediate step between the idea and its execution, that is, the moment when geometric rules are expected to meet aesthetic ideals.

Drawings with written dimensions: the problem of the scale

Modern architectural drawings are to a precise, calculated scale. In a plan at 1:100, for example, 1 cm of the drawing corresponds to 100 cm (1 m) in reality. Therefore, by measuring a drawing, one can calculate the dimensions of each element of the actual object or building. Concerning ancient Egypt, the majority of the surviving working drawings (listed in table 3) consist of more or less elaborated plans in which the dimensions were written out beside the parts to which they referred.

---

[5] Herbert Ricke, 'Ein Inventartafel aus Heliopolis im Turiner Museum', *ZÄS* 71 (1935), especially 130–1.

[6] Alan H. Gardiner, *The Ramesseum Papyri*, Oxford: Oxford University Press, 1955, pp. 17–8.

[7] See, for example, the five different representations of the pylon of the Great Aten Temple at Amarna (Badawy, *Dessin architectural*, pp. 164–6).

[8] Lists of architectural drawings have been published, among others, by Badawy ('Ancient Constructional Diagrams in Egyptian Architecture', *Gazette des Beaux-Arts* 107 (1986), 51–56), Arnold (*Building in Egypt*, New York/Oxford: Oxford University Press, 1991, p. 8) and Heisel (*Antike Bauzeichnungen*, Darmstadt: Wissenschaftliche Buchgesellschaft, 1993, chapter 2). Other sketches are listed by Brunner-Traut, including seven in *Die Altägyptischen Scherbenbilder*, Wiesbaden: Steiner, 1956, pp. 120–3 and the representation of a decorated doorway in Brunner-Traut, *Egyptian Artists' Sketches*, Istanbul: Istanbul, Nederlands Historisch Archaeologisch Institut, 1979, pp. 22–5. The latter, and three among those listed by Heisel – the sketch of an unidentified plan (p. 96) and the sketch of a column (p. 137), both from Deir el-Medina, and the sketch of a column from Kalabsha (Siegler, *Kalabsha*, p. 39, fig. 17) – have not been considered here, because of their rough descriptive character. The Eighteenth Dynasty sketch on an ostracon representing a funeral (Gardiner Alan H., 'An Unusual Sketch of a Theban Funeral', *PSBA* 35 (1913), 229) and the Nineteenth Dynasty map of the gold mines (latest publications: James A. Harrell and V. Max Brown, 'The Oldest Surviving Topographical Map from Ancient Egypt (Turin Papyri 1879, 1899 and 1969)', *JARCE* 29 (1992), 81–105 and Jac. J. Janssen, 'An Exceptional Event at Deir el-Medina', *JARCE* 31 (1994), 91–7), although both undoubtedly very interesting from many points of view, do not add any useful dimensional information.

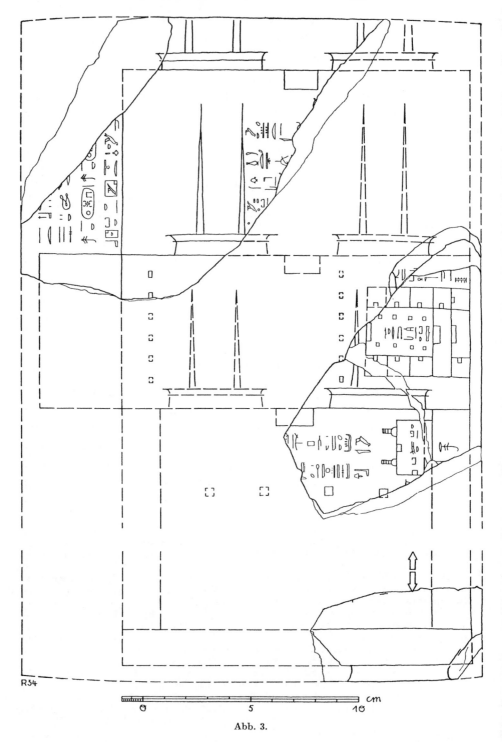

Abb. 3.

Fig. 52: Slate tablet from Heliopolis representing a temple and two reconstructions by Ricke (from *ZÄS* 71, figs. 3, 6 and 7).

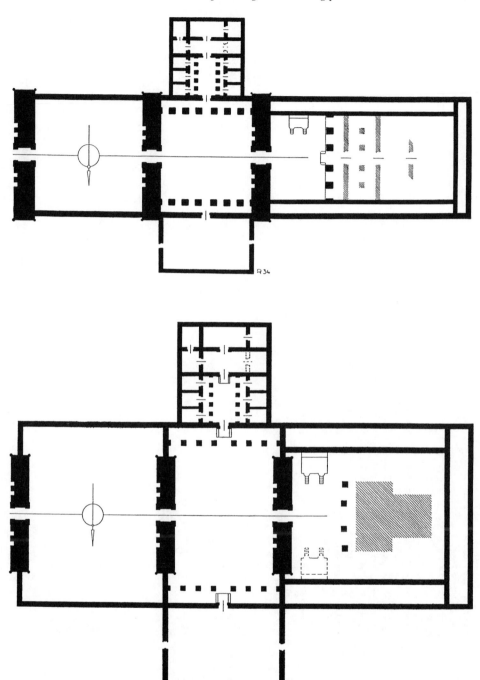

Fig. 52: (*cont.*)

Table 3. *Architectural sketches and drawings*

Object represented	Material	Date	Provenance	Location	Bibliography
Diagram with coordinates	ostracon	Third Dynasty	Saqqara	Cairo Museum 50036	Gunn, *ASAE* 26, pp. 197–202; Daressy, *ASAE* 27, pp. 157–60.
Layout of a garden or temple	sandstone slab	Mentuhotep (Eleventh Dynasty)	Deir el-Bahari	Metropolitan Museum of Art 22.3.30	Winlock, *Deir el-Bahri*, p. 50: Arnold, *Mentuhotep*, p. 23, fig. 9.
Plan of a building	paving slab	Senwosret I (Twelfth Dynasty)	Lisht	Metropolitan Museum of Art 14.3.15	Arnold, *Senusret I*, p. 98, fig. 4.7.
Plan of a building	papyrus	Amenemhat III (Twelfth Dynasty)	Middle Kingdom tomb in the area of the Ramesseum	Berlin, P. Ram. B	Gardiner, *Ramesseum*, p. 18, fig. 2.
Plan of a temple at Heliopolis	slate tablet	Middle Kingdom	Heliopolis	Turin Museum 2682	Ricke, *ZÄS* 71, pp. 111–33.
Plan of a tomb	ostracon	Eighteenth Dynasty	Thebes, tomb of Senenmut (n. 71)	Cairo Museum 66262	Hayes, *Sen-mut*, p. 15, pl. 7; Dorman, *Senenmut*, p. 26, note 52.
Plan of a peripteral chapel (?) on a canal	wooden board	Eighteenth Dynasty	Dra Abu el-Naga (?)	Metropolitan Museum 14.108	Davies, *JEA* 4, pp. 194–9.
Sketch plan of a house	ostracon	Eighteenth Dynasty?		Cairo Museum	
Sketch plans of houses	ostracon	Amarna Period (Eighteenth Dynasty)		Floor of the Broad Hall, Great Palace, Amarna	Pendelbury, *City of Akhenaten* III, pl. 36.4–5.
Sketch of a peripteral chapel	ostracon	Eighteenth–Nineteenth Dynasty	Deir el-Bahari	British Museum 41228	Glanville, *JEA* 16, pp. 237–9; Van Siclen, *GM* 90, pp. 71–7.
Plan of a temple	papyrus	Early Nineteenth Dynasty	Thebes?	Berlin, Ägyptisches Museum und Papyrussamlung SMB P 15781	Müller, *Festschrift Eggebrecht*, pp. 67–9.
Four-pillared chamber	ostracon	Nineteenth Dynasty	Valley of the Kings	Cairo Museum 51936	Englebach, *ASAE* 27, pp. 72–5; Reeves, *CdE* 61, pp. 42–9.
Plan of the tomb of Ramses IV	papyrus	Twentieth Dynasty		Turin Museum, Papyrus 1885 (verso)	Carter and Gardiner, *JEA* 4, pp. 130–58.
Plan of the tomb of Ramses IX	ostracon	Twentieth Dynasty	Valley of the Kings	Cairo Museum 25184	Daressy, *Revue Archéologique* 32, pp. 235–40.
Sketch of stairs and door of a tomb	ostracon	Twentieth Dynasty	Valley of the Kings	Cairo Museum?	Clarke and Engelbach, *Ancient Egyptian Masonry*, p. 52; Reeves, *CdE* 61, pp. 43–9.
Plan of a colonnaded court	ostracon	Twentieth Dynasty	Dra Abu el-Naga, tomb of Ramsesnakht (n. K93.11)		Polz, *MDAIK* 53, pp. 233–40.
Sketch plans of the pyramids on top of tombs 14 and 15	ostracon	Eighteenth–Twentieth Dynasty	Soleb, tomb 14		Leclant, *Orientalia* 31, p. 134.
Sketch of a large building		New Kingdom?	Limestone quarry at Sheikh Said		Davies, *Ancient Egypt* 1917, pp. 21–5.
Sketch plan of a pyramid	terracotta jar	Late Period	Meroe		Bonnet, *Genava* 28, p. 59.
Sketch of half the vertical section of a pyramid		Late Period		Meroe, chapel of pyramid Beg. 8	Hinkel, *ZÄS* 108, pp. 107–12.

Only in a few cases do some elements of the plans seem to correspond to the written measures; that is, they seem to be to scale, but in the same representation other parts do not follow the same rule.

Although written dimensions provide useful information, in virtually all cases in which we cannot match a drawing with a particular building, a precise reconstruction of the object represented is very difficult.[9] Some drawings are very rudimentary, as if they were abbreviated sketches providing only the most useful information about the plan, the rest being taken somehow for granted. A good example of this kind of representation is a sketch of a shrine on an ostracon (Eighteenth Dynasty), of which two tentative reconstructions have been made (fig. 53). Glanville suggested that the plan might refer to a shrine surrounded by a square court, with two rows of three pillars on the right and left, although he admitted that the distance between the pillars and what he had interpreted as a wall was entirely conjectural.[10] Charles Van Siclen, however, suggested that the outer line represented the external alignment of a row of pillars running all around the inner shrine, and that the sketch would therefore represent a peripteral bark shrine.[11] In any case, it appears clear that the plan on the ostracon was a very abbreviated representation, meant to provide a few useful hints for the construction of a building, the nature of which must have been already clear to the person who sketched the plan. Whether he was referring to another, more complete and detailed plan, or whether he simply had in mind a conventional type of building, for which no further explanation was necessary, is difficult to establish.

The sketch of a four-pillared chamber (Twentieth Dynasty) from the Valley of the Kings[12] (discussed again in the next chapter, see fig. 70) and the plan of a subterranean tomb (Eighteenth Dynasty), found among the debris of Senenmut

---

[9] See, for instance, Davies' reconstruction of the sketch of building from the Sheikh Said Quarry at Amarna, in Norman de Garis Davies, 'An Architectural Sketch at Sheikh Said', *Ancient Egypt* 1 (1917), 21–5.

[10] S. R. K. Glanville, 'Working Plan for a Shrine', *JEA* 16 (1930), 237–9.

[11] Charles C. Van Siclen III, 'Ostracon BM41228: A Sketch Plan of a Shrine Reconsidered', *GM* 90 (1986), 71–7. The rectangular outline of peripteral chapels was sometimes very elongated, as in the chapel in the courtyard of the VII Pylon at Karnak, two chapels at el-Kab and two at Elephantine, now completely destroyed (Borchardt, *Tempel mit Umgang*, pls. 19, 20, 21 and 23). At other times it approached a square, as in the chapel of Senusret I at Karnak and the chapel at Kuban. The badly destroyed chapel at Amada may have been square (Borchardt, *Tempel mit Umgang*, p. 56, fig. 19 and pl. 22.). On the ostracon, it is written that the length and breadth of the chamber are equal, thus suggesting a square space. Van Siclen, however, preferred to follow the example of the chapels at Karnak and Kuban, and suggested that for each pair of dimensions written on the ostracon, one should be considered internal and the other external. The outer enclosure would therefore be rectangular, rather than square, with a small difference between the two sides. In his reconstruction, he derived the missing architectural and numerical data (e.g. number and dimensions of pillars and distance between them) from the average dimensions of other similar contemporary constructions. The exact design and distribution of the pillars may be open to conjecture (see also Polz D., 'An Architect's Sketch from the Theban Necropolis', *MDAIK* 53 (1997), pp. 233–40), but a definitive result is unlikely to be found, since the pillars and the space between them were usually not the same along longer and shorter sides.

[12] Reginald Engelbach, 'An Architect's Project from Thebes', *ASAE* 27 (1927), 72–6; Nicholas C. Reeves, 'Two Architectural Drawings from the Valley of the Kings', *CdE* 61 (1986), 43–9.

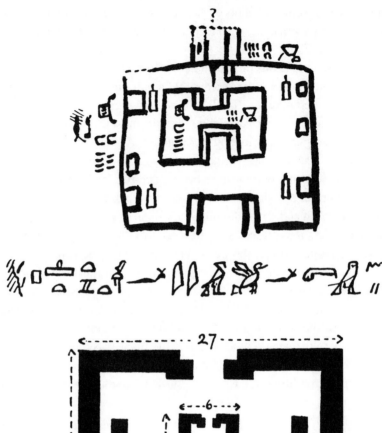

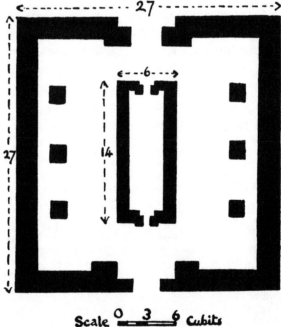

Fig. 53: Ostracon BM 41228 (Eighteenth Dynasty), reconstruction of the plan by Glanville (both from *JEA* 16, fig. 1) and by Van Siclen (from *GM* 90, fig. 3).

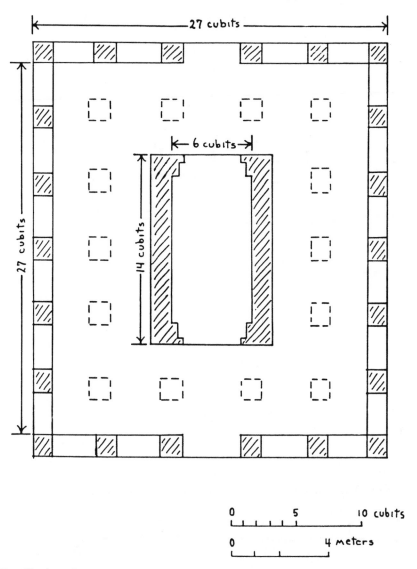

Fig. 53: (*cont.*)

but referring to another tomb[13] (fig. 54), are both on ostraca and are very similar in concept to the sketch of the shrine which we have just considered. They are rough representations, not to scale, providing dimensional information by means of written indications. In both cases, the dimensions are given by means of strokes,

[13] William C. Hayes, *Ostraka and Name Stones from the Tomb of Sen-mut (No. 71) at Thebes*, Metropolitan Museum of Art Egyptian Expedition 15, New York: Metropolitan Museum of Art, 1942, p. 15, pl. 7; Peter Dorman, *The Tombs of Senenmut: The Architecture and Decoration of Tombs 71 and 353*, New York: Metropolitan Museum of Art, 1991, p. 26, note 52.

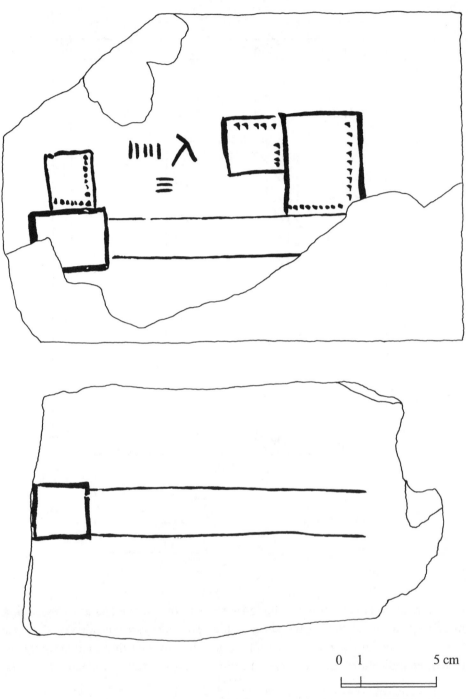

Fig. 54: Sketches of a subterranean tomb, from the tomb of Senenmut (Eighteenth Dynasty), (drawn after Hayes, *Sen-mut*, pl. 7).

each representing one cubit (thus in the plan of a subterranean tomb the three rooms, from left to right, appear to be 7×7, 5×4 and 9×9 cubits, whereas the corridor was 15 cubits long and 3 cubits wide). The fact that they are drawn on ostraca points to their being working drawings meant to be used in rough conditions, but at least in the case of royal tombs, it is possible that a more precise plan had been drawn beforehand, as we shall see later in this chapter.

The Eighteenth Dynasty plan on a wooden board of an enclosure on a canal (fig. 55) is accompanied by some written dimensions: the internal enclosure appears to be 29 cubits long and probably 23 cubits, 2 palms and 2 fingers wide; the two flights of stairs were 10 cubits long; the external enclosure was 32 cubits long; and the rectangular enclosure close to the water was 21 cubits and 4 palms long. This drawing was identified by Norman de Garis Davies as an architect's survey, since the measures were expressed in cubits, palms and fingers, with a precision which, in his opinion, would have not been required in a project.[14] His suggestion, as we shall see in the next chapter, agrees with the results of a careful examination of documents related to works in royal tombs, where dimensions given in whole cubits seem to correspond to projects, while those given in cubits, palms and fingers seem to be the result of surveys. It is worth observing that the majority of documents on wooden boards appear to have been exercises of onomastica and mathematics, model letters and copies of literary texts.[15] This plan, too, might have been an exercise.

The interpretation of the drawing is not easy, especially because the direction of the two flights of stairs is not clear. Three different interpretations of the central space have so far been suggested, according to three different interpretations of the direction of the stairs: a pool, a room and a platform.[16] The position of the building in connection with the water must have been very important, since the canal was probably drawn first (as the compression of the rear part of the enclosure seems to suggest) and great care was taken to represent the mass of water by means of the usual pattern of broken lines. It is very difficult to establish beyond any doubt the function of the complex, but its position in relation to the thick wall, indicating a large enclosure, and to the water might suggest a parallel with the small peripteral chapel of Thutmosis III at Karnak, the entrance of which pierces the wall of the court of the VIII Pylon and points towards the Sacred Lake[17] (fig. 56). The central enclosure might be a simple outline of the area covered by the peripteral

---

[14] Norman de Garis Davies, 'An Architect's Plan from Thebes', *JEA* 4 (1917), 194–9. The board, purchased by Davies from a dealer, apparently comes from the area of Thebes.

[15] In general, see *LÄ*, vol. v, pp. 703–9.

[16] The first and the second from Davies, *JEA* 4, 198, and the third from Badawy, *Dessin architecturale*, p. 202, fig. 239.

[17] Borchardt, *Tempel mit Umgang*, pp. 90–3; Jean Lauffray, 'Les travaux du Centre Franco-Egyptien d'études des temples de Karnak de 1972 à 1977', *Cahiers de Karnak* VI, Cairo: IFAO, 1980, fig. 1.

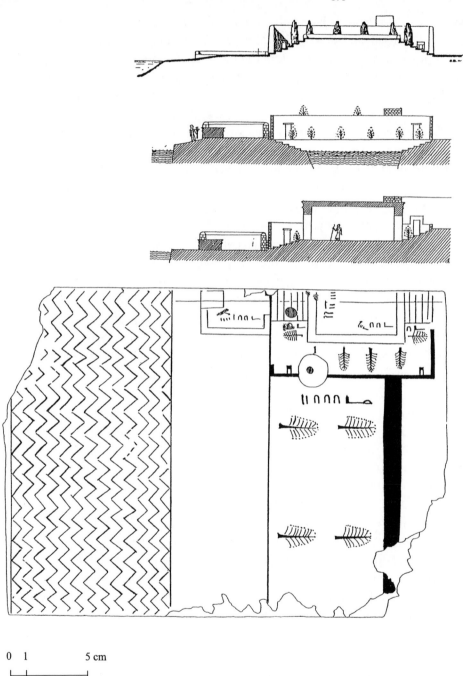

0   1   5 cm

Fig. 55: Plan on a wooden board (Eighteenth Dynasty), (after Davies, *JEA* 4, pl. 38); reconstructions of the plan by Badawy (upper drawing, from *Dessin architecturale*, fig. 239) and by Davies (second and third drawings, from *JEA* 4, 198).

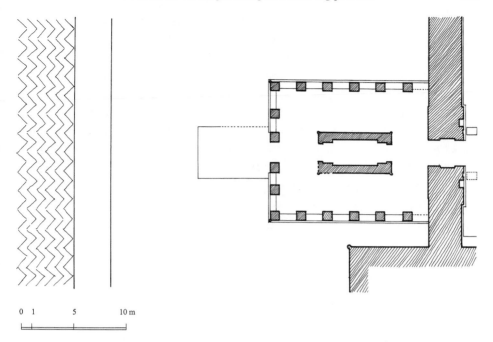

0 1   5   10 m

Fig. 56: Plan of the peripteral temple of Thutmosis III (Eighteenth Dynasty) facing the Sacred Lake in the temple of Karnak (drawn after Borchardt, *Tempel mit Umgang*, pl. 19 and Lauffray, *Karnak VI*, fig. 1).

shrine, approached by two flights of stairs running along the axis. In this case, the written dimensions would correspond to the outline of the shrine: length and breadth of the basement and length of the two stairs. The smaller enclosure, the rectangular feature that Davies interpreted as an altar and Badawy as a ramp, may have been a door. The plan could therefore be a survey of the surroundings of a peripteral shrine; once its outline was established, the plan of the building itself might have appeared as the sketch on the ostracon mentioned above.

Although they are not absolutely precise, some dimensions of the drawing appear to correspond to the written values, to a scale of one to twenty-eight – that is, one finger to the cubit (each finger on the board represented one cubit in reality). Davies interpreted the plan as 'a scale reduction badly plotted out'[18] but, since no 'precise' scale drawings have survived, I wonder whether we do justice to the ancient architect when we accuse him of having been careless. If we expect from the ancient drawings the same concept of precision as in our modern scale drawings, we shall be disappointed. As we have seen, it was not unusual for the ancient architects to indicate in their sketches only the most important data, ignoring what was probably classified as obvious. In this case, even if some elements were drawn

[18] Davies, *JEA* 4, 196.

to scale, other elements, such as the secondary doors piercing the outer enclosure, the trees, and probably the steps, were not.

While drawing, the architect probably counted the cubits using the fingers marked on his cubit rod. The fact that he actually used a rod can be easily inferred from the neatness of the lines. Nevertheless, he probably did not mean to draw a scale drawing in our modern sense, that is, a drawing which others could measure in order to gain information on the object represented. In fact, since he ran out of space, he 'compressed' the upper part of the plan, but took care to write that the breadth of the garden (or possibly the length of the stairs) had to be 10 cubits, the same as below. He aimed to draw a plan in which the parts were represented in fairly realistic proportions and counted the fingers as cubits, but beyond that one was expected to read the labels, not to measure the lines.

Two of the most spectacular architectural drawings from ancient Egypt are the plan on an ostracon of KV 6, tomb of Ramses IX,[19] and the plan on papyrus of KV 2, tomb of Ramses IV[20] (see chapter 4). They are not to scale, as a comparison between original plan, scale representation of the written dimensions and modern plan clearly proves (figs. 69 and 70). In both cases, Davies noted that the proportions of the plan were not correct, but nevertheless suggested a scale of about 1:28 (the same as the plan on wooden board) for the tomb of Ramses IV, and of about 1:220 (very close to a supposed scale 1:224, in which $\frac{1}{8}$ of a finger, about 0.23 cm, would be equal to 1 cubit) for the tomb of Ramses IX.[21] Drawings meant to be to scale but hampered by such an approximation, however, would be quite useless. If there is a similarity between written and drawn dimensions, it may simply depend on the attempt to keep a visual proportion between the parts, without involving geometrical proportions while drawing the lines. This is certainly the case of the sketch of a shrine box on an ostracon[22] (Nineteenth–Twentieth Dynasty). It is a message to a craftsman asking him to make four boxes, an example of which was rapidly sketched and completed by two written measures referring to its height, 5 palms, and breadth, 4 palms. Reymond Weill noted that height and breadth of the sketch were in a ratio very close to 5:4 but, once more, there is no need to suppose an approximate scale. If the shape of the object to be represented was clear, an eyeball sketch could reproduce its proportions with a remarkable

[19] Georges Daressy, *Ostraca, CG*, Cairo: SAE, 1901, p. 35 and pl. 32, and 'Un plan égyptien d'une tombe royale', *Revue Archéologique* 32 (1898), 235–40.

[20] Karl Richard Lepsius, 'Grundplan des Grabes König Ramses IV. in einem Turiner Papyrus', *Abhandlungen der Königlichen Akademie der Wissenschaften zu Berlin* 1867, Philosophische und historische Abhandlungen, 1–22; Howard Carter and Alan H. Gardiner, 'The Tomb of Ramses IV and the Turin Plan of a Royal Tomb', *JEA* 4 (1917), 130–58. For a photograph, see Ernesto Scamuzzi, *Museo Egizio di Torino*, Torino: Edizioni d'Arte Fratelli Pozzo, 1964, pl. 87.

[21] Davies, *JEA* 4, pp. 196–7.

[22] Raymond Weill, 'Un épure de stéréotomie dans une pièce de correspondance du Nouvel Empire', *Recueil de Travaux* 36, Paris 1916, pp. 89–90; Alan H. Gardiner, 'Some Coptic Etymologies', *PSBA* 38 (1916), 181–5.

Table 4. *Full-size geometrical sketches*

Object represented	Date	Location	Bibliography
Guidelines for the sloping sides of Mastaba 17	Third–Fourth Dynasty	Meidum, corners of Mastaba 17	Petrie, *Medum*, pp. 11–13, pl. 8.
Sketch of an elliptical vault	Twentieth Dynasty	Valley of the Kings, tomb of Ramses VI	Daressy, *ASAE* 8, pp. 237–40.
Sketch of an ellipse	Twentieth Dynasty?	Temple of Luxor	Borchardt, *ZÄS* 34, pp. 75–6.
Sketch of a column	Ptolemaic Period	Temple of Philae	Borchardt, *ZÄS* 34, pp. 70–4.
Sketch of cavetto cornice	Ptolemaic Period	Temple of Edfu	Borchardt, *ZÄS* 34, pp. 74–5.
Sketch of a capital	Roman Period	Quarry at Gebel Abu Foda	Petrie, *Season in Egypt*, p. 33.
Sketch of a Hathor-headed capital	Roman Period	Quarry at Gebel Abu Foda	Petrie, *Season in Egypt*, p. 33.
Sketch of a capital	Roman Period	Temple of Kalabsha	Siegler, *Kalabsha*, p. 37.

degree of accuracy, without necessarily being a conscious, calculated scale drawing.

In conclusion, the surviving evidence suggests that architectural working drawings were meant to convey a general idea of the arrangement and proportions of the space. The transmission of precise numerical data was delegated to written instructions instead. All the information we do not find in the drawings, including many basic details of the elevation, probably belonged to a long consolidated building practice. Small-scale architectural drawings, therefore, seem to have been just quick reminders of a few details of buildings which were created directly as volumes in the three-dimensional space.

Full-size geometrical sketches of architectural details

Besides lines and marks, which generally helped the workmen keep alignment and position during the construction,[23] full-size sketches were sometimes used to design relatively small-scale architectural details (table 4). Although from a chronological

---

[23] Traces of guidelines and control marks can often be found in ancient monuments. Arnold provided an useful summary of this kind of evidence (*Building in Egypt*, pp. 16–22). Zero-level lines can be seen at the pyramid of Menkaura (George A. Reisner, *Mycerinus, the Temple of the Third Pyramid at Giza*, Cambridge, Mass.: Harvard University Press, 1931, pp. 76–7) and Neuserra (Ludwig Borchardt, *Das Grabdenkmal des Königs Ne-user-re*; Leipzig: Hinrichs, 1907, p. 154, fig. 129) and in the Mastabat el-Fara'un (Arnold, *Building in*

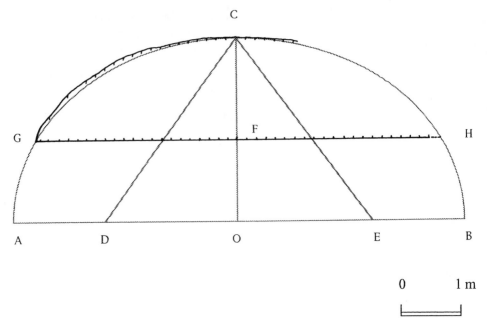

0   1 m

Fig. 57: Sketch of a Twentieth Dynasty elliptical vault (drawn after Daressy, *ASAE* 8, fig. 1).

point of view the evidence on the subject is, as often happens, very uneven, it is nevertheless possible to establish interesting connections which seem to suggest continuity in the methods employed by the ancient workmen.

There is the case of the Twentieth Dynasty sketch of an elliptical vault discovered by Georges Daressy in the Valley of the Kings (fig. 57). Just outside the tomb of Ramses VI, he noted a sketch, carved in the rock, which represented the outline of the vault covering the burial chamber.[24] Daressy demonstrated that the curve was part of an ellipse, which had been probably drawn first on the ground by means of ropes and pegs, then measured and transferred to the wall, where it could be checked by the workmen engaged in the quarrying. A certain degree of elasticity in the ropes and the subsequent process of transfer to the wall can be used to account for the slight irregularities of the sketch. The horizontal line appears to have been divided into regular intervals by means of little strokes, which correspond to a

Egypt, p. 17, fig. 1.14.), while whitewashed bands on three sides of the shaft of the pyramid at Zawyet el-Aryan provided a surface for red vertical control lines (Alexandre Barsanti, 'Fouilles de Zaouiét el-Aryân (1904–5)', *ASAE* 7 (1906), 262–5, figs. 2 and 4). Marks and written instructions on stone blocks and setting marks for columns and pillars are also frequent. One of the most interesting sets of guidelines, those used for the sloping sides of Mastaba 17 at Meidum (W. M. Flinders Petrie, *Medum*, London: Nutt, 1892, pp. 11–3 and plate 8), may be even considered a full-size sketch. They will be discussed in Part III, which is entirely devoted to pyramids.
[24] Georges Daressy, 'Un tracé egyptienne d'une voûte elliptique', *ASAE* 8 (1908), 234–41.

series of marks cutting the curve. Its rise, therefore, could be easily measured at set intervals, and the measures then transferred down into the tomb.

This must have been the same principle which had led an unknown hand, fifteen centuries earlier, to draw the diagram on an ostracon found at Saqqara in the area of the Step Pyramid (fig. 58).[25] On the rough surface of the limestone flake, red lines describe a curve divided into intervals by vertical lines, the height of which is written in cubits, palms and fingers. The horizontal distance between the lines is not given, both their equidistance and its value, one cubit, undoubtedly being taken for granted. Daressy discovered that the curve was part of a circumference, cut at a certain distance from its diameter,[26] as in the case of the later elliptical vault. This implies that the first horizontal distance on the right did not correspond to one whole cubit, as Battiscombe Gunn had suggested.[27] Also, in this case the curve probably had been drawn somewhere and then measured at regular intervals. Half of it, with its basic dimensions, was rapidly sketched and then used to carry out the work. In this case, little mistakes in reporting the measures from the ground to the ostracon can be noted.[28]

Even if many centuries divide the Third Dynasty diagram and the Twentieth Dynasty elliptical vault, the method used in the construction seems to have been the same. In the earlier example, the vault corresponded to part of a circumference, while in the later case it referred to an ellipse, which prompts further interesting remarks. Both geometrical figures could be easily traced with the aid of ropes and pegs. In the case of the circumference, a fixed peg acted as centre, while another one, connected to the first by a length of cord (the radius), traced the circle while being dragged all the way round. The method to construct an ellipse is basically the same, with the difference that the ellipse has two centres, which we call foci, around which the moving peg must rotate. In the case of the elliptical vault of Ramses VI, the position of the two foci and the proportions of the ellipse were determined by means of the 3-4-5 triangle.[29] Daressy[30] noted that the sides of the triangles which he called COD and COE (cf. fig. 57) were equal to 4 cubits, $5 + \frac{1}{3}$ cubits and $6 + \frac{2}{3}$ cubits, which correspond to the numbers 3, 4 and 5 multiplied by $1 + \frac{1}{3}$. This seems to imply that the Egyptians not only used the 3-4-5 triangle to trace right angles, but that they were also aware that similar triangles could be obtained by varying the dimensions, but keeping unaltered the proportions between the sides. This is

[25] Battiscombe Gunn, 'An Architect's Diagram of the Third Dynasty', *ASAE* 26 (1926), 197–202. See also Max Hoberman, 'Two Architect's Sketches', *JSAH* 44 (1985), 380–3.

[26] Georges Daressy, 'Tracé d'une voûte datant de la IIIe dynastie', *ASAE* 27 (1927), 157–60.

[27] Compare Gunn, *ASAE* 26, fig. 3 and Daressy, *ASAE* 27, 159.   [28] Daressy, *ASAE* 27, 158–9.

[29] Choisy suggested that the Egyptians used the 3-4-5 triangle to design parabolic vaults, but did not include any details about location or date of specific examples (Auguste Choisy, *L'art de bâtir chez les Egyptiens*, Paris: Gauthier-Villars, 1904, p. 46). For the use of right-angled triangles to draw the profile of vaulted chambers in the pyramid of Amenemhat III see Arnold, *Amenemhet III.*, pp. 78–9.

[30] Daressy, *ASAE* 8, 238.

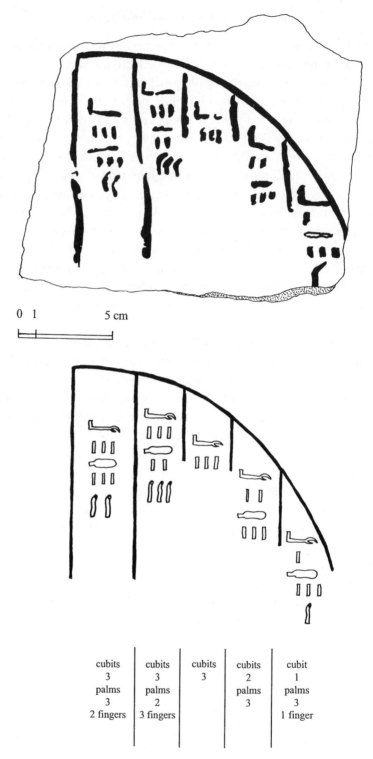

	cubits	cubits	cubits	cubits	cubit
	3	3	3	2	1
	palms	palms		palms	palms
	3	2		3	3
	2 fingers	3 fingers			1 finger

Fig. 58: Diagram of a curve (Third Dynasty), with hieroglyphic transcription (drawn after Gunn, *ASAE* 26, figs. 1 and 2).

an important point, which might have had a significant function in the project and construction of pyramids, as we shall see in Part III.

The construction of an ellipse based on the 3-4-5 triangle could have proceeded in the following way. After the horizontal line had been traced, the vertical line at a right angle was traced by means of a 3-4-5 triangle (or one of its multiples). In the case of the elliptical vault, the side corresponding to 3 was placed on the horizontal line (fig. 59a). Two of the three pegs used to set the triangle also determined the basic proportions of the ellipse: one corresponded to one of the foci, the other to the maximum height of the curve. The second focus could be easily placed in a symmetric position along the horizontal line. A rope, its extremes tied together, stretched around the foci and the moving peg (fig. 59b), would then determine the trajectory of the latter, that is, the ellipse (fig. 59c). Even if this is not related to ancient Egypt, it may be interesting to add that the 3-4-5 triangle and other triplets are supposed to have been used to trace the layout of elliptical and egg-shaped megalithic monuments in Western Europe as early as 3000 BC.[31]

The full-size sketch of a column in the section of the Temple of Philae built under Ptolemy VI Philometor in the second century BC[32] and the sketch of a capital in the Roman quarry at Gebel Abu Foda[33] (fig. 60) provide further evidence about the use of mathematics in the design of architectural details. Ludwig Borchardt noted that they were both designed using special subdivisions of the cubit which did not necessarily correspond to precise values in terms of palms and fingers, but which could be more easily expressed as $\frac{1}{2}$, $\frac{1}{4}$, $\frac{1}{8}$ and $\frac{1}{16}$ of a cubit.

In general, this was not an uncommon method. Not only the cubit, but also the *setat* (unit of measurement for areas) and the *hekat* (unit of measurement of volumes) were sometimes divided into successive halves.[34] There is ample evidence that the division of the cubit into fractions, not necessarily corresponding to palms and fingers, was widely used for practical purposes, at least in architecture, along with the usual division into palms and fingers. John Legon, for example, noted that in the Old Kingdom Palermo Stone the height of the Nile was expressed using both systems.[35] Another example is the Middle Kingdom Reisner Papyri, which also contain palms and fingers and fractions of cubit,[36] while the Building Texts of the Ptolemaic period, as we shall see, only contain fractions of cubits.

---

[31] See, for instance, the summary published by B. L. Van der Waerden, *Geometry and Algebra in Ancient Civilizations*, Berlin/Heidelberg/New York/Tokio: Springer-Verlag, 1983, pp. 16–22.

[32] Ludwig Borchardt, 'Altägyptische Werkzeichnungen', *ZÄS* 34 (1896), 70–4.

[33] W. M. Flinders Petrie, *A Season in Egypt*, London: Field, 1887, p. 33, pl. 25; Borchardt, *ZÄS* 34, 74.

[34] One *setat* was equal to one square *khet*, which corresponded to a linear measure of 100 cubits. It could be divided into narrow strips 1 *khet* long and 1 cubit wide, and portions of it could be expressed as $\frac{1}{2}$, $\frac{1}{4}$ and $\frac{1}{8}$ of a *setat*, corresponding to a certain number of 1-cubit strips. The *hekat*, a common unit of volume, was also subdivided into $\frac{1}{2}$, $\frac{1}{4}$, $\frac{1}{8}$, $\frac{1}{16}$, $\frac{1}{32}$ and $\frac{1}{64}$ (Peet, *Rhind Mathematical Papyrus*, p. 25 and 122; Gillings, *Mathematics*, pp. 173 and 210–11; Robins and Shute, *Rhind Mathematical Papyrus*, pp. 13–5).

[35] Legon, *DE* 35, 65.

[36] William K. Simpson, *Papyrus Reisner I*, Boston: Museum of Fine Arts, 1963, pp. 124–6.

a

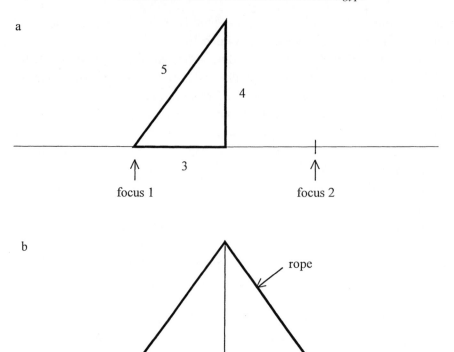

b

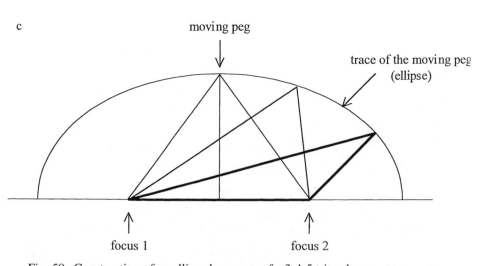

Fig. 59: Construction of an ellipse by means of a 3-4-5 triangle.

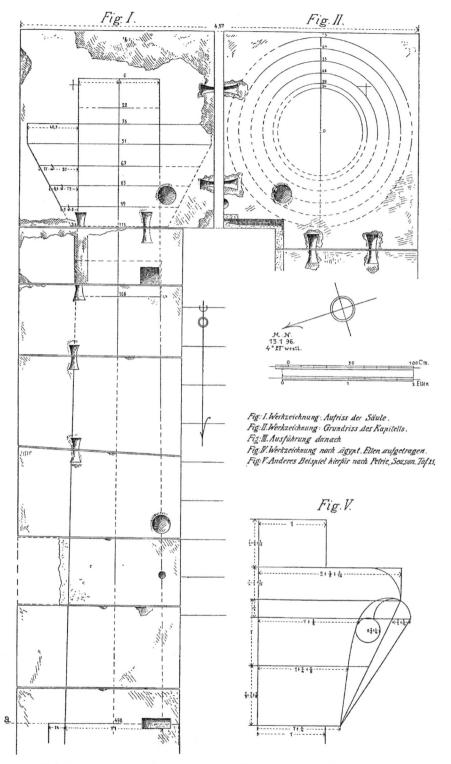

Fig. 60: Sketch of a Ptolemaic column at Philae and of a Roman capital, and reconstruction of their proportions according to Borchardt (from *ZÄS* 34, pls. 3 and 4).

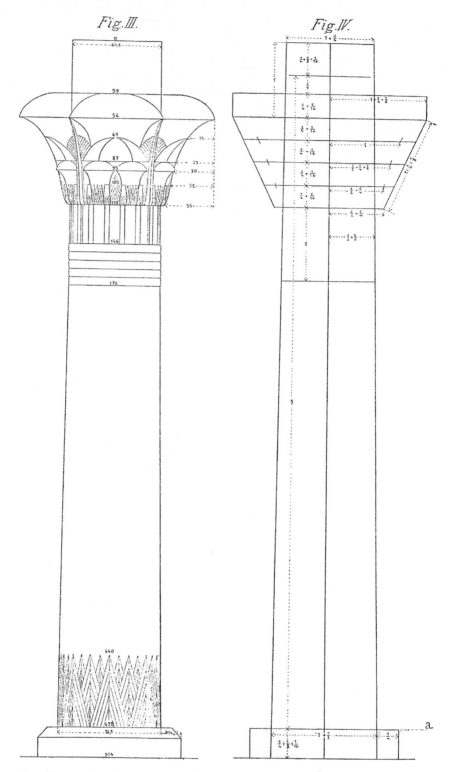

Fig. 60: (cont.)

The peculiarity of the design of this Ptolemaic column is that not only do the fractions belong to this alternative way of dividing up the cubit, but also they appear to express the use of a module corresponding to $\frac{1}{16}$ of a cubit. This characteristic can be visualised with the aid of a document that has nothing to do with our Ptolemaic column, but is nevertheless the product of exactly the same mathematical process: a late Byzantine division table. This contains the division of 15 by the numbers from 1 to 15 and of 16 by the numbers from 1 to 16, calculated in the typical Egyptian way. Probably this tablet belonged to a series giving the division of several numbers, but only 15 and 16 have survived.[37] Here is the translation of the part concerning the number 16:

Number 16.

The 16th part   of $1 = \frac{1}{16}$

           of $2 = \frac{1}{8}$

           of $3 = \frac{1}{8} + \frac{1}{16}$

           of $4 = \frac{1}{4}$

           of $5 = \frac{1}{4} + \frac{1}{16}$

           of $6 = \frac{1}{4} + \frac{1}{8}$

           of $7 = \frac{1}{4} + \frac{1}{8} + \frac{1}{16}$

           of $8 = \frac{1}{2}$

           of $9 = \frac{1}{2} + \frac{1}{16}$

           of $10 = \frac{1}{2} + \frac{1}{8}$

           of $11 = \frac{1}{2} + \frac{1}{8} + \frac{1}{16}$

           of $12 = \frac{1}{2} + \frac{1}{4}$

           of $13 = \frac{1}{2} + \frac{1}{4} + \frac{1}{16}$

           of $14 = \frac{1}{2} + \frac{1}{4} + \frac{1}{8}$

           of $15 = \frac{1}{2} + \frac{1}{4} + \frac{1}{8} + \frac{1}{16}$

           of $16 = 1$

The dimensions of column and capital correspond to some of the results. For instance, the value $\frac{1}{4} + \frac{1}{16}$, expressing the distance between the parallel lines dividing the capital, corresponds to $\frac{5}{16}$, that is, 5 times $\frac{1}{16}$ of a cubit. Taking $\frac{1}{16}$ as the module, this means that these lines are five modules apart. Seemingly, the radius just below the capital corresponded to ten modules ($\frac{1}{2} + \frac{1}{8}$), the lower radius of the capital to twelve modules ($\frac{1}{2} + \frac{1}{4}$), and so on. As in other similar cases, the final result might be rather complicated if expressed in palms and fingers, but was nevertheless relatively simple in terms of geometrical subdivisions of the cubit. This

---

[37] Thompson, *Ancient Egypt* 2, pp. 52–4; Kurt Sethe, *Von Zahlen und Zahlworten bei den alten Ägyptern*, Strasburg: Trübner, 1916, p. 70. See, for example, the similar tablet on an ostracon with the division of 31 for the first 31 integers in Sethe, *Zahlen und Zahlworten*, pp. 71–2.

introduces another important subject, the adoption of a module in architecture in the design not only of architectural details, but also of entire buildings.

The use of square grids and the idea of a module

From the Middle Kingdom onwards, ancient Egyptian artists used square grids to design human figures and to establish the general layout of two-dimensional scenes. They do not appear to have been tied by any strict rule, and were perfectly able to reproduce the same proportions without the help of grids.[38] Guidelines and grids were also used in sculpture, as a number of surviving unfinished pieces show,[39] and architectural details might be also designed in this way, as the Roman sketch of a Hathor-headed capital in a quarry at Gebel Abu Foda[40] shows (fig. 61).

Turning to buildings, there is no evidence that the ancient architects used square grids to design their projects on papyrus, but square grids might have been used to lay down the plans on the ground. After having fixed the central axis and its orthogonal, tracing parallel lines to these two initial directions would have helped to measure distances, to check right angles and in general to fix on the ground the position of the various elements. If this method was employed, it may have left a trace in the repetition of one or more basic dimensions, and this is what scholars have been looking for.

Alexander Badawy included square grids in his list of 'elements of harmonic design',[41] and suggested the use of square modules of different sizes, the side-length of which could vary from round measures such as 5, 10 or 12 cubits, to odd dimensions such as $11 + \frac{2}{3}$ or $13 + \frac{1}{3}$ cubits, and from small lengths such as 1.75 or 2.6 cubits up to incredible modules of $94 + \frac{1}{2}$ or 104 cubits. Zygmunt Wysocki claimed to have discovered the use of a module equal to $1 + \frac{1}{2}$ royal cubit in a portico and in the sun court of the upper terrace in the Eighteenth Dynasty temple of Hatshepsut at Deir el-Bahari,[42] Karl Georg Siegler suggested the

---

[38] Robins, *Proportion and Style*, pp. 45 and 165; see also Eric Iversen, *Canon and Proportions in Egyptian Art*, Warminster: Aris and Phillips, 1975 and Gay Robins, 'Canonical Proportions and Metrology', *DE* 32 (1995), 91–2.

[39] To the Late Period belong a number of the so-called 'trial pieces', blocks laid out for sculpture with the aid of guidelines (Robins, *Proportion and Style*, pp. 177–81), an unfinished sphinx (Badawy, *Gazette des Beaux-Arts* 107, pp. 55–6) and a papyrus with the drawing on a grid of plan and front view of another sphinx (Heinrich Schäfer, *Von Ägyptischer Kunst*, Wiesbaden: Harrassowitz, 1963, p. 339, fig. 325).

[40] Petrie, *Season in Egypt*, p. 33, pl. 25; Arnold, *Building in Egypt*, p. 47 and fig. 2.26.

[41] Badawy, *Ancient Egyptian Architectural Design*, p. 21. In a short article, Badawy also suggested that the decoration in some Old Kingdom tombs was arranged in registers corresponding to the same module used by the architect to design the plan ('Composition murales à système modulaire dans les tombes égyptiennes de l'Ancien Empire', *Gazette des Beaux-Arts* 97 (1981), 49–52).

[42] Zygmunt Wysocki, 'The Result of Research, Architectonic Studies and of Protective Work over the Northern Portico of the Middle Courtyard in the Hatshepsut Temple at Deir el-Bahari', *MDAIK* 40 (1984), 329–49, and also 'The Temple of Queen Hatshepsut at Deir el-Bahari – The Results of Architectural Research over the North Part of the Upper Terrace', *MDAIK* 43 (1986), 274, figs. 5 and 8.

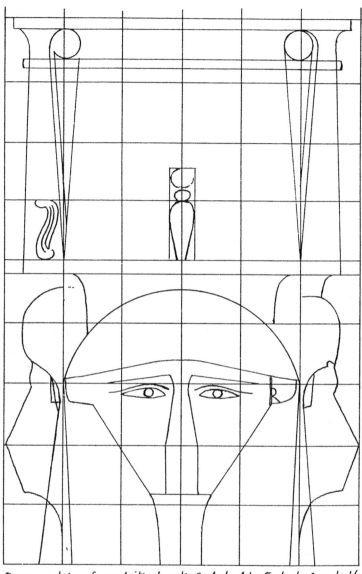

Draught of capital at Gebel Abu Fodeh. scale 1/20

Fig. 61: Sketch of a capital at Gebel Abu Foda, Roman (from Petrie, *Season in Egypt*, pl. 25).

use of five different modules in the construction of the Roman temple of Kalabsha,[43] and Jean-François Carlotti detected the use of several different ratios and modules in the temple of Karnak.[44]

---

[43] Siegler, *Kalabsha*, p. 22 and pls. 9–12, 16, 21 and 22.   [44] Carlotti, *Cahiers de Karnak* x, pp. 65–94.

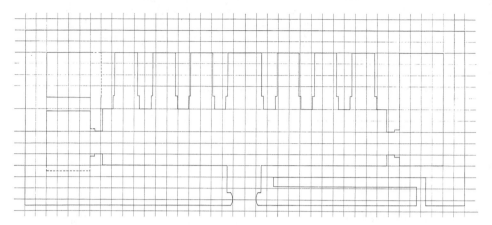

Fig. 62: Plan of the temple of Qasr el-Sagha with a superimposed 1-cubit grid (from Arnold and Arnold, *Qasr el-Sagha*, pl. 27a).

It is important, however, to note that a square grid superimposed on a plan may be useful to highlight some geometrical aspects of a building, as in Dieter Arnold's study of the Middle Kingdom temple of Qasr el-Sagha[45] (fig. 62), but that in many cases the same result might have been achieved even without the aid of such a device.[46] For instance, a theoretical 40×60 cubit courtyard could have been planned with the aid of a 1, 2, 4, 5, 10 or 20-cubit grid (see, for example, fig. 63 and compare again with fig. 43), but also without any of them, by simply establishing two orthogonal dimensions, as many of the surviving drawings do. We may conclude that it is possible that orthogonal lines on the ground were used to lay down the plan, even if they were not organised into strictly regular square grids.

In general, a modular pattern may also be the result of the use of a modular element. In 1899, for instance, Auguste Choisy suggested that in ancient Egypt the use of standardised mud-bricks produced a modular pattern,[47] but his conclusions were not based on a large variety of archaeological remains. Modern studies have proved that the dimensions of mud-brick in ancient Egypt varied from a smaller size used in the Early Dynastic Period to larger versions adopted from the Old Kingdom onwards, but their proportions remained more or less the same, with a ratio of about 2:1 between length and width.[48] The argument sounds more convincing if

[45] Arnold and Arnold, *Qasr el-Sagha*, p. 18, pl. 22.

[46] Lauffray suggested that the chapel of Hakoris at Karnak could have been laid out according to a module of 54 cm, a value which seems too close to the usual cubit to be a completely different unit of measurement (Lauffray, *Chapelle d'Achôris*, pp. 23–4). Four rods 53.8 cm long were found in the Eighteenth Dynasty tomb of Sennefer, together with a standard cubit rod of 52.7 cm (Bernard Bruyère, *Rapport sur les fouilles de Deir el Médineh (1927)*, Cairo: IFAO, 1928, pp. 55–6 and pl. 8). A list of useful references on the subject can be found in Lauffray, *Chapelle d'Achôris*, p. 24, note 32.

[47] Choisy, *Histoire de l'architecture*, p. 52.

[48] Alan J. Spencer, *Brick Architecture in Ancient Egypt*, Warminster: Aris and Phillips, 1979; Barry J. Kemp, 'Soil (Including Mud-brick Architecture)', in Paul T. Nicholson and Ian Shaw (eds.), *Ancient Egyptian Materials and Technology*, Cambridge: Cambridge University Press, 2000, especially p. 87.

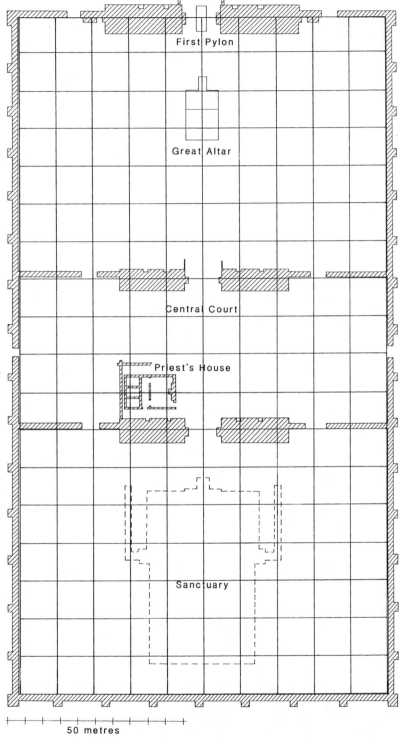

First Pylon

Great Altar

Central Court

Priest's House

Sanctuary

50 metres

Fig. 63: Plan of the Small Aten Temple at Amarna (Eighteenth Dynasty), with 20-cubit grid according to Spence, left, and with 18-cubit grid according to Mallinson, right (from Kemp and Rose, *CAJ* 1, figs. 4 and 6.

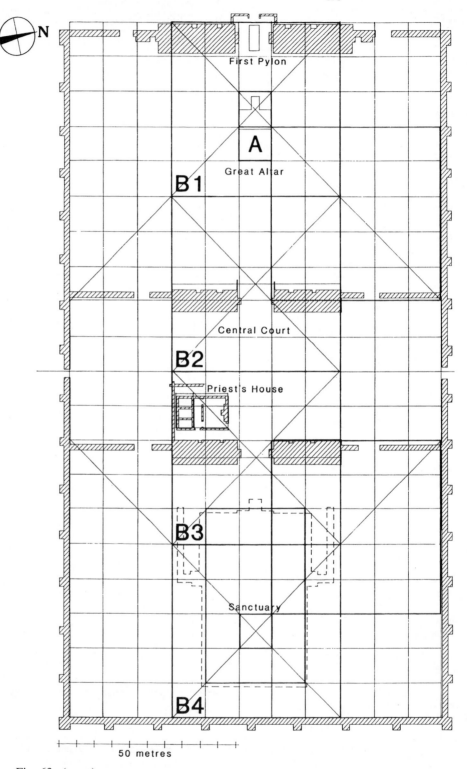

Fig. 63: (cont.)

applied to the Eighteenth Dynasty stone architecture at Amarna. Here the majority of the blocks appear to have had fixed dimensions, about 1 cubit for the length and about half a cubit for the breadth.[49] Provided that the stones were laid out without significant gaps between them and according to the solution adopted at the corners (different junctions between 1-cubit blocks or blocks of a special shape), the final length of a wall might correspond to a whole number of cubits. Achieving round dimensions in their buildings, however, might not have been the reason why the builders of Amarna used 1-cubit blocks. One of their main concerns was to build a lot and quickly, and it is possible that it was decided to establish a fixed, easy dimension for the blocks to be quarried for all the monuments, so that they could be easily moved around and used anywhere they were required.[50]

Square grids and modules in architecture appear to have been used in Greece during the Hellenistic Period, when cultural influences across the Mediterranean were stronger. From the fourth century BC onwards, the once irregular column spacing and the position of columns and walls of Greek temples started being laid out on the basis of a uniform square grid, and there is evidence that some plans might have been designed with the aid of drawings. In the late Hellenistic period, Greek architects adopted a modular system in their temples, that is, a basic dimension whose multiples and submultiples regulated the layout of the whole building.[51] It is possible that at some point these methods were imported into Egypt, as the second century BC sketch of a column from the Ptolemaic temple of Phylae seems to suggest, and that they even influenced the construction of several Meroitic temples in the modern Sudan. According to Friedrich Hinkel, in some of these buildings the façade happens to be 16 times a module corresponding to the diameter of a column or, when there are no columns, the thickness of a wall.[52]

Concerning the earlier Egyptian architecture, from the general appearance of their working drawings, the lack of scale, and the abbreviated way used to convey information, it is clear that drawings were not the only method employed by the ancient architects to plan and visualise their buildings. The surviving drawings barely provide enough information about the two-dimensional layout of the plans, and do not seem to have been the principal instrument to take decisions about the three-dimensional aspects. This gap between the schematic drawings and the actual buildings may have been filled by architectural models, which might have been used to visualise in advance the real appearance of the construction

---

[49] Günther Roeder, *Amarna-Reliefs aus Hermopolis*, Wissenschaftliche Veröffentlichungen Pelizeus-Museum zu Hildesheim 6, Hildesheim: Gesterberg, 1969, p. 9.

[50] On the subject, see Barry J. Kemp, 'Tell el-Amarna 2000–01', *JEA* 87 (2001), 17.

[51] James J. Coulton, *Greek Architects at Work*, London: Paul Elek, 1977, pp. 66 and 71.

[52] Friederich W. Hinkel, 'Säule und Interkolumnium in der meroitischen Architektur. Metrologische Vorstudien zu einer Klassifikation der Bauwerke', *Studia Meroitica* 10 (1984), 231–67; 'Ägyptische Elle oder griechischer Modul?', *Das Altertum* 33/3 (1987), 150–62; also 'The Process of Planning in Meroitic Architecture' in Davies (ed.), *Egypt and Africa*, pp. 220–5.

Table 5. *Architectural models of funerary and religious monuments*

Building represented	Material	Date	Provenance	Location	Bibliography
Model of a step pyramid	limestone	?	Memphis	University College London UC 16519	Petrie, *Labyrinth*, p. 35.
Model of the pyramid of Hawara?	limestone	Twelfth Dynasty	Hawara	University College London UC 14793	Petrie, *Labyrinth*, p. 35.
Model of the funerary apartment of a pyramid	limestone	Twelfth Dynasty	Dahshur	Cairo Museum	Arnold, *Amenemhet III.*, pp. 86–8.
Model of a temple of Seti I	Basement: quartzite (missing parts: limestone and other stones, bronze)	Nineteenth Dynasty	Tell el-Yahudiya	Brooklyn Museum 49183	Badawy, *Wilbouriana* 1, pp. 1–23.
Model of (part of) the temple of Tôd	limestone	Late Period	Tôd	Louvre E 14762	Bisson de la Roque, *Tôd*, p. 154.

without the distortions and illusions produced by the adoption of the graphic conventions necessary to reproduce a three-dimensional reality on a two-dimensional surface.

Architectural models

Votive objects

Models representing buildings are not rare from ancient Egypt, but we shall focus on a small number only (table 5). The majority were votive or decorative objects and can provide useful information about interesting architectural details, such as materials, type of construction and decorations.[53] The most famous group of models comes from the Twelfth Dynasty tomb of Meketra and includes representations of his house, of cattle-rearing, bread- and beer-making, a spinning- and weaving-shop, a carpenter shop, some offering-bearers and a number of boats.[54] A peculiar example of architectural model that is worth mentioning is the T-shaped basin with miniature quay and steps found in front of the main entrance to a chapel of

---

[53] See, for example, Aylward M. Blackman, 'A Painted Pottery Model of a Granary', *JEA* 6 (1920), 206–8 for the painted pottery model of a granary; Rainer Stadelmann, 'Ein bemaltes Hausmodell in der ägyptischer Sammlung der Universität Heidelberg', *MDAIK* 18 (1962), 54–8 for a painted pottery model of a house. For the pottery soul-houses, see the photographs in W. M. Flinders Petrie, *Gizeh and Rifeh*, BSAE ERA 13, London, 1907, chapter 6 and corresponding plates; see *LÄ*, vol. V, pp. 806–13 for a general bibliography.

[54] Herbert E. Winlock, *Models of Daily Life in Ancient Egypt from the Tomb of Meketre at Thebes*, Metropolitan Museum of Art, Egyptian Expedition 18, Cambridge, Mass.: Harvard University Press, 1955.

the Workmen's Village at Amarna.[55] In general, these models are quite realistic in terms of proportions, since men and cattle, women and looms, bearers and offerings are represented in a coherent size in comparison to one another. There is no need, however, to assume that they were realised to a consciously calculated scale.

In a model (just as in a drawing) the similarity in terms of shape, arrangement and even relative size of the spaces may be respected, but at the same time the dimensions of the model may not correspond to a precise reduction of the dimensions of the actual building. Nevertheless, attempts to find a calculated scale have been carried out on a couple of models, one representing a temple of Seti I and the other the Ptolemaic temple at Tôd, with uncertain results. They are likely to have been votive objects, rather than working models, and a precise reduction to scale does not seem to have been the main concern of the sculptors who carved them.

The remains of the first consist of a large rectangular quartzite block, found at Tell el-Yahudiya and now in the Brooklyn Museum in New York, which appears to have been the base of a precious and elaborate model of a temple erected or planned by Seti I. The inscriptions running all round the front and two sides describe the various elements of the missing superstructure, which consisted of separately made elements to be inserted into the sockets cut in the base (fig. 64). Alexander Badawy reconstructed the missing parts by combining their description with similar elements that have survived in other New Kingdom temples.[56] For the sphinxes, he used the proportions of those of Hatshepsut and Thutmosis III, for the two colossi he referred to statues of Akhenaten and Ramses II, while the obelisks were reconstructed after the obelisk now in Piazza del Popolo in Rome, originally erected by Seti I himself. The breadth of the doorway in comparison with the size of the sockets for the pylon led Badawy to the conclusion that the portal was a monumental gateway with an Amarna-style broken lintel, rather than a typical pylon, which would have had more elongated towers and a narrower doorway.

After 'having reconstructed the elements of the model into a harmonious whole',[57] Badawy attempted an evaluation of its scale. The restored elements, however, having been given internal coherent proportions, cannot be considered of any help, and in fact Badawy himself concentrated his calculations on the sole original element of the base which could provide any information: the flight of stairs. He suggested that 1 palm in the model corresponded to 3 cubits in the actual temple, that is, a ratio of 1:18 if the small cubit (6 palms) was used (1 palm in the model $= 3 \times 6$ palms in the temple), or 1:21 if the royal cubit (7 palms) was chosen as the unit of measurement (1 palm in the model $= 3 \times 7$ palms in the temple). Using these

---

[55] Barry J. Kemp, 'Preliminary Report on the el-Amarna Expedition, 1979', *JEA* 66 (1980), 14 and 'Patterns of Activity at the Workmen's Village', *Amarna Reports I*, London: EES, 1984, chapter 1, p. 11.

[56] Badawy, *Dessin architecturale*, figs. 236a and 236b and 'A Monumental Gateway for a Temple of King Seti I – An Ancient Model Restored', *Miscellanea Wilbouriana* 1 (1972), 1–23.

[57] Badawy, *Miscellanea Wilbouriana* 1, p. 4.

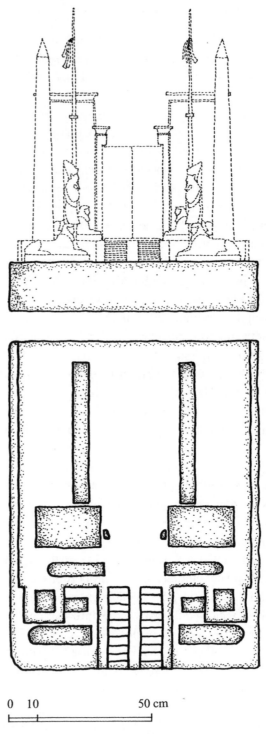

0   10   50 cm

Fig. 64: Plan of the basement of the model of a temple of Seti I (Nineteenth Dynasty), showing the sockets carved to accommodate architectural elements and sculptures, and frontal view of Badawy's reconstruction of the entire model (drawn after Badawy, *Miscellanea Wilbouriana* 1, figs. 2 and 6).

two scales, Badawy calculated two possible real values for the restored elements. The obelisks, for example, would have been 1.250 m wide at the base and 11.433 m high if the scale was 1:18, and 1.575 m wide and 14.406 m high if the scale was 1:21. Since, however, the model cannot be compared with any existing temple, and since we cannot be sure that the missing elements of the model followed the proportions of the actual monument, these calculations do not lead to any definite conclusion.

Badawy suggested that this model could be a surviving example of a particular feature of New Kingdom and Late Period scenes depicting foundation ceremonies. When the king is shown performing the purification of the completed temple and its presentation to the god, the temple is represented as a miniature shrine. Badawy suggested that little models of the construction existed and that the basement found at Tell el-Yahudiya belonged to one of them. In a literal interpretation of the foundation scenes, the Brooklyn model would have just about the right size in comparison with the figures of the king and the gods. It is possible, however, that the little shrine which appears in scenes depicting foundation ceremonies was just a symbolic representation of the whole temple, reduced in size and appearance to a 'hieroglyph' to be inserted in the scene.

Even if the connection with the foundation ceremonies cannot be proved, several clues suggest that this model was indeed a votive object. The first clue lies in the materials: the inscriptions on the basement list the missing parts together with the materials of which they were made, that is, bronze for the doors and white crystalline, *mesdet* and *bekhen* stone for the rest, including even the flagstaffs. Apart from the first, they differ from the materials usually employed in similar elements of real temples. The second clue is in its design: the model represents the entrance of a sacred enclosure and the artist has focused on the composition of the external elements, such as pylon, door, obelisks, statues and sphinxes, that is, the elements which would be the distinctive features of that building from an external, public point of view. The internal space is just outlined by the two parallel walls, while the back is ignored.

It might be suggested that this was a study for the design of the façade of a temple, but then the variety and preciousness of the materials employed in the model (and carefully described in the inscriptions) would be difficult to explain. The presence all round the base of the figure of Seti I kneeling and presenting offerings also seems to confirm the votive character of the object. Whether the artist maintained in the model the proportions of the façade of the actual temple or simply represented its more distinctive features without respecting their numerical ratios, it is impossible to ascertain. The second hypothesis, however, seems more likely.

A fragment of a peculiar architectural model, dating to the Late Period, was found at Tôd. It is the plan of the northern corner of the first hall of the temple, in which

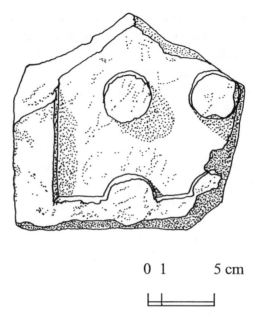

0 1   5 cm

Fig. 65: Fragment of a model of the northern corner of the first hall of the Ptolemaic temple at Tôd (drawn after the photograph published by Bisson de la Roque, *Tôd*, p. 154).

the base of the walls, and free-standing and engaged columns, are cut at 6 mm from the level of the floor (fig. 65). Bisson de la Roque published a photograph and a short description of the object, in which he identified the architectural elements. In both the model and the actual temple, the distance between the two free-standing columns is shorter than the distance between the latter and the two engaged columns. In the model, the first distance is 7.5 cm, which is exactly 1 palm, while the second is 8 cm. In the text, Bisson de la Roque wrote that these dimensions corresponded to 4.50 m and 4.80 m in the actual temple, thus attributing a scale of 6:100 to the model.[58] However, according to the published plan of the temple, the distance between free-standing columns is significantly less than the 4.50 m given by the text; even assuming that the drawing is not absolutely precise, the aerial photograph included at the beginning of the volume seems to confirm that the proportions of the plan are more reliable than the dimensions given in the text.

Without a new survey to establish the precise dimensions of that part of the temple, it is safer for the moment to abandon the attempt to calculate a scale and conclude that the model is a miniature plan outlined by means of simple units of measurement, not necessarily corresponding to the actual construction. In the model the diameter of the bases of the columns corresponds to 2 fingers (about 3.7 cm); the

[58] Bisson de la Roque, *Tôd*, p. 154. This scale, even if wrong, can be better expressed as 1:60 palms.

distance between the axes of free-standing columns, as we have seen, corresponds to 1 palm (7.5 cm); and the distance between free-standing and engaged columns (8 cm) can be expressed as 1 palm $+\frac{1}{4}$ finger. The artist might have chosen to represent the plan of the temple (or a part of it) in an approximate but realistic way, choosing 'simple' dimensions such as 1 palm and 2 fingers for the main elements. In this case, it is likely that this model was part of a votive object, rather than an architectural plan.

Finally, it is worth mentioning the model of a step pyramid found at Memphis by Petrie, which he thought might be the a model of the 'step pyramid of Saqqareh'[59] (fig. 66). This model cannot be identified with a precise monument for several reasons. First of all, nothing is known about the circumstances of its discovery, apart from the fact that it was found at Memphis,[60] and its date is impossible to establish. The model consists of a large limestone block cut in at least seven steps, of which six still remain, while only a fragment of the seventh survives. It is the representation of a step pyramid, but it does not seem to have been a working model, since it lacks the precision that this would have required. The overall appearance of a step pyramid is well rendered, but the steps are very roughly outlined, their corners are blunted and irregular, and there is a consistent discrepancy in the depth of the steps of two adjacent sides.[61]

If it represented the pyramid of Djoser, as Petrie suggested, it must be noted that the model does not show the specific feature of that pyramid, that is, its rectangular plan. The model cannot be identified with certainty as any existing step pyramid. Its outline, that is, the imaginary line connecting the steps from the ground to the top, is about 63°, much steeper than the funerary monuments of Djoser (about 52°), Sekhemkhet (about 50°), the so-called Layer Pyramid at Zawiyet el-Aryan

---

[59] W. M. Flinders Petrie, *The Labyrinth, Gerzeh and Mazghuneh*, BSAE ERA 21, London, 1912, p. 35. Photographs of both models were published by Iorweth E. S. Edwards, *The Pyramids of Egypt*, London: Penguin Books, 1993 (revised edition), pl. 61.

[60] Petrie, *Labyrinth*, 35. According to Edwards (*Pyramids*, p. 260) the model was purchased and not directly found by Petrie.

[61] This model, therefore, does not provide any answer to the discussion about the exact shape of the steps, that is, whether they had all the same 'riser' (as they are generally represented) or whether it diminished towards the top (as suggested by Vyse and Perring in *Operations Carried On at the Pyramids of Gizeh*, London: Fraser, 1840–2, pl. A, according to whom the steps were 22, 21, 20 19, 18 and 17 cubits high, and Legon in 'The 14:11 Proportion at Meydum', *DE* 17 (1990), 15–22), and whether the 'tread' was flat or sloping. The major step pyramids are generally reconstructed with sloping steps (as in Rainer Stadelmann, *Die Ägyptischen Pyramiden*, Mainz: Von Zabern, 1985, figs. 18 and 19 and Edwards, *Pyramids*, figs. 6 and 13). The pyramid of Meidum is usually represented with flat steps (Vito Maragioglio and Celeste Rinaldi, *L'architettura delle Piramidi Memfite*, Torino: Artale, 1963–77, vol. III, pl. 2, fig. 2; Stadelmann, *Pyramiden*, fig. 21, although in *LÄ*, vol. IV, p. 1220 he adopted sloping steps; see also Jean-Philippe Lauer, *Le mystère des pyramides*, Paris: Presses de la Cité, 1988, p. 235 and Gay Robins and Charles Shute, 'The 14 to 11 Proportion in Egyptian Architecture', *DE* 16, 1990, 75–80 for calculations of their proportions) and its satellite might have had the same shape (Maragioglio and Rinaldi, *Piramidi* MDAIK 38 (1980), 83–95, fig. 3) suggested flat steps for their reconstructions of the step pyramid at Sinki. Jánosi suggested two possible reconstructions of the casing of GIIIb and c, of two queens of Menkaura: one with flat and one with sloping steps (Peter Jánosi, *Die Pyramidenanlagen der Königinnen*, Vienna: Österreichischen Akademie der Wissenschaften, 1996, pp. 86–7 and fig. 33).

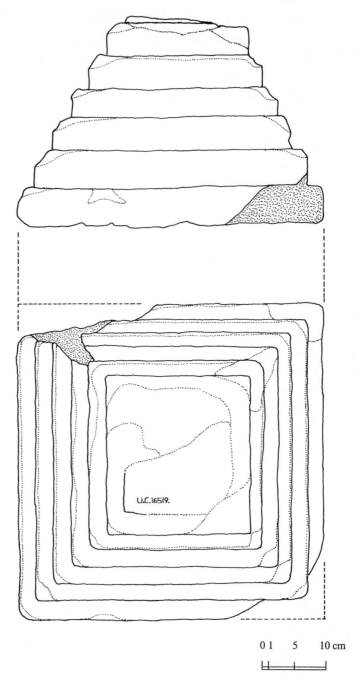

0 1   5   10 cm

Fig. 66: Plan and elevation of the model of a step pyramid (date unknown), Petrie Museum of Egyptian Archaeology, University College London, UC 16519.

(about 47°) and the original pyramid at Meidum (about 52°). Nothing precise is known about the slope of the unfinished northern pyramid at Zawiyet el-Aryan and of the 'destroyed' pyramid 29 at Saqqara, and very little can be said of the various small step pyramids scattered all over Egypt, dating to the reign of Huni, which were possibly cenotaphs or landmarks of the royal power, rather than tombs.[62] However, it is unlikely that the outline of any of these monuments reached the 63° of the model, a slope which would only be achieved very late in the history of true pyramids. Therefore, this model does not seem to have been specifically connected with the project or the construction of a step pyramid. It may have been a votive or decorative object, such as the basis for a divine image, but the absolute lack of information about its finding-spot and its date prevents any precise conclusion.

Working models

Among the mass of votive objects, there are a few architectural models that can be related to the planning and building process. The most important one is the model of a funerary apartment in a pyramid, probably dating to the late Twelfth Dynasty, which was found carefully buried in the Valley Temple of Amenemhat III at Dahshur[63] (fig. 67). The model is not to a calculated scale, the rooms being grouped and represented in a clear, but schematic and abbreviated way. Dieter Arnold suggested that this may have been an early project for the interior of the Hawara pyramid, used by the architects to study a first distribution of the rooms. The project was later modified, and possibly a more precise and detailed model was then realised to assist the builders during the construction of the monument.

Curiously enough, at Hawara Petrie found a limestone fragment which he identified as a model of the ruined pyramid of Amenemhat III.[64] This fragment (fig. 68) consists of a small limestone pyramid with four smooth faces and a very irregular and rough base. Narrow tool marks are visible all around the uppermost part, and the slope of its faces is about 47°–48°. The casing of the pyramid of Hawara has completely disappeared, apart from a few loose blocks, from which Petrie obtained three different values: 48°45′, 49°51′ and 52°45′, the lowest being very close to the slope of the model.[65] It would be tempting to see this small pyramidal fragment as another piece of a large model of the Hawara complex prepared by the architects of Amenemhat III, but unfortunately there is no evidence that this was the case. It

---

[62] Günter Dreyer and Werner Kaiser, 'Zu den kleinen Stufenpyramiden Ober- und Mittelägyptens', *MDAIK* 36, 1980, 43–59. According to the reconstruction of the step pyramid at Sinki by Dreyer and Swelim, its outline may have been around 50° (Dreyer and Swelim, *MDAIK* 38, fig. 3).
[63] Arnold, *Amenemhet III.*, pp. 86–8.   [64] Petrie, *Labyrinth,* p. 35 and pl. 27.
[65] W. M. Flinders Petrie, *Kahun, Gurob and Hawara*, London: Kegan Paul, Trench and Trübner, 1890, p. 13.

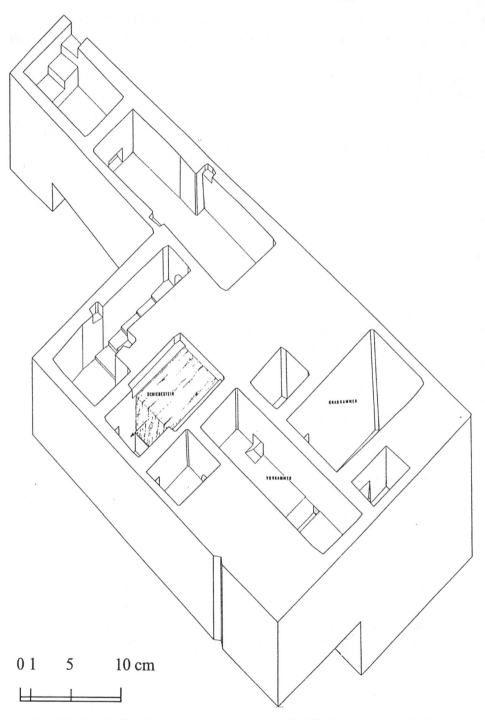

0 1   5   10 cm

Fig. 67: Model of the funerary apartment in a late Twelfth Dynasty pyramid (from Arnold, *Amenemhet III.*, pl. 66).

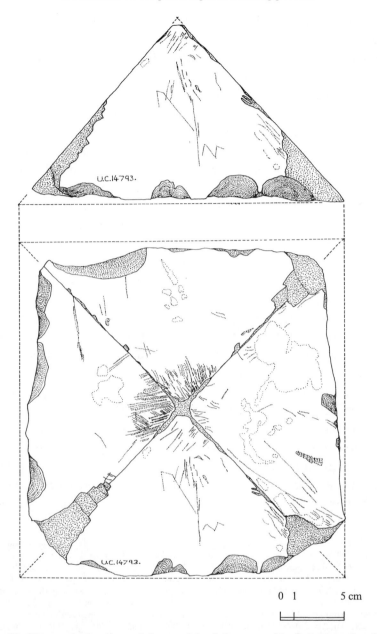

U.C.14793.

U.C.14793.

0 1   5 cm

Fig. 68: Plan and elevation of the model of the pyramid of Amenemhat III at Hawara (?) (Twelfth Dynasty), Petrie Museum of Egyptian Archaeology, University College London, UC 14793.

might have been an independent model or even the upper part of a pyramidion, the capstone of a pyramid.[66]

To the Ptolemaic period belong a number of architectural models representing capitals or portions of columns, which do not show any indication of having been parts of larger models.[67] Their dimensions range from a few centimetres to almost one metre. Some of the small models are just approximations of architectural details, while others, especially the largest, were carved with a certain precision. Some of them might have been votive objects without any direct link with the building process, but in the case of the most accurate examples I would suggest that their function corresponded to that of the Greek *paradeigmata*, the models of architectural elements such as triglyphs and capitals that were provided by the architects at the beginning of the works to illustrate the details of their projects. In the Hellenistic period, while Egypt was ruled by the Ptolemies, these models might have been to a precise scale.[68] Since all the small models of columns and capitals found in Egypt seem to belong to the Ptolemaic period, it is not illogical to suppose that their function was the same of the *paradeigmata*.

The doubt remains whether this system was imported from Greece to Egypt or the other way around, but what it is really important is that during the Hellenistic Period these methods were spread and transmitted across the Mediterranean. This suggests that a comparison with the more abundant Greek sources on architects and architectural projects might cast new light on some still obscure aspects of ancient Egyptian architecture, at least concerning the planning and building process adopted from the seventh century BC onwards, when monumental architecture started to appear in Greece. For the previous periods, we can rely only upon the available archaeological material found in Egypt. Among all the uneven and discontinuous evidence, a unique chance to follow the methods used by architects and workmen from the beginning to the end of the planning and building process is provided

[66] The little pyramid does not rest on a proper base, since the lower edge seems broken, rather than unfinished, and it is not even horizontal. It might even be suggested that this was not a model of the pyramid, but the uppermost part of its capstone, the pyramidion, if only Middle Kingdom kings did not appear to have preferred dark stones for their pyramidia. On the other hand, it must be borne in mind that nothing is known about the pyramidia of Middle Kingdom secondary pyramids. In the area of the pyramid of Hawara, there are the remains of the tomb of Neferuptah, daughter or queen of Amenemhat III, reconstructed by Farag and Iskander as a mud-brick pyramid cased with limestone (Nagib Farag and Zaky Iskander, *The Discovery of Neferwptah*, Cairo: Government Press, 1971). Absolutely nothing, however, remains of the superstructure. Maragioglio and Rinaldi assumed the existence of a pyramid only because its plan was almost square (Vito Maragioglio and Celeste Rinaldi, 'Note complementari sulla tomba di Neferu-Ptah', *Orientalia* 42 (1973), 357–69) and recently Jánosi concluded that there is no evidence at all that the tomb had the form of a pyramid (*Pyramidenanlagen*, p. 70).

[67] See, for example, the five fine models held in Berlin (nos. 991–995 in Staatliche Museen Preussischer Kulturbesitz, *Ägyptisches Museum Berlin,* Berlin: Östlicher Stülerbau, 1967, p. 101 and corresponding plate, also published by Badawy, *Gazette des Beaux-Arts* 107, p. 55), the three models held in Cairo (nos. 33395-7, in Campbell C. Edgar, *Sculptor's Studies and Unfinished Works, CG,* Cairo: SAE, 1906, pp. 49–50 and pl. 20). Models of various size are held in several major museums.

[68] Coulton, *Greek Architects*, pp. 55–7.

by the material accumulated in years of studies on Deir el-Medina and the royal necropoleis, to which the next chapter is entirely dedicated.

Projects and works in the Nineteenth and Twentieth Dynasty royal tombs

Documents on the works

The Valley of the Kings, the Valley of the Queens and Deir el-Medina, the village that housed the workmen in charge of the royal necropoleis, provided a large number of documents directly or indirectly relating to the quarrying of the royal tombs. The surviving fragments of texts on various subjects allow us to catch a glimpse of what life in the village and in the valleys must have been like about thirty-three centuries ago. Life at Deir el-Medina rotated around the construction of tombs. A precise hierarchy regulated the activity of workmen divided into gangs, chief workmen, guardians, doorkeepers, scribes, administrators and policemen. Their families formed a lively community in the village, and the boys that were expected to remain there and join the group of workmen were called 'children of the Tomb'.[69]

Among the mass of material including personal letters, administrative records, requests of supplies and private quarrels, there are a number of documents (texts and drawings on ostraca and papyri) that more strictly deal with the architectural aspect of the work. The majority are short texts recording the progress of the work to a certain date, but there are also more or less detailed drawings of elements or whole tombs. Some of these documents were listed and studied by Jaroslav Černy, who also suggested a first identification of the descriptions with existing tombs.[70] Demarée then published a list including a number of other documents, and classified the material into three groups: plans, lists of measurements and journals.[71] More recently, after the work of the Theban Mapping Project in the Valley of the Kings, it finally has been possible to compare the ancient documents with reliable surveys of the tombs as they were completed.[72] This comparison yielded interesting information on many aspects of the work and allowed the correct identification of the tombs described on some of the documents.[73] Table 6 lists all of these documents accompanied by an updated select bibliography.[74]

---

[69] Jaroslav Černy, *A Community of Workmen at Thebes in the Ramesside Period*, BdE 50, Cairo: IFAO, 1973.

[70] Jaroslav Černy, *The Valley of the Kings*, BdE 61, Cairo: IFAO, 1973, pp. 23–34.

[71] R. J. Demarée, ' "Royal Riddles" ', in R. J. Demarée and A. Egberts (eds.), *Village Voices*, Leiden: Centre of Non-Western Studies, Leiden University, 1992, pp. 9–18.

[72] Theban Mapping Project, *Atlas of the Valley of the Kings*, Cairo: American University in Cairo Press, 2000.

[73] Corinna Rossi, 'The Plan of a Royal Tomb on O. Cairo 25184', *GM* 184 (2001), 45–53; 'The Identification of the Tomb Described on O. BM 8505', *GM* 187 (2002), 97–9; also *JEA* 87, 73–80.

[74] In comparison with Černy's and Demarée's lists, this one includes also Ostracon Strasburg H.122 (K. A. Kitchen, *Ramesside Inscriptions*, VII, Oxford: Blackwell, 1989, pp. 288–9; see also Koenig Yvan, *Les ostraca hiératiques inédits de la Bibliothèque nationale et universitaire de Strasbourg*, DFIFAO 33, Cairo: IFAO, 1997, pls. 44–7, and Cathleen A. Keller, 'The Draughtsmen of Deir el-Medina: A Preliminary Report', *NARCE* 115

All of the texts and drawings concern works done in the Valley of the Kings and the Valley of the Queens in about two hundred years, between the reigns of Ramses II and Ramses IX. They provide a large amount of information on several aspects of the planning and building process, from the symbolic function of each architectural element to some of the technical solutions adopted during construction, from the theory of the project to the practice of the quarrying process.

The function of each part of a tomb was mirrored by its specific title[75] (see figs. 69 and 71). The internal corridors, generally up to four in total, were called 'god's passages', while the external approach bore the name of 'god's passage which is upon the sun's path'. Niches called 'the sanctuaries in which the gods of the west/east repose' could be found on both sides of the third corridor, while the small recesses placed at the end of the fourth corridor were called 'doorkeeper's rooms'. The last corridor led to a 'hall of hindering', or 'hall of denial of access', where, in the earliest tombs, a deep vertical shaft was quarried. This may be followed by a 'chariot hall', also called 'another hall of repelling rebels', sometimes followed by a 'hall of truth'. The burial chamber was called 'house of gold' or 'the hall in which one rests'. In some cases there were further corridors, and secondary rooms and recesses, called 'resting place of the gods' and 'treasuries'.[76] Not all of these chambers appear in every tomb, and some of these terms are to be found also in the descriptions of tombs of queens and princes.

It is sometimes difficult to draw a line between practical and symbolic functions. The 'hall of hindering' or 'hall of denial of access', the room occupied by the vertical shaft, may have had a function of protection not only from ill-intentioned intruders, as its title seems to suggest, but also from sudden floods, that must have proved particularly disruptive for very steep tombs like the earliest examples in the Valley of the Kings.[77] A practical reason may well have had a symbolic counterpart; in fact, it has been suggested that, at least for the Eighteenth Dynasty tombs, the

(1981), 14). This list does not include, however, Ostracon Michaelides 71 (*verso* 2–3), which mentions the opening of a chamber in a late Nineteenth Dynasty tomb (Hans Goedicke and F. Edward Wente, *Ostraka Michaelides*, Wiesbaden: Harrassowitz, 1962, p. 20 and pl. 69), and Ostracon Cairo 72452, which refers to the beginning of the work in the tomb of Tawosret (K. A. Kitchen, *Ramesside Inscriptions*, vol. IV, Oxford: Blackwell, 1982, p. 404. See also Hartwig Altenmüller, 'Bemerkungen zu den Königsgrabern des Neuen Reiches', *SAK* 10 (1983), 25–61, especially 45, note 52, and 'Der Begräbnistag Sethos' II.', *SAK* 11 (1984), 37–47, corrected by Wolfgang Helck, 'Drei Ramessidische Daten', *SAK* 17 (1990), pp. 205–14, especially 208–10), since neither of them contain information on the dimensions of these tombs. For Ostracon BM8505, Ostraca Cairo 25581 (*recto*), 25538, 25536 (*recto*) and 25537, Ostraca Turin 57036 and 57037, see respectively: S. Birch, *Inscriptions in Hieratic and Demotic Character in the Collections of the British Museum*, London: British Museum, 1868; Jaroslav Černy, *Ostraca Hiératiques*, *CG*, Cairo: SAE, 1935; Jesús López, *Catalogo del Museo Egizio di Torino*, Serie Seconda – Collezioni, vol. III, Fascicolo I: Ostraca ieratici, Milano: Cisalpino-La Goliardica, 1978.

[75] Carter and Gardiner, *JEA* 4, 130–58; Černy, *Valley of the Kings*, pp. 23–34; Demarée, *Village Voices*, pp. 9–18. See also Erik Hornung, 'Struktur und Entwicklung der Gräber im Tal der Könige', *ZÄS* 105 (1978), 59–66.

[76] See the scheme of an ideal tomb by Demareé, *Village Voices*, figs. 1 and 2.

[77] Elizabeth Thomas, *Royal Necropoleis of Thebes*, Princeton, 1966, p. 278 and 'The "Well" in Kings' Tombs of Bibân el-Molûk', *JEA* 64 (1978), 80–3; Raphael Ventura, 'The Largest Project for a Royal Tomb in the Valley of the Kings', *JEA* 74 (1988), 139.

well might be symbolically connected to the subterranean 'aquatic region' of the Amduat.[78] Either because the importance of this symbolic link faded, or because the practical considerations of construction were stronger than anything else, when the slope of the later tombs decreased considerably (together with the potential damage due to a sudden flood), the floor of the 'hall of hindering' ceased to be cut away and the well disappeared.

Texts and drawings providing the dimensions of various elements of a tomb use as a unit of measurement the royal cubit, divided into seven palms, each divided into four fingers.[79] From the comparison between the descriptions contained in these documents and the actual tombs as they were completed, it is possible to reconstruct some interesting aspects of the way the space was perceived, measured and represented. For example, there is a striking lack of any record of the slope of the corridors, which may be one of the reasons why in a few cases newly quarried tombs ran into older burials. It might even be suggested that the risk of colliding with older tombs, of which only the position of the entrance was known, was one of the reasons for the progressive reduction of the slope of the later tombs. Another important point is that the Egyptians apparently measured the length of a sloping corridor along the actual surface of the floor, unlike our modern plans, where we represent and measure its projection on a horizontal plane.[80] This assumption is in line with the fact that ancient Egyptian architectural drawings were not drawn to a calculated scale, and lacked any type of foreshortening or 'flattening' due to a projection on an ideal plane.

Another interesting aspect is the passage from the theory of the project to the practice of the construction. In the case of royal tombs, as probably in the more general cases of rock-cut tombs or temples, the characteristics of the rock and the techniques of excavation must have had a constant and significant influence on the development of the work.[81] A number of more or less important details must have depended on a certain degree of improvisation. For example, one of the four niches in KV 6, tomb of Ramses IX, the one above KV 55, was left unfinished in order to avoid a collision with another subterranean tomb.[82] In the Amarna Royal Tomb, Lehner suggested that the axis of the corridor labelled as 1 was not at a right angle with the corridor B in order to avoid interference with the

---

[78] Friedrich Abitz, *Die religiöse Bedeutung der sogenannten Grabräuberschächte in den ägyptischen Königsgräbern der 18. bis 20. Dynastie*, Wiesbaden: Harrassowitz, 1974, and Claude Vandersleyen, 'Le sens symbolique des puits funéraires dans l'Egypte ancienne', *CdE* 50 (1975), 151–7.

[79] About the use of other units of measurements see the discussion about the *neby* in Hayes, *Sen-mut*, pp. 21–2; Claire Simon, 'Le *nbi* at le canon de proportions', *JEA* 79 (1993), 157–77, challenged by Gay Robins, 'On Supposed Connections Between the "Canon of Proportions" and Metrology', *JEA* 80 (1994) 191–4; Elke Roik, 'Auf der Suche nach dem "true *nbj* measure" ', *DE* 34 (1996), 91–115, challenged by John A. R. Legon, 'The quest for the true *nbj* measure', *DE* 36 (1996), 69–78.

[80] Rossi, *JEA* 87, 73–80.   [81] Černy, *Valley of the Kings*, p. 9.

[82] Nicholas C. Reeves and Richard H. Wilkinson, *The Complete Valley of the Kings*, London: Thames and Hudson, 1996, p.169.

room γ (fig. 45).[83] Significant changes in the plan were adopted in emergencies, such as a collision with another tomb. In the worst accident, Sethnakht abandoned the tomb he had started (KV 11) when its straight axis collided with KV 10, the tomb of Amenmesse. Later Ramses III took over and completed the tomb along a shifted axis, adopting a rising corridor as a solution to avoid the underlying chamber of KV 10.[84]

Recording the progress: from the project to the survey

From the study of these documents as a group, it is possible to suggest a reconstruction of the whole building process from the project to the actual monument. The general dimensions of tombs must have been decided in advance, as it is proved by Papyrus Turin 1923 and related fragments, and by Ostracon Cairo 25184, containing the plan of a tomb identified as KV 6, the tomb of Ramses IX (fig. 69). Papyrus Turin 1923 is a peculiar and complicated text that records the calculations carried out by the scribe to establish how many cubic cubits had to be removed in one year in order to complete in three years the project of enlargement of KV 9, started for Ramses V and then taken over by Ramses VI.[85] The dimensions of rooms and corridors are expressed in whole cubits, just as in Ostracon Cairo 25184, the plan identified as the project for KV 6 (Ramses IX). This tomb, apart from minor variations, seems to have been completed according to the general design envisaged by the plan on ostracon, but not necessarily to the dimensions anticipated by the project.[86]

In general, it seems that the projects were laid out according to a set of simple, linear dimensions expressed by whole numbers of cubits, which were meant to act as a guide but not as a strict rule. The three surviving corridors mentioned in Ostracon Cairo 25184 and the first two of Papyrus Turin 1923, for example, are all supposed to be 30 cubits long (*c.* 15.70 m), and the other dimensions are always rather 'simple' numbers of whole cubits, but in fact only a few corridors in the whole Valley of the Kings, including those of KV 6 (Ramses IX), ever reached that length. We may conclude that at the very beginning of the work an official plan was drawn, probably on papyrus, containing the design of the internal arrangement of the tomb and a general idea of its size based on simple sets of dimensions. Apparently, the slope was not one of the aspects taken into account in advance. If such a general plan on a papyrus ever existed, no example has survived, but Ostracon Cairo 25184,

[83] Lehner, Martin, *Royal Tomb at el-Amarna*, p. 7.
[84] Reeves and Wilkinson, *Complete Valley of the Kings*, pp. 159–61.
[85] Ventura, *JEA* 74, 145. Another case where the volume of rock to be removed for each room was recorded is Ostracon Strasburg H.122.
[86] Rossi, *GM* 184, 45–53.

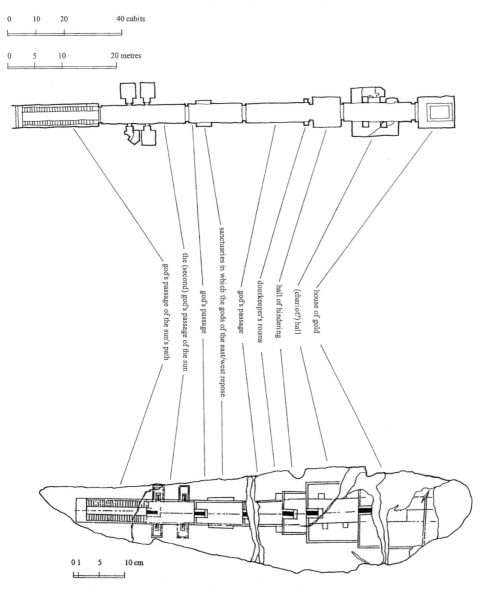

Fig. 69: Ostracon Cairo 25184 (drawn after the photograph published by Daressy, *Ostraca*, pl. 32; the hieratic text accompanying the drawing has been omitted) and plan of KV 6, the tomb of Ramses IX, Twentieth Dynasty (drawn after Weeks, *NARCE* 105, sheet 7; names of chambers taken from Černy, *Valley of the Kings*, chapter III and Demarée, *Village Voices*, figs. 1 and 2).

Table 6. *Documents on the architectural work in some Nineteenth and Twentieth Dynasty tombs*

Document	Contents	Tomb	Attribution	Bibliography
Papyrus Cairo 86637 (*verso* XX)	List of parts of a tomb with dimensions	Unknown (time of Ramses II)	Černy (*Valley of the Kings*, p. 25) by palaeography	Bakir, *Cairo Calendar*, p. 56, pls. 50 and 50a.
Ostracon Michaelides 53	List of parts of a tomb with dimensions	Unknown (first half of the Nineteenth Dynasty)	Demarée (*Village Voices*, p. 14), by palaeography	Goedicke and Wente, *Ostraka Michaelides*, p. 22, pl. 81.
Ostracon Cairo 25581 (*recto*)	List of parts of a tomb with dimensions	Unknown (time of Merenptah)	Černy (*Valley of the Kings*, p. 25) by palaeography	Černy, *Ostraca*, pp. 29 and 52*, pl. 52.
Ostracon Michaelides 92	List of parts of a tomb with dimensions	Unknown (time of Merenptah)	Demarée (*Village Voices*, p. 14), by palaeography	Goedicke and Wente, *Ostraka Michaelides*, p. 22, pl. 81.
Ostracon Berlin B + British Museum 65944 (Nash 10)	List of parts of a tomb with dimensions	Uncertain (possibly Amenmesse or Seti II)		Unpublished.
Ostracon Cairo 25538	List of parts of a tomb with dimensions	KV 15-Seti II	Černy (*Valley of the Kings*, p. 26) by the name of the vizier	Černy, *Ostraca*, pp. 16 and 34*, pl. 23.
Ostracon Cairo 51936	Sketch of a four-pillared hall	Uncertain (possibly Seti II or Siptah)	Reeves, Rossi, by comparison with the plan	Engelbach, *ASAE* 27, pp. 72–5; Reeves, *CdE*61, pp. 43–9.
Ostracon Cairo 25536 (*recto*)	List of work done in a tomb with dimensions	KV 47-Siptah	Černy (*Valley of the Kings*, p. 26) by the name of the vizier	Černy, *Ostraca*, pp. 16 and 33*, pl. 23.
Ostracon Cairo 25537	List of work done in a tomb with dimensions		Černy (*Valley of the Kings*, p. 26) by the name of the vizier	Černy, *Ostraca*, pp. 16 and 34*, pl. 22.
Ostracon DeM (private collection)	List of doors of a tomb with dimensions	Unknown (late Nineteenth or early Twentieth Dynasty)	Demarée, by palaeography	Demarée, *Village Voices*, pp. 9–18.
Ostracon Strasburg H.112 (*recto* and *verso*)	List of work done in a tomb with dimensions	QV 44-Khaemwaset (son of Ramses III)	By comparison with the plan	Kitchen, *Ramesside Inscriptions* VII, pp. 288–9; Koenig, *Ostraca hiératiques*, p. 9, pls. 44–7; Keller, *NARCE* 115, p. 14.
Ostracon Turin 57036	List of parts of a tomb with dimensions	Sons of Ramses III	López, by the name of the king	López, *Ostraca*, p. 28.
Ostracon Turin 57037	List of parts of a tomb with dimensions		López, by palaeography	López, *Ostraca*, p. 28.
Papyrus Turin 1885 (*recto*)	Plan of a tomb with dimensions	KV 2-Ramses IV	Lepsius, by comparison with the plan	Lepsius, *Abhandlungen* 1867, pp. 1–22; Carter and Gardiner, *JEA* 4, pp. 130–58.
Ostracon Cairo (number not known)	Sketch of flight of stairs and door		Reeves, by comparison with the plan	Clarke and Engelbach, *Ancient Egyptian Masonry*, p. 52, fig. 52; Reeves, *CdE* 61, pp. 43–9.
Papyrus Turin 1885 (*verso*)	List of parts of a tomb with dimensions	KV 9-Ramses V–VI	Gardiner, by chronology	Carter and Gardiner, *JEA* 4, pp. 144–9.
Papyrus Turin 1923 (*verso*) + fragments	List of parts of a tomb with dimensions		Černy (*Valley*, p. 25) by the regnal year	Ventura, *JEA* 74, pp. 137–56.
Ostracon British Museum 8505 (*recto* and *verso*)	List of parts of a tomb with dimensions	QV 51-Queen Isis (Ramses VI)	Rossi, by comparison with the plan	Birch, *Inscriptions*, pl. 6; Černy and Gardiner, *Ostraca* I, pl. 82, 3; Rossi, *GM* 187, pp. 97–9.
Ostracon Cairo 25184	Plan of a tomb with dimensions	KV 6-Ramses IX	Daressy, by comparison with the plan	Daressy, *Revue Archéologique* 32, pp. 235–40; Rossi, *GM* 184, pp. 45–53.

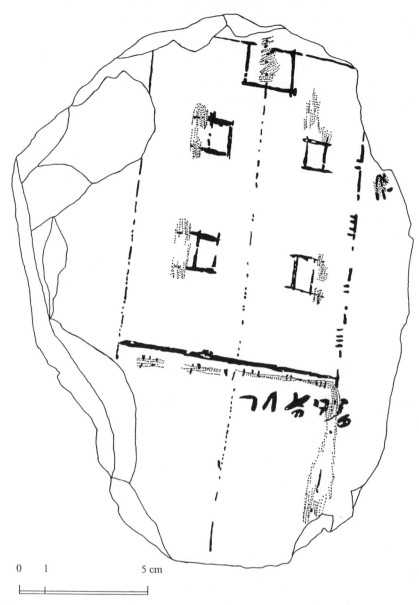

0   1   5 cm

Fig. 70: Ostracon Cairo 51936, Nineteenth Dynasty (drawn after comparison between the original and the photograph published by Engelbach, *ASAE* 27, unnumbered plate).

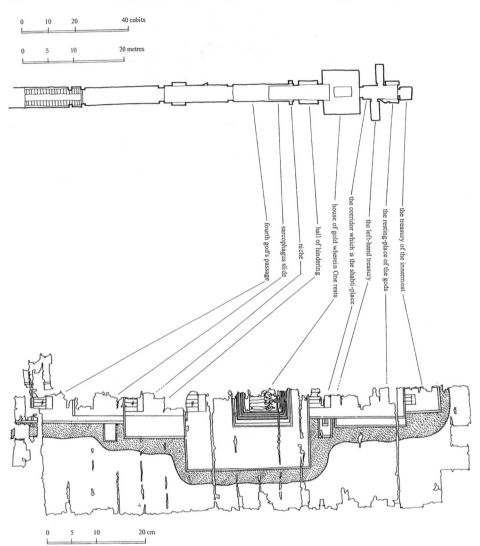

Fig. 71: Papyrus Turin 1885 (drawn after Scamuzzi, *Museo Egizio di Torino*, pl. 87; the hieratic text accompanying the drawing has been omitted) and plan of KV 2, the tomb of Ramses IV, Twentieth Dynasty (drawn after Weeks, *NARCE* 109, p. 10; names of chambers taken from Carter and Gardiner, *JEA* 4).

the plan of KV 6 (Ramses IX), could be a working copy of this initial plan, meant to be used on the spot by the architect to direct the excavation.

After the beginning of the digging, progress was then recorded from time to time on ostraca and papyri. These documents (the majority of those listed in table 6) enumerate elements of the tomb, completed at a certain date, with their exact dimensions expressed in cubits, palms and fingers. Since, evidently, the dimensions of the actual tomb were not expected to correspond exactly to the general, initial plan, the measurements of the completed elements were probably recorded to prove not only that the work was being carried out, but also that it was being carried out with accuracy. It was at this stage that many details were decided, probably including the final dimensions of the chambers. Ostracon Cairo 51936, for instance, contains the sketch of a four-pillared room (of Seti II or Siptah) and bears traces of the train of thought of the ancient draughtsman, who seems to have drawn lines and numbers, changed his mind a couple of times and scratched the surface of the ostracon to cancel what he had discarded[87] (fig. 70). This ostracon, therefore, probably represents a working plan made on the spot to decide the final dimensions of that pillared hall, presumably until that moment only vaguely established.

Finally, from the existence of Papyrus Turin 1885 *recto*, it may be inferred that at the very end of the work a final survey took place in order to record every important detail. This papyrus contains one of the most fascinating ancient Egyptian architectural drawings, the plan of KV 2, tomb of Ramses IV (fig. 71). That this was a survey and not a project may be inferred by the fact that the sarcophagus is represented in its place surrounded by a nest of wooden shrines. This drawing was not just a technical reminder, but a careful and decorative representation of the completed work, embellished by details such as the miniature sarcophagus and the hatched surface representing the mountain into which the tomb had been quarried. Again, as in the case of other surveys, the written dimensions are expressed in cubits, palms and fingers.

In general, if we consider the whole process from the initial project to the development of the work down to the actual tomb, the final result appears to be a compromise between ritual ideas and practical considerations, which does not seem to leave room for the idea that dimensions could have been of specific, numerical interest. In the case of rock-cut tombs, the nature of the work and of the rock might have a strong influence on the final result, whereas in the case of a building started and built on a flat surface the dimensions could be established in advance on the ground. This is probably what the Egyptians did in their foundation ceremonies, which will be the subject of the next chapter.

---

[87] Engelbach, *ASAE* 27, 72–6; Reeves, *CdE* 61, 43–9.

4

Foundation rituals

Foundation ceremonies

The ritual sequence

From the First Dynasty down to the Ptolemaic Period the Egyptians performed a ritual ceremony for the foundation of sacred buildings in which practical and symbolic actions were closely interlaced. In the elaborated version of the Ptolemaic Period,[1] this ceremony consisted of ten different steps:

- the king departs from his palace;
- the king arrives on the site of the new temple;
- the king and the goddess Seshat[2] drive into the ground two poles around which a rope is extended. This operation is called *pd-šsr*, 'stretching the cord'. Some of the spells which are associated with this scene explicitly state that in this way the orientation of the temple and its four corners were fixed;[3]
- the king digs the foundation trench down to the water-table, 'as far as the limit of Nun', the primeval ocean;[4]
- the king moulds four bricks for the four corners of the temple;[5]

---

[1] For a translation of the texts of the foundation ceremonies, see Pierre Montet, 'Le rituel de fondation des temples égyptiennes', *Kêmi* 17 (1964), 74–100. For a detailed description of the sequence, see also James Morris Weinstein, 'Foundation Deposits in Ancient Egypt', Ph.D. thesis, University of Pennsylvania, 1973, chapter 1. For the foundation rituals in general see also E. Lefébure, *Rites égyptiennes, construction et protection des édifices*, BCA 4, Paris: Leroux, 1890 (chapters 3–6 are dedicated to temples) and Alexandre Moret, *Du caractère religieux de la royauté pharaonique*, Paris: Leroux, 1902, chapter 4.

[2] For the history and function of the goddess Seshat see Gerald A. Wainwright, 'Seshat and the Pharaoh', *JEA* 26 (1940), 30–40.

[3] *Edfu* II, 31; III 105; III 167; VII 44–5. Johannes Dümichen, *Baugeschichte des Denderatempels*, Strasburg: Trübner, 1877, pls. 60 and 66.

[4] *Edfu* II, 60.

[5] According to Montet, the four bricks represented the thousands of bricks which were employed for the foundation of the four corners, which were the weakest points of the structure (*Kêmi* 17, p. 89). Weinstein suggested instead that, even if stone was the building material for New Kingdom and Ptolemaic temples, bricks were inserted in order to recall the ancient practice of using light materials ('Foundation Deposits', pp. 12–3).

– the king pours sand in the foundation trench, thus providing a compact surface on which to build;[6]
– the king places a number of stone or metal plaques at the four corners of the temple. In the representations in the Temple of Edfu, the plaques are seventeen,[7] while at Dendera they are twenty-four;[8]
– the king moves into place the first stone block;
– the king purifies the completed temple by throwing natron all around the building,[9] represented as a small shrine;
– the king presents the temple to the god. Once more, the temple is represented as a miniature.

The action corresponding to the third step in the Ptolemaic ritual, the 'stretching of the cord', appears to have been the name of the foundation ceremony already at the time of the Palermo Stone, which records two similar events.[10] A worn out door-jamb of King Khasekhemwy, rediscovered by chance in the Cairo Museum by Reginald Engelbach, seems to have been covered with a representation of a foundation ceremony[11] (fig. 72), although the surface is too erased to allow a precise interpretation of the details. The best Old Kingdom representations of this ceremony are a fragmentary relief showing Snefru and Seshat hammering poles[12] (fig. 73) and a large fragment from the sun temple of Neuserra, which shows the king kneeling in front of a foundation deposit and then performing twice the 'stretching of the cord' together with a goddess[13] (fig. 74).

References to the foundation ceremonies became quite common in the Middle Kingdom.[14] In this period the ritual placing of votive offerings in foundation deposits at special points of important buildings[15] also assumed a more precise

---

[6] It is not unlikely that the sand had also a symbolic meaning, recalling the primeval mound which emerged from the Nun.

[7] Montet, *Kêmi* 17, p. 91. [8] Dümichen, *Baugeschichte*, pl. 52.

[9] According to Blackman and Fairman, 'the Rite of Consecration of a temple employed at Edfu consisted partly, if not entirely, in a version of the Opening of the Mouth, the sequence and character of the ceremonies composing the rite suggesting that first of all it was performed on behalf of the cult-statues (. . .) and that then the "Mouth of the Temple" itself was opened' (Aylward M. Blackman and Herbert W. Fairman, 'The Consecration of an Egyptian Temple According to the Use of Edfu', *JEA* 32 (1946), 85).

[10] Edouard Naville, 'La Pierre de Palerme', *Recueil des Travaux* 25 (1903), especially 70 and 73 and pl. 1 A; Heinrich Schäfer, *Ein Bruchstück Altägyptischer Annalen*, Berlin: Königliche Akademie der Wissenschaften, 1902, pp. 22 and 29; Toby A. H. Wilkinson, *Royal Annals of Ancient Egypt: The Palermo Stone and Its Associated Fragments*, London/New York: Kegan Paul International, 2000, pp. 111–2 and 139.

[11] Reginald Engelbach, 'A Foundation Scene of the Second Dynasty', *JEA* 20 (1934), 183–4.

[12] Ahmed Fakhry, *The Monuments of Sneferu at Dahshur*, Cairo: Government Press, 1961, vol. II, part I, p. 94 and figs. 84–95.

[13] Ludwig Borchardt and Heinrich Schäfer, 'Vorläufiger Bericht über die Ausgrabungen bei Abusir im Winter 1899/1900', *ZÄS* 38 (1900), 97 and pl. 5. For further bibliographical references see Weinstein, 'Foundation Deposits', p. 42, note 19.

[14] For the foundation ceremony for the Eleventh Dynasty temple at Tôd see Bisson de la Roque, *Tôd*, pp. 100–1, 1521 and pl. 25, no. 2; for the temple at Heliopolis of Senusret I, see Adriaan de Buck, 'The Building Inscription of the Berlin Leather Roll', *Analecta Orientalia* 17 (1938), 48–57, especially 53.

[15] Not only religious buildings: foundation deposits were found at the four corners of the interior fortification walls in the fortress at Semna South (Weinstein, 'Foundation Deposits', pp. 84–5). During the Eighteenth Dynasty, foundation deposits were also adopted for obelisks (p. 102) and royal palaces (p. 103).

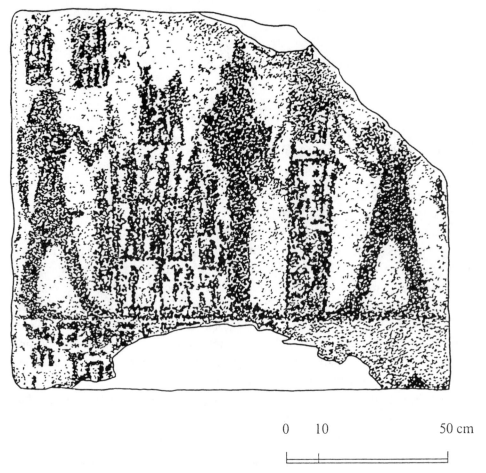

0   10   50 cm

Fig. 72: Scene from a foundation ceremony from the reign of Khasekhemwy,
Second Dynasty (drawn after the photograph published by Engelbach, *JEA* 20,
pl. 24).

character (if compared with the scanty Old Kingdom remains and the absolute
lack of First Intermediate Period material) and shows a strong continuity in terms
of position and objects with the New Kingdom, when the tradition appears to be
consolidated.[16] The ritual was developed and enriched through the New Kingdom
down to the Ptolemaic Period (fig. 75). The scenes related to the foundation ceremony of Thutmosis III at Karnak[17] and Medinet Habu[18] and of Amenhotep III and

---

[16] Weinstein, 'Foundation Deposits', p. 3 and chapter 3.

[17] Paul Barguet, *Le Temple d'Amon-Rê à Karnak*, RAPH 21, Cairo: IFAO, 1962, pl. 31.

[18] Paul Barguet, 'Le rituel archaïque de la fondation des temples de Medinet-Habou et de Louxor', *RdE* 9 (1952),
1–22 for a translation of the texts.

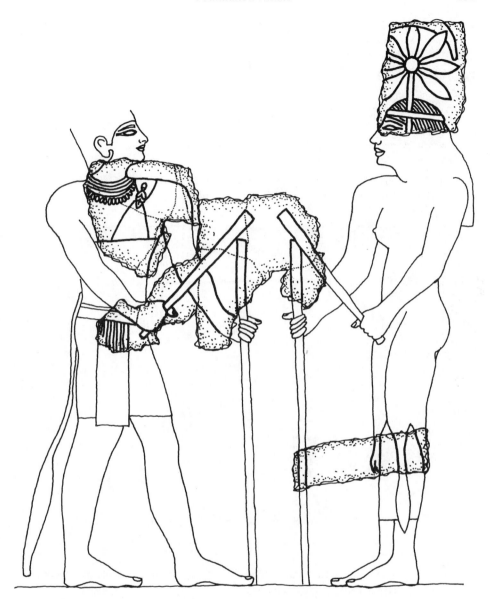

Fig. 73: Fragmentary foundation scene from the valley temple of Snefru at Dahshur, Fourth Dynasty (drawn after Fakhry, *Monuments of Sneferu*, fig. 89).

Ramses II[19] at Luxor seem to be a shorter version of the more elaborated representations in the Ptolemaic temples of Edfu, Dendera and Philae.

The ceremony of 'stretching the cord' corresponds to the first practical act in the foundation of a temple: the sacred area was outlined and at the same time the

---

[19] Donald B. Redford, 'The Earliest Years of Ramses II and the Building of the Ramesside Court at Luxor', *JEA* 57 (1971), 110–9, especially 114–5.

Fig. 74: Scene from a foundation ceremony from the sun temple of Neuserra, Fifth
Dynasty (from Borchardt and Schäfer, *ZÄS* 38, pl. 5).

Fig. 75: Scene from the foundation ceremony of the Ptolemaic temple of Dendera
(from Dümichen, *Baugeschichte*, pl. 64).

orientation and dimensions of the building were laid down. Apart from the late
development of the whole ritual, the essence of this initial act must have remained
the same from Early Dynastic times. This is also mirrored by the Egyptian word for
'to found' and for 'plan' (or 'foundation'), (*snṯ*), written with a looped cord as
a determinative.[20] This word, clearly referring to the ancient connection between

---

[20] Alexander Badawy, 'Philological Evidence about Methods of Construction in Ancient Egypt', *ASAE* 54 (1957),
57.

cord and plan, was nevertheless commonly used also for New Kingdom rock-cut tombs,[21] where the sacred area could not be delimited in advance as for a temple built on flat ground.[22] The ceremony of 'stretching the cord' is actually mentioned only in connection with temples, and the only indirect reference to this ceremony for a tomb is an ink drawing on an ostracon of the Goddess Seshat hammering a pole from the Valley of the Kings.[23]

There is no reference in any inscription or relief to foundation ceremonies for royal or private tombs, but the presence of foundation deposits does seem to suggest that some kind of ritual was performed, possibly derived from the standard foundation ceremonies for temples. In the temples, foundation deposits were usually placed at the corners and at special points of the building, while in the case of tombs they were dug in the area in front of the entrance.[24] It is uncertain whether the deposits in this case were meant to symbolically encircle the whole tomb, or simply to 'protect' the entrance. James Weinstein has suggested that there always should have been five pits, corresponding thus to the usual arrangement for temples: four at the corners and one along the main axis.[25]

The ceremony of 'stretching the cord' is described as consisting of two actions: $\bar{\delta}$, *pḏ-šs(r)* and $\unicode{x2001}$, *wḥᶜ wꜣwꜣt*. The first can be translated as the 'stretching of the cord' itself,[26] while the second can be translated as 'loosening' or 'unravelling the cord'. It may be intended as 'unravelling the (ball of) cord',[27] an obvious initial action for the ceremony of 'stretching the cord'. Since, however, the 'unravelling of the cord' always follows the 'stretching of the cord', the second action might actually refer to the moment when, having fixed the outline of the building, the cord was unravelled across it in order to mark significant points or subdivisions of the area.[28] Badawy even suggested that *wḥᶜ wꜣwꜣt* might be translated as the 'spreading of the plan-net'.[29] He tailored this translation onto his theory of the use of a Harmonic System in which cords played an important part, but nevertheless the overall meaning of this sentence may be correct.

---

[21] Černy, *Valley of the Kings*, p. 22.

[22] Badawy (*ASAE* 54, pp. 51–74.) mentioned three cases in which the connection between cords and outline is quite clear: 'I levelled this site which is inside the cord-(boundary) to build this monument upon it' (Kurt Sethe, *Urkunden der 18. Dynastie*, Leipzig: Hinrichs, 1905–6, p. 835); 'To fill in the contour-plan with sand as required, to stabilise the work of the sanctuary' (*Edfou* II, 31; see also Moret, *Caractère religieux*, p. 134); 'To fill in the contour of the Hathor-temple', which he derived from photos of Dendera.

[23] Cairo Museum, *CG* 24917; Georges Daressy, *Fouilles de la Vallée des Rois (1898–1899)*, *CG*, Cairo: SAE, 1902, pl. 52.

[24] Weinstein, 'Foundation Deposits', figs. 15 and 21. See for example the foundation deposits corresponding to the various stages of enlargement of the temple of Hatshepsut at Deir el-Bahari in Zygmunt Wysocki, 'The Temple of Queen Hatshepsut at Deir el-Bahari: The Raising of the Structure in View of Architectural Studies', *MDAIK* 48 (1992), 233–50. For the deposits at Deir el-Bahari, see also Herbert E. Winlock, 'The Egyptian Expedition 1924–5', *BMMA* 21, 3 (1926), especially 16–8.

[25] Weinstein, 'Foundation Deposits', pp. 105–8 and figs. 2, 3, 7, 19.

[26] Badawy, *ASAE* 54, 54–5.   [27] Montet, *Kêmi* 17, 78–81.

[28] Weinstein, 'Foundation Deposits', p. 12. See also the foundations of Amarna buildings in the following section.

[29] Badawy, *Ancient Egyptian Architectural Design*, pp. 9–10.

Fig. 76: Land-surveyors from the Eighteenth Dynasty tomb of Amenhotepsesi (from Davies, *Two Officials*, pl. 10).

Cords and geometry

The use of cords for land measuring and surveying is comparatively well attested in Eighteenth Dynasty art. Representations from the Theban tombs of Menna, Amenhotepsesi, Khaemhat and Djeserkaraseneb show a group of men in the act of measuring the standing crop by means of a rope[30] (fig. 76). Three statues which represent Senenmut, Amenemhat-Serer and Penanhor as 'overseers of the fields', kneeling and holding a large ball of rope, the tool of their task, also date to the Eighteenth Dynasty.[31] As already mentioned, the unit of measurement for long distances was the *khet*, corresponding to 100 cubits, and the common unit of area was the *setat*, corresponding to one square *khet*. Since the number 100 was represented by means of a coil of rope (𓍢), it might be concluded that cords 100 cubits long were actually employed for land-surveying.[32] In the scene from the tomb of Menna, the cord carried by the men is clearly divided by means of knots, which Arnold suggested were placed at 1-cubit intervals.[33]

---

[30] On the subject see Suzanne Berger, 'A Note on Some Scenes of Land-Measurement', *JEA* 20 (1934), 54–6 and Ludwig Borchardt, 'Statuen von Feldmessern', *ZÄS* 42 (1967), 70–72. For the tomb of Menna see also Colin Campbell, *Two Theban Princes, Kha-em-uast and Amen-khepeshf, Menna, a Land-Steward, and Their Tombs*, Edinburgh: Oliver and Boyd, 1910, p. 87 and the unnumbered plate on the page before; for Amenhotepsesi see also Norman de Garis Davies, *The Tombs of Two Officials of Thutmosis the Fourth*, TTS 3, London: EES, 1923, p. 11, plate 10.

[31] Jacques Vandier, *Manuel d'archéologie égyptienne*, Paris: Picard, 1952–78, vol. III: Text, pp. 476–7 and *Manuel* III: Plates, p. 164 (1, 3, 6). For Senenmut see also Paul Barguet, 'Une statuette de Senenmut au Musée du Louvre', *CdE* 28 (1953), 23–7; for Penanhor see also Borchardt, *ZÄS* 42, 72.

[32] Arnold, *Building in Egypt*, p. 252. Reisner suggested that the sign 𓏴 (*s3*) represented a measuring rope, 'taking the end loops as handles and the side loops as tags marking the ells' (*Mycerinus*, p. 78, note 1). It may be worth adding that fields, presumably measured by means of cords, were sometimes triangular in shape. MMP problem 4, RMP problems 51 and 53 deal with the calculation of the area of triangular fields, whereas RMP problem 52 concerns a trapezoidal field. In none of these cases do these triangles bear any similarity to the 3-4-5, the 8:5 or the equilateral triangle (Respectively Struve, *Studien und Quellen* Part A, vol. 1, pp.145–69; Peet, *Rhind Mathematical Papyrus*, pp. 91–7).

[33] Arnold, *Building in Egypt*, p. 252.

There is, of course, a temptation to extend this discussion to architecture. There is ample evidence that cords were used in architecture at various stages of construction, but none to suggest that they had a specific length or were divided into units of measurement. The statue, mentioned above, representing Senenmut holding a ball of rope, might be of a certain interest because Senenmut was also the architect of Hatshepsut. In the inscriptions carved on the base of that statue, however, he is mentioned with titles which only connect him to agricultural activities.[34]

Amarna provides evidence suggesting the use of cords possibly at two different stages in the foundation of buildings: for the ceremony of 'stretching the cord' (attested, however, only by a *talatat* found at Karnak[35]), and during the layout of the plan. Pendlebury reconstructs the method employed at least in the Great Aten Temple, the Hat-Aten and the Palace as follows:

first of all shallow trenches were dug in the virgin soil along the lines the walls were intended to take. These were flooded with white lime plaster on which the exact line of the walls was marked with a taut string dipped in blacking. (. . .) Meanwhile, should any partition walls or light structures such as offering-tables be required inside the building the whole of the interior was flooded with plaster and the exact position of each light party-wall, altar, or offering-table marked out, first with a taut string dipped in black, then by chipping along the lines so drawn.[36]

No traces of knots are recorded. If, at this stage, the cords were employed not only to fix the alignment of the walls, but also to establish the dimensions of the chambers, this absence might be explained by the adoption of other devices to divide the cord, such as painted marks.

Cords wound around stakes, along with other votive objects and offerings, were sometimes found in tombs and foundation deposits.[37] These objects were sometimes classified as 'surveyor's stakes', but their small dimensions seem to suggest that they were used for levelling surfaces or drawing lines.[38] To my knowledge, none of them is recorded as having been subdivided by means of knots or other devices. From New Kingdom literary sources, we know of high-quality ropes up to 1,000, 1,200 and, probably, 1,400 cubits long (about 520, 624 and 728 m) used for the

---

[34] Barguet, *CdE* 28, 24.
[35] Weinstein, 'Foundation Deposits', p. 142, note 141, probably referring to the scene later published by Donald B. Redford, *The Akhenaten Temple Project*, vol. I, Warminster: Aris and Phillips, 1976, pl. 18 no. 6.
[36] Pendlebury, *City of Akhenaten* III, p. 6.
[37] Somers Clarke and Reginald Engelbach, *Ancient Egyptian Masonry*, Oxford: Oxford University Press, 1930, fig. 256; Arnold, *Building in Egypt*, p. 256 and fig. 6.3; Weinstein, 'Foundation Deposits', for Hatshepsut at Deir el-Bahari, deposit B (p. 157), Thutmosis III at Gurna (p. 112) and Deir el-Bahari (pp. 185–6), kiosk at Deir el-Bahari (p. 189) and possibly in the temple of Horus at Aniba (pp. 223–4). For foundation deposits of Thutmosis III, see also Alexander Badawy, 'A Collection of Foundation-Deposits of Thutmosis III', *ASAE* 47 (1947), 145–56, especially 154.
[38] See, for example, the traces of red paint on the cord found at Deir el-Bahari, mentioned in Herbert E. Winlock, 'The Egyptian Expedition 1921–2', *BMMA* 17, 2 (1922), 30–1.

royal bark.[39] Even if not necessarily to this extent, long and strong ropes were used during construction to move blocks, statues, obelisks and other heavy items. According to fragments of ropes which have been recovered, they appear to have been made of relatively coarse plant fibres (palm or papyrus), with a diameter of up to 7–8 cm.[40]

Josef Dorner notes that if these were the cords used for surveying, they would have been suitable only for rough measurements, because, even if painted marks were used instead of bulky knots, the total length of the cord would have been influenced by elasticity and variations in atmospheric humidity.[41] This is not incompatible, however, with the more general and practical purpose of the ceremony of 'stretching the cord', that is, establishing the outline of the sacred area. Ropes made of linen would have been more stable and therefore less problematic, but their use is not well documented.[42] The surviving examples range from the Predynastic Period[43] to the Old[44] and Middle Kingdoms.[45] They are mainly fragments with a diameter of about half a centimeter, apart from the large coil of rope found in the First Dynasty tomb of Hemaka, which is about 1 cm thick.[46]

In general, it seems that cords were used to fix the alignment (astronomical and internal), to establish the overall dimensions of the plan, and to mark the position of walls and other elements. However, as already mentioned in Part I, some scholars believe that cords were also used to design on the ground specific geometrical figures, not necessarily related to the shape of the actual building, in order to establish the proportions of the plan. As a witness, the supporters of this theory have called upon the Greek philosopher Democritus, who lived between the fifth and fourth century BC and, as with many other Greek philosophers and mathematicians, is said to have travelled to Egypt. Clemens of Alexandria reported that Democritus, talking about his travels in foreign lands, declared: 'nobody surpassed me in the composition of lines by means of a drawing, not even

[39] Jac. J. Janssen, *Commodity Prices from the Ramesside Period*, Leiden: Brill, 1975, p. 439.

[40] Donald P. Ryan and David H. Hansen, *A Study of Ancient Egyptian Cordage in the British Museum*, London: British Museum, 1987; see also Jac. J. Janssen, *Two Ancient Egyptian Ship's Logs*, Leiden: Brill, 1961, p. 87 and *Commodity Prices*, p. 438. About the diameter of the ropes, see Reginald Engelbach, *The Aswân Obelisk*, Cairo: SAE, 1922, p. 25 and Boris Catoire, 'Evaluation par le calcul des efforts de traction transmis dans les cordages au cours de l'operation d'abattage de l'obelisque ouest du VIIe pylône', *Karnak VII*, Paris: Recherche sur les Civilisations, 1982, pp. 181–202. In general, see Alfred Lucas and J. R. Harris, *Ancient Egyptian Materials and Industries*, London 1962, pp. 134–6 and Gillian Vogelsang-Eastwood, 'Textiles', in Nicholson and Shaw (ed.), *Ancient Egyptian Materials and Technology*, pp. 268–98.

[41] Josef Dorner, 'Die Absteckung und astronomische Orientierung ägyptischer Pyramiden', Ph.D. dissertation, Innsbruck, 1981, p. 9.

[42] Ropes made of flax were used for net-making (Vogelsang-Eastwood, in Nicholson and Shaw (eds.), *Ancient Egyptian Materials and Technology*, pp. 270 and 272).

[43] Guy Brunton and Gertrude Caton-Thompson, *The Badarian Civilisation*, BSAE ERA 46, London, 1928, p. 67.

[44] Walter B. Emery, *The Tomb of Hemaka*, Cairo: Government Press, 1938, pp. 43–44.

[45] Petrie, *Kahun*, pp. 28 and 35.   [46] Emery, *Tomb of Hemaka*, pp. 43 and pls. 9b and 23b.

those among the Egyptians called *Harpedonaptai*, with whom I spent five years abroad'.[47]

The word *Harpedonaptai* does not occur in any other text. It seems to have been composed by the word *harpedone* (ἀρπεδόνη) and the verb *apto* (ἅπτω), which means (among other similar meanings) 'I tie', 'I stretch'. The *Harpedonaptai* appear thus to have been 'cord-stretchers'.[48] In the mathematical texts, the word *apodeixis* (ἀπόδειξις) is used in the meaning 'proof', and this led some scholars to believe that Democritus actually referred to the demonstration of some mathematical theorem. However, the context of this sentence does not necessarily confirm this interpretation. Here Clemens of Alexandria, a Christian author who lived between the second and the third century AD, is telling stories about various Greek philosophers, paying special attention to their relations with the Egyptians. Giving too much importance to the terms he used may be misleading, and the interpretation of *apodeixis* simply as a 'drawing' (another attested meaning of this word) seems to me acceptable.

At any rate, some scholars, including Badawy, have suggested that the *Harpedonaptai* used cords divided by knots to trace right angles by means of the 3-4-5 triangle.[49] The cord would have been divided into twelve intervals $(3 + 4 + 5 = 12)$ and then stretched around pegs (fig. 28). There is ample evidence of the use of the 3-4-5 triangle and other Pythagorean triplets in several ancient mathematical systems, often in clear connection with the use of cords. For instance, first millennium BC Indian texts describing ritual rules achieved by means of cords, in some cases based on Pythagorean triplets, were actually called *Sulbasutra*, that is, 'texts regulated by the cords'.[50]

The trace of elliptical vault in the tomb of Ramses VI, which has been examined in the previous chapter, seems to suggest that this method was also employed in Egypt. The vault is, however, a relatively small architectural element (and even in this case its irregularities are quite evident), and it is likely that, in order to trace right angles, other more accurate methods were adopted whenever a certain degree of precision was required and when long distances were involved.[51] The texts of the foundation ceremonies mention the 'stretching of the cord' in connection with the fixing of the corners, but this does not imply that the cords were the only

---

[47] Clemens of Alexandria, *Stromata* I, Fr. 68B 299 DK: Γραμμέων ξυνθέσιος μετὰ ἀποδέξιος οὐδείς κώ με παρήλλαξε, οὐδ' οἱ Αἰγυπτίων καλεόμενοι Ἀρπεδονάπται· σύν τοῖσδ' ἐπὶ πᾶσι ἐπ' ἔτεα πέντε ἐπὶ ξείνης ἐγενήθην.

[48] Solomon Gandz, 'Die Harpedonapten oder Seilspanner und Seilknüpfer', *Quellen und Studien zur Geschichte der Mathematik, Astronomie und Physik*, Part B, vol. 1 (1931), especially pp. 256–7.

[49] See Peet, *Rhind Mathematical Papyrus*, p. 32 and Gandz, *Quellen und Studien* 1, p. 257 for bibliographical references.

[50] Van der Waerden, *Geometry and Algebra*, pp. 15–25; Gericke, *Mathematik*, pp. 4–5, 33–4 and 67–8. See Gandz, *Quellen und Studien* 1, pp. 262–4 and 267–72 for references to the use of cords in the Bible.

[51] For suggestions on other methods, see Clarke and Engelbach, *Ancient Egyptian Masonry*, pp. 66–8; Mark Lehner, 'Some Observations on the Layout of the Khufu and Khafre Pyramids', *JARCE* 20 (1983), 7–25 and Arnold, *Building in Egypt*, pp. 14–5 and 252.

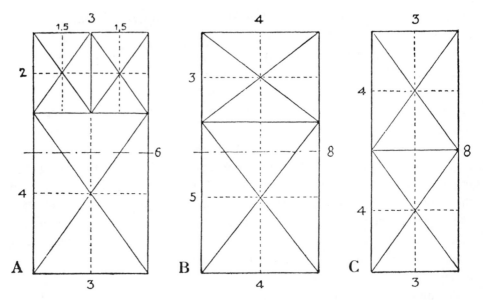

Fig. 77: Figures based on the 3-4-5 triangle according to Lauer (from *BIFAO* 77, fig. 1).

tool employed on this occasion. In fact, the texts describe a succession of ritual actions which are an abbreviated version of all the practical operations which were actually carried out by the architects. The king is represented as easily performing one action after the other, but very likely the inevitable time intervals between stages of construction and many other practical details were omitted from the narrative.[52]

Because of the possibility of constructing right angles, Jean-Philippe Lauer suggested that the Egyptians used the 3-4-5 triangle (to be precise, multiples of this triangle) to design the plans of a number of Old Kingdom buildings.[53] The Twentieth Dynasty elliptical vault seems to suggest that, at least in the New Kingdom, the Egyptians were aware of the possibility of constructing similar triangles (that is, larger or smaller but with the same proportions). However, in the cases when a multiple of the 3-4-5 triangle is supposed to be as large as 100 by 75 cubits, the Egyptians would have had to use long ropes (100 + 75 + 125 = 300 cubits, over 156 m), which, if they were made, as it seems, of vegetal fibres, would have provided a meagre result in terms of precision.

As a starting point, Lauer suggested two possible ways of constructing a double square by means of 3-4-5 triangles (fig. 77), but, as we have already seen in the case

---

[52] Weinstein, 'Foundation Deposits', p. 7.
[53] Jean-Philippe Lauer, 'Le Triangle Sacré dans les plans des monuments de l'Ancient Empire', *BIFAO* 77 (1977), 55–78; see also Audran Labrousse, Jean-Philippe Lauer, Jean Leclant, *Le Temple Haut du complexe funéraire du roi Ounas*, BdE 53, Cairo: IFAO, 1977.

of other geometrical constructions, there is no reason to assume that double squares were necessarily designed by means of this system. Some of Lauer's drawings are as complicated as Badawy's and share the same faults. Arnold, for example, noted that the temple of Qasr el-Sagha is half a cubit too deep to fit the 3-4-5 triangle.[54] Those reproduced in figure 78 are certainly simpler but, for example, the subdivision of 100 cubits into 75 and 25 (respectively $\frac{3}{4}$ and $\frac{1}{4}$ of 100) is not necessarily related to the use of 3-4-5 triangles.

The three Sixth Dynasty funerary temples of Teti, Pepi I and Pepi II are the most impressive examples discussed by Lauer. According to Lauer, small dimensional variations (such as the thickness of the walls of the rear magazines in the temple of Pepi I) were introduced in the construction of the three otherwise identical temples in order to adjust the plan to the 3-4-5 triangle (fig. 79). The fact that this triangle appears to have been employed in the design of the three pyramids corresponding to these temples (see Part III) seems to add weight to Lauer's theory. On the other hand, the temples also appear to have been largely reconstructed, and from the drawings it is unclear whether some key points were part of the original construction or were reconstructed using the proportions of the 3-4-5 triangle. Moreover, Lauer's drawings produce a certain impression because they are removed from their context: the plans apparently designed in accordance with the 3-4-5 triangle are, in fact, just a section of the whole temples. In general, the idea that parts of the funerary complexes were designed according to the proportions of the triangle used for the pyramid is not illogical, but more evidence is necessary to support this suggestion.

In conclusion, cords were certainly used to lay down the plan of a building on the ground, but not necessarily to establish its proportions. For the moment, the connection between 3-4-5 triangles and cords in ancient Egypt seems to remain restricted to the small-scale example of the Twentieth Dynasty elliptical vault. If the 3-4-5 triangle was really used to a larger scale, it is more likely to have been employed as a symbolic figure, rather then as an imprecise large-scale device to fix right-angled triangles. Throughout history, from the Old Kingdom to the Late Period, precision and accuracy have always been important characteristics of the ancient Egyptian architects, who planned and built perfect joints between stone blocks. The final achievement of this ancient tradition is represented by the Ptolemaic temples, where symbolism, aesthetics and technical ability combined in a stunning result. On their walls were carved the so-called Building Texts, which describe the mythical origin and the construction of these temples. These texts will be the last source we will examine.

---

[54] Arnold and Arnold, *Qasr el-Sagha*, p. 17.

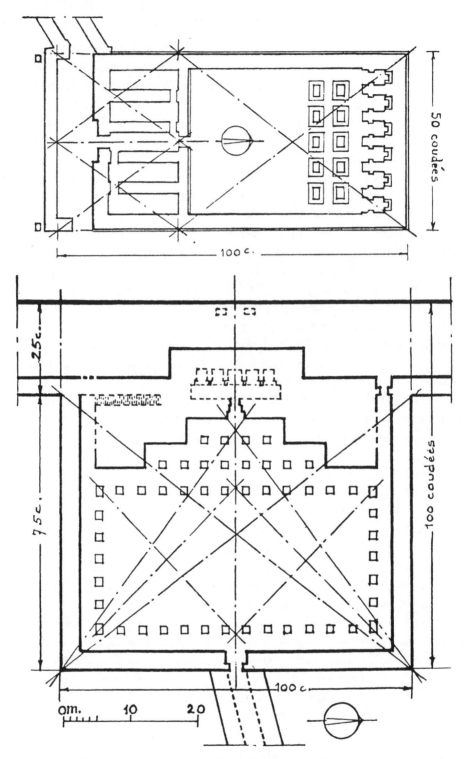

Fig. 78: 3-4-5 triangle in the plans of the valley temple of Snefru at Dashur and of the funerary temple of Khufu (Fourth Dynasty), according to Lauer (from *BIFAO* 77, figs. 4 and 5).

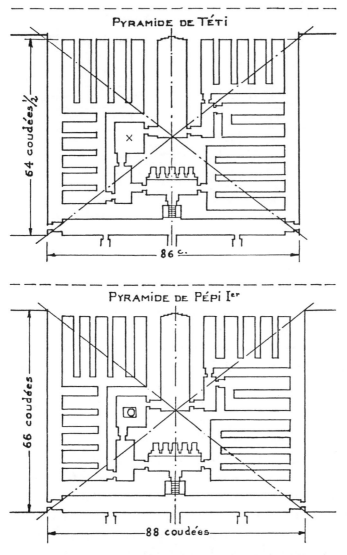

Fig. 79: 3-4-5 triangle in the plan of the funerary temples of Teti, Pepi I and Pepi II (Sixth Dynasty), at Saqqara according to Lauer (from *BIFAO* 77, fig. 13).

Building Texts

The dimensions of the primeval temples

We possess a unique source to study the way the temples built by the Ptolemies in the last three centuries BC were planned: the so-called Building Texts. Engraved on the walls of some temples, they contain numerous references to mythical primeval

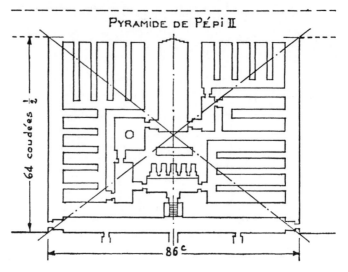

Fig. 79: (*cont.*)

temples and to the construction of the actual sanctuaries. The longest version of these texts survives in the temple of Edfu.[55]

The Ptolemaic temple and the supposed original sanctuaries dedicated to the Falcon and the Sun are described together with their detailed dimensions. Eve Reymond summarised the information we possess about the primeval temples into eight schemes,[56] one of which is reproduced in figure 80. These drawings are not proper plans, but they are nevertheless useful in giving an idea of numbers and forms which were supposedly involved in the design of these temples. The texts seem to describe stages of the progressive enlargement of a Temple of the Falcon and a Solar Temple. They never mention bricks or stone, but often refer to the use of reeds,[57] one of the main building materials of early architecture. In fact, Reymond has pointed out that the outline of the primeval Temple of the Falcon, as described by the texts, shows a certain similarity to the representations of sacred enclosures from the Predynastic to the Early Dynastic Periods.[58]

In the Ptolemaic Period many temples were re-built above pre-existing temples, but it is not easy to reconstruct the appearance of these earlier sanctuaries. At

---

[55] In general, see Eve A. E. Reymond, *The Mythical Origin of the Egyptian Temple*, Manchester: Manchester University Press, 1969, p. 1, note 1 and chapter 4. For Edfu, see Heinrich Brugsch, 'Bau und Maße des Tempels von Edfu', *ZÄS* 8 (1870), 153–61; 9 (1871), 32–45 and 137–44; 10 (1872), 1–16 and 'Eine neue Bauurkunde des Tempels von Edfu', *ZÄS* 13 (1875), 113–23; de Wit Constantin, 'Inscriptions dédicatoires du Temple d'Edfou', *CdE* 36 (1961), 56–97 and 277–320. For Dendera, see Johannes Dümichen, 'Bauurkunde der Tempelanlagen von Edfu', *ZÄS* 8 (1870), 1–13; 9 (1871), 25–32, 88–98, 105–12; 10 (1872), 33–42; 11 (1873), 109–19. For Philae, see Heinrich Brugsch, 'Bautexte und Inschriften', *Thesaurus Inscriptionum Aegypticarum*, vol. VI, Leipzig: Hinrichs, 1891, pp. 1235–406.

[56] Reymond, *Mythical Origin*, figs. 4–11.   [57] Reymond, *Mythical Origin*, pp. 225 and 230.

[58] Reymond, *Mythical Origin*, pp. 217–8 and fig. 3. See also W. M. Flinders Petrie, *The Royal Tombs of the Earliest Dynasties*, Part II, London: EEF, 1901, plates 3A (no. 5) and 10 (no. 2) and Badawy, *Dessin architecturale*, pp. 10–16.

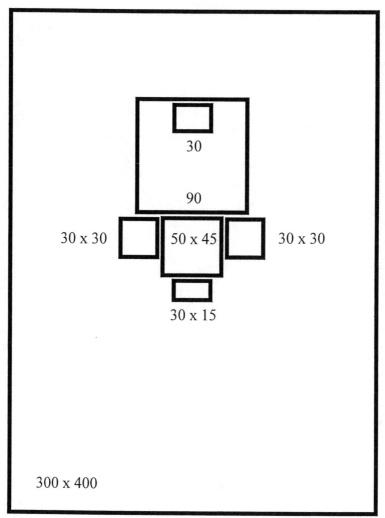

Unit of measurement: cubit

Fig. 80: Final stage of the Primeval Temple of the Falcon according to the Edfu texts (drawn after Reymond, *Mythical origin*, fig. 6).

Edfu, for instance, in order to make room for the large Ptolemaic temple, the New Kingdom stone temple was completely demolished, apart from one of its pylons, which was retained and used as a secondary entrance to the first courtyard.[59] All we know is that the New Kingdom temple was laid at 90° with respect to the Ptolemaic temple, that it must have been much smaller, and that it was probably surrounded by an enclosure wall.[60] In the temple of Satet at Elephantine, where it

---

[59] Alexandre Barsanti, 'Rapport sur la découverte à Edfou des ruines d'un temple Ramesside', *ASAE* 8 (1908), 233–6; Louis A. Christophe, 'Le pylone "Ramesside" d'Edfou', *ASAE* 55 (1958), 1–23.
[60] The surviving pylon, slightly asymmetrical, does not show any trace of orthogonal walls joining its internal side, thus suggesting that it was part of an enclosure wall that surrounded an inner sanctuary.

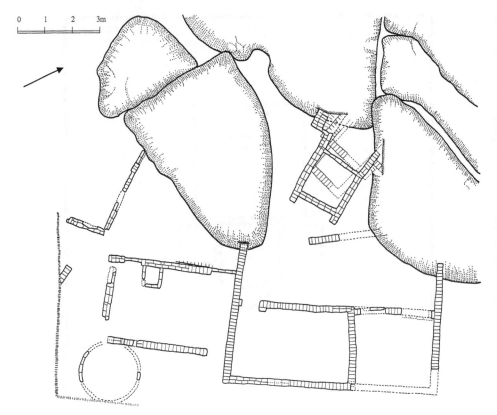

0   1   2   3m

Fig. 81: Predynastic temple of Satet at Elephantine (drawn after Dreyer, *Elephantine VIII*, fig. 1).

was possible to study the stratification from the Ptolemaic Period down to the level of the Predynastic Period, the remains of the early mudbrick temple are smaller and less regular than the early enclosures described by the Edfu texts (fig. 81). In this case the link with the past was not just theoretical, because a deep shaft connected the Eighteenth Dynasty temple with the Old Kingdom level.[61] Another example is provided by the unique remains of the predynastic ceremonial centre at Hierakonpolis, which consist of an earlier complex of wood and mat structures to which mudbrick walls and other elements were gradually added[62] (fig. 82). Even if

---

[61] Cf. Günter Dreyer, *Elephantine VIII, Der Temple der Satet. Die Funde der Frühzeit und des Alten Reiches*, AV 39, Mainz: Von Zabern, 1986, figs. 1–5 and plates 1–4.

[62] Renée Friedman, 'The Ceremonial Centre at Hierakonpolis Locality HK29A', in Jeffrey Spencer (ed.), *Aspects of Early Egypt*, London: British Museum Press, 1996, pp. 16–35; for a colour photograph and a computer reconstruction, see Vivian Davies and Renée Friedman, *Egypt*, London: British Museum, 1998, pp. 26–7. Hoffmann suggested a possible reconstruction of the temple in 1987, but since then excavations brought to light other features (cf. figs. 11a and 11b in Friedman, in Spencer (ed.), *Aspects of Early Egypt*). The plan of the site reprinted in figure 82 is based on the data collected before 1996. In 2002 the Hierakonpolis Expedition, under the direction of Dr Renée Friedman, resumed the excavation of the temple site and further changes and additions to both the plan and the reconstruction are likely to be suggested by the excavators in the near future.

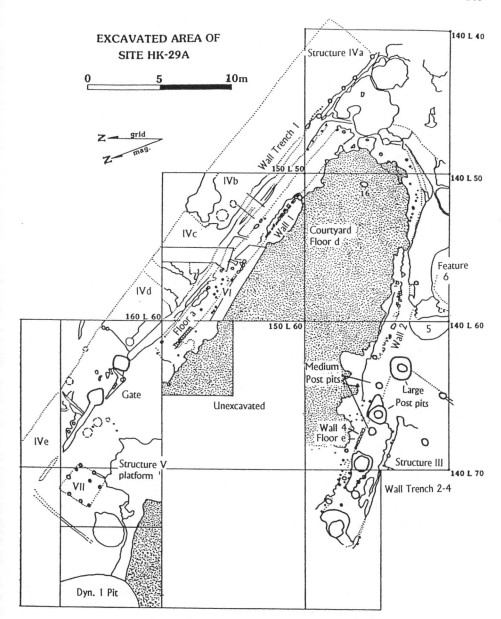

Fig. 82: Plan of the Predynastic ceremonial centre at Hierakonpolis, named HK29A, according to the data collected before 1996 (from Friedman, in Spencer (ed.), *Aspects of Early Egypt*, fig. 2).

this complex appears to be larger than the Elephantine sanctuary, it has very little in common with the data provided by the Edfu texts.

In general, the enclosures described by the Building Texts appear to be more 'Ptolemaic', in terms of size and regular shape, than 'Predynastic'. Although the Edfu texts repeated refer to the Ptolemaic temple as having being laid out following what was written in the ancient texts, this might be simply explained by the desire to highlight their continuity with the past.[63] In general, the fact that some dimensions of the final stage of the Solar Temple can be also found at Edfu[64] may be interpreted in two ways. Either this temple was built using 'numbers' taken from a textual tradition (the origin of which is, however, difficult to establish), or the theoretical dimensions of the primeval temple were purposely taken from the already planned dimensions of the Ptolemaic temple, in order to create a suitable ancestor for the latter.

The measures given by the texts for all the stages of the two primeval temples are very simple: always whole numbers of cubits, mainly multiples of 10, with the exception of a few measures containing its half, the number 5. When the enclosures are not square, no recurrent ratio can be detected between long and short sides. The dimensions of these schematic plans show the same characteristics of those encountered in the study of architectural drawings containing projects: simple dimensions, which seem to be composed by accretion, following no other overall geometrical rule than the alignment along the central axis. If these dimensions really come from an ancient tradition, it does not seem that they had been based on a complicated geometrical design. If, instead, they were attributed to the ancient temples by the Egyptian priests, it does not seem that there was any attempt to associate the ancient architects with pyrotechnic geometrical patterns. This is an important point, because it suggests that the tradition (real or made up) only provided examples of a very linear and simple design. This is especially interesting because the dimensions of the actual Ptolemaic temples, on the other hand, appear to be the result of rather complicated calculations.

The dimensions of the temples at Edfu and Dendera

Parts of the texts engraved on the walls of the temple of Edfu (started by Ptolemy III in 237 BC and completed by Ptolemy VIII Euergetes II in 142 BC[65]) and Dendera (started under Ptolemy XII Auletes in 54 BC and completed in 20 BC[66]) contain a

---

[63] References to the conformity of the temple to the ancient tradition are contained in *Edfu* IV 4.8, VII 3.4, 6.2, 12.2, 18.9–10 (de Wit, *CdE* 36, pp. 92, 282, 287, 301–2, 316).

[64] Reymond, *Mythical Origin*, pp. 318–9.

[65] For the history of the Edfu temple, see Dieter Arnold, *Temples of the Last Pharaohs*, New York/Oxford: Oxford University Press, 1999, pp. 169–71, 198–202 and 209, and fig. 170.

[66] For the history of the Dendera temple, see Arnold, *Temples of the Last Pharaohs*, pp. 212–6 and plan VI.

description of their various chambers together with their dimensions. In both cases, the rooms are described starting from the central chapel at the back of the sanctuary and then following the order indicated by the progressive numbers in figure 83. For each room, the texts give length and breadth in cubits and fractions of cubit (table 7; the horizontal subdivisions correspond to groups of chambers).[67] In the texts the chambers are not numbered, but are described using their names.

As in the sketch of a column in the Ptolemaic temple of Philae and the sketch of a Hathor-headed capital at Gebel Abu Foda, the fractions of the cubit are not expressed in palms and fingers. At Edfu all of the fractions belong to the series $\frac{2}{3}$, $\frac{1}{3}$, $\frac{1}{6}$, where each term is half the preceding one. At Dendera, the fractions involved are more complicated and do not appear to belong to a single series. Curiously enough, these rather complicated numbers have failed to appeal to the imagination of the numerologists, who, to my knowledge, have never attempted an explanation.

The recurrent mentions of 'perfect' and 'exactly calculated' dimensions in the Building Texts convinced Daumas and Badawy that these temples were laid out by means of a set of precise mathematical rules.[68] Descriptions of the temples or of some of their parts, vaguely stating that they are 'perfect', 'exact', 'beautiful' or 'excellent', can be found scattered throughout the Building Texts.[69] Bearing in mind that it is unlikely that a temple would ever be described as 'imperfect' or 'inexact' or by means of any other reductive expression, at the same time it appears clear that complicated calculations must have been performed to establish the dimensions of the various architectural elements of these temples.

About the temple of Edfu, we are told that 'its length is perfect, its height is exact, its perimeter is exactly calculated, all its cubits are close to excellence. Exact-of-cubits is said to be its name. Its foundations, moreover, are where they should be, as the ancestors did for the first time'.[70] This passage and other similar texts do not say much about the nature of the mathematical rules adopted to establish the plan. However, there are two texts from the Mammisi at Dendera (built, over an original core by Nectanebo I, under Ptolemy VI, X and XI and then Augustus), which seems to suggest the existence of a special relationship between the length

---

[67] The data for Edfu are taken from Sylvie Cauville and Didier Devauchelle, 'Les mesures réelles du temple d'Edfou', *BIFAO* 84 (1984), 23–34, those for Dendera from Sylvie Cauville, 'Les inscriptions dédicatoires du temple d'Hathor à Dendera', *BIFAO* 90 (1990), 83–114.

[68] François Daumas, *Les mammisis des temples égyptiens,* Annales de l'Université de Lyon 3/32, Paris, 1958, p. 366; Badawy, *Ancient Egyptian Architectural Design*, pp. 6–13.

[69] See, for example, *Edfu* IV 4.7–8; VII 2.6, 2.9, 6.5, 8.7–8, 10.12, 11.8–9, 12.1–2, 13.1, 17.9 and 19.6 (de Wit, *CdE* 36, pp. 64–5, 280, 288, 298, 300–2, 313, 315 and 317); Daumas, *Mammisis des temples égyptiens*, pp. 342–3 and Emile Chassinat, *Le Mammisi d'Edfou*, MIFAO 16, Cairo: IFAO, 1939, p. 6, translated by Daumas, *Mammisis des temples égyptiens*, p. 292.

[70] *Edfu* IV 4.7–8, translated into French by De Wit, *CdE* 36, pp. 64–5. Revised English translation on the basis of Penelope Wilson, *A Ptolemaic Lexikon*, OLA 78, Leuven: Uitgeverij Peeters en Department Oosterse Studies, 1997.

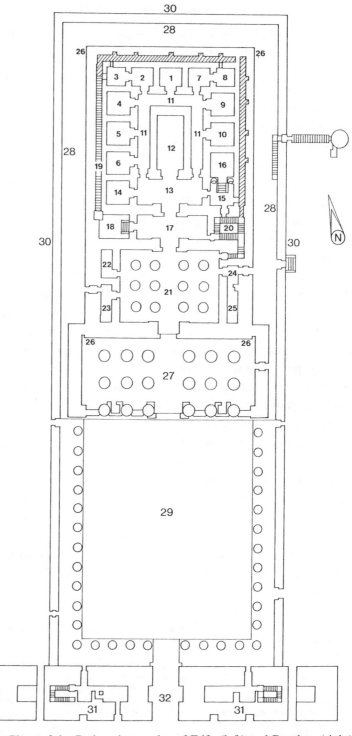

Fig. 83: Plans of the Ptolemaic temples of Edfu (left) and Dendera (right) with numbering of the rooms (respectively from Cauville and Devauchelle, *BIFAO* 84, fig. 4, and from from Cauville, *BIFAO* 90, fig. 1).

SYLVIE CAUVILLE

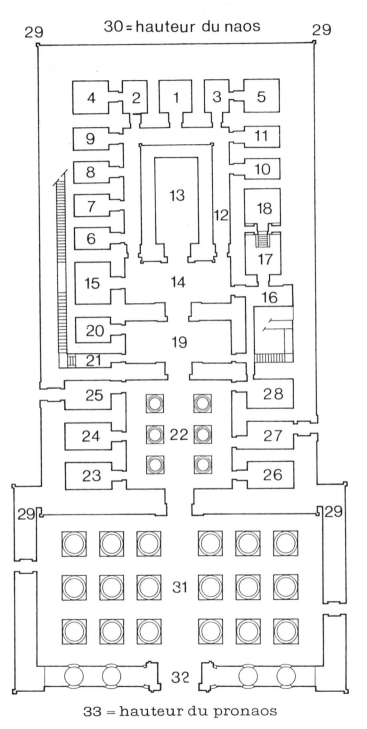

Fig. 83: (*cont.*)

Architecture and Mathematics in Ancient Egypt

Table 7. *The dimensions of some chambers of the Ptolemaic temples of Edfu and Dendera according to the Building Texts*

	Edfu			Dendera	
	Dimensions (in cubits)			Dimensions (in cubits)	
N° chamber	east/west	north/south	N° chamber	east/west	north/south
1	8 + 1/3	6 + 2/3	1	8	8
2	7 + 1/6 + 2/3	6 + 2/3	2	6	8
7	7 + 1/6 + 2/3	6 + 2/3	3	6	8
3	6 + 2/3	6 + 2/3	4	8 + 1/2 + 1/10	8
8	6 + 2/3	6 + 2/3	5	8 + 1/2 + 1/10	8
4	8	8	6	8 + 1/2 + 1/10	5 + 1/4 + 1/24
5	8	8	7	8 + 1/2 + 1/10	5 + 1/4 + 1/24
6	8	8	8	8 + 1/2 + 1/10	5 + 1/4 + 1/24
14	8	8	9	8 + 1/2 + 1/10	5 + 1/4 + 1/24
			15	8 + 1/2 + 1/10	10
9	8	8	10	8 + 1/2 + 1/10	5
10	8	8	11	8 + 1/2 + 1/10	5
15	8	8	16	8 + 1/2 + 1/10	5
16	8	8	17	8 + 1/2 + 1/10	10
			18	8 + 1/2 + 1/10	8 + 1/6
11	3 + 1/3 + 2/3		12	4 + 1/6	28 + 1/2
12	10 + 1/3	19 + 1/6 + 2/3	13	10 + 1/2	21 + 1/2
13	23 + 2/3	9	14	26	10
17	25 + 1/6 + 2/3	8	19	26	10
18	10	9	20	8 + 1/2 + 1/10	6
19	(lacuna)		21	12 + 1/2 + 1/10	3 + 1/3
20	10	8 + 1/2			
21	37 + 1/6 + 2/3	25 + 1/6 + 2/3	22	26	26
22	4	10	23	11 + 1/3	6 + 1/2
23	4	13	24	11 + 1/3	6 + 1/2
24	4	7	25	11 + 1/3	6 + 1/2
25	4	11	26	11 + 1/3	6 + 1/2
			27	11 + 1/3	6 + 1/2
			28	11 + 1/3	6 + 1/2
26	63	105	29	67 + 1/5	112
27	75	36	31	81 + 2/3	48 + 1/2
28	90	113			
29	80	90			
30	90	240			
31	120	21			
32	26 + 2/3		32	15	

and the breadth of the temple. One states that 'the length is perfect, the breadth is according to the need, the depth and the thickness are exactly calculated',[71] and the second says that 'its length is exact, its breadth is according to the spell'.[72] The second is especially interesting because of the presence of the word here rendered as 'spell' (*ꜣis*), translated as 'sentence' by Daumas, and as 'formula' by a confident Badawy.[73] The latter thought he had found a justification for the use of triangles, which may, in fact, describe the length and breadth of spaces by means of their bases and heights. In his reconstructions, however, a triangle never describe the outline of a whole temple, and Badawy does not seem to have taken into account the most obvious possibility: that the actual length and breadth of the whole rectangular outline of the temples may be related to one another.

At Edfu and Dendera, a significant correspondence can be found in the proportions of the central blocks, those started respectively by Ptolemy III and Ptolemy XII. The majority of the dimensions given by the texts refer to the internal outline of the various chambers, measured at ground level.[74] For the rectangular outlines of the sanctuaries (indicated by the numbers 26 for Edfu and 29 for Dendera), instead, the external dimensions are given: 105×63 cubits for Edfu and $112 \times 67 + \frac{1}{5}$ cubits for Dendera. By means of a simple calculation, it can be ascertained that, although the dimensions are different, in both cases the ratio between the short and the long side is the same. The short side appears to have been derived by calculating $\frac{1}{2} + \frac{1}{10}$ of the long side: at Edfu $105 \times (\frac{1}{2} + \frac{1}{10}) = 63$, and at Dendera $112 \times (\frac{1}{2} + \frac{1}{10}) = 67 + \frac{1}{5}$. If, instead, the short side was established first, the long side would have been derived by multiplying the short side by $1 + \frac{2}{3}$, reciprocal of $\frac{1}{2} + \frac{1}{10}$. Therefore, either the numbers 105 and 112, or the pair 63 and $67 + \frac{1}{5}$, seem to have been the initial values chosen for these two temples. Their origin, however, is obscure: whether these numbers had a symbolic meaning, or whether they were derived from the pre-existing temples, remains, for the moment, uncertain. At any rate, it is tempting to imagine that these were the dimensions fixed on the ground in the foundation ceremonies.

It is difficult to find other mathematical connections, because the Building Texts do not provide, for instance, the thickness of the walls, which must have played an important role in the calculation of all the other dimensions.[75] Luckily the Dendera temple has been carefully surveyed by the architect Pierre Zignani, whose excellent work has highlighted the extreme precision of the ancient builders in many aspects

---

[71] Frieze, southern side, in François Daumas, *Le mammisis de Dendara*, Cairo: IFAO, 1959, p. 100, translated into French by Daumas, *Mammisis des temples égyptiens*, p. 360. Translation into English on the basis of Wilson, *Ptolemaic Lexikon*.

[72] Frieze, northern side, in Daumas, *Mammisis de Dendara*, p. 100, translated into French by Daumas, *Mammisis des temples égyptiens*, p. 362. Translation into English on the basis of Wilson, *Ptolemaic Lexikon*.

[73] Badawy, *Ancient Egyptian Architectural Design*, p. 9.   [74] Cauville and Devauchelle, *BIFAO* 84, 34.

[75] Cauville and Devauchelle reconstructed the two different thicknesses of the walls around the central sanctuary in *BIFAO* 84, 27–8 and fig. 3.

of the construction.[76] On the basis of this survey it will be possible to compare the ancient texts and the actual monument, and to try to reconstruct the planning process that generated those complicated dimensions, at least in the case of the Dendera temple.

Without a similarly detailed survey, it will be difficult to proceed with such research for the other temples. At Kom Ombo, the equivalent of the central nuclei of Edfu and Dendera (the portion of the temple built under Ptolemy VI–VIII[77]) might have been planned on the basis of the same ratio between length and breadth that is found at Edfu and Dendera (breadth equal to $\frac{1}{2} + \frac{1}{10}$ of the length or, vice versa, length equal to $1 + \frac{2}{3}$ of the breadth). Instead, the main sanctuaries at Philae (the part built by Nectanebo II and Ptolemy II) and at Kalabsha (built under the Roman emperor Augustus) were built according to different proportions. Only Dendera and Kalabsha have been so far surveyed in a detailed way, and more work is necessary before any conclusions can be drawn.

Even if, for the moment, the planning process cannot be reconstructed, it is clear that at least the Edfu and Dendera temples (but there is no reason not to extend the discussion to other Ptolemaic temples) were built on the basis of extremely detailed projects, supported by complicated calculations, traces of which remain in the dimensions included in the Building Texts. During the Ptolemaic rule, even if the function of the king was always officially acknowledged, the foundation, construction, decoration and maintenance of the temples was largely left in the hands of the local priests.[78] Therefore, in this period it is particularly difficult to draw a line between Egyptian tradition and foreign influences.

The Greek-speaking Ptolemies were the successors of Ptolemy, general of Alexander the Great, who managed to keep Egypt for himself after the collapse of the large empire conquered by the Alexander in his thirteen years of reign. The cultural scene in the Mediterranean had changed considerably since the pyramid age. After the collapse of the New Kingdom (eleventh century BC) and the confused Third Intermediate Period, Egypt had been invaded twice by the Persians, had been annexed to the empire of Alexander in 332 and then ruled by the Ptolemaic Dynasty of Macedonian origins. By the first century BC, however, the balance of the military power in the Mediterranean was rapidly shifting north-west in the direction of Rome. Eventually Egypt became part of the Roman empire in the year 30 BC, after the deaths of Antony and Cleopatra VII.

---

[76] Pierre Zignani, 'Espaces, lumières at composition architecturale au temple d'Hathor à Dendara. Résultats préliminaires', *BIFAO* 100 (2000), 47–77.

[77] For the history of the Kom Ombo temple, see Arnold, *Temples of the Last Pharaohs*, pp. 187–9, 220, 232–5, fig. 188 and plan XIII.

[78] Günther Hölbl, *A History of the Ptolemaic Empire*, London/New York: Routledge, 2001, chapter 3 and 9.

The changes that took place are significant, and even if the architecture built in Egypt in the last three centuries BC and then under the Romans is strictly related to the ancient tradition of the country, it cannot be excluded that foreign influences combined with the old traditions. For instance, as already mentioned, Friedrich Hinkel suggested that some of the contemporary Meroitic monuments, erected in the modern Sudan, were built using a module inspired by the Greek architecture. As for the Ptolemaic temples, an interesting detail is that the group of fractions $\frac{1}{2} + \frac{1}{10}$ (which can also be expressed as $\frac{3}{5}$) corresponds to a value of 0.6 which might be interpreted once more as an approximation of the Golden Section. The Edfu and Dendera temples were built when this proportion had already been codified in Greece and probably imported into Egypt (see Part I). Doubt remains, however, as to what degree this knowledge would have penetrated Egyptian culture and how receptive the Upper Egyptian priests, who were in charge of planning and building large the Egyptian-style temples commissioned by their Greek rulers, would have been.

From the plan to the building

The picture that appears at the end of this study of ancient Egyptian documents on the planning and building process shows that the ancient architects used a combination of drawings, models and written specifications to describe and create their buildings. None of these methods, alone, pretended to be exhaustive in the description of the actual building,[1] but each could provide partial information on the final result.

Where entire buildings were concerned, drawings had the function of describing the general arrangement and the overall proportions, whilst the precise dimensions were indicated by written specifications. The limited available surface on which architects could draw, moreover, prevented the drawings from being able to describe large buildings with a great degree of detail. Ostraca larger and heavier than a certain limit would have been uncomfortable to handle and, apart from a few exceptions, the average papyri were less than 50 cm high.[2]

The absence of scale drawings sweeps away any attempt to prove that complicated mathematical patterns were used in the project. That they were absent in the practice of construction, too, is suggested by the fact that the most successful and convincing analyses of the dimensions of ancient Egyptian monuments are those based on simple measurements. Some excellent examples of this are Dieter Arnold's studies on the temple of Mentuhotep at Deir el-Bahari[3] and of the pyramid complex of Amenemhat III at Dahshur.[4] Seemingly, the surviving projects of royal tombs suggest that the ancient architects started, if possible, from round measures.[5]

---

[1] Clarke and Engelbach, *Ancient Egyptian Masonry*, p. 48; Arnold, *Building in Egypt*, p. 7.
[2] Smith and Stewart, *JEA* 70, 55; Bridget Leach and John Tait, 'Papyrus', in Nicholson and Shaw (eds.), *Ancient Egyptian Materials and Technology*, p. 237; see also Coulton, *Greek Architects*, p. 53. In the case of the Gurob papyrus, the representation of a shrine on a square grid, there is clear evidence that the basic dimensions of the shrine were chosen in advance to fit the available papyrus surface and corresponded to simple values on the cubit rod (4 palms for the width, 6 for the depth and 8 for the height, that is, depth and height were respectively one and a half and twice the width). Only after this, the surface of the papyrus was then divided by means of a square grid, possibly based on a side-length of $\frac{1}{18}$ of the height from basement and frieze.
[3] Arnold, *Temple of Mentuhotep*, pp. 29–31.   [4] Arnold, *Amenemhet III.*, p. 63.
[5] See also Ludwig Borchardt, 'Das Grab des Menes', *ZÄS* 36, 87–105, especially 104–5.

In the case of free-standing buildings, the small discrepancies between theoretical numbers and actual dimensions can be ascribed to the intrinsic approximation in a stone construction. In other cases, such as in the rock-cut tombs, a significant difference between the planned measures and the final result might have been considered absolutely irrelevant. In general, for the presence in the dimensions of fractions of a cubit, it does not seem necessary to take into account complicated values such as $\sqrt{2}$, π or ϕ.

In relation to drawings, architectural models might have represented a later or contemporary step. The model of the funerary apartment of a pyramid found at Dahshur seems to pick up the trail where architectural drawings left off. After the general arrangement of the spaces was established by means of a few lines on ostracon or papyrus, one or more three-dimensional visualisations may have been prepared before the final calculations gave way to the beginning of the works. It may be concluded that it is likely that ancient Egyptian architects adopted a method similar to that of the Greek architects of the seventh and sixth century BC; that is, they built their buildings directly in three dimensions, with the support of written specifications, sketches and three-dimensional specimens.[6]

In other words, Ancient Egyptian architects probably shared with the Greek architects what Jim Coulton referred to as the incomplete preliminary planning: whilst the overall dimensions and general disposition of fourth-century Greek temples were established before the work was started, a number of details were left to be decided at a later stage at full scale. This also explains the various attempts to solve the problem of the angle contraction in the Doric order – that is, how to combine the length of the alternating metopes and triglyphs with the intercolumniation in order to have a triglyph, and not a metope, next to the angle. The various solutions adopted by the architects suggest that in many cases they were worked out when the building had reached that stage, and not earlier.[7]

Greek architects probably did not adopt a modular system before the late Hellenistic period, whereas earlier architects might have used a method similar to that described by Vitruvius for the Ionic order. In his *De Architectura*, the Doric order appears to be based on a fixed common module, while in the Ionic order the various elements are derived from one another and form a sort of chain, where the ratios between widely separated parts may be difficult to calculate.[8] As Coulton

---

[6] See, for instance, the famous Arsenal inscription, dating around 330 BC, which acted as a written project for the arsenal to be built in the Pireus (Jens A. Bundgaard, *Mnesicles, a Greek Architect at Work*, Oslo: Scandinavian University Books, 1957, pp. 117–32, especially p. 123).

[7] Coulton, *Greek Architects*, pp. 60–64; by the same author, 'Incomplete Preliminary Planning in Greek Architecture: Some New Evidence', in Jean-François Bommelaer (ed.), *Le dessin d'architecture dans le sociétés antiques*, Strasburg: Université des Sciences Humaines de Strasbourg, 1985, pp. 103–21; see also Vitruvius, *Ten Books on Architecture*, fig. 62.

[8] Vitruvius, *Ten Books on Architecture*, III.5 and IV.3.

concluded, 'Vitruvius' rules for the Ionic order are arranged so that the colonnade could be designed as the building went up'.[9]

The temples built in Egypt under the Ptolemies might have been affected by the significant cultural changes that were taking place in the Mediterranean basin during the Hellenistic period.[10] A closer comparison between Greek and Egyptian architecture is likely to yield more interesting results, but it is essential, first of all, to carry out detailed surveys of other Ptolemaic temples. The lack of reliable surveys is, in general, the greatest obstacle for a research on proportions in architecture, especially when the complexity of a monument such as a temple (not only Ptolemaic) cannot be satisfactorily represented by a two-dimensional plan. There is, however, one group of monuments, relatively well-surveyed in their apparent simplicity, which allow a study of their geometry from the beginning to the end of their history. They are the pyramids.

[9] Coulton, *Greek Architects*, p. 66.
[10] For the Roman architecture and architectural design see Mark Wilson Jones, *Principles of Roman Architecture*, New Haven and London: Yale University Press, 2000.

Part III

The geometry of pyramids

Combining the knowledge

Compared to a temple, a pyramid is certainly simpler from a geometrical point of view. It consists of a square base and four triangular faces, and can be measured by means of a few parameters, such as side-length of the base, height of the face, height of the pyramid, slope of the face and slope of the corner. However, this geometrical simplicity does not necessarily imply that in practice measuring a pyramid is always easy, nor does it prevent theoretical reasoning from being marred by confusion and mistakes.

Besides their simple geometry, another important element is the fact that, unlike other monuments, some of the ancient mathematical sources provide first-hand evidence about the calculations involved in the planning process. Many obscure points still remain to be clarified, but at least we possess some basic information such as, for instance, the way the ancient architects measured the slope of a pyramid.

Another important point is that pyramids have been relatively well-studied, at least those built during the Old and the Middle Kingdoms. Even if materials and building techniques changed over the years, these monuments form a homogeneous group which can be studied as a whole. At the end of the Middle Kingdom there was a significant break in the history of pyramids, and their construction was resumed after two centuries on a completely different basis. Not many New Kingdom pyramids have survived, and in general our knowledge of these monuments is scant and fragmentary. The later Meroitic pyramids belong to yet another group, clearly inspired by the small New Kingdom pyramids rather than by the large Old Kingdom funerary monuments. But the Old and Middle Kingdom pyramids together form a large and consistent group of buildings which allow the reconstruction of the evolution of their constructional problems and building techniques.

For all these reasons, Old and Middle Kingdom pyramids provide a good chance to try to reconstruct the mathematical background of a group of monuments. By combining all the information we possess on their history and on the ancient mathematics involved in their planning process with the picture that emerges from the more general study of the relationship between architecture and mathematics outlined in Part I and II, it is possible not only to clarify some important aspects of pyramid construction, but also to fill the gaps of our knowledge by means of suggestions that, even if difficult to prove with certainty, are at least compatible with ancient mathematics.

5

Symbolic shape and constructional problems

The form

Pyramidal form and solar cult

Although built in different dimensions, forms, and materials, and performing different functions, pyramids were constructed throughout the history of ancient Egyptian architecture. The monuments themselves, their chronological succession, and the symbolism and the constructional problems associated with them have been thoroughly studied by Reiner Stadelmann, Jean-Philippe Lauer, Dieter Arnold, Mark Lehner and Martin Isler, among others. It is also worth mentioning here the impressive amount of material collected on many Old Kingdom pyramids by Vito Maragioglio and Celeste Rinaldi, and the comprehensive report on the Old and Middle Kingdom secondary pyramids published by Peter Jánosi. Here, as an introduction to the subject, I will summarise the most important steps in the evolution of these monuments.

From the Old Kingdom until the beginning of the New Kingdom, pyramids were essentially royal symbols. Rectangular mud-brick mastabas were used as funerary monuments by kings and nobles of the early period at Saqqara and at Abydos. At least two kings of the Second Dynasty, Hetepsekhemwy and Ninetjer, build large underground complexes at Saqqara, where, at the beginning of the Third Dynasty, Djoser erected his innovative funerary complex. The large mastaba, originally intended to cover the pit of the burial chamber surrounded by an intricate set of underground galleries, was enlarged twice before a new expansion of the volume took place. The basically flat, almost two-dimensional rectangular tumulus was turned into a massive, three-dimensional stepped monument pointing to the sky. The first step pyramid was born.

Step pyramids were started by Sekhemkhet and Khaba(?), successors of Djoser, but both monuments remained unfinished.[1] The second-ever completed step pyramid was built at Meidum between the end of the Third and the beginning of the Fourth Dynasty, by Huni or his son Snefru. It had been originally conceived as a seven-step pyramid but was rapidly enlarged with the addition of an eighth step. Snefru then built two pyramids with smooth faces (the Bent Pyramid and the Red Pyramid at Dahshur), and by the end of his reign he also cased the Meidum Pyramid and turned it into another true pyramid.[2] From this point onwards, large true pyramids were built for almost every Old and Middle Kingdom king and for many of their queens, although other forms were probably adopted in some cases.[3] Pyramids were essentially funerary monuments, but there is also evidence of a number of small step pyramids, probably belonging to the Third Dynasty, scattered along the Nile. Their exact function is unclear, although it is generally assumed that they served as symbols of royal power.[4]

The Seventeenth Dynasty Theban kings were buried under small mud-brick pyramids at Dra Abu el-Naga. Buried among them was probably Ahmose, founder of the Eighteenth Dynasty, who also built another, larger pyramid acting as cenotaph at Abydos. After that, tombs were no longer marked by any pyramidal superstructure: the Theban mountain itself acted as a huge pyramid, and instead of building the superstructure, the Eighteenth, Nineteenth and Twentieth Dynasty kings just quarried their subterranean funerary apartments into it. Among the most famous of these are the beautifully decorated tomb of Seti I, the huge KV5, built for the sons of Ramses II, and, obviously, the tomb of Tutankhamun. After a break of about two centuries, pyramids re-appeared in funerary architecture. They lost their exclusive royal character and became the main feature of New Kingdom private tombs scattered all over Egypt, from Saqqara to Deir el-Medina, Soleb and Aniba in Lower Nubia, and, during the Twenty-sixth Dynasty, to Abydos. Pyramids were again adopted as royal burials by the Late Period Nubian kings, who built over 180 of these small monuments at el-Kurru, Nuri, Gebel Barkal and Meroe. When the Nubian kingdom collapsed, around AD 350, the history of Egyptian pyramids came to an end.

---

[1] Sekhemkhet chose Saqqara for his so-called 'Buried Pyramid', while Khaba(?) started the monument nicknamed 'Layer Pyramid' at Zawiyet el-Aryan. For the evolution of Djoser's complex, see Jean-Philippe Lauer, *La Pyramide à Degrés. L'Architecture*, Cairo: SAE, 1936.

[2] Rainer Stadelmann, 'Snofru und die Pyramiden von Meidum und Dahschur', *MDAIK* 36 (1980), 437–49.

[3] For their burials at Giza and South Saqqara, Khentkawes (one of the most important queens of the Fourth Dynasty) and later Shepseskaf (successor of Menkaura) chose a mastaba-like superstructure and there is no evidence that GIIIb and GIIIc (queens of Menkaura) at Giza, the pyramid of Neferirkara and the satellite of Neuserra, at Abusir, were ever cased. Jánosi suggested three possible reconstructions for GIIIb and GIIIc: four-step, two-step and bent pyramid (Jánosi, *Pyramidenanlagen*, pp. 86–7).

[4] Dreyer and Kaiser, *MDAIK* 36, 43–59.

Benben *and* benbenet

The sun was one of the principal elements of the ancient Egyptian religion, and was worshipped under various forms. In the ancient town of Heliopolis, the solar cult revolved around the sacred *benben* stone, whose form seems to represent the common origin of pyramids, obelisks and stelae. The stone itself has not survived, but it probably was an elongated, roughly pointed stone of an irregular shape. The stone was stylised in two ways: a pointed, pyramidal form, and a round-topped form. The first was the model for pyramids and obelisks, including the large obelisks of the Fifth Dynasty sun temples; the second can be found in stelae and replicas of the *benben* stone itself.[5]

The pyramidion of pyramids and obelisks bore the same name: *benbenet*, a feminine form of *benben*.[6] The origins and connections of the Egyptian word *benben* are not easy to trace. It has been suggested that there might be a common origin between the word *benben* and the verb *weben*, 'to shine',[7] and in fact Alan Gardiner translated *benben* as 'the radiant one'.[8] John Baines has analysed the connection between the two words and concluded that *benben* is more likely associated with the root *bn(n)*, sometimes also written *bl*.[9] The latter has a sexual meaning and is strictly connected with the theme of the creation of the primeval hill, which was in fact called *benenet*. The connection with the primeval hill also can be found in the tradition which considers the temple as the mound on which the sun rises or descends by itself or by means of a perch, a pole or an obelisk.[10] The *benben* stone was also associated with the heron, the Greek phoenix, called *benw*. A passage from the Pyramid Text shows these linguistic interconnections: 'O Atum-Kheprer, you became elevated on the height, you rose up (*weben*) as the *benben*-stone in the Mansion of the "Phoenix" (*benw*) in Heliopolis'.[11] In general, however, as Baines has pointed out, word-games are double-edged references, since they may link similar but originally unrelated words or things.

Even if the *weben* etymology is doubtful, the *benbenet* (the pyramidion of pyramids and obelisks) is connected, as a matter of fact, with the sun. There is ample

[5] Kemp, *Ancient Egypt*, fig. 30.

[6] Although the vast majority of pyramidia were capstones of pyramidal structures, some might have had simply a votive function (Agnes Rammant-Peeters, *Les pyramidions égyptiens du Nouvel Empire*, OLA 11, Leuven: Departement Oriëntalistiek, 1983, p. x). For the different capstones of Late Period Nubian pyramids, see Friederich W. Hinkel, 'Pyramide oder Pyramidenstumpf? (Teil C und D)', *ZÄS* 109 (1982), 127–47.

[7] Lacau suggested that the meaning of the verb *wbn* was the shining of the rising sun, in opposition to *ḥtp*, the setting sun, and *psd*, the sun at the zenith (Pierre Lacau, 'Les verbes *wbn*, "poindre" et *psd*, "culminer" ', *BIFAO* 69 (1971), 1–9).

[8] Alan Gardiner, *Egypt of the Pharaohs*, Oxford: Clarendon Press, 1961, p. 85.

[9] John Baines, '*Benben*: Mythological and Linguistic Notes', *Orientalia* 39 (1970), 390.

[10] Baines, *Orientalia* 39, 394. See also Alexandre Moret, *Le rituel du culte divin journalier*, Paris: Leroux, 1902, pp. 242–3.

[11] James B. Pritchard, *Ancient Near Eastern Texts*, Princeton: Princeton University Press, 1969, p. 3; Kemp, *Ancient Egypt*, p. 88.

evidence that the pyramidia of Middle and New Kingdom obelisks were often covered with gold, electrum or copper. The oldest of the large standing obelisks is one of a pair which was erected by Senusret I at Heliopolis. Several writers who visited Egypt in different periods described its pyramidion as covered with a cap of copper.[12] Likewise, the pyramidia of the pair of obelisks of Thutmosis I at Karnak were covered with electrum,[13] while in one of the two pairs of obelisks erected by Hatshepsut at Karnak, not only the pyramidion, but also the image of the sky above the head and the ground line under the feet of the eight couples of figures of Hatshepsut and Thutmosis III, carved in sunk relief, were probably inlaid with gold.[14]

As for the pyramidia of pyramids, a block from the causeway of Sahura bears a representation of a group of men dragging a pyramidion: the pyramidion itself is not visible in the scene, but the surviving inscription mentions a *benbenet* covered with gold.[15] A fragmentary text from the pyramid temple of Udjebten, queen of Pepi II, mentions a pyramidion covered with gold, but it is not clear whether it refers to the capstone of that pyramid or to another monument.[16] The pyramidion found at Abusir in the area of pyramids numbered by Lepsius as 24 and 25, possibly built for queens of Neuserra, seems to have been prepared to host a metal cap.[17] The surviving finished pyramidia of Middle Kingdom pyramids are made of dark stone, are inscribed and, in two cases, decorated with a solar motif. Of the pyramidion of Senusret II, the few surviving fragments bear traces of a text.[18] The pyramidia of Amenemhat III[19] and Khendjer[20] were covered by texts and decorated with scenes centred on the solar cult; the motif of the winged sun-disk was repeated on the top of their triangular faces. The decoration of the three surviving sides of the small pyramidion of Merneferra Ay is contained in small squares and shows the king presenting offerings to probably four different gods.[21] As for the later private small pyramids, decorations related to the solar cult can be found on the majority of New Kingdom pyramidia,[22] as well as on the Late Period pyramidia from Abydos.[23]

[12] Labib Habachi, *The Obelisks of Egypt*, London: Scribner's Son, 1977, pp. 47–8.

[13] Habachi, *Obelisks*, pp. 58–9.

[14] Pierre Lacau, 'L'or dans l'architecture égyptienne', *ASAE* 53 (1956), 221–50, especially 243–6.

[15] Zahi Hawass and Miroslav Verner, 'Newly Discovered Blocks from the Causeway of Sahure', *MDAIK* 52 (1996), 181 and fig. 1a.

[16] Gustave Jéquier, *La Pyramide d'Oudjebten*, Cairo: SAE, 1928, p. 18.

[17] Miroslav Verner, 'Excavations at Abusir. Season 1982 – Preliminary Report', *ZÄS* 111 (1984), 73 and 'Abusir Pyramids "Lepsius no. XXIV and no. XXV" ', in *Hommages à Jean Leclant*, vol. I, Cairo 1994, pp. 373–4 and figs. 3 and 4.

[18] W. M. Flinders Petrie, *Lahun II*, BSAE ERA 33, London: Quaritch, 1923, p. 4 and plate 24.

[19] Gaston Maspero, 'Sur le pyramidion d'Amenemhait III à Dachour', *ASAE* 3 (1902), 206–8; Heinrich Schäfer, 'Die Spitze der Pyramide Königs Amenemhat III', *ZÄS* 41 (1904), 84–5; Arnold, *Amenemhat III*, p. 14.

[20] Gustave Jéquier, *Deux Pyramides du Moyen Empire*, Cairo: SAE, 1933, pp. 19–26.

[21] Labib Habachi, 'Two Pyramidions of the XIIIth Dynasty from Ezbet Rushdi el-Kebira (Khata'na)', *ASAE* 52 (1954), 473–4.

[22] Rammant-Peeters, *Pyramidions égyptiens*, especially chapter 7.

[23] Herman J. de Meulenaere, 'Pyramidions d'Abydos', *JEOL* 20 (1967–68), especially 19–20.

Finally, nothing certain can be said about the pyramidia of the Fifth Dynasty sun temples, since the two complexes excavated so far were too damaged to provide any evidence. The ancient names of these temples are completed by a determinative sign in the shape of an obelisk resting on a pedestal, with a solar disk on the top of its pyramidion. This elegant hieroglyph suggests that the top of the obelisk was equipped to catch the sunlight.[24] Ludwig Borchardt, however, pointed out that there is no direct evidence that the pyramidion of the obelisk of Neuserra was covered with gold or another metal.[25]

As high as possible

Obelisks were usually erected in pairs at the entrance of temples and were dedicated to the rising and setting sun.[26] The shining of their golden points in the sunlight must have been spectacular and particularly evocative, because the sun was 'captured' on the top of the obelisks and so kept shining on the temple all day long. The *benbenet* of obelisks had therefore the precise function of acting as an intermediary link for the sun to descend from the sky to the earth. The *benbenet* of pyramids also seems to have been perceived as a point of contact between earth and sky, in both directions, since capstones of pyramids were the first and last points of the landscape to be illuminated by the sun and, at the same time, Pyramid Texts often refer to the pyramids as 'stairs' or 'ramps' for the dead king to reach the sky.[27]

Although there are many analogies between obelisks and pyramids, solar symbolism alone cannot explain the form of the pyramids. Other factors must be considered. The Step Pyramid of Saqqara and the creation of the true pyramid by Snefru represent two turning points, where new ideas were added to the existing forms. But even if the evolution of the pyramid form is visible (the various phases from mastaba to step pyramid can be seen in the north side of the Saqqara pyramid, and the Meidum pyramid displays the entire sequence of actions that turned it from a step into a true pyramid), its reasons cannot be fully explained.

In ancient Egypt it is especially difficult to make a distinction between the original idea and the symbolism which became attached to it and was consequently adopted. The first step pyramid, for instance, might be explained as a pile of superimposed mastabas[28] and/or a huge stair for the king to reach the sky. Seemingly, the first true pyramid might be interpreted as the form to which a step pyramid naturally

[24] Werner Kaiser, 'Zu den Sonnenheiligtümer der 5. Dynastie', *MDAIK* 14 (1956), 103–16.

[25] Friedrich W. von Bissing (ed.), *Das Re-Heiligtum des Königs Ne-woser-re*; Band I: Der Bau, Berlin: Duncker, 1905, p. 12.

[26] Habachi, *Obelisks*, p. 11; Lacau, *ASAE* 53, 242 and 246.

[27] Spells 365, 971, 975, 978, 980, 995, 1089, 1090.

[28] Ahmed Fakhry, *The Pyramids*, Chicago: University Press, 1961, p. 5.

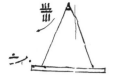 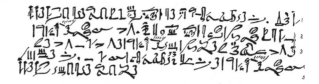

Fig. 84: RMP problem 57: the height of a pyramid is calculated from the base-length and the *seked* (slope), (from Chace, Bull and Manning, *Rhind Mathematical Papyrus*, pl. 79).

turned when covered by sand, and/or a huge ramp to reach the sky,[29] and/or a giant representation of the *benben* stone. Whatever explanation is chosen, the common point seems to be the aim to reach the sky.

True pyramids tried to reach the highest possible point. 'As high as possible' naturally implied 'as steep as possible', for at least two reasons. First of all, a steep slope allowed the architects to reach a high point with a relatively small amount of material. Second, a steeper pyramid seems higher that a flatter one. Reconciling stone and maximum height, however, was not an easy matter, as we shall see in the next chapters.

The technique

Seked, *side-length, diagonals and corners*

Concerning pyramids, our Middle Kingdom sources tell us how the Egyptians calculated the slope of an oblique face, which they called *seked*, from the base-length and the height (and vice-versa, see fig. 84), and the volume of a truncated pyramid (from which it may be inferred that they also calculated the volume of a complete pyramid).

The *seked* was the horizontal displacement of the sloping face for a vertical drop of one cubit, that is, the number of cubits, palms and fingers by which the sloping side had 'moved' from the vertical at the height of one cubit (fig. 85). This method, in fact, defines a right-angled triangle, where one of the two catheti is equal to one cubit and the other corresponds to the *seked* itself. This triangle is proportional to half the vertical section of the pyramid; that is, it is a small version (only one cubit high) of half the vertical section (see also fig. 89). Problems 56, 57, 58, 59 and 60 of the Rhind Mathematical Papyrus (RMP) contain calculations involving the *seked* of pyramids obtained by dividing half of the base by the height, that is, by finding the ratio between the two catheti of the triangle corresponding to half the vertical section of the pyramid. Four RMP problems refer to pyramids, the fifth possibly to a

---

[29] Fakhry, *Pyramids*, p. 8; Kurt Mendelsohn, *The Riddle of Pyramids*, London: Thames and Hudson, 1974, plate 24.

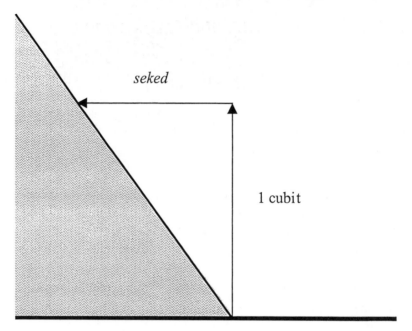

Fig. 85: *Seked* of a sloping face according to the Rhind Mathematical Papyrus.

pillar.[30] They are accompanied by rough sketches of small and steep pyramids, the first four resting on bases and topped by a dark pyramidion and showing a steeper slope than the *seked* provided by the corresponding problems.

It is interesting to note that all of the problems deal with the calculation of the *seked* of faces of pyramids and other sloping constructions, never of their corners. From a practical point of view, however, the corner must have played an important role, since its alignment was the only visible line which could be checked in order to avoid the pyramid rotating around its vertical axis during construction. At the centre of the top step of the Meidum pyramid, for example, there is a hole in the masonry which may be interpreted as a socket for a rod which would act as a visual reference during the construction of the uppermost section of the casing, when the four corners must meet the base of the pyramidion.[31]

Only two ancient 'plans' of pyramids survive: two sketches on ostraca, one dating to the New Kingdom and the other to the Late Period. The first, found at Soleb, represents the plan of two pyramids identified as the superstructures of the tombs numbered 14 and 15.[32] The second, sketched on a Meroitic jar, has been interpreted as the representation of a small pyramid resting over an underground oval burial,

---

[30] Since the *seked* given by this problem is 1/4, Badawy thought that this could refer to the slope of his harmonic triangle 1:4 (Badawy, *Ancient Egyptian Architectural Design*, pp. 57–8.

[31] Mark Lehner, *The Complete Pyramids*, London: Thames and Hudson, 1997, p. 100; Isler Martin, *Sticks, Stone and Shadows. Building the Egyptian Pyramid*, Norman: University of Oklahoma Press, 2001, pp. 210–1.

[32] Jean Leclant, 'Fouilles et travaux au Soudan, 1955–1960', *Orientalia* 31 (1962), 134, note 8 and fig. 3.

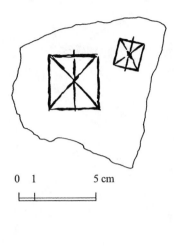

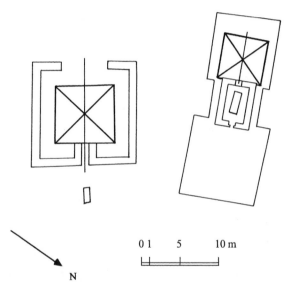

Fig. 86: New Kingdom ostracon from Soleb representing two pyramids and plan of pyramids 14 and 15 at Soleb (left, drawn after Leclant, *Orientalia* 31, fig. 3) and sketch of a pyramid on top of a tomb on a Meroitic jar (drawn after Bonnet, *Genava* 28, fig. 29).

in front of which an offering-table was placed (both in fig. 86).[33] In both cases, the two lines drawn across the plan may be interpreted as the two diagonals of the base or as the projection of the corners. In addition, the Soleb sketch also indicates the main axis of the monuments.

The diagonals of the base played an important role during the construction, but it was the side-length of the pyramid that was established first, as can be deduced by several observations. First of all, the side-length usually consists of a whole number

[33] Charles Bonnet, 'Les fouilles archéologiques de Kerma (Soudan)', *Genava* 28 (1980), 59.

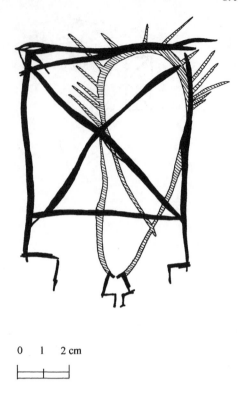

0   1   2 cm

Fig. 86: (*cont.*)

of cubits: if the first choice were the diagonal, the side-length would have seldom corresponded to a simple number. Second, whenever pyramids were built around and on an already existing rock core, this would have prevented the measurement of the diagonal in the initial phase of the construction (although, at a later stage, the diagonals themselves might have been used to check the regularity of the plan). Finally, the orientation of the faces of the pyramids towards the four cardinal points indicates that establishing the sides, and not the diagonals, was the initial act of the construction.

Methods for obtaining the slope

Around the corners of Mastaba 17 at Meidum, Petrie found a series of diagrams that seem to imply that the slope of the corner was a consequence of the slope of the faces.[34] Petrie found four L-shaped mud-brick walls which had been built beneath the ground level around the four corners of the mastaba and which acted as a guide to check its slope (fig. 87). The construction of the sloping walls of the mastaba

---

[34] Petrie, *Medum*, pp. 11–3 and pl. 8.

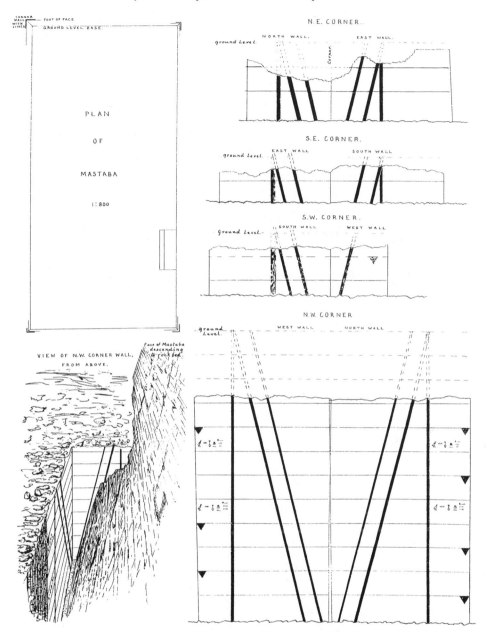

Fig. 87: Petrie's drawings of the diagrams at the four corners of Mastaba 17 (Third to Fourth Dynasty) at Meidum (from *Medum*, pl. 8).

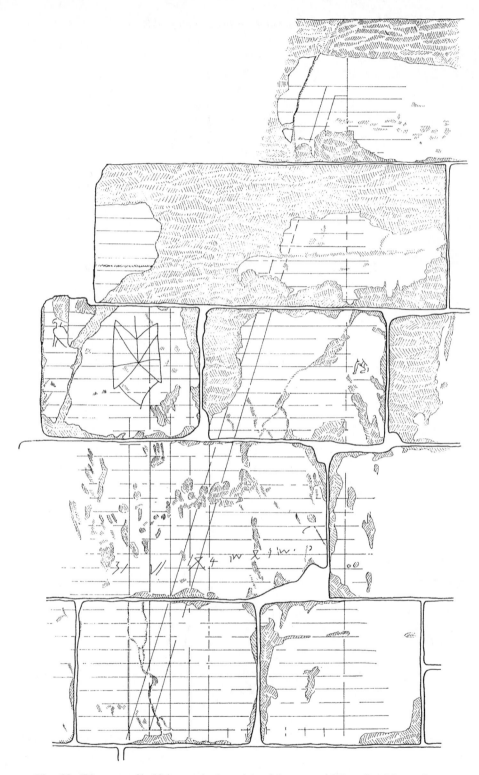

Fig. 88: Diagram of half the vertical section of the pyramid Beg. 8 at Meroe drawn on the wall of its chapel, left, and its reconstruction, right (from Hinkel, *ZÄS* 108, figs. 4 and 5).

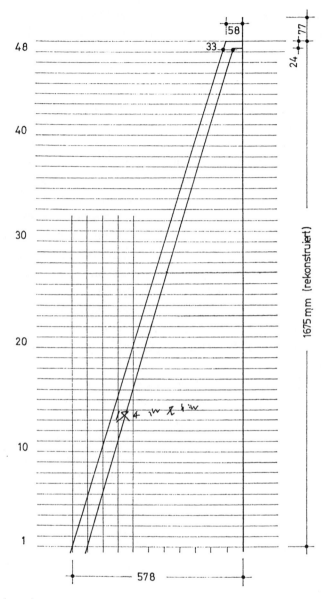

Fig. 88: (*cont.*)

began from the rock bed, which was not perfectly flat. For this reason, the architects fixed a zero-line, built the L-shaped walls and marked on them the projection of the dimension which the mastaba was intended to have at the ground level. From these points downwards, horizontal lines were drawn on the walls at the distance of one cubit to mark the depth of the rock bed. Two oblique black lines were traced to represent the projection on the walls of the underground sloping faces. At some point, two other lines were drawn parallel to the first pair, and the mastaba was enlarged by the short distance between them. In this way, regardless of the depth of the rock bed, the masons could start the construction of a sloping side which would reach the surface at the 'right' point; that is, the emerging construction would have had the established dimensions.[35] The slope of the sides was constructed by keeping the visual alignment with the line drawn on the wall. The slope of the corner, therefore, was merely the meeting point of the two sloping faces.

Mastaba 17 was built in one single stage and is contemporary with the large Third–Fourth Dynasty pyramid attributed, at least in its final phase, to Snefru.[36] The diagram found by Petrie is an exceptional document, since it is our only Old Kingdom source concerning the construction of sloping walls. There is only one other original source of this kind and it dates to twenty-one centuries after Mastaba 17: the diagram found on the north wall of the chapel of Pyramid 8 at Meroe.[37] It represents half of the vertical section of a pyramid, consisting of a vertical line, corresponding to the axis of the pyramid, a horizontal ground line and forty-eight horizontal lines drawn across the sketch at regular intervals, probably representing the horizontal masonry courses (fig. 88). The slope, about 72°, is very close to the slope of the face of other Meroitic pyramids. More than two thousand years divide Mastaba 17 of Meidum and Pyramid 8 of Meroe, but in both cases the slope of the face, not of the corner, is the starting point.

If, for some reason, it was necessary to express the *seked* of the corner in cubits and palms, this could have been easily calculated from the *seked* of the face. As we have seen before, the *seked* corresponds to one of the catheti of a right-angled triangle (which represents half the vertical section of the pyramid), the other cathetus being equal to one cubit. In a theoretical small-scale model of a pyramid which is one cubit high, half of its base would be equal to the *seked* of the face. As a consequence, half of its diagonal would be equal to the *seked* of the corner[38] (fig. 89).

Martin Isler suggested that pyramids were built in three stages: a stepped nucleus was erected first, then its steps were filled to achieve a smoother outline, and finally the casing was added and then smoothed moving from the top downwards.[39] The slope must have been decided in advance, but it was in the final stages of construction that precision really mattered. Helped probably by sighting stations, the workmen positioned the casing blocks row after row.

---

[35] It may be noted that, probably for symbolic reasons, the architects chose to start the sloping sides from the hidden rock bed, rather than build a vertical platform up to the ground level and then the mastaba on top of it.

[36] For the attribution of the pyramids of Meidum and Dahshur, see Stadelmann, *MDAIK* 36, 437–49.

[37] Friederich W. Hinkel, 'Pyramide oder Pyramidenstumpf? (Teil A)', *ZÄS* 108 (1981), 107–12.

[38] See Gillings' interpretation of the *remen* mentioned in Part I, p. 88, note 4 (Gillings, *Mathematics*, pp. 208–9); also Gay Robins and Charles Shute, 'Irrational Numbers and Pyramids', *DE* 18 (1990), 47.

[39] Isler, *Sticks, Stone and Shadows*, chapters 9–13.

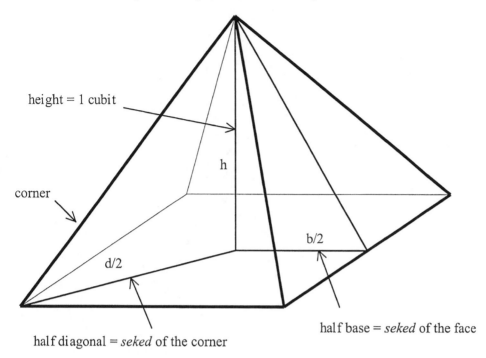

height = 1 cubit

h

corner

b/2

d/2

half base = *seked* of the face

half diagonal = *seked* of the corner

Fig. 89: Geometrical relationships in a pyramid one cubit high.

As Mark Lehner described the process, the casing blocks arrived at their final destination roughly prepared but with the lower surface already dressed. After they had been smoothed on both sides and laid out, the upper surface of the whole row was dressed as far as the line marking the external edge of the following row. This operation was repeated row after row by calculating the slope of the face on the spot, and the final smoothing removed all the external extra stone as far as that line. Traces of the process are visible in the unfinished casing of the pyramid of Menkaura. The vertical section of the casing blocks, therefore, were trapezoidal and the slope of each block may have been marked on both sides with the aid of a right-angled triangle in the shape of the *seked* chosen for that pyramid (fig. 90).[40]

---

[40] Lehner, *Complete Pyramids*, p. 220 and figures p. 221. It is generally accepted that from the Fourth Dynasty onwards the masonry of pyramids was laid out on horizontal beds, leaving to the Third Dynasty step pyramids the sloping accretion layers. Horizontal beds would reduce the stress toward the centre and the chambers built in the body of the pyramid: this was probably the reason, for example, why the architects of the Bent Pyramid turned to horizontal beds half way up during the second stage of construction (Lehner, *Complete Pyramids*, p. 102). The recent excavation of Djedefra's pyramid at Abu Rawash (Michel Valloggia, 'Fouilles archéologiques à Abu Rawash (Egypte), rapport préliminaire de la campagne 1995', *Genava* 43 (1995), 65–72), however, provided contrasting evidence. Only two small areas were cleared on the north side, the north-east corner and a section beside the descending corridor. The masonry has long disappeared, but the rock retained the shape of flat beds in the first case, and sloping in the second. Valloggia assumed that the final slope of the pyramid, about 52°, was obtained by placing casing blocks with a slope of 64° on a bed with a slope of 12°: the composition of the two slopes would produce a final result of 52° (64°–12° = 52°). The subject will be discussed again later.

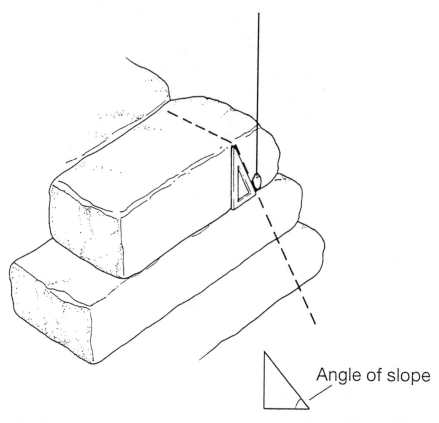

Fig. 90: Method for obtaining the slope in a pyramid according to Lehner (*Complete Pyramids*, p. 220).

Seemingly, for the later small Meroitic pyramids, Friedrich Hinkel suggested that the architects adopted a right-angled triangle designed according to the proportions of half the vertical section of the pyramid to check the slope during construction. One or more wooden triangles with these proportions might have been fixed on top of the platform corresponding to any intermediate stage of the building process and acted as a guide, as represented in figure 91.[41]

It is unclear whether three-dimensional models of pyramids were prepared in advance and exactly what their practical use could have been. Of the two surviving models of pyramids already mentioned, the step pyramid does not seem to have been a working model, and nothing certain can be concluded about the function of the fragment identified by Petrie as a model of the pyramid of Amenemhat III at Hawara. It is certainly more refined than the step pyramid, but, provided it was really a model, it is impossible to establish whether it was prepared before

[41] Friederich W. Hinkel, 'Pyramide oder Pyramidenstumpf? (Teil B)', *ZÄS* 109 (1982), 27–61.

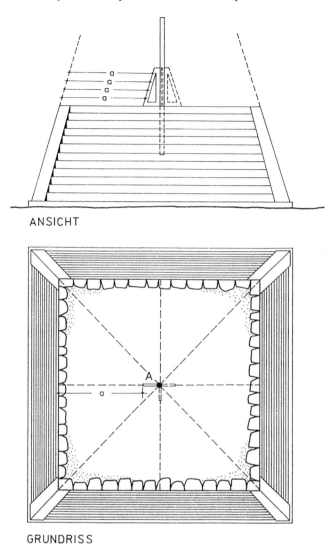

ANSICHT

GRUNDRISS

Fig. 91: Method for obtaining the slope in a Meroitic pyramid according to Hinkel
(*ZÄS* 109, figs. 19 and 20).

or after completion of the pyramid which it is supposed to represent. Finally, it
is worth mentioning that there is evidence, in at least three cases, that pyramidia
were prepared while the corresponding pyramids were still under construction (see
next chapter), but whether or not they were used as models on the spot remains
unclear.

In conclusion, establishing the *seked* means establishing a right-angled triangle corresponding to the proportions of half the vertical section of the pyramid.
Although no archaeological evidence has survived, it is possible that wooden tools

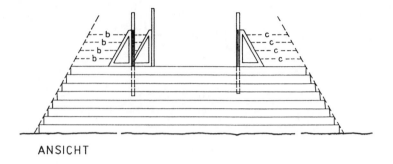

ANSICHT

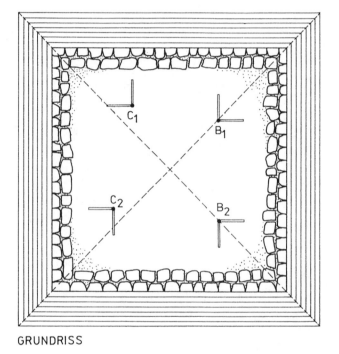

GRUNDRISS

Fig. 91: (*cont.*)

with this shape existed and were used during the construction, as suggested by Lehner and Hinkel. The choice of the triangle – that is, of the slope – might depend on a number of reasons, but certainly a decisive factor was the final size of the monument, or rather the volume of stone involved.

Dimensions and proportions

Nabil Swelim has suggested that the pyramids were built according to the 'angle of repose' of the material, that is, the natural angle in which any heaped matter remains without changing its form.[42] Well-laid courses of stone, however, would allow the adoption of a wider range of possible slopes, especially as the working technique (junctions between stones, arrangement and dimensions of the rows) improved. It is true, however, that larger pyramids had to deal with significant structural problems, while the relatively small amount of stone involved in the construction of smaller pyramids was likely to cause less trouble to the architects.

Throughout the whole history of Egyptian pyramids, smaller pyramids were generally steeper than larger ones (with the exception of some satellite pyramids which were built using the same slope as the main pyramid). Among the largest and medium-size pyramids, only two reached 56°, while the smaller ones reached over 63° already in the Old Kingdom. The surviving Eighteenth and Nineteenth Dynasty pyramidia reveal that the small mud-brick pyramids which were built on the top of the underground burials were even steeper, the average slope being about 70°. Similar slopes can be found in the Late Period pyramidia of Abydos and in the later Meroitic pyramids.

The struggle between ideal aims and practical problems is clearly visible in the early history of the Bent Pyramid, the first pyramid intentionally started from the beginning as true, built by Snefru at the beginning of the Fourth Dynasty. The final form of this monument is the result of three changes of slope, due to repeated structural problems[43] (fig. 92). The first project consisted of a pyramid with a side-length of 300 cubits and a slope of about 60°. Evidence of this first construction can be found in the western and northern descending corridors at the points where the new portion of corridor joins the original. This first project reached, therefore, at least the height of the west corridor, before being abandoned. Serious structural problems must have appeared at this stage, and the architects decided to incorporate this original pyramidal stump into a larger and less steep pyramid. Therefore, they enlarged the base to 362 cubits and adopted a slope of about 54°30′, but this change of plan did not stop the problems. There is ample evidence that the pyramid was subjected to enormous forces caused by a settling in the masonry, probably accompanied (or caused) by a sinking of the foundation rock. The blocks of the casing of the east face appear to have been crushed, and there are numerous cracks both in the descending corridor at the junction between the first, internal and second, external pyramid and in the lower part of the corridor.[44] The situation deteriorated to the point that, when the pyramid reached the height of 90 cubits, a

---

[42] Dreyer and Swelim, *MDAIK* 38, 95.

[43] Varille suggested that the pyramid was intentionally designed in this shape. According to him, everything in the complex was double: two entrances, two descending corridors, two porticullises, two apartments, etc. and, therefore, two slopes (*A propos des pyramides des Snefru*, Cairo 1947. For a review, see Arpag Mekhitarian, *CdE* 47 (1949), 63–5). On the subject, see also John A. R. Legon, 'The Geometry of the Bent Pyramid', *GM* 116 (1990), 65–72 and 'The Problem of the Bent Pyramid', *GM* 130 (1992), 49–56.

[44] Maragioglio and Rinaldi, *Piramidi* III, pp. 58–62.

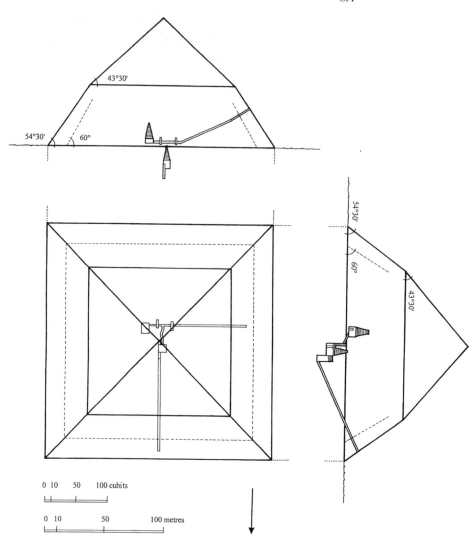

Fig. 92: Plan and section of the Bent Pyramid, Fourth Dynasty (drawn after Maragioglio and Rinaldi, *Piramidi* III, and Stadelmann, *Pyramiden*, p. 90).

radical decision was taken. In order drastically to reduce the weight on the already damaged core, a change in the slope was decided and the pyramid was completed using a slope of about 43°30′.

The care which the architects showed in completing the Bent Pyramid (all the casing was smoothed) proves that this pyramid was far from being perceived as a failure. If the idea was to build a giant representation of the *benben* stone, the Bent Pyramid might be considered quite a good result. In any case, warned by the previous experience, the architects probably chose the safe slope of the upper part of the Bent Pyramid to build the second pyramid attributed to Snefru, the Red Pyramid. Although similar structural problems were less likely to occur in a small pyramid, the satellite of the Bent Pyramid was built using the same 'flat' slope of the upper part of the main pyramid. This pattern, main and satellite pyramids with the same slope, was rapidly substituted by two independent slopes already at the beginning of the Fifth Dynasty: the smaller pyramids were left free to reach the sky according to their own possibilities.

6

The proportions of pyramids

Analysing true pyramids

Numerological theories

It is virtually impossible to mention all of the theories that have been suggested to explain the geometry of Egyptian pyramids. Many of them are based on more or less imaginative interpretations. At best, they are incorrect simply because they are based on our modern mathematics, with little respect for the ancient Egyptian system, but in the worst cases no field of human knowledge has been left untouched by those who aim to find hidden meanings in these ancient monuments.

The pyramid of Khufu, being the largest and the most famous (and, in fact, often simply called the 'Great Pyramid'), has especially inspired complicated mathematical interpretations. They are usually based on the assumption that the pyramid was planned and built using mathematical principles such as π (the ratio between diameter and circumference in a circle) and ϕ (the number of the Golden Section). Useful summaries of the history of the most famous mathematical theories have been published by Jean-Philippe Lauer[1] and Franco Cimmino, among others.[2] In particular, Roger Herz-Fischler has listed all of the theories suggested so far on the pyramid of Khufu alone.[3] Over time, the proportions of this pyramid have been explained, in turn, on the basis of the equality between corner and base-length, or between base-length and apothem (height of the face); by assuming that the ratio between side-length and apothem was 5:4, or that the ratio between the side-length and the height was 8:5 or ϕ; by suggesting that the circumference of a circle with radius equal to the height of the pyramid was equal to the perimeter of the base of the pyramid, or that the area of the square constructed on the height was equal to

[1] Lauer, *Les mystère des pyramides*, Paris: Presses de la Cité, 1988, part III.
[2] Franco Cimmino, *Storia delle piramidi*, Milano: Rusconi, 1990, chapter 2.
[3] Roger Herz-Fischler, *The Shape of the Great Pyramid*, Waterloo: Wilfrid Laurier University Press, 2000.

the area of a face of the pyramid; and by deriving the vertical section of the pyramid from the heptagon or from a golden triangle.

Many scholars have attempted to 'read' the geometry of pyramids in terms of mythological or esoteric significance. These theories are mainly based on incorrect starting points, inappropriate connections and unjustified interpretations, but evidently appeal to the imagination in such a powerful way that their multiplication and diffusion shows no downward trend. Their importance may be evaluated in sociological and psychological terms, and their contents compared with their own contemporary cultural background. They are representative of the modern culture which generated them, rather than of the ancient culture to which they refer. Herz-Fischler, for instance, briefly analysed the social and intellectual background of many of these theories and pointed out that some of them are true products of Victorian Britain.[4]

One of the most famous works on the subject was *The Great Pyramid: Why Was It Built? & Who Built It?*, published in 1859 by John Taylor, who concluded that the Great Pyramid must have been built by the race of the 'Children of Israel' rather than by the idolatrous Egyptians. The dimensions of the pyramid reflected the dimensions of the earth (diameter and circumference) after the Deluge, but also incorporated, in its interior, 'antediluvian measures'.[5] The pyramid was meant to 'serve as record and memorial, to the end of time, of the Measure of the Earth, and secondly, to form a Standard of measures of length, capacity, and weight, to which all nations might appeal, as to a common authority'.[6] According to Taylor, the English inch was also invented at that time. Charles Piazzi-Smyth, Professor of Astronomy and Astronomer Royal of Scotland, adopted these ideas and produced a number of publications on the subject.[7] He agreed that the Great Pyramid could not have been built by the Egyptians ('we find in all its finished parts not a vestige of heathenism, nor the smallest indulgence in anything approaching to idolatry, no Egyptology of the kind denounced by Moses and the prophets of Israel, nor even the most distant allusion to Sabaism'[8]) and concluded that the pyramid of Khufu had been built using the so-called 'pyramidal inch', an imaginary unit of measurement corresponding to an equally imaginary 'sacred cubit'. The well-known Egyptian royal cubit was hastily discarded as an idolatrous and profane unit of measurement invented by Cain.[9]

Biblical fanaticism, merged with numerological interpretation, generated a number of imaginative theories. Moreux, for example, calculated that, by multiplying the

---

[4] Herz-Fischler, *Great Pyramid*, chapter 18.
[5] John Taylor, *The Great Pyramid: Why Was It Built? & Who Built It?*, London: Longman, Green and Roberts, 1859, pp. 297–9.
[6] Taylor, *Great Pyramid*, p. 224.
[7] The two most important are Charles Piazzi-Smyth, *Life and Work at the Great Pyramid*, Edinburgh: Edmonston and Douglas, 1867 and *Our Inheritance in the Great Pyramid* (4th edn), London: Straham and Co., 1880 (1864).
[8] Piazzi-Smyth, *Our Inheritance*, p. 5.   [9] Piazzi-Smyth, *Our Inheritance*, pp. 343–7.

perimeter of the Great Pyramid by the square of its height, the result was very close to π (incidentally, at that time the base of Khufu's pyramid was unmeasurable because it was covered by sand). He also asserted that the architects of the Great Pyramid were able to calculate the length of the polar radius of the earth, the distance between earth and the sun, the length of the earth's orbit during twenty-four hours, the length of the cycle of the precession of the equinoxes, the exact length of the solar, astronomical and leap year, the exact distribution of the emerged lands, and so on.[10]

The cogitations of entire generations of pyramidologists (wittily called 'pyramidiots' by Leonard Cottrell[11]) may be summarised in the following passage by Barbarin:

> the key-dates of the history of mankind are shown in the Pyramid by the intersection of the lines of ceilings and floors of corridors and chambers, by the junction of axes, by the intersection of circumferences, thresholds, beginning and end of passages, by the details of the construction.

Among these 'key-dates of the history of mankind' were the signing of the report of the royal commission for the English oil industry, the fall of the Briand government, the beginning of the Anglo-Egyptian crisis and the abolition of Islam as the established religion in Turkey.[12]

Not all of the theories suggested to explain the geometry of pyramids have a biblical and numerological background. The most common fault in many theories, however, is the liberal use of modern mathematical concepts in the attempt to explain the design of ancient monuments. Yet scholars such as Ludwig Borchardt, Jean-Philippe Lauer and Gay Robins have proved that it is possible to explain the geometry of pyramids (and not only of the Great Pyramid) by using the proper mathematical instruments; there is no need to invoke concepts for which we have no evidence that they were known to the ancient architects.[13]

Lauer's simple ratios

One of the most interesting aspects of pyramid construction is the choice of the slope. Jean-Philippe Lauer suggested that the architects adopted 'easy' ratios

---

[10] Quoted by Lauer, *Mystère des pyramides*, pp. 178–83 and Cimmino, *Piramidi*, p. 30.

[11] Leonard Cottrell, *The Mountains of Pharaoh*, London: Pan Books, 1963, especially chapter 11.

[12] Quoted by Lauer, *Mystère des pyramides*, pp. 160–1 and Cimmino, *Piramidi*, p. 31.

[13] See for example Ludwig Borchardt, *Gegen die Zahlenmystik an der Grossen Pyramide bei Gise*, Berlin: Behrend and Co., 1922; Robins and Shute (*DE* 16, 75–80 and *DE* 18, 43–53) challenged the conclusions of Legon (*DE* 10, 33–40) about the supposed use of irrational numbers. Butler, for his analysis of the Giza complex, did use the ancient Egyptian mathematics as a starting point and measured everything in cubits, but some of his conclusions (such as the importance of the height of the base-lines of the Giza pyramids in relation to one another and to the sea-level) remain difficult to explain (Hadyn R. Butler, *Egyptian Pyramid Geometry, Architectural and Mathematical Patterning in Dynasty IV Egyptian Pyramid Complexes*, Mississauga: Benben Publications, 1998).

Table 8. *Proportions of some pyramids according to Jean-Philippe Lauer*

Name of the king and/or location (and dynasty)	Theoretical angle of the pyramid	'Simple ratio' describing the slope of the apothem	'Simple ratio' describing the slope of the corner
Casing of Meidum, Khufu (Fourth), Neuserra (Fifth)	for 51°50′35″ for 51°50′39″	14/11 (5 palms 1/2)	9/10
Snefru: lower part of the Bent Pyramid (Fourth), Amenemhat I (Twelfth)	for 54°27′44″ for 54°44′06″	7/5	1/1
Snefru: upper part of the Bent Pyramid and Red Pyramid (Fourth)	for 43°22′ for 43°19′	17/18	2/3
Khafra (Fourth), Userkaf and Neferirkara (Fifth), Teti, Pepi I, Merenra and Pepi II (Sixth)	53°7′48″	4/3 (3-4-5 triangle)	
Sahura (Fifth)	for 50°11′40″ for 50°28′45″	6/5	6/7
Satellites at Saqqara starting from Djedkara-Isesi (Fifth-Sixth)	63°26′06″	2/1	
Senusret I (Twelfth)	for 49°23′55″ for 49°21′	7/6	14/17

Data from *Observations sur les pyramides*, pp. 258–9.

between half the base and height, and produced a list of over twenty-five pyramids that corroborated his theory[14] (some are shown in table 8). The two terms of these ratios correspond to the two catheti of a right-angled triangle. The ratio $\frac{7}{5}$, for example, means that for every 7 palms measured along the vertical there was a lateral displacement of 5 palms, a perfect example of *seked* as found in the mathematical papyri. Ratios such as $\frac{6}{5}$ or $\frac{17}{18}$, on the other hand, do not correspond to the usual expression of the *seked*, but Lauer noted that the geometrical method could be used independently from the arithmetical calculation. The architects would choose a simple ratio and use small wooden right-angled triangles shaped accordingly to check the slope during construction. In these cases, the expression of the slope in

---

[14] Jean-Philippe Lauer, *Observations sur les pyramides*, BdE 30, Cairo: IFAO, 1960, pp. 87–8 and 258–9; see also pp. 91–7.

terms of *seked* did not have any practical advantage, but, if necessary, it could have been established at any time by means of a simple calculation.[15]

Lauer's theory, although substantially correct, may be extended in several directions. For example, it is possible to take into account more pyramids, and to investigate more thoroughly the nature of the right-angled triangles chosen to represent the slope. In order to achieve this result, the first step has been the compilation of a longer and more detailed list of pyramids which provides essential information about their dimensions, included in the Appendix. On this basis, it has been possible to draw conclusions based on a large number of monuments and not only on a few examples, and to fit other pieces of evidence into the broader picture. Nabil Swelim, for example, has noted and studied the relationship between dimensions and proportions, and suggests that the architects adopted three successive ratios in the design of pyramids. In the earliest pyramids, the height is equal to half the base (that is, the slope of the face is equal to 45°); in a second phase, the height is equal to half the diagonal (that is, the slope of the corner is equal to 45°); in a third phase, the height is equal to the base (with a slope of about 63°30′).[16] These three 'models', however, correspond exactly to only eighteen pyramids out of over eighty listed in the Appendix. What happened in the other cases?

A list of true pyramids

Available data

The Appendix contains select information about over eighty Old and Middle Kingdom pyramids. The name of the owner, the dynasty under which he/she lived, the location, function, material and form of his/her monument are followed by the available information about the dimensions and proportions of the pyramid. Base and slope are listed before the height, because the latter is almost always calculated from the two former factors. The last two columns of the Appendix contain short remarks and list the bibliographical sources for these numerical data. The column labelled 'ratio/triangle' lists the geometrical models adopted for the construction of the various monuments, and will be explained in the next chapter.

Since the aim of the list included in the Appendix is to allow a study of proportions, the pyramids of which nothing is known in terms of dimensions have not been taken into account. They can be found, however, in the complete list of pyramids published by Nabil Swelim, who divided pyramids and pyramid-like monuments into five categories according to their function (funerary pyramids and pyramid-like

---

[15] Lauer, *Mystère des Pyramides*, note p. 229.
[16] Nabil Swelim, *The Brick Pyramid at Abu Rawash, Number 'I' by Lepsius. A Preliminary Study*, Alexandria: Archaeological Society of Alexandria, 1987, p. 68.

monuments; religious pyramids and pyramid-like monuments; and civil pyramid-like monuments).[17] In comparison, the list which will be used here does not contain Third Dynasty step pyramids (both large funerary and small ritual pyramids) and pyramid-like monuments (which have sloping sides, but are not pyramids). Finally, it is important to bear in mind that there may be still several secondary pyramids (either satellites of the king's pyramid or pyramids built for queens) waiting to be discovered in the vicinity of larger pyramids.

Archaeological evidence concerning pyramids is rather uneven, since famous monuments have been studied and measured several times, while other, less attractive remains have been superficially examined and generally neglected, as, for example, Thirteenth Dynasty pyramids. A list like this does not help to fill the already existing gap, since it includes well-studied monuments and necessarily excludes minor remains of which little or nothing is known. The result of the analysis carried out on the whole of the pyramids included in the list, however, is comfortably uniform. Apparently, similar patterns have been used in the designs and constructions of the Old and Middle Kingdoms, and the scanty evidence provided by the less well documented Thirteenth Dynasty pyramids seems to agree with the general tendency.

Pyramidia as alternative sources

The dimensions and proportions of the pyramids can be established with a certain degree of precision only when a portion of the casing is preserved. In many cases, however, the remains give ambiguous results and different authors provide different measures. In a few cases, the casing is completely missing, making any measurement impossible. Paradoxically, even if a pyramid has completely disappeared, its proportions (and a vague idea about its size) can still be reconstructed provided that its pyramidion has survived. In terms of proportions, in fact, the pyramidia of pyramids are exact replicas of the large monuments on the top of which they once lay.

In general, pyramidia can be useful for fixing the exact slope. In the cases of the pyramids of Amenemhat III at Dahshur and Khendjer, for example, the casing blocks provided values between 54° and 56°, while their pyramidia provide the precise value of 54°30'.[18] A number of Old and Middle Kingdom pyramidia have survived, some in relatively good condition, some in fragments. They are listed

---

[17] Nabil Swelim, 'Pyramid Research. From the Archaic to the Second Intermediate Period, Lists, Catalogues and Objectives', in *Hommages à Jean Leclant*, BdE 106/1–4, Cairo: IFAO, 1994, pp. 337–49.

[18] For the pyramidion of Amenemhat III, see Maspero, *ASAE* 3, 206–8; Schäfer, *ZÄS* 41, 84–5; Habachi, *ASAE* 52, 471–9; Arnold, *Amenemhet III.*, p. 14. For the pyramidion of Khendjer, see Jéquier, *Deux Pyramides*, p. 19–26.

Table 9. *List of surviving pyramidia of pyramids*

Owner	Dynasty	Provenance	Present location	Stone	Select Bibliography	Remarks
Snefru	Fourth	Dahshur, Bent Pyramid (?)	Dahshur, east of the Red Pyramid	Limestone	Stadelmann, *MDAIK* 39, pp. 235–6; Rossi, *JEA* 85, pp. 219–22.	Formerly attributed to the Red Pyramid, its slope corresponds to the lower part (second project) of the Bent Pyramid.
Khufu	Fourth	Giza, satellite pyramid	Giza, south-east of the main pyramid	Limestone	Lehner, *Complete Pyramids*, pp. 222–3.	
Queen GIIIa of Menkaura	Fourth	Giza	Giza, south of GIIIa	Limestone	Jánosi, *Studia Aegyptiaca*14, pp. 306–14.	
Khentkawes, Queen of Neferirkara	Fifth	Abusir	?	Black granite	Verner, *ZÄS* 107, p. 158.	Corner fragment survives.
Queen of Neuserra? (Lepsius 24 or 25)	Fifth?	Abusir	?	Basalt (with metal cap?)	Verner, *Hommages à Leclant*, vol. 1, pp. 371–8; Rossi, *JEA* 85, pp. 219–22.	Very similar to the pyramidion found at Ezbet Rushdi and attributed to the Thirteenth Dynasty.
Iput II, Queen of Pepi II	Sixth	South Saqqara	?	Limestone	Jéquier, *Neith et Apouit*, p. 46	May belong to the main pyramid or to the satellite.
Senusret II	Twelfth	Lahun	?	Black granite (inscribed)	Petrie, *Lahun* II, p. 4 and pl. 24.	A number of fragments survive.
Amenemhat III	Twelfth	Dahshur	Cairo Museum 35133, 35745	Dark grey granite (inscribed)	Maspero, *ASAE* 3, pp. 206–8; Schäfer, *ZÄS* 41, pp. 84–5; Arnold, *Amenemhet III.*, p. 14.	
Khendjer	Thirteenth	South Saqqara	Cairo Museum 53045	Black granite (inscribed)	Jéquier, *Deux Pyramides*, pp. 19–26.	
Merneferra Ay	Thirteenth	Ezbet Rushdi	Cairo Museum 43267	Dark grey granite (inscribed)	Habachi, *ASAE* 52, p. 472.	
Unknown king	Thirteenth	South Saqqara	Cairo Museum 54855	Black granite (unfinished)	Jéquier, *Deux Pyramides*, pp. 58–60.	
			Cairo Museum 54856	Black granite (unfinished, truncated pyramid)	Jéquier, *Deux Pyramides*, pp. 58–60.	The outline of a flatter pyramidion was drawn on one of the sides.
Unknown king	Thirteenth	Ezbet Rushdi	?	Basalt (with metal cap?)	Habachi, *ASAE* 52, pp. 475–6.	

in table 9.[19] Of the pyramids of Khafra, Udjebten and Senusret III, the actual capstones are lost, but their bases survive.[20] The oldest pyramidion is the one found in fragments in the area of the Red Pyramid at Dahshur. It has been assembled, reconstructed and placed in front of that pyramid, but it probably belongs to another pyramid, perhaps to one of the stages of construction of the Bent Pyramid. Its slope (about 54°30′) corresponds to the slope of the lower part of this monument, and it is possible that this pyramidion was prepared after the first variation of the project (when the slope was reduced from about 60° to 54°30′) and then discarded when the second variation (from 54°30′ to about 43°30′) made it useless.[21]

It is necessary, at this point, to explain a few geometrical details which may prove rather confusing. We may describe a pyramid by means of three triangles. The first is the vertical section parallel to a side of the base, which stands at right-angles to the base. The second is the vertical section along the diagonal of the base, also at right-angles to the base, which, however, need not be taken into account in this discussion. The third corresponds exactly to each face of the pyramid, and since the faces converge to the vertical axis, these triangles lie on oblique planes. The height of the face is usually called apothem, and must not be confused with the height of the vertical section (shorter), which is the actual height of the pyramid (fig. 93).

In a frontal representation of a pyramid (elevation), the oblique face undergoes a shortening and ends up corresponding to the outline of the vertical section. One must pay attention to interpret the available drawings of pyramidia in the correct way, that is, to avoid confusing faces and vertical sections (and their respective slopes). This is relatively easy in the case, for instance, of Gustave Jéquier's drawings of the decoration on the four faces of the pyramdion of Khendjer[22] (one is reproduced in fig. 94). One just has to remember that these are, obviously, full views of the faces, and therefore steeper than the pyramidion. Other drawings, however, are very ambiguous, and so potentially misleading for the reader. One case is certainly represented by the drawing of four pyramidia published by Labib Habachi[23] (but see also note 26 below). There each pyramidion is represented by means of its plan (a square crossed by two diagonals) and a triangle corresponding to a full view

[19] A list of pyramidia was published by Arnold (*Amenemhet III.*, p. 15). Since then, four other Old Kingdom pyramidia have been discovered: the capstone of the satellite of Khufu (Lehner, *Complete Pyramids*, p. 222–3), the pyramdion of GIIIa for a queen of Menkaura (Peter Jánosi, 'Das Pyramidion der Pyramide GIII-a', *Studia Aegyptiaca* 14 (1992), pp. 306–14), a fragment of the pyramidion of Khentkawes (Miroslav Verner, 'Excavations at Abusir. Season 1978/1979 – Preliminary Report', *ZÄS* 107 (1980), 158–69), and a pyramidion in the area of the pyramids Lepsius 24 and 25 at Abusir, probably for queens of Neuserra (Verner, *ZÄS* 111, 73 and *Hommages Leclant*, vol. I, pp. 373–4 and figs. 3 and 4). In Arnold's list, the Thirteenth Dynasty basalt pyramidion found at Ezbet Rushdi (Habachi, *ASAE* 52, 475–6) was not included.

[20] They are included in Arnold's list. For Khafra, see Lepsius, *Denkmäler*, p. 27; for Udjebten, see Gustave Jéquier, 'Rapport préliminare sur les fouilles exécutées en 1925–1926 dans la partie méridionale de la nécropole Memphite – La Pyramide de la Reine Oudjebten', *ASAE* 26 (1926), 48–9 and *Oudjebten*, pp. 3–5; for Senusret III, see Vyse and Perring, *Operations*, p. 61.

[21] Corinna Rossi, 'Note on the Pyramidion Found at Dahshur', *JEA* 85 (1999), 219–22.

[22] Jéquier, *Deux Pyramides*, figs. 17–20.   [23] Habachi, *ASAE* 52, pl. 19.

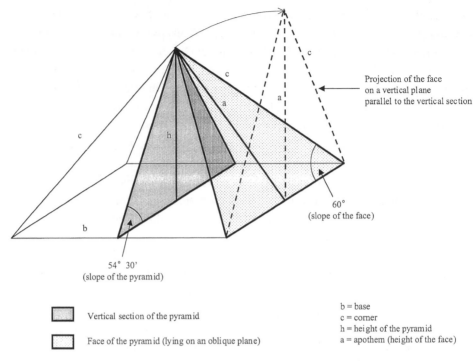

Fig. 93: Relationship between face and vertical section in a pyramid.

of one of its faces (not its shorter elevation). In this case, the reader may be led to conclude that the pyramidia were steeper than in reality (see the difference between the shorter and flatter vertical section, the oblique face and the steeper and higher vertical projection of the latter marked with a broken line in fig. 93).

There are further complications to bear in mind. In a pyramid in which the vertical section is an equilateral triangle, the slope of the face (that is, the slope of the apothem) corresponds to 60° (a *seked* of 4 palms). In this case, the apothem happens to be equal to the side-length of the base; that is, the face of the pyramid is a triangle in which base and height are equal (fig. 95, upper register). When, instead, the *seked* of a pyramid is 5 palms, corresponding to about 54°30′, it is the corner of the pyramid that is equal to the side-length of the base (fig. 95, lower register). This means that, in this case, the oblique face of the pyramid is equal to an equilateral triangle. That a *seked* of 5 palms generates four faces corresponding to four equilateral triangles could not have escaped the attention of the Egyptian architects. This characteristic becomes especially visible in the pyramidia. The Middle Kingdom capstones of Amenemhat III and Khendjer, for example, are large blocks in which all the edges (base and corners) have the same length, about 187 cm for the former (probably 3 cubits 4 palms) and about 141 cm for the latter (probably 2 cubits 5 palms).

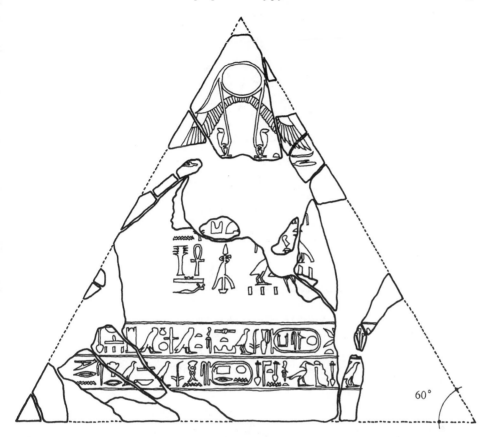

60°

Fig. 94: West face of the pyramidion of Khendjer, Thirteenth Dynasty (drawn after Jéquier, *Deux pyramides*, fig. 18).

In the case of the pyramid at South Saqqara built by an unknown king of the Thirteenth Dynasty, the pyramid itself is badly destroyed and does not provide any information about its slope.[24] Two unfinished pyramidia, however, were found abandoned at the entrance of the subterranean apartment. One had almost been completed, while the other, in the shape of a truncated pyramid, was left in a less advanced state after probably undergoing several changes. The first pyramidion has a base of about 157–8 cm and irregular corners ranging from 141 to 147 cm. Therefore its height can be established as about 92–3 cm and its slope as about 50°–51°.[25] The second pyramidion is truncated, and according to its dimensions (168 cm for the lower base, 60–2 cm for the upper base and 117 cm for the corner), it is possible to establish that its slope is about 60°. On one of its faces, red lines

[24] Jéquier, *Deux Pyramides*, p. 60.
[25] Height and slope mentioned by Arnold, 121 cm and 57° (with a question mark, *Amenemhet III.*, p. 15), refer to the face of the pyramidion: 121–3 cm is, in fact, the apothem.

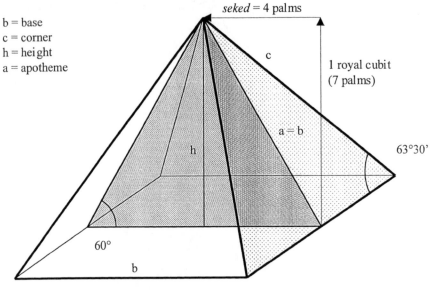

b = base
c = corner
h = height
a = apotheme

seked = 4 palms

c

1 royal cubit
(7 palms)

a = b

h

63°30'

60°

b

Vertical section = equilateral triangle
slope of the pyramid = 60° (*seked* = 4 palms)

Face = triangle with base equal to height (apotheme)

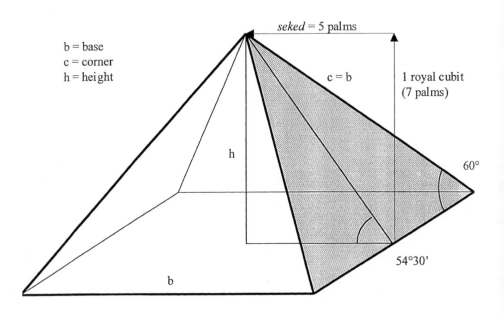

b = base
c = corner
h = height

seked = 5 palms

c = b

1 royal cubit
(7 palms)

h

60°

54°30'

b

Face = equilateral triangle
slope of the pyramid = 54°30' (*seked* = 5 palms)

Fig. 95: Equilateral triangle as vertical section and face of a pyramid.

had been traced, probably in order to carve from that block a flatter pyramidion that might have had a final slope of *c.* 43°30′.[26]

One of the two pyramidia might have been planned for a secondary pyramid, of which, however, no trace has been recorded. If they both belonged to the same pyramid, then the final slope of the monument seems to have been either 50°–51° or about 43°30′. As for the initial slope of 60° of the truncated pyramidion, it is impossible to establish whether it represented traces of an initial plan for that or for another pyramid.

In the case of the Thirteenth Dynasty king Merneferra Ay, all we know about his pyramid depends on his pyramidion, found in the area of Ezbet Rushdi. No traces of the pyramid have been found so far and the capstone is the only clue about its proportions, and very likely about its dimensions as well. It is logical to assume that large pyramids were topped by relatively large pyramidia; therefore, since Merneferra Ay's pyramidon is much smaller than the other surviving Middle Kingdom capstones (Amenemhat III and Khendjer's, but also the two unfinished from South Saqqara), it is likely that his pyramid was not very large in total. The fragments of this pyramidion have been incorporated in a plaster reconstruction on display in the Cairo Museum and its dimensions appear to be about 85–6 cm for the base, 92–3 cm for the corner and about 82 cm for the apothem, giving a height of about 70 cm and a slope of about 58°–59°. Although the plaster reconstruction is not very regular and makes it difficult to establish the original side-length precisely, it is very unlikely that the slope of this pyramidion exceeded 60°.

Thus the additional information derived from the pyramidia may integrate the measurements taken directly on the surviving pyramids. By listing in chronological order all the available data, similarities and trends appear more clearly and make it possible to reconstruct the development of the choice of the geometrical models adopted by the ancient architects.

[26] Gustave Jéquier published a sketch of this face, which shows the axis, a first pair of lines slightly flatter than the slope of the pyramidion, and a second pair of lines connecting on the central axis and probably giving the final intended form (*Deux pyramides*, fig. 42). The pyramidion is on display in the Egyptian Museum in Cairo, but unfortunately the lines have completely disappeared. Jéquier's drawing is rather ambiguous, since he drew the outline of the face, rather than the outline of the pyramidion. In this way, the slope of the block seems to be about 63°, instead of the actual 60°. On the face, the two lines indicating the outline of the new pyramidion are inclined at 48° and, on the basis of this drawing, it might be concluded that a modification from about 62°–63° to about 48° had been planned (Arnold, *Amenemhet III.*, p. 15.) The actual slope of the face, however, is 60°, and the new pyramidion was drawn along this oblique plane. Provided that the proportions in Jéquier's drawing are precise, by projecting its height twice, the final slope of the new pyramidion can be established as about 43°30′.

7

Pyramids and triangles

Geometrical models

Approximation and seked

In order to give a quick and clear impression, the slopes of the pyramids in the list have been expressed in degrees. Some measurements are more precise than others, and can be expressed in degrees, minutes and sometimes also seconds. However, the extreme precision of such data may be misleading, since virtually all the measurements have been taken from small surviving parts of the casing and sometimes even from loose blocks.

Of course every slope, even those differing from one another by a fraction of a degree, can be expressed in an equally detailed way by means of cubits, palms, fingers and smaller fractions. It is worth asking, though, if extreme precision is really important. Was it really possible to control fractions of degrees in the largest pyramids? The final smoothing of the faces removed quite a lot of extra stone, and slight mistakes and imperfections of the surface must have been corrected by this last operation. The precision of the construction is certainly documented, whenever they have survived, by last courses of casing blocks and pyramidia, but, for the whole surface of entire pyramids, a certain approximation should be allowed. It is probably useless to make a distinction, for example, between the 51°40′ of Queen GIc, the 51°50′ of Queen GIa and GIb, the 51°52′ of Meidum and the 51°53′ of Khufu, or between 56° of the satellite of Sahura and Senusret III and 56°18′ of Unas, or between 54°30′ of Amenemhat III at Dahshur and Khendjer and 54°21′ of Queen Atmu-Neferu, and probably even between all the values ranging from 54° and 55°23′ measured by Petrie along the very irregular lower part of the Bent Pyramid. I will assume that pyramids with a very similar slope were designed according to the same proportion, allowing an approximation of about a half degree. This limit is absolutely arbitrary, but the approximation itself has to be limited in such a way that both similarities and differences between the proportions of pyramids can be preserved, and a half degree seems a good starting point. All the slopes mentioned below in degrees, therefore, are meant as approximate values.

Establishing the *seked* of a pyramid means, as we have seen, choosing a right-angled triangle. This is true from a purely geometrical point of view, but may also be true from a practical, constructional point of view. As it has already been suggested, wooden triangles, probably in the shape of right-angled triangles, might have been used to check the slope during construction. The various values of the *seked* (that is, the various right-angled triangles) adopted in the course of history must not be considered as a homogeneous group. They were probably not all invented at the same time, but were introduced from time to time by the ancient architects who were experimenting with new solutions. For simplicity, these geometrical models are listed below in order of descending slope, but it is important to stress that this succession does not reflect a chronological order. They are:

- *seked* of 2 palms, corresponding to a slope of about 74°;
- *seked* of 3 palms, corresponding to a slope of about 67°;
- *seked* 3 palms + 1 finger, corresponding to a slope of about 65°;
- *seked* of $\frac{1}{2}$ cubit (equal to 3 palms + 2 fingers), corresponding to a slope of about 63°30′;
- *seked* of 3 palms + 3 fingers, corresponding to a slope of about 62°;
- *seked* of 4 palms, corresponding to a slope of about 60°;
- *seked* of $\frac{2}{3}$ cubit (equal to about 4 + $\frac{2}{3}$ palms), corresponding to a slope of about 56°;
- *seked* of 5 palms, corresponding to a slope of about 54°30′;
- *seked* of 5 palms + 1 finger, corresponding to a slope of about 53°;
- *seked* of 5 + $\frac{1}{2}$ palms (equal to 5 palms + 2 fingers), also called $\frac{14}{11}$ triangle after the pyramid of Khufu (see below), corresponding to a slope of almost 52°;
- *seked* of 5 palms + 3 fingers, corresponding to a slope of almost 51°;
- *seked* of 6 palms, corresponding to a slope of about 49°30′;
- a *seked* of probably 7 palms + 1 finger (equal to 1 cubit + 1 finger), corresponding to a slope of about 43°30′; and
- *seked* of possibly 7 + $\frac{2}{3}$ palms (equal to 1 cubit + $\frac{2}{3}$ palm), corresponding to a slope of about 42°30′.

These are the *sekeds* of all the true pyramids listed in the Appendix to this book, plus two slopes (first and second) only found in New Kingdom and Late Period pyramids. This list does not pretend to be exhaustive and is based on a certain degree of approximation. For instance, I have interpreted a slope of 56° as the result of the adoption of a *seked* of $\frac{2}{3}$ of a cubit, that is, 4 + $\frac{2}{3}$ palms, but a slightly different *seked* of 4 palms + 3 fingers would give a very similar result. The same doubts arise for the odd 7 + $\frac{2}{3}$ palms, by means of which I have tried to respect Petrie's measurement of the slope of the pyramid of Senusret II at Lahun (about 42°30′), assuming that this value is absolutely precise. It must be borne in mind, however, that *sekeds* of 7 palms + 2 fingers or 7 palms + 3 fingers would produce very similar results. All

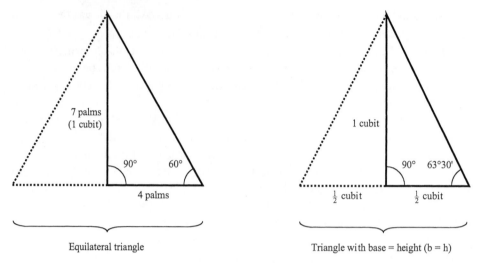

Equilateral triangle   Triangle with base = height (b = h)

Fig. 96: *Sekeds* corresponding to an equilateral triangle, and to a triangle in which base = height.

these values, therefore, must not be treated as absolute definitions, but as convenient descriptions. One finger corresponds to a value between $1°30'$ and $2°$, and some values of the *seked* have been approximated on this basis. The approximation of half a degree suggested above would therefore correspond to a third or a quarter of a finger, between 0.4 and 0.6 cm.

All of these *sekeds* correspond to right-angled triangles, that is, to half the vertical section of the pyramid. However, the triangle corresponding to the whole vertical section of the pyramid may have had an independent identity in the cases of the equilateral triangle and the triangle in which base and height are equal, to which the next section is dedicated.

Equilateral and b = h triangles

In a pyramid with a *seked* of 4 palms, the entire vertical section is an equilateral triangle.[1] A *seked* of $\frac{1}{2}$ cubit, instead, generates a pyramid in which the base (b) is equal to the height (h). Therefore, a triangle with this proportion will be called from now onwards a 'b = h triangle' (fig. 96).

The importance of the equilateral triangle is difficult to establish. According to Maragioglio and Rinaldi[2] (but not Dorner[3]), the first version of the Bent Pyramid was meant to have a slope of $60°$; that is, its section was supposed to correspond to

---

[1] Incidentally, this is one of the two ratios suggested by Choisy for constructing an equilateral triangle.
[2] Maragioglio and Rinaldi, *Piramidi* III, p. 58.
[3] Josef Dorner, 'Form und Ausmaße der Knickpyramide', *MDAIK* 42 (1986), 54 and 'Die Form der Knickpyramide', *GM* 126 (1992), 41.

an equilateral triangle. The fact that this seems to have been the outline chosen for the first true pyramid ever built might suggest that this triangle was regarded with a certain attention. As we have seen before, in a pyramid with a vertical section equal to an equilateral triangle (*seked* of 4 palms), its faces correspond to b = h triangles. When, instead, the *seked* is 5 palms, the faces of the pyramid correspond to equilateral triangles. These two *sekeds*, 4 and 5 palms, were used in the first two projects of the Bent Pyramid. It would be difficult, however, to establish whether the architects (who therefore seem to have begun using the equilateral triangle as vertical section and then attempted to use it as face of their pyramid) used these variations based on this geometrical figure voluntarily, or whether the 'presence' of the equilateral triangle in one or both projects is just a coincidence.

Leaving aside pyramids for a moment, from a drawing by Herbert Ricke, it seems that the pyramidion of the obelisk in the sun temple of Userkaf might have corresponded to an equilateral triangle.[4] According to Ludwig Borchardt's reconstruction, the pyramidion of the obelisk of Neuserra seems to have had a slope of about 63°, which means a b = h triangle. He pointed out, however, that these proportions were arbitrary[5] and did not publish any details of the casing blocks.

In conclusion, the equilateral triangle does not seem to have been very successful in providing the vertical section of pyramids (although it can be found, voluntarily or not, as the face of many pyramids), while the b = h triangle, instead, was widely used from probably the Fifth Dynasty onward for small and secondary pyramids. In both cases it is likely that the starting point was the triangle corresponding to the entire vertical section of the pyramid, and that the *seked*-like right-angled triangle was consequently derived from it.

Seked $5\frac{1}{2}$ palms, generally called $\frac{14}{11}$ triangle

Different from the cases mentioned above, the so-called $\frac{14}{11}$ triangle has been mistaken for an independent triangle, while, in fact, its origin is a pure *seked*-like ratio.

The $\frac{14}{11}$ triangle corresponds to half the vertical section of the pyramid of Khufu, and several authors have noted that this ratio had been already employed in the casing of the Meidum Pyramid. Probably a number of theories on the proportions of the pyramid of Khufu have been fuelled by the problematic Proposition 2 by Archimedes on the calculation of the area of a circle, which says that 'the area of the circle is to the square on its diameter as 11 to 14'.[6]

---

[4] Herbert Ricke, *Der Sonnenheiligtum des Königs Userkaf*, vol. I, Cairo: Schweizerisches Institut fur agyptische Bauforschung und Altertumskunde in Kairo, 1965, fig. 8.
[5] Von Bissing, *Ne-woser-re*, p. 12.
[6] Archimedes, *Measurement of a Circle*, p. 448. This text is likely to have been largely reworked (Knorr, *Archive for History of Exact Sciences* 35/4, pp. 281–324).

Jean-Philippe Lauer suggested that this slope depended on the standard proportions of the Third Dynasty step pyramids. According to him, the most obvious slope for the casing to turn a step pyramid into a true pyramid was the angle of the line connecting the edges of the steps, and that therefore the angle of the smooth face was implicit in the proportions of the steps.[7] John Legon, however, has argued that it is not certain whether the step pyramid at Meidum was built using the same proportions as the step pyramid at Saqqara, and it is not even clear whether or not the steps were equal to one another.[8] If not, the line connecting the corners of the steps was not unique, and the slope could be chosen among a range of values.

A slope which was too flat or too steep would have implied the use of a large amount of stone to fill in the missing volume around, respectively, the lower or the upper part of the stepped core. It might be suggested, therefore, that the architects chose an average slope from the results of their calculations, but I prefer to consider the problem from another point of view.

The correspondence of the ratio $\frac{14}{11}$ and the dimensions of the pyramid of Khufu is more evident than the connection with the same ratio and the dimensions of the Meidum Pyramid. The numbers 14 and 11 are equivalent to 280 and 220, the height and half the base of the pyramid of Khufu ($14 \times 20 = 280$; $11 \times 20 = 220$). The ratio between 175 and $137\frac{1}{2}$ (respectively the height and the half-base of the Meidum Pyramid) is the same, but it is certainly less evident (175 and $137\frac{1}{2}$ would correspond to 12.5 times 14 and 11).

The ratio $\frac{14}{11}$ corresponds to a *seked* of $5\frac{1}{2}$. In the right-angled triangle of the *seked*, the height is 7 palms (1 cubit), half of 14, and the base is $5\frac{1}{2}$ palms, half of 11 (fig. 97). The use of the numbers 14 and 11, therefore, is misleading. The numbers 280 and 220 of the pyramid of Khufu (multiples of 7 and $5\frac{1}{2}$, and therefore of 14 and 11) are the result of the first voluntary use of the *seked* of $5\frac{1}{2}$ palms, but it was this *seked*, and not the numbers 14 and 11, that was employed in the casing of the Meidum Pyramid. The numbers 14 and 11 are not causes, but consequences of the choice of that *seked*. The reasons for this choice will appear clearer in the outline of the evolution of the early pyramids presented in the next section.

Pythagorean triplets

It is possible that some of the slopes listed above might have been obtained by means of some of the so-called Pythagorean triplets, triplets of whole numbers corresponding to the sides of right-angled triangles, which have been already discussed in Part I and II in connection with the Theorem of Pythagoras (Part I) and the use of cords to lay down plans of buildings (Part II).

---

[7] Lauer, *Mystère des pyramides*, p. 234, Robins and Shute, *DE* 16, 75–80.   [8] Legon, *DE* 17, 15–20.

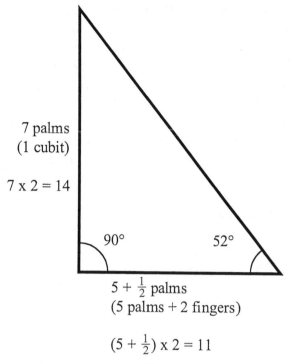

7 palms
(1 cubit)

7 x 2 = 14

90°   52°

$5 + \frac{1}{2}$ palms
(5 palms + 2 fingers)

$(5 + \frac{1}{2})$ x 2 = 11

Fig. 97: *Seked* of $5\frac{1}{2}$ palms, also called $\frac{14}{11}$ triangle.

As we have seen, there seems to be only one written mathematical source containing certain information on the use of three triplets in Egypt, and it is a Demotic papyrus dating possibly to the third century BC, which contains nine problems dealing with the Theorem of Pythagoras and mentions the triplets 3-4-5, 5-12-13 and 20-21-29.[9] It is worth noting that these are just three of the triplets which might have been used in the construction of pyramids, but it must not be forgotten that over two thousand years divide the supposed first use of a triplet in a pyramid and this mathematical papyrus. Various textual sources and archaeological sites have been searched for evidence of the knowledge of Pytahgorean triplets in ancient Egypt, but with unconvincing results.

According to Beatrice Lumpkin, two problems from the Middle Kingdom papyrus Berlin 6619 deal with squares of numbers in a way that strongly suggests knowledge of the properties of the Pythagorean triplets, although they are never specifically mentioned.[10] Her interpretation, however, did not seem conclusive to Robert Palter.[11] Rory Fonseca saw traces of the use of the 3-4-5 triangle in

[9] Parker, *Demotic Mathematical Papyri*, pp. 3–4 and 35–40.
[10] Beatrice Lumpkin, 'The Egyptians and Pythagorean Triples', *HM* 7 (1980), 186–7.
[11] Robert Palter, 'Black Athena, Afrocentrism, and the History of Science', in Mary R. Lefkowitz and Guy MacLean Rogers (eds.), *Black Athena Revisited*, Chapel Hill: University of North Carolina Press, 1996, p. 237.

problems 57, 58 and 59 of the RMP, problem 6 of the Moskow Mathematical Papyrus (MMP) and problem LV-4 of the Kahun Papyrus, and examples of the triplet 5-12-13 in lines H-30 and I-2 of the Reisner Papyrus, all dating to the Middle Kingdom.[12] None of these cases, however, seems particularly convincing. The RMP problems, for instance, deal with *sekeds* of pyramids corresponding to the proportions of a 3-4-5 triangle, but the actual 3-4-5 triangle is never mentioned. Concerning the other problems, MMP problem 6 and Kahun LV-4 simply contain two areas of 12 square cubits of which the reader is asked to find the sides, which are equal to 3 and 4. Again, the 3-4-5 triangle is not necessarily involved. The same happens with lines H-30 and I-2 of the Reisner Papurys I, which refer to two chambers 12 cubits long and 5 cubits wide.[13] Although it is true that these dimensions correspond to numbers belonging to Pythagorean triplets (and therefore it may be suggested that these rooms were designed after them), the Reisner Papyrus lists so many spaces with different proportions that the presence of the numbers 5 and 12 in only two cases does not seem to be significant at all.

Another interpretation for which there may be an alternative explanation is Meyer-Christian's suggestion that Djoser used Pythagorean triplets in his Saqqara complex to design the subterranean apartments of the south tomb and of the step pyramid. In this case, the triplets would have been used to establish the slope of the descending passages and to fix specific points.[14] The same geometrical result, however, could also have been obtained without the use of triplets. The slope of the passage of the south tomb is rather irregular, but averages 26°30′, the same slope as that of the descending passage of the step pyramid, which can be easily explained by the adoption of a *seked* of $\frac{1}{2}$ cubit, which was widely used in the descending corridors of later pyramids as well.[15]

Even if all of these suggestions are questionable, generally speaking the knowledge of some triplets in ancient Egypt is not incompatible with the surviving mathematical sources. It is not necessary to suggest that the Egyptians were acquainted with more or less complicated versions of the Theorem of Pythagoras as early as the Old Kingdom. The peculiarity of the Pythagorean triplets – that is, the fact that they correspond to right-angled triangles in which the three sides are equal to whole numbers – is not necessarily related to the relationship between their squares. If they were used in ancient Egypt, it was probably in their simplest version of right-angled triangles easy to construct, as the Twentieth Dynasty trace of an elliptical vault, for instance, suggests. Pyramids might be the best clue we possess about the use of some triplets as a simple practical device to construct right angles.

---

[12] Rory Fonseca, 'The Geometry of Zoser's Step Pyramid at Saqqara', *JSAH* 45 (1986), 333–4.
[13] Simpson, *Papyrus Reisner I*, pp. 124–6.
[14] W. Meyer-Christian, 'Der "Pythagoras" in Ägypten am Beginn des Alten Reiches', *MDAIK* 43 (1987), 195–203.
[15] Rossi, *JEA* 87, 73–80.

The first pyramid which corresponds to the proportions of the 3-4-5 triangle is the pyramid of Khafra, but the voluntary use of this triangle might have been introduced later. The *seked* corresponding to this triangle is 5 palms 1 finger,[16] and may have been adopted by Khafra after Khufu had used the slightly flatter *seked* of 5 palms 2 fingers, as will be explained in the next section. It is not until the Sixth Dynasty that the dimensions of the pyramid clearly reflect this proportion in their standard side-length of 150 cubits and height of 100 cubits. Half their vertical section is a right-angled triangle 75 cubits long and 100 cubits high, clearly multiples of 3 and 4 ($3 \times 25 = 75$ and $4 \times 25 = 100$). It is unlikely that the Egyptians would not have noticed this proportion. As we have seen, Jean-Philippe Lauer even suggested that the same proportion was used in the funerary temples attached to these pyramids,[17] although their use, in this case, remains somewhat doubtful (see Part II).

The 3-4-5 triangle is certainly the most famous among the triplets, but certainly not the only one.[18] Since they corresponded to right-angled triangles easy to construct, if some of them were known by the Egyptians, it is possible that they were, at some point, adopted as models. If the workmen used wooden triangles to check the slope of the pyramid, a 3-4-5 triangle, for example, would have been the ideal tool for easily and quickly obtaining a *seked* of 5 palms 1 finger. If this is the case, it is not impossible that other Pythagorean triplets might have been adopted beside the 3-4-5. Alexandre Varille, for example, noted the correspondence between the Red Pyramid and the triplet 20-21-29.[19] Unfortunately, there is no agreement among scholars about the actual dimensions of this pyramid (see Appendix). The measurements taken by John Perring, 420 cubits for the base and 200 for the height, would correspond to a triplet 20-21-29 (half the vertical section of this pyramid would be a right-angled triangle 210 cubits long and 200 cubits high, clearly multiples of 21 and 20). It may be observed that, if we accept these dimensions, in this case the corresponding Pythagorean triplet would certainly have been an easier way to express the slope not only in comparison with the odd *seked* 7 palms + 1 finger, but also with the not-that-simple ratio $\frac{17}{18}$ that Lauer suggested to explain the slope of this pyramid.

The *seked* of possibly 3 palms 3 fingers of Iput I (Queen of Teti) and Nofru (Queen of Senusret I), corresponding to about 62°, might have been obtained by means of the

---

[16] Robins and Shute, *DE* 18, 43–53.

[17] Lauer, *BIFAO* 77, 55–78. Neumann and Ogdon claimed to have identified three geometrical models, corresponding to the '3-4-5 proportion', the '14-to-11' and the '3-to-7 relationship', which were allegedly used not only in the construction of pyramids, but also in the design of small-scale objects (Claudio Neumann and Jorge R. Ogdon, 'A New Approach to Ancient Egyptian Objects. A Preliminary Report on Statue Louvre E.12627', *DE* 10 (1988), 55–68).

[18] For a list, see Artemas Martin, 'On Rational Right-angled Triangles', *Proceedings of the Fifth International Congress of Mathematicians, Cambridge 1912*, Cambridge: Cambridge University Press, 1912, pp. 40–58, table pp. 57–8.

[19] Quoted in Maragioglio and Rinaldi, *Piramidi* III, p. 128.

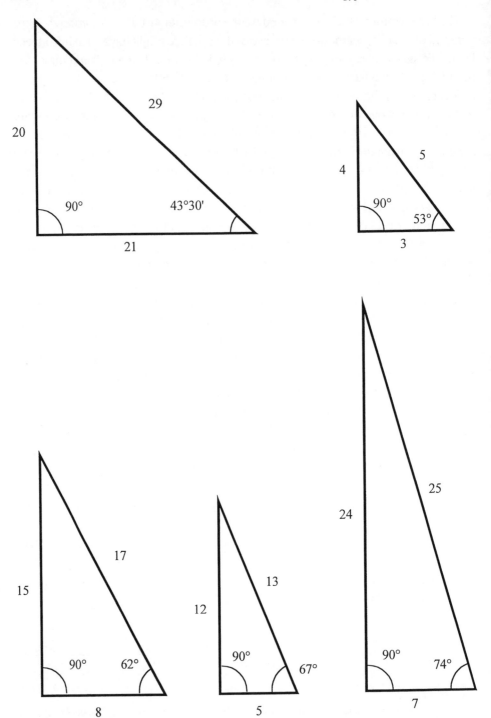

Fig. 98: Pythagorean triplets possibly employed as models in the construction of pyramids (to different scales).

triplet 8-15-17. Seemingly, a *seked* of 3 palms (corresponding to about 67°) might have been achieved by means of the triplet 5-12-13 and a *seked* of 2 palms (about 74°) by means of the triplet 7-24-25. The last two *sekeds* were only employed in New Kingdom and Late Period pyramids and appear to have been the most common slopes of those periods, as we shall see in the last chapter.

In conclusion, the various *sekeds* of pyramids work perfectly well even without the introduction of the Pythagorean triplets. However, it is not impossible that at least some of these triplets might have been used by the workmen to construct right-angled triangles which would help them to check the slope during construction (fig. 98). If this was the case, there is no need to assume that these triplets had any symbolic meaning. They might have simply represented a convenient choice for the architects, because the proportions of the triangles corresponding to triplets could be easily transmitted to the workmen and the corresponding right-angled triangles could be easily reproduced by anyone without constant supervision.

The geometrical models that might have been adopted by the ancient architects have been listed together in a certain order for simplicity, but considering them as a well-defined and uniform group would be a mistake. In antiquity, some of them might have been better expressed as typical *sekeds*, some as triangles, and some possibly as Pythagorean triplets. Other models, not mentioned here, might have been used. The important fact is that this type of geometrical model allows a consistent analysis of the Old and Middle Kingdom pyramids, and might prove significant for a future, more detailed study of New Kingdom pyramids as well.

The evolution of the form

Old Kingdom pyramids

The evolution of pyramid slopes may be explained using the right-angled triangles described in the previous section. Their development is visualised in fig. 99. Apart from a few additional notes, this discussion is based on the bibliographical references included in the Appendix, which, therefore, will not be repeated here.

The starting point is the work of Snefru at Meidum and Dahshur. At the end of his reign, Snefru left three completed true pyramids, the relative chronology of which has been the subject of several studies[20] (fig. 100). The Bent Pyramid underwent two changes of plan. According to the first project, the vertical section of the pyramid might have been an equilateral triangle, with a *seked* of 4 palms,

---

[20] See expecially Mendelsohn, *Riddle*, pp. 88 and 114 and Stadelmann, *MDAIK* 36, 437–49. Mendelsohn suggested that the variation in the slope of the Bent Pyramid was decided after the collapse of the casing of the pyramid of Meidum. Stadelmann, however, disagrees and convincingly reconstructed the chronology of Snefru's reign and of his pyramids in a different way, a reconstruction which I will also follow. See also Rainer Stadelmann, 'Die Pyramide des Snofru in Dahschur. Zweiter Bericht über die Ausgrabungen an der nördlichen Steinpyramide', *MDAIK* 39 (1983), 225–41.

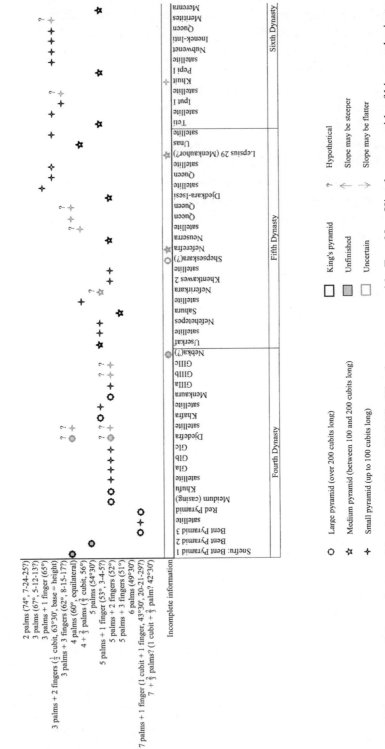

Fig. 99: Diagram of the evolution of the slope of Old and Middle Kingdom true pyramids. Four New Kingdom pyramids of kings and private individuals have been added at the end for comparison.

2 palms (74°, 7-24-25?)
3 palms (67°, 5-12-13?)
3 palms + 1 finger (65°)
3 palms + 2 fingers ($\frac{1}{2}$ cubit, 63°30', base = height)
3 palms + 3 fingers (62°, 8-15-17?)
4 palms (60°, equilateral)
4 + $\frac{2}{3}$ palms (2/3 cubit, 56°)
5 palms (54°30')
5 palms + 1 finger (53°, 3-4-5?)
5 palms + 2 fingers (52°)
5 palms + 3 fingers (51°)
6 palms (49°30')
7 palms + 1 finger (1 cubit + 1 finger, 43°30', 20-21-29?)
7 + $\frac{2}{3}$ palms? (1 cubit + $\frac{1}{3}$ palm? 42°30')

Incomplete information

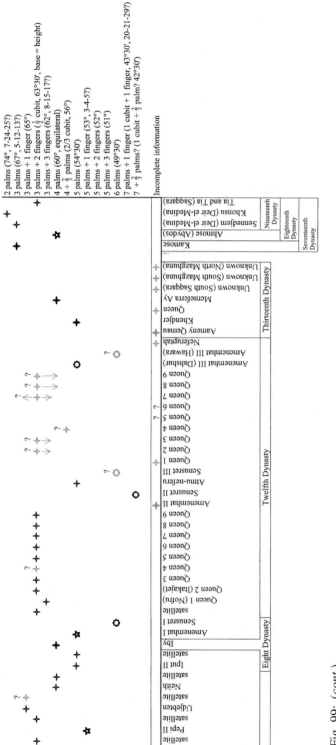

Fig. 99: (cont.)

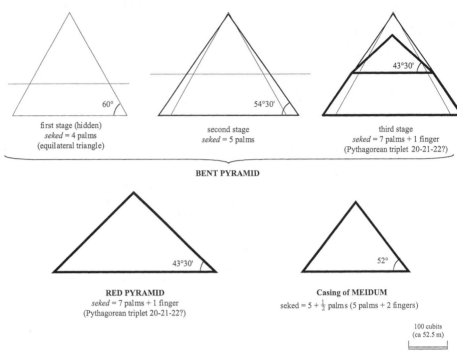

Fig. 100: Pyramids of Snefru (Fourth Dynasty).

corresponding to a slope of 60°. Josef Dorner, however, suggested that the original pyramid might have had a slope of about 58°30′, that means a *seked* of 4 palms 2 fingers. However, the Bent Pyramid is not very regular altogether (Petrie measured values from 54° to 55°23′ for the lower part), and the internal pyramid can only be measured at the junctions in the corridors. It is not unlikely that the original *seked* may have been indeed 4 palms, corresponding to 60°, and that Dorner measured an irregularity of the construction. A *seked* of 4 palms 2 fingers (about 58°30′), in fact, does not appear to have been used in any other pyramid, while 4 palms (60°), although probably not as often as other ratios, was adopted in a number of cases from the Old, Middle and New Kingdoms down to the Late Period. At any rate, when the architects were forced to turn to a second project, the base of the pyramid was enlarged and the *seked* was increased from 4 (or $4\frac{1}{2}$) to 5 palms; that is, the slope was reduced from about 60° (or 58°30′) to about 54°30′. Eventually, they were forced to make a second variation in the plan, and a very flat slope (about 43°30′) was chosen to complete the pyramid.

The slope of the upper part, 43°30′, corresponds to a *seked* of probably 7 palms 1 finger (1 cubit 1 finger). It is possible that, in this case, there might be a connection with the Pythagorean triplet 20-21-29. In the Red Pyramid, which was built immediately afterwards, the dimensions 200 for the height and 210 for half the base show a striking correspondence with the 20 and 21 of the triplet. This triplet gives a slope of about 43°30′, very close to the slope of the upper part of the Bent Pyramid. Even if, as we have seen, there is no agreement among scholars about the precise proportions of both the Bent and the Red Pyramid, it may be assumed that the architects, after the problems encountered during the construction of the Bent Pyramid, adopted, for the Red Pyramid, the 'safe' slope of the upper part of the other. If, on the contrary, the upper part of the Bent Pyramid was started after the beginning of the construction of the Red Pyramid, the 'safe' slope of the latter (based on the Pythagorean triplet 20-21-29?) might have been adopted to complete the former. The exact slope of the satellite of the Bent Pyramid is uncertain, but it might have been the same as the Red Pyramid, and therefore as the upper part of the Bent Pyramid itself.

The Meidum Pyramid was cased by Snefru in the last years of his reign, while he was also building the Red Pyramid. The geometry of the original step pyramid suggested to the architects a certain range of possibilities for the slope of the casing, and previous experiences narrowed the choice. Leaving aside the 'flat' triplet 20-21-22, after the 4 palms (or $4\frac{1}{2}$) of the first project and the 5 palms of the second project of the Bent Pyramid (which had both 'failed'), the architects who cased Meidum attempted a further step: a half palm more, to $5\frac{1}{2}$ palms, that is, 5 palms + 2 fingers.

The Bent Pyramid, the Red Pyramid and Meidum were the pyramids which stood in the Egyptian desert when Khufu started the construction of his funerary monument (fig. 100). If the aim of the architects was to build a pyramid as steep as possible, the obvious model to refer to was the pyramid of Meidum. The Bent Pyramid had been started with the best of intentions, but experience had also taught that a flatter slope was more secure, and between the flatter Red Pyramid and the steeper pyramid of Meidum, the latter was the obvious choice.

The exact slope of the pyramid of Khufu's successor Djedefra at Abu Rawash is not clear. According to Maragioglio and Rinaldi, it was 60°, corresponding to a *seked* of 4 palms. This would mean that the king might have attempted to succeed where Snefru had failed – that is, in the construction of a pyramid corresponding to an equilateral triangle – and it would also explain why he cautiously reduced the side-length by one-third. However, recently Michel Valloggia suggested that Djedefra might have chosen a slope of $5\frac{1}{2}$ palms, the same slope as Meidum and Khufu. If this is the case, it is possible that the small size of the pyramid simply reflected the advanced age of the king.

Anyway, the choice of Abu Rawash, the highest point of the plateau, a few kilometres north of Giza, suggests a clever and ambitious nature. His pyramid might have been smaller than the others, but it was visually and physically closer to the sky; an important achievement for the king who appears to have been the first to adopt the title of Son of Ra. Unfortunately, the king died a few years after the pyramid was started, and his monument was never completed.

When Khafra started his pyramid at Giza, his aim must have been to maintain the level of Khufu's pyramid and, at the same time, to spare material and to improve the impulse toward the sky. He chose, therefore, a shorter side-length, 410 instead of 440 cubits, and increased the steepness of the slope by 1 finger, from 5 palms + 2 fingers to 5 palms + 1 finger. This actually produced a significant difference in the final volume, 2,100,000 m^2 against the 2,590,000 m^2 of Khufu.[21]

Amongst the five large true pyramids which had been completed so far (three by Snefru, one by Khufu, one by Khafra), the pyramid of Khufu was the largest and the one of Khafra was the steepest (see fig. 101). In terms of the ratio between volume and steepness, this record was preserved throughout the entire history of Egyptian architecture. To reach a steeper slope, the dimensions had to be drastically reduced. From this point onwards, many pyramids were built using the slopes of Meidum/Khufu and Khafra as models. For his pyramid, Menkaura appears to have chosen the Meidum/Khufu model, even if on a much smaller scale. According to Valloggia's calculations, it seems that the pyramids of Djedefra and Menkaura might have been absolutely identical in terms of the dimensions of their superstructures (fig. 101).

In the Old Kingdom, at least eleven pyramids followed the model of Meidum/ Khufu and seven the model of Khafra. New attempts to increase the slope were carried out in the construction of smaller pyramids, with the adoption of the *seked* $\frac{2}{3}$, corresponding to a slope of about 56°, and the use of the triangle in which the base is equal to the height, corresponding to a slope of about 63°30'. For their pyramids, Fifth Dynasty kings seem to have preferred the *seked* 5 palms 2 fingers of Meidum and Khufu, with the exceptions of Userkaf, who used the *seked* 5 palms 1 finger of Khafra,[22] and Sahura, who turned to a flatter 5 palms 3 fingers.[23] It is unclear whether the pyramid of Neferirkara was meant to be cased or to be left as a step pyramid. In 1909 Ludwig Borchardt suggested that its final slope might have been about 53°, the same as Khafra's 5 palms 1 finger.

In the satellite of Djedkara, the *seked* 3 palms 1 finger, corresponding to a steep 65° (actually the steepest slope of Old and Middle Kingdom pyramids) appears for the first time. The pyramid at Saqqara, formerly identified as a queen of Djedkara, was the first case in which a triangle with a base equal to the height (b = h triangle) was employed. With Teti, the first king of the Sixth Dynasty, the *seked* 5 palms 1

---

[21] Stadelmann, *MDAIK* 36, 438.

[22] Jean-Philippe Lauer, 'Le temple haut de la pyramide du roi Ouserkaf', *ASAE* 53 (1954), 121; Maragioglio and Rinaldi, *Piramidi* vii, p. 12.

[23] The slope of the pyramid of Sahura, about 50°54' according to Maragioglio and Rinaldi, can be easily explained by means of a *seked* of 5 palms + 3 fingers. Lauer's simple ratio $\frac{6}{5}$ is interesting because might be associated with a measurement based on the small cubit (6 palms instead of 7). See also Ludwig Borchardt, *Das Grabdenkmal des Königs Sahu-re'*, Leipzig: Hinrichs, 1910.

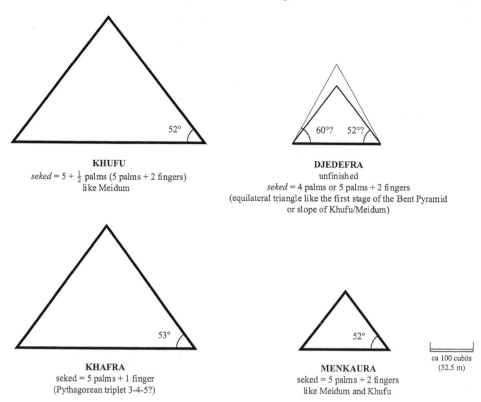

Fig. 101: Pyramids of Khufu, Djedkara, Khafra and Menkaura (Fourth Dynasty).

finger of Khafra became the favourite model for the main pyramid. As explained above, the dimensions of the four Sixth Dynasty royal pyramids (Teti[24], Pepi I, Merenra and Pepi II[25]), 150 cubits for the side-length and 100 for the height, might even reflect a conscious use of the 3-4-5 triangle. During the same period, the b = h triangle was used for satellites and queens by Teti[26] and Pepi I. The pyramid of Iput I (queen of Teti), instead, had a *seked* of 3 palms 3 fingers (about 62°), which might have been obtained by means of the triplet 8-15-17, while the satellite pyramid of Teti had a vertical section corresponding to a b = h triangle (*seked* of 3 palms 2 fingers, about 63°30'). The pyramid of the other queen of Teti, Khuit, was too damaged to provide any detail about the layout, but a few loose blocks gave a slope of about 63°. Its slope might have been equal to that of the other queen, or to the slope of Teti's satellite.

[24] Vito Maragioglio and Celeste Rinaldi, *Notizie sulle piramidi di Zedefrâ, Zedkarâ Isesi e Teti*, Torino: Artale, 1962, p. 45.

[25] Gustave Jéquier, *Le Monument Funéraire de Pepi II*, Cairo: SAE, 1938, p. 6.

[26] For Teti's satellite, see Jean-Philippe Lauer and Jean Leclant, *Le Temple Haut du complexe funéraire du roi Téti*, BdE 51, Cairo, 1972, p. 37, and Maragioglio and Rinaldi, *Notizie*, p. 53.

Beside his own pyramid, Pepi I built a satellite for himself, 30 cubits long, and four pyramids for his queens, each 40 cubits long. The *seked* adopted for each of the five minor pyramids may have been half a cubit, that is, the b = h triangle. Only the slope of Meritites' monument is unknown, but it is likely to have been equal to the others. The case of Pepi II is different. For his queens Neith and Iput II, he probably adopted *sekeds* of 4 and 5 palms. Gustave Jéquier excavated both pyramids and measured from blocks *in situ* 61° for the slope of the pyramid of Neith and its satellite,[27] and 55° for the monument of Iput II, which must be considered only as an approximation, since it was taken from a few irregular blocks.[28]

The pyramid of Iput II might have had a *seked* of 5 palms (*c*. 54°30′), while the 61° of the Pyramid of Neith is obviously very close to 60°, that is, to a *seked* of 4 palms. If the pyramid of Iput was built with a *seked* of 5 palms, a *seked* of 4 palms for the pyramid of Neith has a certain degree of analogy. If this is correct, then this small pyramid (only 46 cubits long, about 24 m) represented another attempt to achieve the elusive 4 palm *seked*, and perhaps the first to succeed.[29] A value of 61° is also close to the slope given by the triplet 8-15-17, corresponding to about 62°, which had been probably employed in the pyramid of Iput I. For Udjebten, queen of Pepi II, the steep 3 palms 1 finger (about 65°) was again adopted, apparently for the second and last time. The slope of this pyramid was measured by Jéquier from the base of the pyramidion, the only surviving piece of casing, which provided a value of 65°. Peter Jánosi, however, suggested that the rest of the monument had the standard slope of about 63° (probably corresponding to the b = h triangle) and that only the upper part was steeper. By analogy with the two other queens, the small satellite of Udjebten might have had the same slope of the main pyramid.

In the First Intermediate Period, Iby possibly tried to revive once more Snefru's idea, and started a relatively small pyramid (60 cubits of side-length, *c*. 31.5 m) using the *seked* of 4 palms of an equilateral triangle.[30] Once more, this triangle did not bring any luck: the pyramid was left unfinished.

Middle Kingdom pyramids

With a few exceptions, the Middle Kingdom kings seem to have used *sekeds* of 4, 5 and 6 palms for their pyramids and the b = h triangles for their satellites and queens.

---

[27] Gustave Jéquier, *Les Pyramides des Reines Neit et Apouit*, Cairo: SAE, 1933, p. 12.

[28] Jéquier, *Neit et Apouit*, p. 45.

[29] The slope of the pyramids Lepsius 24 and 25, perhaps built for the queens of Neuserra, is uncertain (see Appendix).

[30] Gustave Jéquier, *La Pyramide d'Aba*, Cairo: SAE, 1935, p. 3. Of another monument of this period, built by Khui, very little is known: it is unclear whether it was a mastaba or a pyramid (Raymond Weill, *Dara; campagne de 1946–1948*, Cairo: Government Press, 1958, Lehner, *Complete Pyramids*, pp. 164–5).

The first two pyramids were built at Lisht by Amenemhat I, who used a *seked* of 5 palms,[31] and by his successor Senusret I, who chose 6 palms.[32] Senusret I built ten secondary pyramids around his own, one satellite and nine for his queens. In nine pyramids out of ten, including the satellite, base and height are equal to 30 cubits, corresponding to a slope of 63°30'. The pyramid of the most important queen, Nofru, had a base of 40 cubits and a slightly flatter slope. Its *seked* was 3 palms 3 fingers (about 62°), possibly obtained by means of the triplet 8-15-17, exactly the same dimensions and proportions of Iput I, queen of Teti. In the construction of his pyramid, Senusret I was the first to adopt an internal skeleton of walls at right-angles to one another. In this case, the compartments between these walls were filled by stone slabs.

Amenemhat II used the same system, but filled the compartments with sand. According to De Morgan, who worked in 1894–5, the superstructure of his pyramid was too damaged to provide any information about its proportions,[33] but it is possible that future research may be able to cast some light on these ruined remains. Senusret II also adopted the same constructional technique, but filled the spaces with mud-bricks. His pyramid seems to have been very flat, with a slope, according to Petrie,[34] averaging 42°37' (possibly corresponding to a *seked* of 7 palms $\frac{2}{3}$, even flatter than the 7 palms 1 finger of the Red Pyramid). This would be the only case in which this slope was ever used throughout the entire history of the Egyptian pyramids. The choice of such a flat slope might be connected with the change of material. At any rate, the architects soon seem to have recovered their courage.

The complex of Senusret III at Dahshur has been recently excavated by Dieter Arnold.[35] The slopes of the main pyramid and of the nine secondary pyramids are not easy to measure, but it is possible to attempt an interpretation of the remains. Senusret III may have looked back at the funerary complex of Senusret I as a model for his own complex. He appears to have chosen a slope of more or less 50°, perhaps corresponding to the 6 palms (49°30') that Senusret I had used for his own pyramid. Like his name-sake predecessor, Senusret III also built a large number of secondary pyramids, some now in a very bad state of preservation. Nothing is known of pyramids 5 and 6, but the side-length of the other pyramids ranged from 32 cubits (pyramids 1, 2, 3 and 4), to 42 cubits (8 and 9) and up to 50 cubits (pyramid 7). Apart from pyramid 4, which seems to have been flatter (56°–58°, perhaps a *seked* of $\frac{2}{3}$), the slope of the others appears to have been steeper than 60°.

[31] Gustave Jéquier and J.-E. Gautier, *Fouilles de Licht*, MIFAO 4, Cairo, 1902, p. 89.

[32] Dieter Arnold, *The Pyramid of Senwosret I*, Metropolitan Museum of Art Egyptian Expedition 22, New York: Metropolitan Museum of Art, 1988, p. 64.

[33] Jaques De Morgan, *Fouilles à Dahchour en 1894–1895*, Vienna: Holzhausen, 1903, p. 30.

[34] Petrie, *Lahun II*, pp. 3–4.

[35] All data kindly provided by Dieter Arnold. More details are forthcoming in his *The Pyramid Complex of Senwosret III at Dahshur. Architectural Studies*, New Haven and London: Yale University Press, 2002.

Pyramids 2 and 3 may have measured 61°–63°, pyramid 7 may have ranged between 61° and 66°, and pyramids 8 and 9 may have ranged between 60° and 64°.

Although it is entirely possible that each pyramid was constructed according to a different slope, the comparison with the complex of Senusret I may suggest a different interpretation. As in the Lisht complex, several secondary pyramids of Senusret III (at least 2, 3, 7, 8 and 9) might have been built according to the same slope, either 62°30′ or 63°30′. The first of these slopes corresponds to a *seked* of 3 palms 3 fingers (8-15-17 triplet?) that had been used for Queen Nofru of Senusret I and, several generations earlier, for Iput I, queen of the Fifth Dynasty king Teti. The second slope corresponds to a b = h triangle, used for all the other secondary pyramids of Senusret I.

The successor of Senusret III, Amenemhat III, used a *seked* of 5 palms (about 54°30′) for his pyramid at Dahshur. He also built a pyramid at Hawara, which might have had a slope ranging between 48°45′, 49°51′ and 52°25′ (measurements taken by Petrie). It is therefore possible that the king chose a *seked* of 5 palms for Dahshur (as Amenemhat I), and then one of 6 palms (*c.* 49°30′, as Senusret I and possibly Senusret III) for Hawara.

The Thirteenth Dynasty king Khendjer built for himself a pyramid with the same slope as the one of Amenemhat III at Dahshur, topped by the beautifully decorated pyramidion mentioned earlier. As we have seen, two unfinished pyramidia were found in the area of the unidentified pyramid south of Khendjer, which is now completely destroyed. If the pyramidia which had been almost completed was intended for that pyramid, then this monument might have had a *seked* of 5 palms 3 fingers (about 51°, as Sahura). The final stage of the other pyramidion, the truncated one, apparently about 43°30′, might have corresponded to a *seked* of 7 palms $\frac{1}{3}$, which may also be obtained by means of the triplet 20-21-29.

The pyramid of Merneferra Ay has not been located, but according to the fragments of his pyramidion it appears to have had a slope of about 60°, which means that the original *seked* might have been 4 palms. The pyramid of Ameny Qemau has been found, but its slope is unknown.[36] It is possible to say only that its side-length was probably 100 cubits, like the pyramid of Khendjer.

The Thirteenth Dynasty basalt pyramdion found at Ezbet Rushdi shows a slope of 60° (4 palms), but nothing is known about the monument to which it belonged. An extremely similar pyramidion (same material, same slope, one palm of difference between their bases, same preparation for a metal cap) has been found at Abusir. It has been tentatively attributed to a queen of Neuserra (Fifth Dynasty), but it may be worth bearing in mind that in that area there might be the remains of

---

[36] Vito Maragioglio and Celeste Rinaldi, 'Note sulla piramide di Ameny 'Aamu', *Orientalia* 37 (1968), 325–39 and Nabil Swelim and Aidan Dodson, 'On the Pyramid of Ameny-Qemau and its Canopic Equipment', *MDAIK* 54 (1998), 319–34.

unexcavated Thirteenth Dynasty pyramids.[37] If the Abusir pyramidion dates indeed to the Thirteenth Dynasty, it may be concluded that, after all, the *seked* 4 palms (60°) met with a certain success at the end of the Middle Kingdom.

New Kingdom and Late Period pyramids

As soon as the era of the great pyramids ends, finding a pattern in the proportions of the later, smaller pyramids becomes extremely difficult. The primary reason is that the precise slope of New Kingdom and Late Period pyramids is often unknown, either because the monuments were too damaged for any measurement, or simply because it was not recorded. Sometimes clues about the slope can only be derived from photographs and drawings, and in these cases the data must be handled with care. Although a good frontal photograph of a small object, such as a pyramidion, may be considered a reliable source, in the case of drawings, even if there is no reason to distrust them *a priori*, the possibility of inaccurate or misleading reproductions (as in the case of some of the surviving pyramidia) must be taken into account. The observations contained in this section cannot be considered final conclusions, since they are based on too small a percentage of the once existing monuments to provide reliable evidence in the search for geometrical patterns. It is interesting to note, however, that, although the available data are largely incomplete, it seems possible to detect a certain degree of continuity with the past.

In general, New Kingdom and Late Period pyramids were much smaller and steeper than their Old and Middle Kingdom counterparts. The reduced dimensions of the structures certainly allowed the architects to adopt a series of ratios which were difficult or impossible to use in the earlier, larger monuments. For example, the surviving New Kingdom pyramidia show slopes covering almost every possible value from 60° to 80°.[38]

After the decline of the strong Twelfth Dynasty, the still poorly documented Thirteenth Dynasty pyramids seem to have tried to keep up with the dimensions of the earlier monuments. In contrast, the Theban Seventeenth Dynasty opted for smaller and steeper plastered mud-brick pyramids, clustered in their necropolis at

---

[37] The surviving casing blocks of Lepsius 24, possibly built for a queen of Neuserra (Fifth Dynasty), provide slopes ranging from 57°30′ to 62°42′, thus matching the 60° of the pyramidion (Miroslav Verner, 'Excavations at Abusir. Season 1987 – Preliminary Report', *ZÄS* 115 (1988), 170 and *Hommages Leclant* I, p. 373). For other Fifth Dynasty pyramids in the area of Abusir, see Miroslav Verner, 'Eine zweite unvollendete Pyramide in Abusir', *ZÄS* 109 (1982), 75–8, 'Excavations at Abusir. Season 1980/1981 – Preliminary Report', *ZÄS* 109 (1982), 157–66 and 'Excavations at Abusir. Season 1985/1986 – Preliminary Report', *ZÄS* 115 (1988), 77–83. For the possible Thirteenth Dynasty pyramids in the area of Abusir, see Richard Lepsius, *Denkmäler aus Aegypten und Aethiopien*, Leipzig: Hinrichs, 1897, pl. 32 and Aidan Dodson, 'Two Thirteenth Dynasty Pyramids at Abusir?', *VA* 3 (1987), 231–2; for other Thirteenth Dynasty pyramids, see also Aidan Dodson, 'The Tombs of the Kings of the Thirteenth Dynasty in the Memphite Necropolis', *ZÄS* 114 (1987), 36–45.

[38] Rammant-Peeters, *Pyramidions égyptiens*, pp. 108–10.

Dra Abu el-Naga.[39] The pyramid attributed to Kamose, for example, was just eight metres square but had a slope of about 67°,[40] probably corresponding to a *seked* of 3 palms. All of the other pyramids seem to have almost completely disappeared, apart from a few traces. A fragment of the pyramidion of Sekhemra-Wepmaat Intef V provides the slope of his lost pyramid, 60° (that is, a *seked* of 4 palms, corresponding to an equilateral triangle),[41] while not more that a mud mass remains of the superstructure of tomb K94.1.[42]

Ahmose, successor of Kamose and founder of the Eighteenth Dynasty, was probably buried at Dra Abu el-Naga under a relatively small pyramid, but also built for himself a larger pyramid-cenotaph at Abydos, with a side-length of probably 100 cubits and a slope of 60° (4 palms).[43] His tomb has not yet been located, but when this happens, it will be interesting to compare the proportions of his two pyramids. After Ahmose, Eighteenth Dynasty kings turned to entirely subterranean tombs, and for a couple of centuries pyramids were abandoned. Towards the end of the Dynasty, however, the pyramidal shape was resumed again, this time by the artists and workmen of Deir el-Medina, who built for themselves small tombs in the cliff adjoining their village.

Although the proportions of only a few monuments are known, some of them seem to correspond to familiar patterns. There is, for instance, a significant presence of slopes of about 67° and 74°. The former is attested by the tombs of Sennedjem,[44] Aamaket[45] and Iry[46] (data provided by their pyramidia, in the last two cases taken from photographs) and possibly Nakht Min[47] (from a photograph of the reconstructed tomb), while the latter may have been used for the tombs of Khonsu,[48] Qaha[49] and possibly Turbay[50] (from photographs and drawings of their pyramidia). These two values correspond to *sekeds* of 3 and 2 palms, and might have been obtained by means of the Pythagorean triplets 5-12-13 and 7-24-25. As for the other surviving pyramidia from Deir el-Medina, their slopes seem to range

[39] Herbert E. Winlock, 'The Tombs of the Kings of the Seventeenth Dynasty at Thebes', *JEA* 10 (1924), 217–77; Daniel Polz, 'Bericht über die erste Grabungskampagne in der Nekropole von Dra' Abu el-Naga/Theben West', *MDAIK* 48 (1992), 109–30; 'Bericht über die 2. und 3. Grabungskampagne in der Nekropole von Dra' Abu el-Naga/Theben West', *MDAIK* 49 (1993), 227–38; 'Bericht über die 4. und 5. Grabungskampagne in der Nekropole von Dra' Abu el-Naga/Theben West', *MDAIK* 51 (1995), 109–30.

[40] Winlock, *JEA* 10, 273.   [41] Winlock, *JEA* 10, 234.

[42] Polz, *MDAIK* 51, 224; see also Howard Carter, 'Report on the Tomb of Zeser-ka-ra Amenhetep I, Discovered by the Earl of Carnarvon in 1914', *JEA* 3 (1916), pl. 19.

[43] David Randall-MacIver and Arthur C. Mace, *El Amrah and Abydos*, London: EEF, 1902, pp. 75–6; Edward R. Ayrton, Charles T. Currelly and Arthur E. P. Weigall, *Abydos III*, London: EEF, 1904, p. 37; see also Stephen Harvey, 'Monuments of Ahmose at Abydos', *EA* 4 (1994), 3–5.

[44] Bernard Bruyère, *La tombe n° 1 de Sennedjem à Deir el Médineh*, MIFAO 8, Cairo: IFAO, 1959, pp. 16–8, pls. 10–11 (about these plates, see also Rammant-Peeters, *Pyramidions égyptiens*, p. 202, note 2).

[45] Bernard Bruyère, *Rapport sur les fouilles de Deir el Médineh (1928)*, Cairo: IFAO, 1929, p. 95, fig. 53.

[46] Bernard Bruyère, *Rapport sur les fouilles de Deir el Médineh (1930)*, Cairo: IFAO, 1933, pp. 92–3, figs. 26–7.

[47] Bruyère, *Deir el Médineh (1927)*, pp. 117–20, figs. 80–1.   [48] Bruyère, *Sennedjem*, pp. 14–6, pl. 9.

[49] Bruyère, *Deir el Médineh (1930)*, pp. 92–3, figs. 26–7.

[50] Bernard Bruyère, *Rapport sur les fouilles de Deir el Médineh (1933–1934)*, Cairo: IFAO, 1937, p. 27 and pl. 8.

from about 63° (one case, measured on a drawing, from tomb 1150,[51] was probably generated by the adoption of a b = h triangle) to 68° (one case, from tombs 1301 and 1302[52]), 69° (one case, measured on a drawing, from tomb 1138[53]) and 70°–71° (two cases, one measured on a drawing,[54] the other from the tomb of Nebnefer[55]). Fragments of a number of other pyramdia survive, but they are too damaged to provide any useful information.[56]

In the Ramesside period, small pyramids were also built at Saqqara: the tomb of Tia and Tia (a sister of Ramses II and her namesake husband), for example, was completed by a small pyramid, about 10 × 10 cubits, made of rubble encased with limestone and built at the back of the offering-room.[57] Its slope, measured on the drawings of its lost pyramidion,[58] seems to have been about 63°, possibly corresponding to a *seked* of 3 palms 2 fingers or a triangle b = h. Another Nineteenth Dynasty pyramidion, found at Gurob by Petrie,[59] provides a slope of about 67°, given by a *seked* of 3 palms, possibly by means of the triplet 5-12-13.

Although two-dimensional, decorative representations are not necessarily reliable in terms of proportions, it is interesting to note that, among the representations of Eighteenth and Nineteenth Dynasty Theban tombs containing pyramids published by Nina Davies,[60] eight have a slope of about 74° (*seked* of 2 palms, perhaps the triplet 7-24-25), five a slope of about 67° (3 palms, perhaps the triplet 5-12-13), two (irregular) a slope of about 60° (4 palms), one a slope of 48°, one 79° and one (irregular) 83°. Again, there is a predominance of the two values of about 74° and 67°, possibly corresponding to the triplets 7-24-25 and 5-12-13.

Among the surviving New Kingdom pyramidia, the base is often rectangular, rather than square,[61] and there are, in fact, cases of pyramids resting on rectangular bases, such as tomb 1225 at Deir el-Medina[62] and a number of small pyramids at Aniba, in Lower Nubia.[63] In these cases, the pyramids had therefore two different slopes, one for each pair of opposite faces. If Bernard Bruyère's measurements are correct, the pyramid of tomb 1225 might have had a slope of about 63°30′ (b = h triangle) for the pair of short sides and a slope of about 66° (possibly a *seked* of 3 palms, corresponding to the triplet 5-12-13) for the pair of long sides. As for the Aniba pyramids, in two cases the difference between the sides is very small, and in a

[51] Bruyère, *Deir el Médineh (1928)*, p. 29, fig. 19.   [52] Bruyère, *Deir el Médineh (1933–1934)*, p. 11, fig. 2.
[53] Bruyère, *Deir el Médineh (1928)*, pp. 14–6.   [54] Bruyère, *Deir el Médineh (1928)*, p. 29, fig. 19.
[55] Rammant-Peeters, *Pyramidions égyptiens*, n. 74, p. 110.
[56] They are listed by Rammant-Peeters, *Pyramidions égyptiens*, pp. 108–10.
[57] Geoffrey T. Martin, *The Hidden Tombs of Memphis*, London: Thames and Hudson, 1991, pp. 112–4 and fig. 64, p. 102.
[58] Martin, *Hidden Tombs*, pp. 114–5.   [59] Petrie, *Kahun*, pl. 12.
[60] Nina M. Davies, 'Some Representations of Tombs from the Theban Necropolis', *JEA* 24 (1938), 25–40.
[61] Rammant-Peeters, *Pyramidions égyptiens*, especially 108–10; see also Karol Mysliwiec, 'Zwei Pyramidia der XIX. Dynastie aus Memphis', *SAK* 5 (1977), 139–55.
[62] Bruyère, *Deir el Médineh (1930)*, pp. 22–3.
[63] Georg Steindorff, *Aniba*, Glückstadt: Augustin, 1937, pp. 50–1.

third case the height or the slope are not given, preventing therefore any calculation. The bases of the small pyramids built at another Nubian site, Soleb, also seem to have been rectangular although it has been suggested that their final shape was that of step pyramids.[64] To conclude the subject of private pyramids, a number of pyramidia dating to the Late Period (Twenty-fifth to Thirtieth Dynasty) were discovered at Abydos. Fourteen of them were published by Herman de Meulenaere,[65] and from the seven published photographs it seems that six had a slope of about 74° and one of about 66°, again *sekeds* of 2 and 3 palms, possibly corresponding to the triplets 7-24-25 and 5-12-13.

From the Twenty-fifth Dynasty onward, the Nubian kings built over 180 small pyramids for themselves and their relatives at el-Kurru, Nuri, Gebel Barkal and Meroe. The largest monuments were over 26 m long, whereas the side-length of the rest varied from 12 to 8, 6 and even 4 m. The slope of these monuments, whenever it has been recorded, seems to range between 60° and 69° at Nuri and between 67° and 74° at Barkal and Meroe.[66] Traces of the use of the Egyptian cubit as a unit of measurement have been found in several Meroitic monuments,[67] but it is unclear whether the system used to measure the slope was the same.[68] Hopefully future research on these monuments will clarify this point.

In conclusion, New Kingdom and Late Period small pyramids may have been built according to geometrical models consistent with the large Old and Middle Kingdom monuments. Although the archaeological evidence is far from even, it seems that the *sekeds* 4, 3 and 2 palms (corresponding to 60°, 67° and 74°) were often used. The first generates an equilateral triangle, while the second and the third might have been obtained by means of the Pythagorean triplets 5-12-13 and 7-24-25. Further excavation is needed to clarify the geometry of these little monuments and to verify whether these suggestions are correct.

Finally, it may be interesting to note that pyramids were adopted as tombs by rich people in Rome during the I century BC, when contacts with Egypt became

---

[64] Jean S. F. Garnot, 'Les fouilles de la nécropole de Soleb', *BIFAO* 58 (1959), 165–73.

[65] de Meulenaere, *JEOL* 20, 1–20.

[66] All data taken from Dows Dunham, *The Royal Cemeteries of Kush*, vol. I: *El Kurru*, Cambridge Mass.: Harvard University Press, 1950; vol. II: *Nuri*, Boston: Museum of Fine Arts, 1955; vol. III: *Decorated Chapels of the Meroitic Pyramids at Meroë and Barkal*, Boston: Museum of Fine Arts, 1952; vol. IV: *Royal Tombs at Meroë and Barkal*, Boston: Museum of Fine Arts, 1957; vol. V: *The West and South Cemeteries at Meroë*, Boston: Museum of Fine Arts, 1963.

[67] See Hinkel in Davies (ed.), *Egypt and Africa*, pp. 220–5 and *Sudan and Nubia* 4, pp. 18–9.

[68] Friedrich Hinkel (*Sudan and Nubia* 4, pp. 18–9 and especially fig. 6) suggested that some Meroitic pyramids were designed with the 8:5 ratio. Differently from Badawy's 8:5 triangle, this time 5 corresponded to the base and 8 to the height. Hinkel based his conclusions on the sketch of half the vertical section of pyramid Beg 8. In this drawing, the height of the pyramid is crossed by 48 horizontal lines that probably represent the masonry courses. If the height is divided into 8 parts (each corresponding to 6 courses), then half of the base (platform on top excluded) of the pyramid appears to be equal to 2.5 parts. It may be observed, however, that the ratio 8:5 does not really appear in this monument. With the addition of the breadth of the upper platform, the base of the pyramid will eventually correspond to more than 5 units, and the slope may be derived from the ratio between 8 and 2.5, but not between 8 and 5.

more intense. They were remarkable monuments, about 30 m long and up to 50 m high, with slopes averaging 68°, clearly inspired by New Kingdom rather than Old Kingdom pyramids.[69] Their connection with the Nubian pyramids is uncertain, since the first imperial ambassadors appear to have been sent to that region only a century after the construction of the most important Roman pyramids.[70] A detailed study of their proportions might yield interesting results about the use of geometrical models based on a different metrological system. Unfortunately, however, many of them have completely disappeared.

[69] Carla Alfano, 'Pyramids in Rome', *GM* 121 (1991), 7–17.
[70] Norman Neuerburg, 'Greek and Roman Pyramids', *Archaeology* 22 (1969), 115.

Interpreting the slope of pyramids

In general, Old and Middle Kingdom pyramids appear to have been built on the basis of a number of geometrical models represented by right-angled triangles, which might have acted as guides during construction. A brief examination of the later pyramids seems to point in the same direction. Old Kingdom main pyramids follow a slow but constant tendency to increase their steepness. This evolution was interrupted in the Middle Kingdom, probably because of a change in building technique and the introduction of mud-brick instead of stone for the inner core, but it was resumed again after the first experiments. Secondary pyramids, however, follow two different patterns: until Userkaf, satellites and pyramids of queens had the same slope as the main pyramid but then, starting from Sahura, they became steeper. After two attempts with a *seked* of $\frac{2}{3}$ cubit, the *seked* $\frac{1}{2}$ cubit became the model for the majority of the secondary pyramids down to the end of the Middle Kingdom.

Once the pyramids have been classified according to their proportions, it is possible to ask further questions. Khufu, for example, used the slope which Snefru had adopted to finish Meidum. It is difficult to establish, however, to whom the kings who later adopted this slope meant to refer. Unlike any other king, the figure of Snefru, the 'Beneficent King',[1] was worshipped down to the Ptolemaic Period, while Khufu's pyramid remained the largest ever built in ancient Egyptian history. If the size of the pyramid was perceived as an important achievement, then Khufu and Khafra, who built the first and second largest monuments, must have occupied an important place. If, instead, it was the figure of the king that mattered, then the Meidum pyramid might have been the model for subsequent kings who wished to associate themselves with Snefru.

Another interesting question concerns the cases where the adoption of a specific model cannot be explained by structural reasons. As we have seen, smaller pyramids were steeper than the larger ones, and in general dimensions could make the

---

[1] Battiscombe Gunn, 'Notes on Two Egyptian Kings', *JEA* 12 (1926), 251.

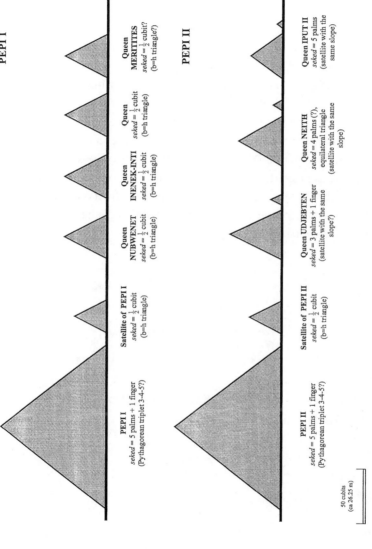

Fig. 102: Pyramids of Pepi I, Pepi II, their satellites and their queens (Sixth Dynasty).

difference in terms of steepness. But why, for example, did the Fifth Dynasty kings prefer Meidum/Khufu as the model for their pyramids, while the Sixth Dynasty kings chose Khafra? The two slopes are very similar, and the medium size of these pyramids did not impose on the architects any specific restriction. Within the choice of slope, was there a direct reference to one of the three kings? It may be noted that these two slopes, the most common in the Old Kingdom, were completely abandoned in the Middle Kingdom.

Similar observations can be made about secondary pyramids as well. For instance, Pepi II built for himself a main pyramid and a satellite which were equal to those of Pepi I. However, Pepi I had built three equal pyramids for his queens, whereas Pepi II chose three different models for the pyramids of his queens (used also for their tiny satellites), even if their bases are very similar to one another (fig. 102). Likewise, the pyramid of Nofru, the most important queen of Senusret I, was larger and flatter than the other nine secondary pyramids of the same king. Yet the largest among the secondary pyramids of Senusret III was also the steepest. Is there any connection between proportions of the pyramid and rank, importance or any other characteristic of the owner of the tomb? Therefore, the final question is: in addition to the practical reasons for the choice of one or another of these forms, was there a symbolic reason as well?

An overview

Paradoxically, the faults and merits of many theories on the proportions in ancient Egyptian architecture share a common origin: the continuity between ancient Egypt and the Western culture. Listing the faults of some nineteenth- and twentieth-century interpretations of the proportions in the ancient Egyptian architecture is very easy. The desire to find links with the past led at times to the attribution of later meanings to earlier documents and also to the misuse of mathematical concepts, while legitimate sources such as ancient texts or drawings were set aside or ignored. Finding geometrical connections in (a drawing on a sheet of paper that represents the plan of) an Egyptian monument proved to be relatively easy, after all.

However, this kind of study also has some merits. The focus on continuity with the past, while sometimes admittedly exaggerated, encouraged research on transmission of knowledge from culture to culture. Egypt certainly had an influence on Greece (and obviously vice-versa), and even if by means of re-interpreted or re-invented forms, it continued to influence the development of Western culture for centuries. It is important to make a distinction between what ancient Egypt was (that is, what we reconstruct today on the basis of the available archaeological and textual sources) and what 'ancient Egypt' meant to Francesco Colonna, author of the fantastic novel *Hypnerotomachia Poliphili* (late fifteenth century); to the Rosacrucians and their ideals; to Athanasius Kircher, author of the *Oedipus Aegyptiacus* and other studies (seventeenth century); to Cagliostro, the Freemasons, and their symbolism; to Giovan Battista Piranesi and his engravings; to Johann Wolfgang von Goethe, collector of *aegyptiaca* (second half of the eighteenth century); to Friedrich Schinkel, author of the scenography for Mozart's *The Magic Flute* (1815); and to the spectators of Giovanni Belzoni's exhibition of Egyptian mummies (1842).[1] Once we make this distinction, we may even say that probably the ancient

---

[1] Erik Hornung, *The Secret Lore of Egypt*, translated by David Lorton, Ithaca and London: Cornell University Press, 2001. See also Jurgis Baltrusaitis, *La quête d'Isis. Essai sur la légende d'un mythe*, Paris: Flammarion, 1985.

Egyptians would have been happy to see how many secret meanings, symbols and geometrical constructions have been found 'hidden' in their monuments.

In general, concerning the interpretation of the archaeological and textual remains, the adoption of the correct mathematical point of view is essential to obtain results which are consistent with the other aspects of the Egyptian culture. One should never forget that Middle Kingdom pyramids were contemporary with the Rhind Mathematical Papyrus, not with Euclid's *Elements*, Archimedes' *Measurements of a Circle*, or Plutarch's *De Iside et Osiride*.

The question of a psychological tendency towards the choice of some geometrical figures remains open. The human mind has not changed much, and there may be archetypal patterns related to the organisation of space that have been adopted throughout history by various cultures, and that can be detected by means of simple psychological experiments. However, architecture is more than a rectangle on paper. We must sometimes ask ourselves whether we seek to see too much in two-dimensional plans of ancient architecture, considering that ancient architects do not seem to have relied much on drawings, after all.

The majority of the architectural drawings and written sources on the architectural planning and building process in ancient Egypt belong to the New Kingdom, for which we can reconstruct a coherent picture. New Kingdom architecture was imagined, planned and built in three dimensions. It is possible that, the more conventional the building, the less explanations were required. In general, however, drawings, written specifications and models were all used to describe different aspects of construction, but none of them was generally expected to provide an exhaustive description of the final result. There is no evidence to assume that the Old and Middle Kingdom architects followed a different method, and it may be concluded that a significant change in the planning process took place in Egypt, just as in the Greek world, only in the Hellenistic period.

For the Old and Middle Kingdom, pyramids provide a good chance to study the development of a type of monument over several centuries and to combine the information we possess about history, symbolism and construction techniques with the ancient mathematical sources. The results of this study agree entirely with the information we possess on New Kingdom architecture, thus confirming once more a certain degree of continuity between these periods. From a geometrical point of view, temples and other buildings are not as simple as pyramids, but hopefully future studies will find a key to read the ancient mathematical background of some of their architectural elements or even of entire buildings.

The search for the rules used by the ancient Egyptian architects is far from exhausted, but must be conducted with respect for the ancient sources and always keeping in mind the practical aspects of construction. The moral of the story may be that looking for interconnections can be extremely productive, but one must never forget the weight of stone, and one must always avoid getting trapped in a vague search for a secret for the sake of it. Because, as Umberto Eco concludes,

a plot, if there is to be one, must be a secret. A secret that, if we only knew it, would dispel our frustration, lead us to salvation; or else the knowing of it in itself would be salvation. Does such a luminous secret exist? Yes, provided that it is never known. Known, it will only disappoint us. (. . .) There are not 'bigger secrets', because the moment a secret is revealed, it seems little. There is only an empty secret. A secret that keeps slipping through your fingers.[2]

---

[2] Umberto Eco, *Il Pendolo di Foucault*, Milano: Fabbri-Bompiani, 1988, English edition: *Foucault's Pendulum*, translated by W. Weaver, London: Vintage, 2001, pp. 620–1.

Appendix

List of Old and Middle Kingdom true pyramids

King/owner	Dynasty	Location	Function	Material	Form	Base (cubits)	Slope (degrees)	Height (cubits)	Ratio/Triangle	Remarks	Source
Snefru	Fourth	'Bent Pyramid' Dahshur South	cenotaph?	stone	true, bent					Total height: 200	Perring, in Vyse, *Operations* III, p. 67; Petrie, *Season in Egypt*, p. 30; Maragioglio and Rinaldi, *Piramidi* III, p. 58; Dorner, *MDAIK* 42, p. 54 and *GM* 126, p. 41; Legon, *GM* 130, pp. 49–56.
					Project 1 (hidden)	300	60°?	(260°?)	4 palms? (equilateral?)	Dorner suggested a slope of about 58°30', possibly a *seked* of 4½ palms.	
					Project 2 (lower part)	362	54°30' (average)	up to 90	5 palms	Perring measured 54°14'26", Petrie values between 55°23' and 54°, Dorner 55°00'30'. Pyramidion of this stage survives (?).	Rossi, *JEA* 85, pp. 219–22.
					Project 2 (upper part)	236	43°01'30"	110, up to 200	20–21–22?	Perring and Petrie measured 42°59'26" and 43°05'.	
			satellite	stone	true	100	44°34'?		20–21–22?	Petrie's measures are uncertain. Slope as the upper part of the Bent Pyramid?	Petrie, *Season in Egypt*, p. 31.
Snefru	Fourth	'Red Pyramid' Dahshur North	tomb?	stone	true	420	43°36'	200	20–21–22	Slope as the upper part of the Bent Pyramid? Perring cleared the corners and measured 43°36'11", Petrie measured 44°36' without clearing the base; Polz measured 45°.	Perring, *Pyramids*, pp. 63–5; Petrie, *Season in Egypt*, p. 27; Stadelmann, *MDAIK* 39, p. 253.

(cont.)

(cont.)

King/owner	Dynasty	Location	Function	Material	Form	Base (cubits)	Slope (degrees)	Height (cubits)	Ratio/Triangle	Remarks	Source
Snefru	Fourth	Meidum	cenotaph?	stone	stepped, later cased	275	51°52′	175	$5\frac{1}{2}$ palms		Petrie, *Medum*, p. 6.
			satellite	stone	stepped	50					Maragioglio and Rinaldi, *Piramidi* III, p. 26.
Khufu	Fourth	Giza	tomb	stone	true	440	51°53′	280	$5\frac{1}{2}$ palms	Slope as Meidum.	Maragioglio and Rinaldi, *Piramidi* IV, p. 18.
			satellite	stone	true	40	51°50′		$5\frac{1}{2}$ palms	Pyramidion survives.	Jánosi, *Pyramidenanlagen*, p. 182: Lehner, *Complete Pyramids*, pp. 222–3.
Queen GIa (Khufu)			tomb	stone	true	$90\frac{1}{3}$ (average)	51°50′		$5\frac{1}{2}$ palms		Jánosi, *Pyramidenanlagen*, p. 184.
Queen GIb (Khufu)			tomb	stone	true	$91\frac{1}{2}$ (average)	51°50′		$5\frac{1}{2}$ palms		Jánosi, *Pyramidenanlagen*, p. 184.
Queen GIc (Khufu)			tomb	stone	true	$87\frac{1}{2}$ (average)	51°40′		$5\frac{1}{2}$ palms?		Jánosi, *Pyramidenanlagen*, p. 184.

Name	Dynasty	Location	Type	Material	True	Base	Angle		Seked	Notes	Reference
Djedefra	Fourth	Abu Rawash	tomb	stone	true	202?	60? 52°?		4 palms? (equilateral?) $5\frac{1}{2}$ palms?	Unfinished. Maragioglio and Rinaldi suggested a side-length of 200 c (104.6 m) and from loose blocks a slope of 60° (*seked* of 4 palms). According to Valloggia, the side 202 c and the casing was placed on a horizontal bed at one corner and on a 12° sloping bed along the face. He found casing blocks with a slope of c. 64° that combined with the counter-slope of the bed would produce a final slope of 52°, similar to Meidum/Khufu.	Maragioglio and Rinaldi, *Piramidi* v, p. 12 and pl. 2; Valloggia, *Geneva* 43, pp. 68–9 and 72.
			satellite	stone	true?	50	?		4 palms? (equilateral?) $5\frac{1}{2}$ palms?	It probably had the same slope of the main pyramid. Maragioglio and Rinaldi thought this could be the pyramid for a queen of Djedefra.	Jánosi, *Pyramidenanlagen*, p. 182.
Khafra	Fourth	Giza	tomb	stone	true	410	53°10′	273	5 palms 1 finger (3-4-5)		Maragioglio and Rinaldi, *Piramidi* v, p. 50.
			satellite	stone	true	40	53°10′		5 palms 1 finger (3-4-5)		Maragioglio and Rinaldi, *Piramidi* v, p. 88.

(cont.)

(cont.)

King/owner	Dynasty	Location	Function	Material	Form	Base (cubits)	Slope (degrees)	Height (cubits)	Ratio/Triangle	Remarks	Source
Menkaura	Fourth	Giza	tomb	stone	true	202?	c. 52°?	125?	5 1/2 palms?	Vyse and Petrie suggested a slope of 51°, but disagreed on the side-length (respectively 207 c and 202 c). Goyon measured 196 c, Maragioglio and Rinaldi 202. According to Robins the slope is that of Meidum/Khufu.	Maragioglio and Rinaldi, *Piramidi* VI, p. 38; Robins, *DE* 18, p. 46.
Queen GIIIa (Menkaura)			tomb	stone	true	84	52°15'		5 1/2 palms?	Originally satellite of Menkaura. Pyramidion survives.	Jánosi, *Pyramidenanlagen*, p.184.
Queen GIIIb (Menkaura)			tomb	stone	?	60			?	No evidence that this pyramid was ever cased	Jánosi, *Pyramidenanlagen*, p.184.
Queen GIIIc (Menkaura)			tomb	stone	?	60			?	No evidence that this pyramid was ever cased	Jánosi, *Pyramidenanlagen*, p.184.
Nebka?	Fourth?	Zawiyet el-Aryan	tomb	stone	true?	400–410	?	?	?		Maragioglio and Rinaldi, *Piramidi* VI, p. 22.
Userkaf	Fifth	Saqqara	tomb	stone	true	134	c. 53°		5 palms 1 finger (3-4-5)		Labrousse and Lauer, *Ouserkaf*, chapter 22.
			satellite	stone	true	40	c. 53°?	28?	5 palms 1 finger? (3-4-5?)	According to Maragioglio and Rinaldi (*Piramidi* VII, p. 22), the slope might have been that of Userkaf.	Jánosi, *Pyramidenanlagen*, p.182.
Queen Neferhetepes (Userkaf)			tomb	stone	true	50			5 palms 1 finger (3-4-5)	Jánosi (*Pyramidenanlagen*, p.184) reports a slope of 52°, corresponding to 5 1/2	Labrousse and Lauer, *Ouserkaf*, chapter 22.

Name	Dynasty	Location	Type	Material	Form		Slope		Palms	Notes	Reference
Sahura	Fifth	Abusir	tomb	stone	true	150	50°54'	93	5 palms 3 fingers	Borchardt, *Sahu-re'*, p. 27: the slope, difficult to establish, may be about 50° 30'.	Maragioglio and Rinaldi, *Piramidi* VII, p. 46.
			satellite	stone	true	30	56°	22?	$\frac{2}{3}$		Jánosi, *Pyramidenanlagen*, p. 182.
Neferirkara	Fifth	Abusir	tomb	stone	stepped?	200?	?		?	Borchardt and Lauer considered this a true pyramid, with a slope of 53° (3-4-5 triangle?). Maragioglio and Rinaldi established a finished base of 185 c; Stadelmann suggested that the pyramid was not stepped.	Borchardt, *Nefer-ir-ke-re'*, p. 12; Maragioglio and Rinaldi, *Piramidi* VII, p. 116; Stadelmann, *Pyramiden*, p. 171.
Queen Khentkawes (Neferirkara)	Fifth		tomb	stone	true	50	52°		$5\frac{1}{2}$ palms	Fragments of pyramidion survive.	Verner, *ZÄS* 107, p. 158.
			satellite	stone	true	10	52°		$5\frac{1}{2}$ palms		Verner, *ZÄS* 109, p. 157.
Shepseskara?	Fifth	Abusir	tomb	stone	?	220?	52°		?		Verner, *ZÄS* 109, p. 76.
Raneferef (Lepsius 26)	Fifth	Abusir	tomb	stone	true?	125?	?		?	Unfinished.	Maragioglio and Rinaldi, *Piramidi* VII, p. 178.
Neuserra	Fifth	Abusir	tomb	stone	true	150	52°	95.5	$5\frac{1}{2}$ palms		Borchardt, *Ne-user-re'*, p. 99.
			satellite	stone	?	30?	56°?		$\frac{2}{3}$?	No trace of casing: dimensions by analogy with the complex of Sahura.	Maragioglio and Rinaldi, *Piramidi* VIII, p. 32.

(cont.)

(cont.)

King/owner	Dynasty	Location	Function	Material	Form	Base (cubits)	Slope (degrees)	Height (cubits)	Ratio/Triangle	Remarks	Source
Unknown Queen of Neuserra? (Lepsius 24)			tomb	stone	true	60?	60°?		4 palms? (equilateral?)	Slope of loose blocks range from 57°31′ to 62°42′; a pyramidion with a slope of 60° was found in the area.	Verner, ZÄS 115, 115; Hommages Leclant, p. 373.
Unknown Queen of Neuserra? (Lepsius 25)			tomb	stone	true	?	?		?	The attribution of the pyramidion found in the area (see above) is uncertain. See also table 9.	Verner, Hommages Leclant, p. 373.
Djedkara Isesi	Fifth	Saqqara	tomb	stone	true	150	c. 52°		5½ palms	Lauer, Mystère des pyramides, pp. 258–9: base 150, height 100 (3-4-5 triangle).	Maragioglio and Rinaldi, Piramidi VIII, p. 66.
			satellite	stone	true	30	65°	30	3 palms 1 finger	Slope measured from blocks in situ.	Maragioglio and Rinaldi, Piramidi VIII, p. 84.
Unknown (Queen of Djedkara?)	Fifth?	Saqqara	tomb	stone	true	80	63°30′?		b=h	Generally identified as a queen. According to Jánosi, its unusually large dimensions and its position suggest an independent origin.	Maragioglio and Rinaldi, Piramidi VIII, p. 98; Jánosi, Königinnen, pp. 36–7.
			satellite	stone	true	8	63°30′?		b=h?	The side is $\frac{1}{10}$ of the main pyramid. The slope might have been the same.	Maragioglio and Rinaldi, Piramidi VIII, p. 104.
Lepsius 29 (Menkauhor?)	Fifth?	Saqqara	tomb	stone	?	120–130?	?		?	Attribution uncertain; Maragioglio and Rinaldi, Piramidi thought that the visible side-length of 100 cubits corresponded to the core only and therefore suggested 120–130	Maragioglio and Rinaldi, Piramidi VII, p. 62.

Unas	Fifth	Saqqara	tomb	stone	true	110	56°18′	85.5	$\frac{2}{3}$		Lauer, *Observations*, p. 95.
			satellite	stone	true	22	63°		b=h		Jánosi, *Pyramidenanlagen*, p. 182.
Teti	Sixth	Saqqara	tomb	stone	true?	150	?		5 palms 1 finger? (3-4-5?)	Lauer, *Mystère des pyramides*, pp. 258–9: base 150, height 100 (3-4-5 triangle)	Maragioglio and Rinaldi, *Notizie*, p. 45.
			satellite	stone	true	30	c. 63°	30?	b=h		Maragioglio and Rinaldi, *Notizie*, p. 53.
Queen Iput I (Teti)			tomb	stone	true	40	62°		3 palms 3 fingers (8-15-17?)	Originally a mastaba	Jánosi, *Pyramidenanlagen*, p. 184.
			satellite	stone	true?	?	?		?		Jánosi, *Pyramidenanlagen*, p. 188.
Queen Khuit (Teti)			tomb	stone	true	40?	?		?		Maragioglio and Rinaldi, *Notizie*, p. 58, Labrousse, *Hommages Leclant*, p. 243.
Pepi I	Sixth	Saqqara	tomb	stone	true	150	c. 53°?	100?	5 palms 1 finger (3-4-5)		Lauer, *Mystère des pyramides*, pp. 258–9.
			satellite	stone	true	30	63°30′		b=h	Superstructure almost completely destroyed	Jánosi, *Pyramidenanlagen*, p. 182.
Queen Nubwenet (Pepi I)			tomb	stone	true	40	c. 63°		b=h		Jánosi, *Pyramidenanlagen*, p. 184.
Queen Inenek-Inti (Pepi I)			tomb	stone	true	40	c. 63°		b=h		Jánosi, *Pyramidenanlagen*, p. 184.

(*cont.*)

(cont.)

King/owner	Dynasty	Location	Function	Material	Form	Base (cubits)	Slope (degrees)	Height (cubits)	Ratio/Triangle	Remarks	Source
Unknown Queen (Pepi I)			tomb	stone	true	40	c. 63°		b=h		Jánosi, *Pyramidenanlagen*, p. 184.
Queen Meritites (Pepi I)			tomb	stone	true	40	?		?		Jánosi, *Pyramidenanlagen*, p. 184.
Merenra	Sixth	Saqqara	tomb	stone	true	150	c. 53°?	100?	5 palms 1 finger? (3-4-5?)	Unfinished	Lauer, *Mystère des pyramides*, pp. 258–9.
			satellite	stone	true	30?	63°30'?		b=h		Jánosi, *Pyramidenanlagen*, p. 188.
Pepi II	Sixth	South Saqqara	tomb	stone	true	150	c. 53°	100	5 palm 1 finger (3-4-5)		Jéquier, *Pepi II*, p. 6.
			satellite	stone	true	30	63°	29.5	b=h		Jéquier, *Pepi II*, p. 8.
Queen Udjebten (Pepi II)			tomb	stone	true	45.5	65°	48.5	3 palms 1 finger	Base of the pyramidion survives. Jéquier measued a slope of 65°. Jánosi suggested a slope of 63°.	Jéquier, *Udjebten*, pp. 4–5.
			satellite	stone	true?				?		Jánosi, *Pyramidenanlagen*, p. 188.
Queen Neith (Pepi II)			tomb	stone	true	46	61°	41	4 palms? (equilateral?)	Slope of 61° taken from blocks *in situ*	Jéquier, *Neith et Apouit*, p. 12.
			satellite	stone	true	10	61°		4 palms? (equilateral?)		Jánosi, *Pyramidenanlagen*, p. 188.

Name	Dynasty	Location	Type	Material						Notes	Reference
Queen Iput II (Pepi II)			tomb	stone	true	42	55° c.	30–2	5 palms?	The value of the slope is uncertain.	Jéquier, *Neith et Apouit*, pp. 45–6.
			satellite	stone	true	7–8	55° c.		5 palms?	The pyramidion found in the area may belong to the main pyramid or to the satellite.	Jánosi, *Pyramidenanlagen*, p. 188.
Iby	Eighth	South Saqqara	tomb	stone	true	L. 60	60°?		4 palms?	Unfinished, according to Jéquier similar to Neith.	Jéquier, *Aba*, p. 3.
Amenemhat I	Twelfth	Lisht	tomb	stone	true	160	54°?		5 palms?	According to Jéquier and Gautier the total absence of casing prevented any measurement. Slope as the lower part of the Bent Pyramid.	Jéquier and Gauthier, *Licht*, p. 89; Stadelmann, *Pyramiden*, pp. 233–4.
Senusret I	Twelfth	Lisht	tomb	stone	true	200	49°24'	116	6 palms		Arnold, *Senwosret I*, p. 64.
			satellite	stone	true	35	63°30'	35	b=h		Arnold, *Senwosret I*, p. 73.
Queen 1 Nofru (Senusret I)			tomb	stone	true	40	62°30'		3 palms 3 fingers (8-15-17?)		Jánosi, *Pyramidenanlagen*, p. 184.
Queen 2 Itakajet (Senusret I)			tomb	stone	true	32	63°30'		b=h		Jánosi, *Pyramidenanlagen*, p. 184.
Queen 3 (Senusret I)			tomb	stone	true	32	63°30'		b=h		Jánosi, *Pyramidenanlagen*, p. 184.
Queen 4 (Senusret I)			tomb	stone	true	32	?		?		Jánosi, *Pyramidenanlagen*, p. 184.
Queen 5 (Senusret I)			tomb	stone	true	31	63°30'		b=h		Jánosi, *Pyramidenanlagen*, p. 184.

(cont.)

(cont.)

King/owner	Dynasty	Location	Function	Material	Form	Base (cubits)	Slope (degrees)	Height (cubits)	Ratio/Triangle	Remarks	Source
Queen 6 (Senusret I)			tomb	stone	true	30	63°30'?		b=h?		Jánosi, *Pyramidenanlagen*, p. 184.
Queen 7 (Senusret I)			tomb	stone	true	30	63°30'?		b=h?		Jánosi, *Pyramidenanlagen*, p. 184.
Queen 8 (Senusret I)			tomb	stone	true	30	63°30'?		b=h?		Jánosi, *Pyramidenanlagen*, p. 184.
Queen 9 (Senusret I)			tomb	stone	true	30	63°30'?		b=h?		Jánosi, *Pyramidenanlagen*, p. 184.
Amenemhat II	Twelfth	Dahshur	tomb	stone	true?	100?	?		?	According to De Morgan, it was impossible to establish the dimensions.	De Morgan, *Dahchour 1894–95*, p. 30.; Fakhry, *Pyramids*, p. 216.
Senusret II	Twelfth	Lahun		mud-brick, stone casing	true	200	42°37'	93	7 palms $\frac{2}{3}$?	The flattest pyramid.	Petrie, *Lahun* II, pp. 3–4.
Queen Atmu-neferu (Senusret II)			tomb	mud-brick, stone casing	true	51?	54°21'		5 palms		Petrie, *Lahun* II, p. 8.
Senusret III	Twelfth	Dahshur	tomb	mud-brick, stone casing	true	202 or 204	c. 50°		6 palms?	May have used the same slope of Senusret I.	Arnold, personal communication (forthcoming in *Senwosret III*).
Queen 1 (Senusret III)	Twelfth	Dahshur	tomb		true	32	?		?	Slopes difficult to measure. By analogy with the complex of Senusret I, pyramids 2, 3, 7, 8 and 9 might have had the same slope.	

Name	Dynasty	Site	Type	Material	Construction	Base	Slope	Height	Dimension	Reference
Queen 2 (Senusret III)	Twelfth	Dahshur	tomb		true	32	61°–63°		3 palms 3 fingers (8-15-17?) or b=h	
Queen 3 (Senusret III)	Twelfth	Dahshur	tomb		true	32	61°–63°		3 palms 3 fingers (8-15-17?) or b=h	
Queen 4 (Senusret III)	Twelfth	Dahshur	tomb		true	32	56°–58°		2/3?	
Queens 5 and 6 (Senusret III)	Twelfth	Dahshur	tombs?		?	?	?		?	
Queen 7 (Senusret III)	Twelfth	Dahshur	tomb		true	50	61°–66°		3 palms 3 fingers (8-15-17?), or b=h or 3 palms 1 finger	
Queens 8 (Senusret III)	Twelfth	Dahshur	tomb		true	42	60°–64°		4 palms (equilateral), or 3 palms 3 fingers (8-15-17?) or b=h	
Queens 9 (Senusret III)	Twelfth	Dahshur	tomb		true	42	60°–64°		4 palms (equilateral), or 3 palms 3 fingers (8-15-17?) or b=h	
Amenemhat III	Twelfth	Dahshur	tomb?	mud-brick, stone casing	true	200	54°30′	143	5 palms	Exact slope provided by the pyramidion (slope from loose blocks gave values between 54° and 56°). Arnold, *Amenemhet III.*, p. 9.

(cont.)

King/owner	Dynasty	Location	Function	Material	Form	Base (cubits)	Slope (degrees)	Height (cubits)	Ratio/Triangle	Remarks	Source
	Twelfth	Hawara	tomb?	mud-brick, stone casing	true	200?	48°–52°	?	?	Values of the slope according to Petrie's measurements: 48°45', 49°51', 52°25'.	Petrie, *Kahun*, p. 13.
Queen Neferuptah (Amenemhat III)			tomb	mud-brick, stone casing	true	100?	?		?	Jánosi concluded that there is no evidence that this was a pyramid.	Jánosi, *Pyramidenanlagen*, p. 184.
Ameny Qemau	Thirteenth	South Dahshur	tomb	mud-brick, stone casing	true?	100?	?	?	?	Unfinished, side-length as Khendjer.	Maragioglio and Rinaldi, *Orientalia* 37, 328.
Khendjer	Thirteenth	South Saqqara	tomb	mud-brick, stone casing	true	100	54°30'		5 palms	Exact slope provided by the pyramidion; slope as Amenemhat III.	Jéquier, *Deux pyramides*, p. 30.
Unknown Queen (Khendjer)			tomb	mud-brick, stone casing	true	50	?		?		Jánosi, *Pyramidenanlagen*, p. 184.
Merneferra Ay	Thirteenth	Area of Ezbet Rushdi el-Khebíra?	tomb?	mud-brick, cased with stone?	true	?	60°		4 palms	Slope derived from the surviving fragment of the pyramidion: the location of the pyramid is unknown.	Habachi, *ASAE* 52, p. 30.
Unknown	Thirteenth	South Saqqara	tomb	mud-brick, stone casing	true	80	?		?	Two unfinished pyramidia were found at the entrance: was there a secondary pyramid?	Jéquier, *Deux pyramides*, p. 60.
Unknown	Thirteenth?	South Mazghuna	tomb	mud-brick, stone casing	?	100?	?		?	No casing left	Petrie, *Labyrinth*, p. 41.
Unknown	Thirteenth?	North Mazghuna	tomb	stone	?	?	?		?		Petrie, *Labyrinth*, p. 50.

Bibliography

Abitz, Friedrich, *Die religiöse Bedeutung der sogenannten Grabräuberschächte in den ägyptischen Königsgräbern der 18. bis 20. Dynastie*, Wiesbaden: Harrassowitz, 1974.

Alfano, Carla, 'Pyramids in Rome', *GM* 121 (1991), 7–17.

Altenmüller, Hartwig, 'Bemerkungen zu den Königsgrabern des Neuen Reiches', *SAK* 10 (1983), 25–61.

'Der Begräbnistag Sethos' II', *SAK* 11 (1984), 37–47.

Andrews, Carol A. R., *Amulets of Ancient Egypt*, London: British Museum, 1994.

Archimedes, 'Measurement of a Circle', English translation by Thomas L. Heath, in *Euclid, Archimedes, Nicomachus*, Great Books of the Western World 10, Chicago: Encyclopaedia Britannica, Inc., 1990, 447–51.

Arnheim, Rudolf, *The Dynamics of Architectural Forms*, Berkeley/London: University of California Press, 1977.

Arnold, Dieter, 'Bemerkungen zu den frühen Tempeln von El-Tôd', *MDAIK* 31 (1975), 175–86.

Der Tempel des Königs Mentuhotep von Deir el-Bahari, vol. I: Architektur und Deutung, AV 8, Mainz: Von Zabern, 1974.

The Temple of Mentuhotep at Deir el-Bahari from the Notes of Herbert Winlock, Metropolitan Museum of Art Egyptian Expedition 21, New York: Metropolitan Museum of Art, 1979.

Der Pyramidenbezirk des Königs Amenemhet III. in Dahschur, AV 53, Mainz: Von Zabern, 1987.

The Pyramid of Senwosret I, Metropolitan Museum of Art Egyptian Expedition 22, New York: Metropolitan Museum of Art, 1988.

Building in Egypt, New York/Oxford: Oxford University Press, 1991.

Temples of the Last Pharaohs, New York/Oxford: Oxford University Press, 1999.

The Pyramid Complex of Senwosret III at Dahshur. Architectural Studies, New Haven and London: Yale University Press, 2002.

Arnold, Dieter and Arnold, Dorothea, *Der Temple Qasr el-Sagha*, AV 27, Mainz: Von Zabern, 1979.

Ayrton, Edward R., Currelly, Charles T. and Weigall, Arthur E. P., *Abydos III*, London: EEF, 1904.

Babin, C., 'Note sur l'emploi des triangles dans la mise en proportion des monuments grecs', *Revue Archéologique* 15 (1890), 83–106.

'Note sur la métrologie et les proportions dans les monuments achéménides de la Perse', *Revue Archéologique* 17 (1891), 347–79.

Bács, Tamás A., 'Two Calendars of Lucky and Unlucky Days', *SAK* 17 (1990), 41–64.

Badawy, Alexander, 'A Collection of Foundation-Deposits of Tuthmosis III', *ASAE* 47 (1947), 145–56.

  Le dessin architectural chez les anciens Egyptiens, Cairo: Imprimerie Nationale, 1948.

  'Philological Evidence about Methods of Construction in Ancient Egypt', *ASAE* 54 (1957), 51–74.

  Ancient Egyptian Architectural Design. A Study of the Harmonic System, Near Eastern Studies 4, Berkeley: University of California Press, 1965.

  'A Monumental Gateway for a Temple of King Seti I – An Ancient Model Restored', *Miscellanea Wilbouriana* 1 (1972), 1–23.

  'Composition murales à système modulaire dans les tombes égyptiennes de l'Ancien Empire', *Gazette des Beaux-Arts* 97 (1981), 49–52.

  'Ancient Constructional Diagrams in Egyptian Architecture', *Gazette des Beaux-Arts* 107 (1986), 51–56.

Baines, John, '*Bnbn*: Mythological and Linguistic Notes', *Orientalia* 39 (1970), 389–404.

  'Restricted Knowledge, Hierarchy and Decorum: Modern Perceptions and Ancient Institutions', *JARCE* 27 (1990), 1–23.

Baines, John and Málek, Jaromír, *Atlas of Ancient Egypt*, Oxford: Phaidon, 1984.

Bakir, Abd el-Mohsen, *The Cairo Calendar n° 86637*, Cairo: Government Press, 1966.

Baltrusaitis, Jurgis, *La quête d'Isis. Essai sur la légende d'un mythe*, Paris: Flammarion, 1985.

Barguet, Paul, 'Le rituel archaïque de la fondation des temples de Medinet-Habou et de Louxor', *RdE* 9 (1952), 1–22.

  'Une statuette de Senenmout au Musée du Louvre', *CdE* 28 (1953), 23–7.

  Le Temple d'Amon-Rê à Karnak, RAPH 21, Cairo: IFAO, 1962.

Barsanti, Alexandre, 'Fouilles de Zaouiét el-Aryân (1904–5)', *ASAE* 7 (1906), 256–86.

  'Rapport sur la découverte à Edfou des ruines d'un temple Ramesside', *ASAE* 8 (1908), 233–6.

Benjafield, John, 'A Review of Recent Research on the Golden Section', *Empirical Studies of the Arts* 3 (1985), 117–34.

  Cognition, London: Prentice-Hall International, 1992.

Benjafield, John and Adams-Webber, J., 'The Golden Section Hypothesis', *British Journal of Psychology* 67 (1976), 11–5.

Benjafield, John and Davis, Christine, 'The Golden Section and the Structure of Connotation', *Journal of Aesthetics and Art Criticism* 36 (1978), 423–7.

Benjafield, John and Green, T. R. G., 'Golden Section Relations in Interpersonal Judgement', *British Journal of Psychology* 69 (1978), 23–35.

Benjafield, John and Pomeroy, Edward, 'A Possible Idea Underlying Interpersonal Descriptions', *British Journal of Social and Clinical Psychology* 17 (1978), 23–35.

Berger, Suzanne, 'A Note on Some Scenes of Land-Measurement', *JEA* 20 (1934), 54–6.

Berlyne, D. E., 'The Golden Section and Hedonic Judgement of Rectangles: A Cross-Cultural Study', *Sciences de l'Art – Scientific Aesthetics* 7 (1970), 1–6.

Birch, S., *Inscriptions in Hieratic and Demotic Character in the Collections of the British Museum*, London: British Museum Press, 1868.

von Bissing, Friedrich W. (ed.), *Das Re-Heiligtum des Königs Ne-woser-re (Rathures)*, vol. i: *Der Bau*, Berlin: Duncker, 1905.

Bisson de la Roque, Fernand, *Tôd (1934 à 1936)*, FIFAO 17, Cairo: IFAO, 1937.

Blackman, Aylward M., 'A Painted Pottery Model of a Granary', *JEA* 6 (1920), 206–8.

Blackman, Aylward M. and Fairman, Herbert W., 'The Consecration of an Egyptian Temple According to the Use of Edfu', *JEA* 32 (1946), 75–91.

Bonnet, Charles, 'Les fouilles archéologiques de Kerma (Soudan)', *Genava* 28 (1980), 31–62.

Borchardt, Ludwig, 'Altägyptische Werkzeichnungen', *ZÄS* 34 (1896), 69–76.

'Das Grab des Menes', *ZÄS* 36, 87–105.

Das Grabdenkmal des Königs Ne-user-re', Leipzig: Hinrichs, 1907.

Das Grabdenkmal des Königs Nefer-ir-ke-re', Leipzig: Hinrichs, 1909.

Das Grabdenkmal des Königs Sahu-re', Leipzig: Hinrichs, 1910.

Gegen die Zahlenmystik an der Grossen Pyramide bei Gise, Berlin: Behrend and Co, 1922.

Ägyptische Tempel mit Umgang, Beiträge Bf 2, Cairo 1938.

'Statuen von Feldmessern', *ZÄS* 42 (1967), 70–72.

Borchardt, Ludwig and Schäfer, Heinrich, 'Vorläufiger Bericht über die Ausgrabungen bei Abusir im Winter 1899/1900', *ZÄS* 38 (1900), 94–103.

Borissavliévitch, Miloutine, *Essai critique sur le principales doctrines relatives à l'esthétique de l'architecture*, Paris: Payot, 1925.

Bruckheimer, M. and Salomon, Y., 'Some Comments on R. J. Gillings' Analysis of the 2/n Table in the Rhind Papyrus', *HM* 4 (1977), 445–52.

Brugsch, Heinrich, 'Bau und Maße des Tempels von Edfu', *ZÄS* 8 (1870), 153–61; 9 (1871), 32–45, 137–44; 10 (1872), 1–16.

'Eine neue Bauurkunde des Tempels von Edfu', *ZÄS* 13 (1875), 113–23.

'Bautexte und Inschriften', *Thesaurus Inscriptionum Aegypticarum*, vol. VI, Leipzig: Hinrichs 1891, 1235–406.

Brunner-Traut, Emma, *Die Altägyptischen Scherbenbilder*, Wiesbaden: Steiner, 1956.

Egyptian Artists' Sketches; Figured Ostraka from the Gayer-Anderson Collection in the Fitzwilliam Museum, Cambridge, Istanbul: Istanbul, Nederlands Historisch Archaeologisch Institut, 1979.

Brunton, Guy and Caton-Thompson, Gertrude, *The Badarian Civilisation*, BSAE ERA 46, London 1928.

Bruyère, Bernard, *Rapport sur les fouilles de Deir el Médineh (1927)*, Cairo: IFAO, 1928.

Rapport sur les fouilles de Deir el Médineh (1928), Cairo: IFAO, 1929.

Rapport sur les fouilles de Deir el Médineh (1930), Cairo: IFAO, 1933.

Rapport sur les fouilles de Deir el Médineh (1933–1934), Cairo: IFAO, 1937.

La tombe n° 1 de Sennedjem à Deir el Médineh, MIFAO 8, Cairo: IFAO, 1959.

De Buck, Adriaan, 'The Building Inscription of the Berlin Leather Roll', *Analecta Orientalia* 17 (1938), 48–57.

Bundgaard, Jens A., *Mnesicles, a Greek Architect at Work*, Oslo: Scandinavian University Books, 1957.

Burke, Edmund, *Enquiry into the Origin of our Ideas of the Sublime and Beautiful* (1757), ed. James T. Bolton, Oxford: Blackwell, 1987.

Burkert, Walter, *Lore and Science in Ancient Pythagoreanism*, Cambridge, Mass.: Harvard University Press, 1972.

Butler, Hadyn R., *Egyptian Pyramid Geometry, Architectural and Mathematical Patterning in Dynasty IV Egyptian Pyramid Complexes*, Mississauga: Benben Publications, 1998

Campbell, Colin, *Two Theban Princes, Kha-em-uast and Amen-khepeshf, Menna, a Land-Steward, and Their Tombs*, Edinburgh: Oliver and Boyd, 1910.

Capart, Jean, 'Cahiers de modèles', *CdE* 16 (1941), 43–4.
  'Sur le cahiers de modèles en usage sous l'Ancient Empire', *CdE* 20 (1945), 33–5.
Carlotti, Jean-François, 'Contribution à l'étude métrologique de quelque monuments du temple d'Amon-Rê à Karnak', *Cahiers de Karnak X*, Paris: Recherche sur les Civilisations, 1995, 65–94.
Carter, Howard, 'Report on the Tomb of Zeser-ka-ra Amenhetep I, Discovered by the Earl of Carnarvon in 1914', *JEA* 3 (1916), 147–54.
Carter, Howard and Gardiner, Alan H., 'The Tomb of Ramses IV and the Turin Plan of a Royal Tomb', *JEA* 4 (1917), 130–58.
Catoire, Boris, 'Evaluation par le calcul des efforts de traction transmis dans les cordages au cours de l'operation d'abattage de l'obelisque ouest du VII e pylône', *Cahiers de Karnak VII*, Paris: Recherche sur les Civilisations, 1982, 181–202.
Cauville, Sylvie, 'Les inscriptions dédicatoires du temple d'Hathor à Dendera', *BIFAO* 90 (1990), 83–114.
Cauville, Sylvie and Devauchelle, Didier, 'Les mesures réelles du temple d'Edfou', *BIFAO* 84 (1984), 23–34.
Černy, Jaroslav, *Ostraca Hiératiques*, CG, Cairo: SAE, 1935.
  A Community of Workmen at Thebes in the Ramesside Period, BdÉ 50, Cairo: IFAO, 1973.
  The Valley of the Kings, BdÉ 61, Cairo: IFAO, 1973.
Černy, Jaroslav and Gardiner, Alan H., *Hieratic Ostraca*, Oxford: Oxford University Press, 1957.
Chace, Arnold B., Bull, Ludlow, and Manning, Henry P., *The Rhind Mathematical Papyrus*, Oberlin, Ohio: Mathematical Association of America, 1929.
Chassinat, Émile, *Le Mammisi d'Edfou*, MIFAO 16, Cairo: IFAO, 1939.
Choisy, Auguste, *Histoire de l'architecture*, Paris: Gauthier-Villars, 1899.
  L'art de batîr chez les Égyptiens, Paris: Gauthier-Villars, 1904.
Christophe, Louis A., 'Le pylone "Ramesside" d'Edfou', *ASAE* 55 (1958), 1–23.
Cimmino, Franco, *Storia delle piramidi*, Milano: Rusconi, 1990.
Clarke, Somers and Engelbach, Reginald, *Ancient Egyptian Masonry*, Oxford: Oxford University Press, 1930.
Cook, Theodore, *Spirals in Nature and Art*, London: Murray, 1903.
  The Curves of Life, New York: Holt and Co., 1914.
Cottrell, Leonard, *The Mountains of Pharaoh*, London: Pan Books, 1963.
Coulton, James J., *Greek Architects at Work*, London: Paul Elek, 1977.
  'Incomplete Preliminary Planning in Greek Architecture: Some New Evidence', in Bommelaer Jean-François (ed.), *Le dessin d'architecture dans le société antiques*, Strasburg: Université des Sciences Humaines de Strasbourg, 1985.
Cuomo, Serafina, *Ancient Mathematics*, London/New York: Routledge, 2001.
Daressy, Georges, 'Un plan égyptien d'une tombe royale', *Revue Archéologique* 32 (1898), 235–40.
  Ostraca, CG, Cairo: SAE, 1901.
  Fouilles de la Vallée des Rois (1898–1899), CG, Cairo: SAE, 1902.
  'Un tracé egyptienne d'une voûte elliptique', *ASAE* 8 (1908), 237–241.
  'Tracé d'une voûte datant de la IIIe dynastie', *ASAE* 27 (1927), 157–60.
Daumas, François, *Les mammisis des temples égyptiens*, Annales de l'Université de Lyon 3/32, Paris, 1958.
  Le mammisis de Dendara, Cairo: IFAO, 1959.
Davies, Nina M., 'Some Representations of Tombs from the Theban Necropolis', *JEA* 24 (1938), 25–40.

Davies, Norman de Garis, *The Rock Tombs of El Amarna* I–VI, ASE 13–18, London, 6 vols., 1903–8.

'An Architectural Sketch at Sheikh Said', Ancient Egypt, 1 (1917), 21–5.

'An Architect's Plan from Thebes', *JEA* 4 (1917), 194–9.

The Tombs of Two Officials of Tuthmosis the Fourth, TTS 3, London: EES, 1923.

Davies, Vivian and Friedman, Renée, *Egypt*, London: British Museum, 1998.

Davis, Whitney, *The Canonical Tradition in Ancient Egyptian Art*, Cambridge: Cambridge University Press, 1989.

Dawson, Warren R., 'Some Observations on the Egyptian Calendars of Lucky and Unlucky Days', *JEA* 12 (1926), 260–4.

Demarée, R. J., ' "Royal Riddles" ', in Demarée, R. J. and Egberts, A. (eds.), *Village Voices*, Leiden: Centre of Non-Western Studies, Leiden University, 1992, pp. 9–18.

Diodorus, *Historical Library*, English translation by C. H. Oldfather, London: Heinemann; Cambridge, Mass.: Harvard University Press, 1946.

Dodson, Aidan, 'Two Thirteenth Dynasty Pyramids at Abusir?', VA 3 (1987), 231–2.

'The Tombs of the Kings of the Thirteenth Dynasty in the Memphite Necropolis', *ZÄS* 114 (1987), 36–45.

Dorman, Peter, *The Tombs of Senenmut: The Architecture and Decoration of Tombs 71 and 353*, New York: Metropolitan Museum of Art, 1991.

Dorner, Josef, 'Die Absteckung und astronomische Orientierung ägyptischer Pyramiden', Ph. D. dissertation, Innsbruck University, 1981.

'Form und Ausmaße der Knickpyramide', *MDAIK* 42 (1986), 43–58.

'Die Form der Knickpyramide', *GM* 126 (1992), 39–45.

Dreyer, Günter, *Elephantine VIII, Der Temple der Satet. Die Funde der Frühzeit und des Alten Reiches*, AV 39, Mainz: Von Zabern, 1986.

Dreyer, Günter and Kaiser, Werner, 'Zu den kleinen Stufenpyramiden Ober- und Mittelägyptens', *MDAIK* 36, 1980, 43–59.

Dreyer, Günter and Swelim, Nabil, 'Die kleine Stufenpyramide von Abydos-Süd (Sinki)', *MDAIK* 38, 1980, 83–95.

Dümichen, Johannes, 'Bauurkunde der Tempelanlagen von Edfu', *ZÄS* 8 (1870), 1–13; 9 (1871), 25–32, 88–98, 105–12; 10 (1872), 33–42; 11 (1873), 109–19.

Baugeschichte des Denderatempels, Strasburg: Trübner, 1877.

Dunham, Dows, *The Royal Cemeteries of Kush*, vol. I: *El Kurru*, Cambridge Mass.: Harvard University Press, 1950; vol. II: *Nuri*, Boston: Museum of Fine Arts, 1955; vol. III: *Decorated Chapels of the Meroitic Pyramids at Meroë and Barkal*, Boston: Museum of Fine Arts, 1952; vol. IV: *Royal Tombs at Meroë and Barkal*, Boston: Museum of Fine Arts, 1957; vol. V: *The West and South Cemeteries at Meroë*, Boston: Museum of Fine Arts, 1963.

Eco, Umberto, *Il Pendolo di Foucault*, Milano: Fabbri-Bompiani, 1988; English edition: *Foucault's Pendulum*, translated by W. Weaver, London: Vintage, 2001.

Edgar, Campbell C., *Sculptor's Studies and Unfinished Works*, CG, Cairo: SAE, 1906.

Edwards, Iorweth E. S., *The Pyramids of Egypt*, London: Penguin Books, 1993 (revised edition).

Emery, Walter B., *The Tomb of Hemaka*, Cairo: Government Press, 1938.

Engelbach, Reginald, *The Aswân Obelisk, with Some Remarks on the Ancient Engineering*, Cairo: SAE, 1922.

'An Architect's Project from Thebes', *ASAE* 27 (1927), 72–6.

'A Foundation Scene of the Second Dynasty', *JEA* 20 (1934), 183–4.

Engels, Hermann, 'Quadrature of the Circle in Ancient Egypt', *HM* 4 (1977), 137–40.

Euclid, *Elements*, English translation by Thomas L. Heath, in *Euclid, Archimedes, Nicomachus*, Great Books of the Western World 10, Chicago: Encyclopaedia Britannica, Inc., 1990, 1–396.

Eysenck, Hans J., 'Aesthetic Preferences and Individual Differences', in O'Hare David (ed.), *Psychology of the Arts*, Brighton: Harvester, 1981.

Eysenck, Hans J. and Castle, Maureen, 'Training in Art as a Factor in the Determination of Preference Judgements for Polygons', *British Journal of Psychology* 61 (1970), 65–81.

Fakhry, Ahmed, *The Pyramids*, Chicago: University Press, 1961.

 The Monuments of Sneferu at Dahshur, Cairo: Government Press, 1961.

Farag, Nagib and Iskander, Zaky, *The Discovery of Neferwptah*, Cairo: Government Press, 1971.

Fechner, Gustav T., *Vorschule der Aesthetik*, Leipzig: Breitkopf & Härtel, 1876.

Fletcher, Roland J., 'Space in Settlements: A Mechanism of Adaptation', Ph.D. thesis, University of Cambridge, 1976.

Friberg, Jöran, 'Methods and Tradition of Babylonian Mathematics', *HM* 8 (1981), 277–318.

Friedman, Renée, 'The Ceremonial Centre at Hierakonpolis Locality *HK* 29A', in Spencer, Jeffrey (ed.), *Aspects of Early Egypt*, London: British Museum Press, 1996, pp. 16–35.

Fonseca, Rory, 'The Geometry of Zoser's Step Pyramid at Saqqara', *JSAH* 45 (1986), 333–8.

Fournier des Corats, A., *La proportion égyptienne et les rapports de divine harmonie*, Paris: Trédaniel, 1957.

Fowler, David H., 'A generalisation of the Golden Section', *Fibonacci Quarterly* 20/2 (1982), 146–58.

 The Mathematics of Plato's Academy, Oxford: Oxford University Press, 1987.

Gandz, Solomon, 'Die Harpedonapten oder Seilspanner und Seilknüpfer', *Quellen und Studien zur Geschichte der Mathematik, Astronomie und Physik*, Part B, vol. I (1931), 255–77.

Gardiner, Alan H., 'An Unusual Sketch of a Theban Funeral', *PSBA* 35 (1913), 229.

 'Some Coptic Etymologies', *PSBA* 38 (1916), 181–5.

 The Ramesseum Papyri, Oxford: Oxford University Press, 1955.

 Egypt of the Pharaohs, Oxford: Clarendon Press, 1961.

Garnot, Jean S. F., 'Les fouilles de la nécropole de Soleb', *BIFAO* 58 (1959), 165–73.

Gericke, Helmuth, *Mathematik in Antike und Orient*, Wiesbaden: Fourier, 1992.

Ghyka, Matila C., *Le Nombre d'Or – Rites et rythmes Pythagoriciens dans le développement de la civilisation occidentale*, Paris: Gallimard, 1931.

 The Geometry of Art and Life, New York: Dover, 1946.

Gillings, Richard J., *Mathematics at the Time of the Pharaohs*, Cambridge, Mass.: Massachusettes Institute of Technology Press, 1972.

 'The Mathematics of Ancient Egypt', in *Dictionary of Scientific Biography*, vol. xv, Supplement 1, New York: Scribner, 1978, 681–705.

Gilpin, William, *Three Essays: On Picturesque Beauty; On Picturesque Travel; And On Sketching Landscape*, London: Blamire, 1792.

Glanville, S. R. K., 'The Mathematical Leather Roll in the British Museum', *JEA* 13 (1927), 232–8.

 'Working Plan for a Shrine', *JEA* 16 (1930), 237–9.

Goedicke, Hans and Wente, F. Edward, *Ostraka Michaelides*, Wiesbaden: Harrassowitz, 1962.

Griffith, Francis L., 'Notes on Egyptian Weights and Measures', *PSBA* 14 (1891–2), 403–50.

> *The Petrie Papyri: Hieratic Papyri from Kahun and Gurob*, London: University College, 1897.

> *Hieratic Papyri from Kahun and Gurob*, London: Quaritch, 1898.

Gunn, Battiscombe, 'An Architect's Diagram of the Third Dynasty', *ASAE* 26 (1926), 197–202.

> 'Notes on Two Egyptian Kings', *JEA* 12 (1926), 250–2.

Habachi, Labib, 'Two pyramidions of the XIIIth Dynasty from Ezbet Rushdi el-Kebira (Khata'na)', *ASAE* 52 (1954), 471–9.

> *The Obelisks of Egypt*, London: Scribner's Sons, 1977.

Hambidge, Jay, *The Parthenon and Other Greek Temples: Their Dynamic Symmetry*, New Haven: Yale University Press, 1924

> *The Elements of Dynamic Symmetry*, New Haven: Yale University Press, 1948.

Hannig, Reiner, *Grosses Handworterbuch Agyptisch-Deutsch*, Mainz: von Zabern, 1995.

Harrell, James A. and Brown, V. Max, 'The Oldest Surviving Topographical Map from Ancient Egypt (Turin Papyri 1879, 1899 and 1969)', *JARCE* 29 (1992), 81–105.

Harvey, Stephen, 'Monuments of Ahmose at Abydos', *EA* 4 (1994), 3–5.

Hasitzka, Monika R. M., *Neue Texte und Dokumentation zum Koptisch-Unterricht*, Mitteilungen aus der Papyrussammlung der Nationalbibliothek (later Österreichischen Nationalbibliothek) in Wien XVIII, Vienna: Hollinek, 1990.

Hawass, Zahi and Verner, Miroslav, 'Newly Discovered Blocks from the Causeway of Sahure', *MDAIK* 52 (1996), 177–86.

Hayes, William C., *Ostraka and Name Stones from the Tomb of Sen-mut (No. 71) at Thebes*, Metropolitan Museum of Art Egyptian Expedition 15, New York: Metropolitan Museum of Art, 1942.

Heath, Thomas L., *The Thirteen Books of Euclid's Elements*, 3 vols., Cambridge: Cambridge University Press, 1926.

Heisel, Joachim P., *Antike Bauzeichnungen*, Darmstadt: Wissenschaftliche Buchgesellschaft, 1993.

Helck, Wolfgang, *Historisch-Biographische Texte der 2. Zwischenzeit und neue Texte der 18. Dynastie*, Kleine Ägyptische Texte, Wiesbaden: Harrassowitz, 1983.

> 'Drei Ramessidische Daten', *SAK* 17 (1990), 205–14.

Henszlmann, Emeric, *Théorie des proportions appliquées dans l'architecture depuis la XIIe dynastie des rois égyptiens jusq'au XVIe siècle*, Paris: Bertrand, 1860.

Herodotus, *Histories*, English translation by A. D. Godley, London: Heinemann; Cambridge, Mass.: Harvard University Press, 1946.

Herz-Fischler Roger, *The Shape of the Great Pyramid*, Waterloo: Wilfrid Laurier University Press, 2000.

Hinkel, Friedrich W., 'Pyramide oder Pyramidenstumpf? (Teil A)', *ZÄS* 108 (1981), 105–24.

> 'Pyramide oder Pyramidenstumpf? (Teil B)', *ZÄS* 109 (1982), 27–61.

> 'Pyramide oder Pyramidenstumpf? (Teil C und D)', *ZÄS* 109 (1982), 127–47.

> 'Säule und Interkolumnium in der meroitischen Architektur. Metrologische Vorstudien zu einer Klassifikation der Bauwerke', *Studia Meroitica* 10 (1984), 231–67.

> 'Ägyptische Elle or griechischer Modul?', *Das Altertum* 33/3 (1987), 150–62.

> 'The Process of Planning in Meroitic Architecture', in Davies, W. V. (ed.), *Egypt and Africa*, London: British Museum and Egypt Exploration Society, 1993, pp. 220–5.

> 'The Royal Pyramids of Meroe. Architecture, Construction and Reconstruction of a Sacred Landscape', *Sudan and Nubia* 4 (2000), 11–26.

Hinz, J. M. and Nelson, T. M., 'Haptic Aesthetic Value of the Golden Section', *Journal of British Psychology* 62 (1971), 217–23.

Hoberman, Max, 'Two Architect's Sketches', *JSAH* 44 (1985), 380–3.

Hölbl, Günther, *A History of the Ptolemaic Empire*, London/New York: Routledge, 2001.

Hölscher, U., *The Excavation of Medinet Habu II: The Temples of the Eighteenth Dynasty*, Chicago: University of Chicago, Oriental Institute, 1939.

Hornung, Erik, 'Struktur und Entwicklung der Gräber im Tal der Könige', *ZÄS* 105 (1978), 59–66.

   The Secret Lore of Egypt, translated by David Lorton, Ithaca and London: Cornell University Press, 2001.

Hume, David, 'Of the Standard of Taste' (1777), in Eugene F. Miller (ed.), *Essays: Moral, Political, and Literary*, Indianapolis, Ind.: Liberty Fund, 1987, 226-49.

Imhausen, Annette, *Ägyptische Algorithmen. Ein Untersuch zu den mittelägyptischen mathematischen Aufgabentexten*, Ägyptologische Abhandlungen, Wiesbaden: Harrassowitz, 2003.

Isler, Martin, *Sticks, Stone and Shadows. Building the Egyptian Pyramid*, Norman: University of Oklahoma Press, 2001.

Iversen, Eric, *Canon and Proportions in Egyptian Art*, Warminster: Aris and Phillips, 1975.

Jánosi, Peter, 'Das Pyramidion der Pyramide G III-a', *Studia Aegyptiaca* 14 (1992), 306–14.

   Die Pyramidenanlagen der Königinnen, Vienna: Österreichischen Akademie der Wissenschaften, 1996.

Janssen, Jac. J., *Commodity Prices from the Ramessid Period*, Leiden: Brill, 1975.

   Two Ancient Egyptian Ship's Logs, Leiden: Brill, 1961.

   'An Exceptional Event at Deir el-Medina', *JARCE* 31 (1994), 91–7.

Jéquier, Gustave, 'Rapport préliminare sur les fouilles exécutées en 1925–1926 dans la partie méridionale de la nécropole Memphite – La Pyramide de la Reine Oudjebten', *ASAE* 26 (1926), 48–55.

   La Pyramide d'Oudjebten, Cairo: SAE, 1928.

   Deux Pyramides du Moyen Empire, Cairo: SAE, 1933.

   Les Pyramides des Reines Neit et Apouit, Cairo: SAE, 1933.

   La Pyramide d'Aba, Cairo: SAE, 1935.

   Le Monument Funéraire de Pepi II, Cairo: SAE, 1938.

Jéquier, Gustave and Gautier J.-E., *Fouilles de Licht*, MIFAO 4, Cairo: IFAO, 1902.

Jomard, Edmé F., 'Memoire sur le système métrique des anciens Égyptiens', in Jomard, *Description de l'Egypte, Antiquités, Memoires*, vol. I, Paris: Imprimerie Impèriale, 1809.

   'Remarques at recherches sur les pyramides d'Égypte', in Jomard, *Description de l'Egypte, Antiquités, Memoires*, vol. II, Paris: Imprimerie Impèriale, 1818.

Jones, Mark Wilson, *Principles of Roman Architecture*, New Haven and London: Yale University Press, 2000.

Junge, Friedrich, 'Zur Fehldatierung des sog. "Denkmals memphitischer Theologie", oder Der Beitrag der ägyptischen Theologie zur Geistesgeschichte der Spätzeit', *MDAIK* 29 (1973), 195–204.

Kaiser, Werner, 'Zu den Sonnenheiligtümer der 5. Dynastie', *MDAIK* 14 (1956), 103–16.

Kames, Henry H., *Elements of Criticism*, London: Millar; Edinburgh: Kincaid & Bell, 1765.

Keller, Cathleen A., 'The Draughtsmen of Deir el-Medina: A Preliminary Report', *NARCE* 115 (1981), 7–14.

Kemp, Barry J., 'The Window of Appearance at El-Amarna and the Basic Structure of this City', *JEA* 62 (1976), 81–99.

'Preliminary Report on the el-Amarna Expedition, 1979', *JEA* 66 (1980), 5–16.

'Patterns of Activity at the Workmen's Village', in Kemp, *Amarna Reports I*, London: EES, 1984, chapter 1.

'The Sanctuary of the Great Aten Temple', in Kemp, *Amarna Reports IV*, London: EES, 1987, chapter 8.

Ancient Egypt. Anatomy of a Civilisation, London: Routledge, 1989.

'Outlying temples at Amarna', in Kemp, *Amarna Reports VI*, London: EES, 1995, chapter 15.

'Soil (Including Mud-brick Architecture)', in Nicholson and Shaw (eds.), *Ancient Egyptian Materials and Technology*, Cambridge: Cambridge University Press, 2000, pp. 78–103.

'Tell el-Amarna 2000–01', *JEA* 87 (2001), 16–21.

Kemp, Barry J. and Rose, Pamela, 'Proportionality in Mind and Space in Ancient Egypt', *CAJ* 1:1 (1991), 103–29.

Kielland, Else C., *Geometry in Greek Art*, *Geometry in Egyptian Art*, London: Tiranti, 1955.

Geometry in Greek Art, Oslo: Dreyer, 1983.

Kitchen, K. A., *Ramesside Inscriptions*, vol. IV, Oxford: Blackwell, 1982.

Ramesside Inscriptions, vol. VII, Oxford: Blackwell, 1989.

Knorr, Wilbur R., *The Evolution of the Euclidean Elements*, Dordrecht/Boston: Reidel, 1975.

'Techniques of Fractions in Ancient Egypt and Greece', *HM* 9 (1982), 133–71.

'Archimede's Dimensions of the Circle: A View of the Genesis of the Extant Text', *Archive for History of Exact Sciences* 35/4 (1986), 281–324.

Koenig, Yvan, *Les ostraca hiératiques inédits de la Bibliothèque nationale et universitaire de Strasbourg*, DFIFAO 33, Cairo: IFAO, 1997.

Labrousse, Audran, Lauer, Jean-Philippe, and Leclant, Jean, *Le Temple Haut du complexe funéraire du roi Ounas*, BdÉ 53, Cairo: IFAO, 1977.

Labrousse, Audran and Lauer, Jean-Philippe, *Les complexes funéraires d'Ouserkaf et de Néferhétepès*, BdE, Cairo: IFAO, 2000.

Lacau, Pierre, 'L'or dans l'architecture égyptienne', *ASAE* 53 (1956), 221–50.

'Les verbes *wbn*, "poindre" et *psḏ*, "culminer"', *BIFAO* 69 (1971), 1–9.

Lauer, Jean-Philippe, *La Pyramide à Degrés. L'Architecture*, Cairo: SAE, 1936.

'Le temple haut de la pyramide du roi Ouserkaf', *ASAE* 53 (1954), 119–33.

Observations sur les pyramides, BdÉ 30, Cairo: IFAO, 1960.

'Le Triangle Sacré dans les plans des monuments de l'Ancient Empire', *BIFAO* 77 (1977), 55–78.

Le mystère des pyramides, Paris: Presses de la Cité, 1988.

Lauer, Jean-Philippe and Leclant, Jean, *Le Temple Haut du complexe funéraire du roi Téti*, BdÉ 51, Cairo: IFAO, 1972.

Lauffray, Jean, *Karnak d'Egypte, domaine du divin*, Paris: Centre national de la recherche scientifique, 1979.

'Les travaux du Centre Franco-Egyptien d'études des temples des Karnak de 1972 à 1977', *Cahiers de Karnak VI*, Cairo: IFAO, 1980, 1–65.

La chapelle d'Achôris à Karnak, vol. I, Paris: Recherche sur les Civilisations, 1995.

Lawlor, Robert, *Sacred Geometry, Philosophy and Practice*, London: Thames and Hudson, 1982.

Leach, Bridget and Tait, John, 'Papyrus', in Nicholson and Shaw (eds.), *Ancient Egyptian Materials and Technology*, pp. 227–53.

Leclant, Jean, 'Fouilles et travaux au Soudan, 1955–1960', Orientalia 31 (1962), 120–41.

Lefébure, E., *Rites égyptiennes, construction et protection des édifices*, BCA 4, Paris: Leroux, 1890.

Lefebvre, Gustave, *Le tombeau de Petosiris*, Cairo: SAE, 1923.

Legon, John A. R., 'The 14:11 Proportion at Meydum', *DE* 17 (1990), 15–22.

   'The Geometry of the Bent Pyramid', *GM* 116 (1990), 65–72.

   'The Problem of the Bent Pyramid', *GM* 130 (1992), 49–56.

   'Review article – Measurement in Ancient Egypt', *DE* 30 (1994), 87–100.

   'The Cubit and the Egyptian Canon of Art', *DE* 35 (1996), 61–76.

   'The Quest for the True *nbj* Measure', *DE* 36 (1996), 69–78.

Lehner, Mark, 'Some Observations on the Layout of the Khufu and Khafre Pyramids', *JARCE* 20 (1983), 7–25.

   'The Tomb Survey', in Martin, Geoffrey T., *The Royal Tomb at el-'Amarna II*, ASE 35, London: EES, 1989, pp. 5–9.

   The Complete Pyramids, London: Thames and Hudson, 1997.

Lepsius, Karl Richard, *Die Alt-Aegyptische Elle (aus den Abhandlungen der Königlichen Akademie der Wissenschaften 1865)*, Berlin 1865.

   'Grundplan des Grabes König Ramses IV. in einem Turiner Papyrus', *Abhandlungen der Königlichen Akademie der Wissenschaften zu Berlin* 1867, Philosophische und historische Abhandlungen, 1–22.

   Denkmäler aus Aegypten und Aethiopien, Leipzig: Hinrichs, 1897.

Lichtheim, Miriam, *Ancient Egyptian Literature*, Berkeley: University of California Press, 1973–80.

López, Jesús, *Catalogo del Museo Egizio di Torino*, Serie Seconda – Collezioni, vol. III, Fascicolo I: Ostraca ieratici, Milano: Cisalpino-La Goliardica, 1978.

Lucas, Alfred and Harris, J. R., *Ancient Egyptian Materials and Industries*, London: Arnold, 1962.

Lumpkin, Beatrice, 'The Egyptians and Pythagorean Triples', *HM* 7 (1980), 186–7.

Mackay, Ernest, 'The Origin of Polychrome Borders: A Suggestion', *Ancient Egypt* 4 (1916), 169–73.

Maragioglio, Vito and Rinaldi, Celeste, *Notizie sulle piramidi di Zedefrâ, Zedkarâ Isesi e Teti*, Torino: Artale, 1962.

   L'architettura delle Piramidi Memfite, 8 vols., Torino: Artale, 1963–77.

   'Note sulla piramide di Ameny 'Aamu'', *Orientalia* 37 (1968), 325–39.

   'Note complementari sulla tomba di Neferu-Ptah', *Orientalia* 42 (1973), 357–69.

Martin, Artemas, 'On Rational Right-angled Triangles', *Proceedings of the Fifth International Congress of Mathematicians, Cambridge 1912*, Cambridge: Cambridge University Press, 1912, 40–58.

Martin, Geoffrey T., *The Hidden Tombs of Memphis*, London: Thames and Hudson, 1991.

Maspero, Gaston, 'Sur le pyramidion d'Amenemhait III à Dachour', *ASAE* 3 (1902), 206–8.

Mau, Jürgen and Müller, Wolfgang, 'Mathematische Ostraka aus der Berliner Sammlung', *Archiv für Papyrusforschung* 17 (1962), 1–10.

McManus, I. C., 'The Aesthetics of Simple Figures', *British Journal of Psychology* 71 (1980), 505–24.

Mekhitarian, Arpag, 'Alexandre Varille, *A propos des pyramides de Snefrou*', review article, *CdE* 47 (1949), 63–5.

Mendelssohn, Kurt, *The Riddle of Pyramids*, London: Thames and Hudson, 1974.

de Meulenaere, Herman J., 'Pyramidions d'Abydos', *JEOL* 20 (1967–68), 1–20.

Meyer-Christian, W., 'Der "Pythagoras" in Ägypten am Beginn des Alten Reiches', *MDAIK* 43 (1987), 195–203.

Montet, Pierre, 'Le rituel de fondation des temples égyptiennes', *Kêmi* 17 (1964), 74–100.

Moret, Alexandre, *Du caractère religieux de la royauté pharaonique*, Paris: Leroux, 1902. *Le rituel du culte divin journalier*, Paris: Leroux, 1902.

De Morgan, Jaques, *Fouilles à Dahchour en 1894–1895*, Vienna: Holzhausen, 1903.

Mössel, Ernst, *Die Proportion in Antike und Mittelalter,* Munich: Beck, 1928.

Mueller, Ian, 'Aristotle and the Quadrature of the Circle', in Kretzmann Norman (ed.), *Infinity and Continuity in Ancient and Medieval Thought*, Ithaca and London: Cornell University Press, 1982, pp. 146–64.

Müller, Ingeborg, 'Plan für einen Tempel', in Bettina Schmitz (ed.), *Festschrift Arne Eggebrecht*, Hildesheimer Aegyptologische Beitraege 48, Hildesheim: Gerstenberg, 2002.

Mysliwiec, Karol, 'Zwei Pyramidia der XIX. Dynastie aus Memphis', *SAK* 5 (1977), 139–55.

Naville, Edouard, 'La Pierre de Palerme', *Recueil des Travaux* 25 (1903), 64–81.

Neuerburg, Norman, 'Greek and Roman Pyramids', *Archaeology* 22 (1969), 106–15.

Neugebauer, Otto E. and Sachs, A., *Mathematical Cuneiform Texts*, AOS 29, New Haven: American Oriental Society and the American Schools of Oriental Research, 1945.

Neumann, Claudio and Ogdon, Jorge R., 'A New Approach to Ancient Egyptian Objects. A Preliminary Report on Statue Louvre E.12627', *DE* 10 (1988), 55–68.

Nicholson, Paul T. and Shaw, Ian (eds.), *Ancient Egyptian Materials and Technology*, Cambridge: Cambridge University Press, 2000.

Palter, Robert, 'Black Athena, Afrocentrism, and the History of Science', in Lefkowitz, Mary R. and MacLean, Rogers Guy (eds.), *Black Athena Revisited*, Chapel Hill: University of North Carolina Press, 1996, pp. 209–66.

Parker, Richard A., *Demotic Mathematical Papyri*, Providence, R. I.: Brown University Press, London: Humphries, 1972.

Peet, Eric T., *The Rhind Mathematical Papyrus*, Liverpool: University Press; London: Hodder and Stoughton, 1923.

Pendlebury, J. D. S., *The City of Akhenaten* III, London: EES, 1951.

Perrot, Georges and Chipiez, Charles, *A History of Art in Ancient Egypt*, 2 vols., London: Chapman and Hall, 1833.

Petrie, W. M. Flinders, *A Season in Egypt*, London: Field, 1887.
Kahun, Gurob and Hawara, London: Kegan Paul, Trench and Trübner, 1890.
Medum, London: Nutt, 1892.
The Royal Tombs of the Earliest Dynasties, part II, London: EEF, 1901.
Gizeh and Rifeh, BSAE ERA 13, London: School of Archaeology, 1907.
The Labyrinth, Gerzeh and Mazghuneh, BSAE ERA 21, London: Quaritch, 1912.
Lahun II, BSAE ERA 33, London: Quaritch, 1923.
'Egyptian Working Drawings', *Ancient Egypt* 1 (1926), 24–7.

Piazzi-Smyth, Charles, *Life and Work at the Great Pyramid*, Edinburgh: Edmonston and Douglas, 1867.
Our Inheritance in the Great Pyramid (4th edn), London: Straham and Co., 1880.

Pieper, Max, *Die grosse Inschrift des Königs Neferhotep in Abydos*, Mitteilungen der Vorderasiatisch-aegyptischen Gesellschaft 32, 2, Leipzig: Hinrich, 1929.

Plato, *Meno*, English translation by G. M. A. Grube, Indianapolis, Ind.: Hackett, 1976.

Plutarch, *De Iside et Osiride*, English translation by J. Gwyn Griffiths, Cardiff: University of Wales Press, 1970.

Polz, Daniel, 'Bericht über die erste Grabungskampagne in der Nekropole von Dra' Abu el-Naga/Theben West', *MDAIK* 48 (1992), 109–30.

'Bericht über die 2. und 3. Grabungskampagne in der Nekropole von Dra' Abu el-Naga/Theben West', *MDAIK* 49 (1993), 227–38.

'Bericht über die 4. und 5. Grabungskampagne in der Nekropole von Dra' Abu el-Naga/Theben West', *MDAIK* 51 (1995), 109–30.

'An Architect's Sketch from the Theban Necropolis', *MDAIK* 53 (1997), 233–40.

Pomeroy, Edward, Benjafield, John, Rowntree, Chris and Kuiack, Joanna, 'The Golden Section: A Convenient Ideal?', *Social Behaviour and Personality* 9 (1981), 231–4.

Preliminary Report on Czechoslovak Excavation in the Mastaba of Ptahshepses at Abusir, Prague: Charles University, 1976.

Preziosi, Donald, 'Harmonic Design in Minoan Architecture', *Fibonacci Quarterly* 6/6 (1868): 370–84.

Minoan Architectural Design, Berlin: Mouton, 1983.

Pritchard, James B., *Ancient Near Eastern Texts*, Princeton: Princeton University Press, 1969.

Quatremère de Quincy, Antoine C., *De l'architecture Egyptienne*, Paris: Barrois, 1803.

Dictionnaire Historique d'Architecture, Paris: Le Clere, 1832.

Rammant-Peeters, Agnes, *Les pyramidions égyptiens du Nouvel Empire*, OLA 11, Leuven: Departement Oriëntalistiek, 1983.

Randall-MacIver, David and Mace Arthur C., *El Amrah and Abydos*, EEF 23, London: EES, 1902.

Redford, Donald B., 'The Earliest Years of Ramses II and the Building of the Ramesside Court at Luxor', *JEA* 57 (1971), 110–9.

The Akhenaten Temple Project, vol. I, Warminster: Aris and Phillips, 1976.

Reeves, Nicholas C., 'Two Architectural Drawings from the Valley of the Kings', *CdE* 61 (1986), 43–9.

Reeves, Nicholas C. and Wilkinson, Richard H., *The Complete Valley of the Kings*, London: Thames and Hudson, 1996.

Reisner, George A., *Amulets*, CG, Cairo: SAE, 1907.

Mycerinus, the Temple of the Third Pyramid at Giza, Cambridge, Mass.: Harvard University Press, 1931.

Reymond, Eve A. E., *The Mythical Origin of the Egyptian Temple*, Manchester: Manchester University Press, 1969.

Ricke, Herbert, 'Ein Inventartafel aus Heliopolis im Turiner Museum', *ZÄS* 71 (1935), 111–33.

Der Sonnenheiligtum des Königs Userkaf, vol. I, Cairo: Schweizerisches Institut fur ägyptische Bauforschung und Altertumskunde in Kairo, 1965.

Robins, Gay, 'The Slope of the Front of the Royal Apron', *DE* 3 (1985), 49–56.

Proportion and Style in Ancient Egyptian Art, London: Thames and Hudson, 1994.

'On Supposed Connections Between the "Canon of Proportions" and Metrology', *JEA* 80 (1994), 191–4.

'Canonical Proportions and Metrology', *DE* 32 (1995), 91–2.

Robins, Gay and Shute, Charles, 'Mathematical Bases of Ancient Egyptian Architecture and Graphic Art', *HM* 12 (1985), 107–22.

The Rhind Mathematical Papyrus, London: British Museum Press, 1987.

'The 14 to 11 Proportion in Egyptian Architecture', *DE* 16, 1990, 75–80.

'Irrational Numbers and Pyramids', *DE* 18 (1990), 43–53.

Robson, Eleanor, 'Neither Sherlock Holmes nor Babylon: A Reassessment of Plimpton 322', *HM* 28 (2001), 167–206.

Roeder, Günther, 'Zwei hieroglyphische Inschriften aus Hermopolis (Ober-Ägypten)', *ASAE* 52 (1954), 315–442.

Amarna-Reliefs aus Hermopolis, Wissenschaftliche Veröffentlichungen Pelizeus-Museum zu Hildesheim 6, Hildesheim: Gesterberg, 1969.

Roik, Elke, 'Auf der Suche nach dem "true *nbj* measure" ', *DE* 34 (1996), 91–115.

Rossi, Corinna, 'Note on the Pyramidion Found at Dahshur', *JEA* 85 (1999), 219–22.

'The Plan of a Royal Tomb on O. Cairo 25184', *GM* 184 (2001), 45–53.

'Dimensions and Slope of the Royal Tombs', *JEA* 87 (2001), 73–80.

'The Identification of the Tomb Described on O. BM 8505', *GM* 187 (2002), 97–9.

Rossi, Corinna and Tout, Christopher A., 'Were the Fibonacci Series and the Golden Section Known in Ancient Egypt?', *Historia Mathematica* 29 (2002), 101–13.

Ryan, Donald P. and Hansen, David H., *A Study of Ancient Egyptian Cordage in the British Museum*, London: British Museum Press, 1987.

Scamuzzi, Ernesto, *Museo Egizio di Torino*, Torino: Edizioni d'Arte Fratelli Pozzo, 1964.

Schäfer, Heinrich, *Ein Bruchstück Altägyptischer Annalen*, Berlin: Königliche Akademie der Wissenschaften, 1902.

'Die Spitze der Pyramide Königs Amenemhat III', *ZÄS* 41 (1904), 84–5.

Von Ägyptischer Kunst, Wiesbaden: Harrassowitz, 1963.

Scholfield, P. H., *The Theory of Proportion in Architecture*, Cambridge: Cambridge University Press, 1958.

Schlott-Schwab, Adelheid, *Die Ausmasse Ägyptens nach altägyptischen Texte*, Ägypten und Altes Testament 3, Wiesbaden: Harrassowitz, 1981.

Schwaller de Lubicz, René A, *Le Temple de l'Homme*, Paris: Caractères, 1957.

Sethe, Kurt, *Imhotep, der Asklepios der Aegypter*, Leipzig: Hinrichs, 1902.

Urkunden der 18. Dynastie, Leipzig: Hinrichs, 1905–6.

Von Zahlen und Zahlworten bei den alten Ägyptern, Strasburg: Trübner, 1916.

Shalit, Benjamin, 'The Golden Section Relation in the Evaluation of Environmental Factors', *British Journal of Psychology* 71 (1980), 39–42.

Siegler, Karl Georg, *Kalabsha, Architektur und Baugeschichte des Tempels*, AV 1, Berlin: Mann, 1970.

Silverman, David P., 'Fractions in the Abusir Papyri', *JEA* 61 (1975), 248–9.

Simon, Claire, 'Le *nbi* at le canon de proportions', *JEA* 79 (1993), 157–77.

Simpson, William K., *Papyrus Reisner I*, Boston: Museum of Fine Arts, 1963.

Smith, H. S. and Stewart, H. M., 'The Gurob Shrine Papyrus', *JEA* 70 (1984), 54–64.

de Solla Price, Derek J., 'The Babylonian "Pythagorean Triangle" Tablet', *Centaurus* 10 (1964), 1–13.

Spencer, Alan J., *Brick Architecture in Ancient Egypt*, Warminster: Aris and Phillips, 1979.

Staatliche Museen Preussischer Kulturbesitz, *Ägyptisches Museum Berlin*, Berlin: Östlicher Stülerbau, 1967.

Stadelmann, Rainer, 'Ein bemaltes Hausmodell in der ägyptischer Sammlung der Universität Heidelberg', *MDAIK* 18 (1962), 54–8.
'Snofru und die Pyramiden von Meidum und Dahschur', *MDAIK* 36 (1980), 437–49.
Die Ägyptischen Pyramiden, Mainz: Von Zabern, 1985.
'Die Pyramide des Snofru in Dahschur. Zweiter Bericht über die Ausgrabungen an der nördlichen Steinpyramide', *MDAIK* 39 (1983), 225–41.
Steadman, Philip, *The Evolution of Designs*, Cambridge Urban and Architectural Studies 5, Cambridge: Cambridge University Press, 1979.
Steindorff, Georg, *Aniba*, Glückstadt: Augustin, 1937.
Strabo, *Geography*, English translation by Horace L. Jones, London: Heinemann; Cambridge, Mass.: Harvard University Press, 1959.
Struve, W. W., 'Mathematischer Papyrus des Staatlichen Museums der Schönen Künste in Moskau', *Quellen und Studien zur Geschichte der Mathematik, Astronomie und Physik*, part A, vol. I (1930).
Swelim, Nabil, *The Brick Pyramid at Abu Rawash, Number 'I' by Lepsius. A Preliminary Study*, Alexandria: Archaeological Society of Alexandria, 1987.
'Pyramid Research. From the Archaic to the Second Intermediate Period, Lists, Catalogues and Objectives', in *Hommages à Jean Leclant*, BdE 106/1–4, Cairo: IFAO, 1994, pp. 337–49.
Swelim, Nabil and Dodson, Aidan, 'On the Pyramid of Ameny-Qemau and its Canopic Equipment', *MDAIK* 54 (1998), 319–34.
Taylor, John, *The Great Pyramid: Why Was It Built? & Who Built It?*, London: Longman, Green and Roberts, 1859.
Theban Mapping Project, *Atlas of the Valley of the Kings*, Cairo: American University in Cairo Press, 2000.
Thiersch, August, *Die Proportionen in der Architektur*, Handbuch der Architektur 4, Darmstadt: Bergsträsser, 1883.
Thomas, Elizabeth, *Royal Necropoleis of Thebes*, Princeton, 1966.
'The "Well" in Kings' Tombs of Bibân el-Molûk', *JEA* 64 (1978), 80–3.
Thompson, D'Arcy W., *On Growth and Form*, Cambridge: Cambridge University Press, 1961 (1917).
Thompson, Herbert, 'A Byzantine Table of Fractions', *Ancient Egypt* 2 (1914), 52–4.
Vajda, Steven, *Fibonacci and Lucas Numbers, and the Golden Section*, Chichester: Ellis Horwood, 1989.
Valloggia, Michel, 'Fouilles archéologiques à Abu Rawash (Egypte), rapport préliminaire de la campagne 1995', *Genava* 43 (1995), 65–72.
VandenBroeck, André, *Philosophical Geometry,* Rochester, N.Y.: Inner Traditions International, 1972.
Vandersleyen, Claude, 'Le sens symbolique des puits funéraires dans l'Egypte ancienne', *CdE* 50 (1975), 151–7.
Vandier, Jacques, *Manuel d'archéologie égyptienne*, Paris: Picard, 1952–78.
Van Siclen III, Charles C., 'Ostracon BM41228: A Sketch Plan of a Shrine Reconsidered', *GM* 90 (1986), 71–7.
Ventura, Raphael, 'The Largest Project for a Royal Tomb in the Valley of the Kings', *JEA* 74 (1988), 137–56.
Verner, Miroslav, 'Excavations at Abusir. Season 1978/1979 – Preliminary Report', *ZÄS* 107 (1980), 158–69.
'Eine zweite unvollendete Pyramide in Abusir', *ZÄS* 109 (1982), 75–8.
'Excavations at Abusir. Season 1980/1981 – Preliminary Report', *ZÄS* 109 (1982), 157–66.

'Excavations at Abusir. Season 1982 – Preliminary Report', *ZÄS* 111 (1984), 70–8.
'Excavations at Abusir. Season 1985/1986 – Preliminary Report', *ZÄS* 115 (1988), 77–83.
'Excavations at Abusir. Season 1987 – Preliminary Report', *ZÄS* 115 (1988), 163–71.
'Abusir Pyramids "Lepsius no. xxiv. and no. xxv." ', in *Hommages à Jean Leclant*, vol. i, Cairo: IFAO, 1994, pp. 371–8.
Viollet-le-Duc, Eugène, *Lectures on Architecture* (*Entretiens sur l'architecture*, Paris 1863), English translation by Benjamin Bucknall, New York: Dover Publications, 1987.
Vitruvius, *Ten Books on Architecture*, English translation by Ingrid D. Rowland, commentary and illustrations by Thomas Noble Howe, Cambridge: Cambridge University Press, 1999.
Vogel, Kurt, *Vorgriechische Mathematik*, vol. i, Hannover: Schroedel; Paderborn: Schöningh, 1959.
Vogelsang-Eastwood, Gillian, 'Textiles', in Nicholson and Shaw (eds.), *Ancient Egyptian Materials and Technology*, pp. 268–98.
Vyse, Howard and Perring, John S., *Operations carried on at the Pyramids of Gizeh*, London: Fraser, 1840–2.
van der Waerden, B. L., *Geometry and Algebra in Ancient Civilizations*, Berlin/Heidelberg/New York/Tokio: Springer-Verlag, 1983.
Wainwright, Gerald A., 'Seshat and the Pharaoh', *JEA* 26 (1940), 30–40.
Weeks, Kent R., 'The Berkeley Map of the Theban Necropolis; Preliminary Report 1978', *NARCE* 105 (Summer 1978), Appendix, 18–50.
'The Berkeley Map of the Theban Necropolis; Report of the Second Season, 1979', *NARCE* 109 (Summer 1979), Appendix – Special Supplement, 1–21.
Weill, Raymond, 'Un épure de stéréotomie dans une pièce de correspondance du Nouvel Empire', *Recueil de Travaux* 36, Paris 1916, 89–90.
Dara; campagne de 1946–1948, Cairo: Government Press, 1958.
Weinstein, James Morris, 'Foundation Deposits in Ancient Egypt', Ph.D. thesis, University of Pennsylvania, 1973.
Wilkinson, Gardner, *The Architecture of Ancient Egypt*, London: Murray, 1850.
Wilkinson, Richard H., *Reading Egyptian Art*, London: Thames and Hudson, 1992.
Symbol and Magic in Egyptian Art, London: Thames and Hudson, 1999 (1994).
Wilkinson, Toby A. H., *Royal Annals of Ancient Egypt: The Palermo Stone and Its Associated Fragments*, London/New York: Kegan Paul International, 2000.
Wilson, Penelope, *A Ptolemaic Lexikon*, OLA 78, Leuven: Uitgeverij Peeters en Department Oosterse Studies, 1997.
Winlock, Herbert E., 'The Tombs of the Kings of the Seventeenth Dynasty at Thebes', *JEA* 10 (1924), 217–77.
'The Egyptian Expedition 1921–2', *BMMA* 17, 2 (1922), 19–48.
'The Egyptian Expedition 1924–5', *BMMA* 21, 3 (1926), 3–32.
Excavations at Deir el-Bahri 1911–1931, New York: Macmillan Company, 1942.
Models of Daily Life in Ancient Egypt from the Tomb of Meketre at Thebes, Metropolitan Museum of Art Egyptian Expedition 18, Cambridge, Mass.: Harvard University Press, 1955.
De Wit, Constantin, 'Inscriptions dédicatoires du Temple d'Edfou', *CdE* 36 (1961), 56–97 and 277–320.
Wittkower, Rudolf, *Architectural Principles in the Age of Humanism*, 5th edn, London: Academy Editors, 1998.
Wolff, Odilio, *Tempelmasse*, Vienna: Schroll and Co., 1912.

Wysocki, Zygmunt, 'The Result of Research, Architectonic Studies and of Protective
    Work over the Northern Portico of the Middle Courtyard in the Hatshepsut Temple at
    Deir el-Bahari', *MDAIK* 40 (1984), 329–49.
   'The Temple of Queen Hatshepsut at Deir el-Bahari – The Results of Architectural
    Research over the North Part of the Upper Terrace', *MDAIK* 43 (1986), 267–76.
   'The Temple of Queen Hatshepsut at Deir el-Bahari: The Raising of the Structure in
    View of Architectural Studies', *MDAIK* 48 (1992), 233–54.
Zeising, Adolf, *Neue Lehre von den Proportionen des menschlichen Körpers*, Leipzig:
    Weigel, 1854.
Zignani, Pierre, 'Espaces, lumières at composition architecturale au temple d'Hathor à
    Dendara. Résultats préliminaires', *BIFAO* 100 (2000), 47–77.

Index